Everything you will ever need to know about everything

Katherine Lapworth & Alexandra Fraser

ORION

To my husband, William,
and our lovely children, Harry and Jack.

Alexandra Fraser

Dedicated to the memory of my father,
Paul Lapworth.

Katherine Lapworth

An Orion paperback
First published in 1998 by Orion Media
This revised paperback edition published in 1999 by Orion Books Ltd,
Orion House, 5 Upper St Martin's Lane, London WC2H 9EA

Second impression 2001

A CIP catalogue record for this book is available from the British Library.

ISBN 0-75282-583-6

Printed in Great Britain by The Guernsey Press Co. Ltd, Guernsey, C. I.

▷▷▷ Contents

▷ ▷ ▷ Preface

With hindsight, we should have put on the cover 'WARNING: reading this book could seriously damage your friendships'. We should know. Having worked first on the television series of *Trade Secrets* and now the book, we have barely a friend left between us.

It began in the heady days when we were still invited to dinner parties. Our host only needed to spill some red wine or apologise for the salty soup and we'd dive in with, 'What you need to do . . .' By the time pudding had arrived, we'd shared our wisdom on every subject under the sun. Whatever turn the conversation might take – pets, plumbing, fashion, funerals, the environment or exploration – we'd have a fund of invaluable gems to make everyone's lives a little easier.

So why not keep quiet and let the invitations continue to roll in? The trouble is that, once learned, these trade secrets are addictive. They have been discovered by true professionals over many years in their trade and are so simple and effective that they beg sharing. What amazes us is how many of them were discovered in the first place. What on earth made a pest controller first try toothpaste around a mousehole? How did a desperate, hairy man light on peanut butter as an alternative shaving cream?

Many of the people who contributed to this book are keeping alive dying trades and, in sharing their pearls of wisdom with us, they are passing on real secrets of craftsmanship, and skills that may disappear altogether.

We hope you enjoy reading it as much as we enjoyed compiling it. One final trade secret – do try to keep the tips to yoursel!

Katherine Lapworth
Alexandra Fraser

►►► Anglers

National Federation of Anglers: Bill Coe, Lenny Goulding, Geoff Bibby,
Dr Terry Thomas, Maggie Vaux, Wendy Miller

Avoid accidents. Don't fish during a thunderstorm. Your rod will probably be made from carbon fibre which is an excellent conductor of electricity.

To keep your line free from knots when sea fishing simply punch a couple of holes an inch below the rim on either side of an ice-cream container. Place a small skewer through the spool and place in the holes. Fill the tub with water up to the level of the holes. As it rotates, the line gets wet and you avoid getting in a tangle.

Stop your hook from corroding by placing a few grains of rice in the hook box.

To extract a small lump of meat from a tin, just poke in a straw. A little piece of meat will go up inside the straw. Just blow down the straw to get it out. The meat will be the perfect size and shape for bait.

It's important to keep your maggots warm in winter so that they remain active and wriggly. If you glue polystyrene to the outside of their box they will keep warm and stay lively all day.

To add flavour to your maggots or luncheon meat sprinkle some curry powder on them the night before. The fish love the flavour.

Attract different sorts of fish by dyeing your maggots with food colouring. For example, red maggots attract perch.

To encourage bream to bite melt some molasses in hot water and then mix your groundbait into it. Bream have a sweet tooth and will love this.

To stop your worms from sinking in the weeds when fishing in a lake, inject them with air and they'll float nearer the surface.

To put together a cheap kit remember to look through all the magazines for second-hand equipment.

To stop your canvas tackle bag getting wet always put it inside a heavy-duty plastic bag when on the boat.

Don't harm the environment. Keep your unwanted nylon line and take it home with you; chop it up into pieces so if you do lose it there won't be too much damage done.

Protect your hands from the cold and wet by rubbing petroleum jelly into them before you start fishing.

To keep your feet really warm wrap them in kitchen foil and then put a pair of thick socks over the top. Your feet will stay snug and dry all day.

Don't waste money on expensive moonboots. Just buy your wellies one size too big and line them with some polystyrene.

To catch a really good salmon put an item of clothing that belongs to your wife or girlfriend in with the bait feathers. Salmon respond to female pheromones.

Waders will keep you dry . . . up to the knees and thighs at least. Make sure your bottom stays dry too. Cut some rubber trousers off just below the knees and tuck them inside your waders. You won't look like a fashion-plate but you will be more comfortable than your wet-bottomed friends.

Make sure you are safe when you go fly fishing. Put a life jacket on, especially if you are wading – in deep water your waders can fill up very quickly.

To stop yourself from falling into the water when you are in a boat, always remember to sit down!

Always be prepared for the big catch! Take some black plastic bin liners with you and some bags of ice in a cool box. When the big moment comes, put your catch inside the bin liner and surround it with ice bags. The one that didn't get away will stay frozen for several hours until you can get back to your freezer.

When fishing for carp, try enticing them with luncheon meat, sweetcorn or potatoes.

Get rid of slugs – use them as bait for chub, dace, roach and rudd.

Freshwater catfish aren't fussy when it comes to bait – it seems anything goes. Anglers have been known to try soured clams, ripened chicken entrails, pig liver, coagulated blood and even bits of scented soap!

Try tempting a mullet with banana, bread, cheese, peas or pasta.

Some brown trout are partial to . . . other brown trout. You can tell a cannibal trout by its hooked lower jaw.

Rainbow trout in America have been known to reach 50lbs (22.7kg) in weight; unfortunately, they're a bit weedier in Europe with the maximum weight being around 24lbs (11kg).

You are allowed to fish with a bow and arrow on many American waters. The arrow is tied to the end of the line and the reel is fixed on the bow.

Store fishing lines in a dark place because UV light damages them.

Clean fishing rods with white spirit.

Rinse and dry fishing nets after each use, otherwise they'll rot.

Rinse and hang up your waders to dry straight and upside down to prevent kinks that will make them fracture.

Also rub olive oil in to prevent cracking.

The sooner you pare a fish after catching it, the less mess you'll make.

Use polish on fishing rods to make them water repellent.

To stop fishing hooks going rusty put a couple of drops of vegetable oil in the box with them.

Soak fishing lines after use in washing-up liquid to stop them going rusty.

▶▶▶ Antique Dealers & Restorers

Jane Knapp, Bath; Purdy Mellor, Tamworth; Stephen Zacirelo, Worcester; Peter Hanlon, Crediton; Patrick Beetholm-Smith, Kingsley Gallery, Bath; Maggie Masters, Stow on the Wold

To age a piece of furniture simply mix some furniture varnish with soot, and apply.

To remove a scratch from a table crack open a walnut and rub it along the scratch. Walnuts contain a natural resin that will conceal the scratch.

Make new oak look old – place three tea-bags in hot water and leave some wire wool in the solution overnight. Rub the wire wool over the wood to age it.

To get rid of rings or minor scratches cover them with petroleum jelly and leave for 24 hours. Then rub it into the wood, wipe off the excess and polish as normal.

To darken wood use paraffin wax.

Polish wood with metal polish instead of the normal wood kind and it should come up a treat.

To remove greasy stains from wood mix talcum powder and methylated spirits into a sloppy paste. Paint on to the stain and leave to dry. Brush off.

To get rid of ink stains from furniture soak a piece of cotton wool in water and cover the stain with it. The mark will be drawn out and into the cotton wool.

Nourish furniture wood using a mixture of turpentine, linseed oil and malt vinegar.

To prevent the spread of woodworm treat the wood in May. The woodworm larvae emerge in June and July so this should nip them in the bud!

Even out the legs of old chairs by measuring the length of the shortfall on a piece of wood. Use this as a measurement to cut the other legs down to the same length.

To check the originality of handles look inside the drawer. If there are extra holes, the handles will have been added later.

To clean a gilded ceramic plate, simply soak it overnight in fabric conditioner and water. If there is no gilding, then soak in a weak bleach solution.

Clean brass handles with lemon juice.

Remove brown stains from an old print by rubbing the paper with breadcrumbs.

To clean the tops of old books gently rub with breadcrumbs.

To restore a wet book put sheets of blotting paper between the pages of the first half. Place an even weight on top and gently dry with a hair-dryer. Repeat the process for the other half of the book.

Clean valuable old books with vellum bindings by dipping cotton wool in milk and gently wiping over the covers. Finally, clean off with a soft, dry cloth.

Preserve the shine on a slate hearth by spraying with WD40.

Stop cast iron from rusting by wiping with olive oil or sunflower oil.

To remove the craze on ceramic ware soak the piece in baby disinfectant.

To repair cracks in papier mâché use a little Polyfilla and sand down carefully. Then paint to match, and varnish.

If you want to impress coin collectors don't polish a coin: use an old toothbrush and scrub it with hot water.

An easy way to identify silver is simply to sniff it. Silver has a stronger smell than plate.

To read faded silver hallmarks light a candle. Let the soot settle over the hallmark and then place a piece of sticky tape over the soot. Transfer the tape onto a piece of paper and read the hallmark. Or you could breathe on a hallmark. The condensation should make it stand out more clearly.

To polish silver effectively use your fingers.

Plated silver should not be stored away – use it.

To realign the teeth of a fork put them in a vice and close it over the four prongs until they have become straight.

Broken beads on frames can be replaced using dried split peas or lentils.

To restore bead work hand wash in lukewarm water and blow dry gently with a hair-dryer.

Clean velour upholstery with a solution of warm water and washing-up liquid. Dip some muslin into the mixture and wipe over the fabric.

Bring a shine to tortoiseshell by rubbing it with almond oil.

To remove marks from tortoiseshell rub talcum powder over the mark with a cotton rag.

To protect ivory polish with a little almond oil and a soft cloth.

To clean coral lightly sponge with a weak detergent solution.

Stop brass from tarnishing by spraying it with furniture polish and leaving it to dry. This covers the brass with a thin layer of wax which protects it.

Clean a copper kettle by covering it with brown sauce and leaving overnight. Wash it off next morning and admire your reflection in the shiny surface!

To unstick a decanter stopper place in the fridge for 24 hours. Eight times out of ten, the stopper should then come out! For the other two occasions when it doesn't . . .

Remove a stuck stopper from an antique bottle by mixing two parts alcohol to one part glycerine and one part salt. Paint on the join between the stopper and the bottle neck and leave for 24 hours.

To clean a narrow-necked vase fill with water and pop in a couple of denture-cleaning tablets.

To fill a crack in pottery heat the piece slowly to 110 °C / 225 °F / Gas Mark ¼. This should open the crack slightly, allowing you to fill it with glue. Wipe off any excess and allow the piece to cool.

For hairline cracks put the plate in a saucepan of milk and boil for 45 minutes. The crack should disappear.

To age a new piece of stone cover it in yoghurt. In a few weeks, it will have acquired an 'I've been here for ages' look.

To clean delicate oil paintings there's no need for fancy fluids. Spit on to a cotton-wool bud and gently rub the surface of the painting. Test a small area first (in case your spit is too corrosive).

To remove any slack from an oil painting gently tap the small wooden wedges at each corner of the stretcher with a hammer.

To clean antique luggage use saddle soap.

If you want to get an even, thin layer of adhesive, gently roll the glue around a cocktail stick and then apply to the surface.

To prevent Araldite from looking too yellow add a small amount of titanium powder.

If you want to preserve stuffed animals, it's a good idea to conceal a few mothballs in their glass case.

Give a stuffed animal a brilliant smile, wipe its teeth with a wet wipe to whiten its fangs.

To clean dark fur dry some bran in the oven, rub it into the fur and then cover with a warm blanket. You should leave it like this for half an hour before shaking the bran out and then brushing the fur.

To clean light fur rub some cornflour into the fur and roll it up in a warm blanket. Leave it like this for 24 hours before shaking out and brushing.

To store textiles cover them up in acid-free tissue paper and roll around a cardboard tube (either from inside your kitchen paper roll or bought from a post office).

To test if something really is silk throw it against a brick wall. If it sticks to the brick then it is the real thing.

If you want to clean unpainted wax items, wipe them down with softened butter.

To replace an antique doll's eyelashes get some false eyelashes and trim them down to a suitable length. Stick in place with a colourless soluble glue.

If your antique doll is having a bad hair day, put a dab of cold cream on a comb and gently separate a lock at a time from the base of the head until you have got it all under control and she looks respectable again.

To improve the lustre and colour of pearls wear them next to your skin as often as possible.

Clean artificial pearls by rubbing carefully with a chamois leather.

To carry your barometer correctly, always hold it at an angle of 95°.

To get the most out of your barometer store it anywhere except under a radiator.

When attending car boot sales, arrive early. The dealers will be out in force then and any bargains will get snapped up early.

Look for sales with school connections especially in wealthy areas.

The best time for sales is early spring and midsummer because that's when people tend to have clear outs, getting rid of 'rubbish' from their homes.

Don't be afraid to haggle – it's part of the fun and most people expect it.

If you are going to be selling at a car boot sale, you should take some loose change, a large umbrella and plastic sheeting (in case it rains) and something to sit on.

Take someone with you so that you can take it in turns to get drinks, keep an eye on the stall and deal with the rush . . . if there is one!

Don't put everything out at once – keep some good bits and pieces back so that you aren't left with a lot of old rubbish.

Make sure that friends and family turn up and hang around your stall. If you've got a crowd there, it will attract other people.

Look out for people who offer quite a bit of money for a large number of items – they are often professional dealers or collectors who have spotted something they want on your stall.

Surface dirt can be removed from an oil or acrylic painting by rubbing with a bit of old bread.

When cleaning the glass of a painting, spray the cleaner on to your duster before polishing, not directly on to the glass. This stops the moisture from damaging the frame.

Clean gilt picture frames with a mixture made from one egg and a teaspoon of bicarbonate of soda.

Costume jewellery can still be expensive. Look after yours by cleaning it with a little baking powder, then brush off any residue with a soft toothbrush.

If you have a treasured teddy . . . keep him looking pucker with carpet shampoo and then just fluff him up afterwards.

Next time you clean your watch you can actually remove scratches on the face too. Just spend 5 or 10 minutes gently rubbing the glass with metal polish, then wipe it off with a soft duster.

▶▶▶ Aromatherapists

Mary Lapworth

Develop your sense of smell. Start with just four essential oils. Find a quiet, undisturbed place and take time to get to know and recognise these smells. Sniff each one separately; see what emotions, memories and feelings they evoke.

Store essential oils in dark amber glass bottles. Your oils, some of which are expensive, will deteriorate in about eight weeks in a clear or plastic bottle.

Oils should be stored away from direct sunlight, in the cool and dark.

Oils will last for about a year if stored properly.

Citrus oils don't last for very long so only buy small amounts at any one time.

To preserve the label, paint with clear nail varnish. This works for medicine bottles, too.

Never buy cheap oils. They *should* be expensive in order to be effective.

Avoid buying fake oils; learn the Latin names, which should appear on the packaging or bottle.

To keep oil fresh never put new oil in an old bottle.

You'll know when an oil has gone bad if it appears cloudy and gives off an unpleasant smell. Essential oils should be clear.

Carrier oils are used to dilute the essential oil. They allow the essential oil to be spread over the body and to be absorbed into the skin properly. They are ideal for dry or sensitive skins. Cold-pressed oils are the best. Sweet almond oil is most commonly used: it's non-allergenic, neutral and can be used for massaging babies.

Choose the right carrier oil – sesame oil is great for stretch marks, walnut balances the nervous system, apricot and peach kernel as well as evening primrose oil are best for cell regeneration. For menstrual problems, use walnut or evening primrose oil.

To make your carrier oils go further, add 5 to 10 per cent of wheatgerm oil which helps to preserve the mixture.

To mix your essential oils with the carrier oil, use a toothpick.

Never put an undiluted essential oil directly on to your skin – except for one drop of tea tree or lavender oil.

Don't take oils internally.

When making up your mixture, add each essential oil a drop at a time.

To store small amounts of mixed oils for a short period put them in an egg cup and cover with clingfilm.

To increase the life of the scent from your oils add some sandalwood oil, which acts as a fixative.

Always do a patch test before applying oils to check that you or whoever you are intending to use the oils on aren't allergic to any of them.

To mix enough oil for a body massage mix ten drops of essential oil with two teaspoons of carrier oil. You will need more carrier oil for a person with a lot of body hair.

When giving a massage, ensure that the room is warm and that you have a suitable, comfortable area to work in. Make sure there are no distractions: take the phone off the hook and send the children round to friends!

Always warm your hands before giving a massage!

Avoid harsh overhead lighting when giving a massage. Candles give a wonderful light and create the right sort of atmosphere.

When you have prepared your oil for massage, make sure it is held in something sturdy that you won't knock over.

Always wash your hands after massaging the feet.

If you're feeling out of sorts or in a bit of a tizz, have a foot massage to calm you down.

To get the most benefit from essential oils in your bath don't put them straight under the hot water tap because they will evaporate too quickly. Instead, put your oils (five to ten drops) into the filled bath and mix around. Keep the door closed so that the vapours don't escape.

If you have sensitive skin, mix the essential oil with a base oil, such as sweet almond or apricot oil, before pouring into the bath.

Before you get into the bath it's a good idea to wash first. This way, you let the oils do their stuff without interference from soap or bubble bath.

Oils are lovely in a bath but can make things slippery. To avoid slip-sliding away, mix the oil with some full-fat milk or dairy cream before adding to the water.

Always wipe the bath down after use. Some essential oils can mark plastic baths if they are left on the surface.

If you are in the sauna, add two drops of eucalyptus or pine oil to ¹/₂ pint/300 ml of water and throw it over the coals. The smell is lovely and the oils are wonderful cleansers and detoxifiers.

For a wonderful foot bath, quarter-fill a washing-up bowl with warm water and add five drops of your favourite essential oil diluted in a cup of vodka (or pure alcohol). Lavender soothes feet while a mixture of four or five drops of peppermint, thyme and rosemary (in whatever balance you prefer) acts as a pick-me-up for tired feet.

Chapped hands will benefit from a soak in some warm water in to which you have added three or four drops of patchouli or comfrey oil.

When using essential oils in a vaporiser, use two to three drops for a small room and six to ten drops for a larger room.

If you don't have a vaporiser, put five drops of essential oil in a small bowl of water and place it on a radiator.

Don't overdo it. Avoid essential oils for 48 hours every week.

Large amounts of clary sage oil can cause drowsiness, so don't use it before driving or operating machinery.

Avoid clary sage if you are on Hormone Replacement Therapy (HRT).

At bedtime, you can put a couple of drops of lavender oil on your pillow to relax you. Ylang-ylang is an alternative choice – it's a great aphrodisiac.

Avoid peppermint oil close to bedtime because it can cause insomnia.

Smelly feet? A couple of drops of pine or parsley oil should help dispel the pong. And you could try some lemongrass oil in your wardrobe.

Make wonderful scented drawer liners by adding a couple of drops of essential oil to some pretty wrapping paper.

Put a couple of drops of your favourite oil on your handkerchief. This is a great idea if you've got a cold.

For a good mouthwash, add three drops of oil to one teaspoon of brandy. Benzoin, camomile, lavender or lemongrass is most effective.

To disinfect a dirty floor add some bergamot, juniper and eucalyptus oils to the final rinsing water.

To make your own inexpensive room spray, add ten drops of your favourite essential oil to a plant spray filled with seven tablespoons of warm water. One tablespoon of vodka or pure alcohol acts as a preservative.

To get the most from your fire put a couple of drops of pine, sandalwood or cedarwood oil on to the wood that you are going to burn. Leave it for an hour before lighting the fire. When the fire is burning, the heat releases the smell into the room.

To help your parties go with a swing add a few drops of clary sage or jasmine to a vaporiser. At Christmas use frankincense (of course), cinnamon, orange, cedarwood or sandalwood.

Insects hate the smell of lemongrass, melissa, eucalyptus, tea tree or citronella oil. Use them when you're eating outside in the summer.

Get rid of fleas by adding a couple of drops of tea tree oil to some water and sponge your dog's coat.

Beware of all the hype surrounding aromatherapy. Don't be taken in by extravagant promises. Of the three hundred and more oils on the market, between fifty and a hundred have actual health benefits.

Don't use aromatherapy to treat serious medical conditions.
It's a great way to treat things such as stress, emotional problems
or minor injuries but it's not the answer to every problem. Don't
use aromatherapy to treat cancer, heart conditions, bad varicose
veins, very high blood pressure, epilepsy or progressive neural
disorders.

If you are pregnant, you must be *very* careful which oils you use.
Some oils have strong diuretic properties while others are
potentially toxic to an unborn foetus. The recommended oils for
pregnancy are: lavender, lemon, neroli, orange, rose, sandalwood,
chamomile and geranium (in small quantities). Avoid chamomile
and lavender in the first few months if you have a history of
miscarriage. If in doubt, talk to a qualified aromatherapist.

▶▶▶ Artists

Francis Hatch, Sherbourne; Antony Whishaw, London; Dave Triffit, Oxford;
Thomsin Smith, Hereford; Mary Jackson, Hampshire; David Peart, Chester

Save on the cost of paint by planning what you are going to do in
a scrap book.

Map out the picture you are going to paint using oil pastels, then
paint over this template.

To kill the stark whiteness of paper stir a tea-bag in to some water
and paint on the water to create a gentle yellowish colour. Use the
paper within four days otherwise fungus will start to grow.

When painting watercolours, use a water-soluble pencil to draw
the outline; it will disappear when you paint over it.

Make your own paint holders by placing empty yoghurt pots into a
Tupperware container. When you have finished, simply snap the lid
back on. This is especially useful if you are painting outdoors.

Create a paintbrush holder from a cardboard tube (from a post office). Plastic holders tend to make the brushes go mouldy.

Keep your paintbrushes in an empty chocolate box.

Store sable brushes away from moths by keeping them in a container.

To make your brushes last longer wrap them in newspaper while they are still damp.

Store paint brushes wrapped in brown paper with a rubber band round them.

Keep your brushes in good condition by putting a drop of linseed oil on each one.

When painting watercolours, dry your paintbrushes flat on a piece of kitchen roll.

Store paintings face to face to protect the surfaces.

Keep white spirit in a jam jar with a lid to stop any evaporation.

Wear waterproof trousers so you can sit anywhere and not get covered in paint.

Wear surgeon's gloves to keep your hands clean.

To clean brushes in the great outdoors fill empty camera film containers with white spirit.

Keep erasers clean – store in empty camera film containers.

Sharpen pencils using a scalpel rather than a Stanley knife.

If the top on a paint tube is stuck on with gunge, simply place the tube in a bowl of hot water for a few minutes and the top will then come off easily.

To get the last squeeze of paint from a tube cut the tube in half.

Remove oil marks from paper by covering with talcum powder, leaving overnight and then brushing off.

If you make a mistake on your oil painting just scrape it off with a razor blade and start again.

Don't spend money buying expensive art fixative, use hairspray instead.

Masking tape makes a good, fine white line – don't get it from art shops (it's too expensive); go to your local DIY shop instead.

Using ordinary water-based paint is cheaper than a conventional primer.

Don't waste paint. Cover your palette with clingfilm if you're taking a break from painting. This will keep the paint fresh for up to two weeks until you are ready to start again.

Don't use ready-made blacks because nothing in nature is totally black. Instead, mix blues and browns together to make a more interesting black.

Create your own brown colour by sieving soil and then cooking it in a saucepan. Mix with acrylic to get a lovely deep colour.

To clean your palette use a mixture of white spirit and soap.

Use an old box on its side for still life. If you cut along the sides, you can lift the lid to adjust the light that is shed on to the still life. This is very good for composition.

Get a really good splatter paint effect by using matchsticks or old toothbrushes.

Create a rust effect by using salt or coffee mixed with the paint.

To get a good, rough texture to your paint simply throw loads of sand into the paint, mix it up and away you go.

Create texture across your canvas by using a garden plant spray filled with liquid paint.

Smooth down highly textured paint with a cheese-grater.

Cheap, effective charcoal sticks can be made from wrapping willow tree branches in tin foil and baking them in the oven.

To paint a large canvas all one colour attach a paintbrush to a broomstick. This saves you from grubbing around on your hands and knees.

Prime paper with white spirit first because this provides an ideal base for oil paint.

Move large canvases around your studio by placing them on roller skates.

To view your painting from another perspective look at it in a mirror.

Stain wooden picture frames using shoe polish.

To dry paintings in a confined space string them up on a washing line. This leaves the floor clear.

Hang pictures using heavy-duty fishing line.

Not all plaster walls are as solid as they seem, so spread the load by placing two hooks in the wall at a distance of half the width of the picture.

To restore old black enamel paintings apply some black shoe polish and then buff off.

Keep oil paintings out of the kitchen because cooking fumes can destroy the paint.

A good way to get airflow in a frame is to use a buffer. Sliced up bits of cork work well.

When cleaning the glass of a painting spray the cleaner onto your duster first before polishing. This stops the moisture from damaging the frame.

Surface dirt can be removed from an oil or acrylic painting using a piece of old bread.

When hanging a painting, make sure that its centre is at eye-level.

►►► Bakers

Geoff Capper, Allen's Pies, Bolton; Stephen Hallam, Old Pie Shop, Melton Mowbray; Lawrie Finch; George Charman; Ron Gardiner; Dean Simpole-Clarke

Have a couple of small freezer bags ready when baking so that you can pop them over your floury hands if the phone rings!

The secret of fantastic bread is always to keep a little bit of dough back from the previous day's batch to add to the new mixture.

If you can't remember whether you've added yeast to your dough, here's a simple test. Take out a small piece of the dough – about gobstopper size – and put it in a cup of hot water. If you didn't put in any yeast, it will immediately sink to the bottom. Dough with yeast in it will rise to the top.

To make authentic-tasting naan or pitta bread, gently warm the flour in a microwave first.

The longer you knead dough, the longer you should leave the dough to develop.

To prevent bread from drying out when baking cover it with a cake tin while it's in the oven.

Don't throw day-old bread away, just brush it with olive oil and toast it in the oven.

For a great rolling pin fill a claret bottle with warm water and replace the cork securely.

Don't rush to get your scones in the oven. Resting them allows the baking powder to become active.

Stop gaping air pockets developing during baking, by soaking some breadcrumbs in water and sprinkling them into your meat pies.

If you haven't got a pastry cutter, use the thoroughly cleaned lid of an aerosol can instead.

When rolling pastry, put it between two sheets of clingfilm. You won't need to use extra flour to stop it sticking to the surfaces and it is easier to turn over, too.

Don't turn your body at an angle when rolling pastry. Turn the pastry around so that you don't hurt your back.

Always let pie pastry dry thoroughly before adding the filling. A skin forms which prevents the filling seeping in during cooking.

Put sugar in a pie, not on it. This gives a much more even flavour, and sugar on a pie often burns.

When slicing apples for pies, put a little salt in the water to stop them discolouring: it has the same effect as adding lemon but it's cheaper.

To cut a sponge cake horizontally take two pieces of wood of equal thickness and of half the depth of the cake, and lie them either side of the cake. Slide the knife in a sawing action across the top of the wood and through the cake.

To cut a loaf of bread, follow the same method as above. Just stand the bread on its end and cut.

Ensure a uniform thickness in pastry by placing two pieces of wood on either side of the pastry and running the rolling pin across the top of the wood.

If you only have very cold butter to hand when baking, try grating it into a warm metal bowl. It will soon become softer and reach the right temperature.

To weigh golden syrup with minimal mess just put the whole tin on the scales and keep spooning the sticky stuff out until the tin has gone down in weight by the amount you need.

Do your cakes always sink? It's not necessarily the opening of the oven door that causes it but the closing. Unless you do it very gently, the sudden movement can cause the cake to sink.

To stop the fruit in cakes from sinking, first wash the fruit, then coat it in glycerine.

To stop glacé cherries from sinking coat them lightly in flour before using.

For a really moist fruit cake, use marmalade instead of candied peel.

Always soak dried fruit overnight – for extra flavour, soak the fruit in apple or orange juice.

For a special-occasion cake, marinate the fruit in your favourite liqueur for a week.

If your cakes always come out cracked, put a dish of cold water in the bottom of the oven before baking.

Before sandwiching your cake together with jam, spread a little butter on each sponge surface. This will stop the cake absorbing all the jam.

Use muslin instead of a sieve when dusting icing sugar through a doily. It is much finer and the effect is so much prettier.

If you want your cake to have a flat top for decorating, spoon out a bit of the mixture from the middle of the tin before baking.

To dry a cake out put it under an anglepoise desk lamp.

Before icing a cake, sprinkle the top with some flour; this will stop the icing running down over the edges.

For a deceptively clever effect, put two colours of icing in a bag and then pipe out. The two-tone effect is stunning.

If you don't have a turntable for decorating a cake, don't worry. Take two plates, sandwich them together back to back with a little cooking oil and place on a damp tea towel to stop the bottom plate slipping. Placed on top, your cake will turn round beautifully.

Royal icing is notoriously difficult to beat with a food mixer. Try fixing the whisk attachment to a variable speed drill instead.

Glacé icings can be horribly sweet. Substituting milk for some of the water gives a creamy texture and reduces the sweetness.

To keep cakes fresh in the tin throw in half an apple.

To create an impressive chocolate bowl brush or pipe lukewarm melted chocolate on to half of an inflated balloon until it's about 3 in/7 cm deep. Allow to cool thoroughly, then carefully burst the balloon (see opposite).

Make your own piping bag by twisting some foil in to a cone and snipping off the bottom.

To tell whether an egg is absolutely fresh put it in a bowl of water. If it is really fresh, it will sink. Older eggs will float.

To remove the stones from cherries use a hair grip stuck into a cork.

Don't waste orange or lemon peel from inside a grater; use a small, clean toothbrush to get it out.

A pinch of salt added to margarine makes whisking quicker.

Store castor sugar with rose petals, lemon zest or cinnamon sticks for extra flavour.

To soften hard brown sugar leave it in a bowl covered with a damp tea towel overnight.

When making meringues you must keep the bowl completely free of grease. Rub the bowl with salt and wash it thoroughly.

To give your meringues a toffee flavour use brown sugar.

A quick way to mark out squares for toffee or fudge is to lightly press a wire cooling tray on to a tin of mixture. The grid marks left behind will be a clear guide to perfect little pieces.

To light a Christmas pudding put brandy in a saucepan and heat gently. Place the warm brandy in a metal soup ladle over a lighted candle until it bursts into flames. Carefully pour over the pudding.

Dried out, stale bread can be revived if you wrap it in kitchen foil and leave on a low heat in the oven for about 10 minutes.

To keep bread moist while baking add a little honey to the dough.

To keep home-baked bread fresh for longer add a couple of teaspoons of vegetable oil to the dough.

Stop mice or mites getting to your flour – put a bay leaf in the packet.

Keep flour in the freezer to keep it for longer.

To stop garlic bread going soggy during cooking wrap it in tin foil.

When kneading dough, stop every two or three minutes to let the dough 'rest'. After resting for a couple of minutes, the dough will be easier to knead.

Flour compacts during storage. Fluff it up before measuring out an amount for a recipe or you'll get too much flour.

If, when heating or baking bread at home, the bread burns and/or has burnt spots on it, cut the spots off and patch up the scars with beaten egg brushed on to the exposed areas. Then keep heating the bread.

To revitalise stale bread plunge the loaf or rolls into cold water for a moment and then bake on a low heat for 10 minutes.

To remove crusts from bread try using a pizza cutter; it will give you a nice neat edge and waste less.

To test whether a loaf of home-made bread is baked properly tap it on top. A hollow sound means that it is baked.

Place a wet towel over your dough, when making bread, to make it rise more quickly.

Make a quiche without the hassle or calories of pastry: simply bake the mixture in a lightly oiled, shallow casserole dish.

To prevent soggy quiche bases brush the pastry with lemon juice and bake blind for three minutes before putting the filling in and cooking fully.

To stop the base and crust of fruit pies going soggy during cooking sprinkle the pastry with flour before putting in the filling.

To stop pastry sticking to your rolling pin when rolling put the pin in the freezer or fridge until it's cold and then continue rolling.

When you've cooked berries for pie fillings, save any left-over juice for topping pancakes and ice-cream.

To avoid soggy pie crusts sprinkle a layer of breadcrumbs over it before cooking.

If, midway through cooking a fruit pie, you notice that the fruit is seeping out, sprinkle salt over the leaking fruit and put it back in the oven. The fruit will become crisp and can easily be removed.

To refresh dried out mincemeat (for mince pies) add brandy or sherry.

To warm bowls that can't go in the oven fill them with boiling water and leave to stand for 5 minutes. Then pour away the water, dry the bowl and serve.

Left-over mashed potato is wonderful in pastry dishes, adding a lovely flavour and texture.

To stop frozen pizzas sticking to the tray or foil during cooking and to make them taste nicer, brush the base with olive oil.

Some pizza take-aways sell off uncollected orders for a reduced price.

Make sweet pizzas – use fruit as a topping and even jam instead of tomato paste.

Never run out of breadcrumbs for stuffings and toppings – keep all your bread ends, pop into a food processor to make crumbs and then freeze in bags.

Try using a packet of stuffing instead of breadcrumbs on scotch eggs for a tasty change.

If you're baking shortbread cookies, try substituting half of your plain flour with cornflour for a really rich taste.

To stop cake mix sticking to your spoon when you're transferring it to a tin, try dipping the spoon in milk beforehand.

To prevent jam tarts from bubbling over whilst cooking sprinkle a few drops of cold water on to them.

Try using tea cakes or hot cross buns for a tastier bread-and-butter pudding.

For an extra rich, tasty fruit cake use cold coffee instead of milk in your fruit cakes.

For a moist fruit cake with extra flavour grate a cooking apple into the mixture.

To make chocolate cookies for parties add a ¼ cup of beer. Or even better, some sherry ...

To check the quality of baking powder put a teaspoon of it into a cup of hot water. If the water bubbles a lot, the baking powder is good. If it doesn't bubble, throw it away.

Do your cakes crumble when cut? After cooling and before cutting, pop them into the freezer for 20 minutes.

To improve the flavour and texture of cakes and to reduce fat at the same time substitute one-third of butter with a mashed banana.

To make fluffier, lighter cakes whip the egg whites separately before adding to the recipe.

To give chocolate cakes an added kick and to give them a rich, brown colour, add a teaspoon of instant coffee granules to the mix.

For a tasty, colourful cake topping mix a little strawberry jam and boiling water into icing sugar.

It sounds obvious, but the best cakes are baked in warm kitchens, so turn on the central heating before you begin baking.

To stop cakes and pastries sticking to the inside of shaped cutters, brush the insides with a little oil.

To stop ice-cream melting in the bowl so quickly put the bowls in the fridge for 30 minutes before serving the ice-cream.

Decorate your cakes with real flowers. To stop the flowers wilting cut a 3-in piece of plastic drinking straw. Bend the end of the straw upwards and tape it. Fill the straw three-quarters full with water and insert the flower stem inside it.

To make your sponge cakes rise add a tablespoon of boiling water to the mix just before putting it in the tin.

Cakes are completely baked when you can stick a skewer in and it comes out clean.

For a delicious pudding add some elderberries to your apple pie.

If your custard goes lumpy, quickly put the base of the pan into some cold water and keep whisking until things are going smoothly again.

To bring out the taste of chocolate in most recipes, add a few coffee granules.

Avoid mess and waste – cut the required amounts of frozen gateaux and cakes while they're still frozen.

If sugar goes hard and lumpy, pop it into your bread bin with a loaf and it will go soft.

If you have trouble slicing lemon meringue pies, try dipping your knife into some hot water before cutting.

Left-over chocolates can be transformed. Melt them in a bowl over hot water, and add nuts and raisins. Cool the mixture, make it into balls and chill. Delicious 'home-made' chocs!

Alternatively spoon the hot mixture over ice-cream for an indulgent dessert.

To avoid sticky fingers when pressing down the base for a cheesecake use a potato masher or the bottom of a mug.

Improve home-made bread-and-butter pudding by adding finely grated carrot – it's a natural sweetener and adds extra texture and colour.

To make individual pavlovas drop the meringue mix on to the baking sheet in large dollops – they are lovely to serve at a dinner party and they also take less time to cook.

Melt your favourite chocolate bar in the microwave, then pour over ice-cream for a delicious treat.

Substitute yoghurt for milk to make lighter scones.

For a crunchy topping for fruit crumbles and sweet tarts grate some bread, then put it in a dish and bake. Mix with demerara sugar to taste and use as required.

To make pretty chocolate curls microwave a chocolate bar for 10 seconds and then use a cheese slice to curl.

If custard 'scrambles' during cooking, put it in a liquidiser with a tablespoon of milk and spin it until it goes smooth again.

If your meringue crust cracks as it cools, spoon cream over it.

Keep brown sugar hard by leaving a slice of apple in the jar.

For firm meringues add a teaspoon of cornflour to the sugar before beating into the egg whites.

To slice baked meringue easily grease the knife with butter before cutting.

To make your mousses more decorative make two different mousses, one with white chocolate and one with dark. Put each in a separate, small, piping bag. Then, put both bags in one large piping bag. Squeeze into a dish and, as the mousse comes out, it will be a beautiful swirl of the two colours. The taste combination of the sweet white chocolate and the bitter dark is lovely too.

To prevent ice crystals forming on ice-cream when stored in the freezer, stretch some clingfilm over the top and press the film on to the surface of the ice-cream. Put the lid on the top and pop it back into the freezer.

For a spicy version of bread-and-butter pudding use malt loaf layered with dates and bananas.

To make more meringue with the same number of eggs add 1 tablespoon of water per egg.

To make beating brown sugar into a cake mix easier put it through a food processor first – it makes it softer.

To prevent nuts sinking to the bottom of cake mixes coat them lightly with flour before adding.

To get the best taste out of nuts in baking toast them first on a baking tray before adding to the mix.

To prevent mould growing on the surface of jam moisten the waxed circle on top of the jar with whisky.

▶▶▶ Beauticians

Midge A. Killen, Amazing Nails, USA; Cathy Bradley, Hydro Springs; Theresa Cook

▷▷ Perfume

Make sure your perfume is working for you – always apply it to your pulse points (behind the ears, nape of the neck, inside the wrists, the temples, the crook of the elbow, behind the knees and on the ankles). Perfume rises, so putting it on your lower body works well.

The higher the concentration of perfume, the longer the scent lasts – *extrait* or perfume has the highest concentration, followed by parfum de toilette and eau de parfum, then eau de toilette, eau de Cologne and, lowest of all, splash Cologne.

▷▷ Skin Deep

Before putting on any face mask, cover your skin with a thin layer of gauze and apply the mask over it. You'll get the benefits of the ingredients seeping through and, when it's time to take the mask off, you can simply peel the gauze away. It's much quicker and you don't damage your skin by scrubbing at stubborn bits of mask.

Give tired skin a boost – use a honey facial. Apply honey to clean skin, leave on for one hour, then rinse off with warm water.

A good emergency face mask can be made from porridge oats mixed with honey.

Cucumber and yoghurt make a great face mask. Blend some mashed cucumber with natural yoghurt and apply to your face. Leave for about 15 minutes, then rinse off with warm water. Cucumber cools and tones while yoghurt acts as a pick-me-up for tired skin.

Make your own facial scrub – use two tablespoons of honey, four or five tablespoons of cornmeal and a tablespoon of ground almonds. Mix them together and then apply to your face. Leave for 5 minutes before rinsing off with warm water and a flannel.

Save your expensive toner – apply it using wet cotton wool. If you use dry, the cotton wool absorbs most of the toner and your skin doesn't get the benefit.

Don't waste cleanser by putting it on to cotton wool that just soaks up most of the cream. Use your finger tips instead and then rinse the cleanser off.

If the weather's very hot and you have a tendency to become 'shiny', make it look deliberate! Wear lip gloss and sheen on your eyelids.

Keep your make-up fresh however hot the conditions – use a quick spray of water every so often.

Loose powder often looks too heavy because it sticks to moisturisers and cleansers. Blot your face with a tissue before you put any powder on.

Apply loose powder with throw-away cotton-wool pads. The puff provided with the powder will quickly build up dirt and won't do your skin any favours.

If you've got a reddish complexion, use a foundation with a greenish tinge. Applied under normal make-up, this will help to neutralise the red.

If you've got a really, *really* bad spot, you'll never be able to cover it up. Instead, turn it into a trendy beauty spot with a dark eyeliner pencil.

Make sure you take your make-up off even when you come in really late after partying the night away. Have a small plastic storage box of ready dampened cotton wool pads by your bed to make the task as easy and quick as possible.

Need a simple make-up remover? Petroleum jelly removes eye make-up, lipstick and blusher.

When using eye cream at night, never put it too close to your eyes or they'll look puffy in the morning.

If you do suffer from puffy eyes first thing in the morning, simply lie down again for 5 minutes with used tea-bags over your eyes.

Open your pores by putting your face over a bowl of hot steamy water. Cover your head with a towel to keep the steam in. If you've got oily skin, stay there for at least 5 minutes.

Remove warts with a solution of one part cider vinegar to one part glycerine. Apply this every day until the warts disappear.

Remove blackheads easily. Mix one tablespoon of Epsom salts with three drops of white iodine and one cup of boiling water. Leave the mixture to cool until warm, and then apply it.

Alternatively, dab neat lemon juice on the blackheads before going to bed. Wash off in the morning with cool water. Repeat for a few nights.

A great way to dry up any pimples is to smear toothpaste on them.

Another way to dry up spots is to dab them with neat lemon juice several times a day.

▷▷ Luscious Lips

To get the deepest, longest-lasting effect from lipstick powder your lips before applying the lipstick.

To mend a broken lipstick carefully melt the broken edges with a lighted match and press them together. Smooth down the join with a toothpick and then leave the lipstick in the fridge for a couple of hours.

▷▷ Eye Eye

Eyeliners need to be really sharp. Try chilling eye pencils in the fridge before sharpening them to get a really pointy point.

Avoid smudgy eyeliner by dipping a wet brush in dark eye shadow and using this to line the eyes instead. It will stay on all day.

When applying mascara, look down directly into a mirror. It makes it impossible to get mascara into the eyes.

After applying mascara, spray a little hair-spray on to the brush and apply a layer to the lashes (avoid this if you have very sensitive eyes).

When you run out of mascara stand the tube in a cup of hot water for a minute. This will loosen the last bit of mascara and allow you to use it for at least two more coats.

Make your own eye make-up remover using one part baby shampoo to twenty parts boiled and cooled water.

▷▷ Nails & Hands

Keep nail polish in the fridge. It dries much more quickly when applied.

Stop the top of the nail varnish from sticking – just rub some petroleum jelly on to the top of the bottle.

If your hands become stained or discoloured rub the skin with half a lemon. Rinse off and dry your hands carefully, then massage in some hand cream because lemon has a drying effect on the skin.

If you get ink stains on your hands rub the stains with a nail brush that you have dipped in vinegar and salt. You could also try rubbing the ink stains with the inside of a banana skin.

Clean grubby nails – especially if you're a smoker – with minty toothpaste.

Don't wipe away excess hand cream – rub it into the cuticles and let it soak in.

Push back cuticles with lollipop sticks.

When filing nails keep going in one direction. Sawing backwards and forwards weakens the edges.

For heavy-duty hand cream, mix virgin olive oil and petroleum jelly together. Rub the mixture into your hands and then put them into freezer bags. Sit and have a cuppa or read the paper while your hands absorb the benefits of this perfect conditioner.

Always protect your hands – try to wear gloves for washing-up, cleaning round the house and gardening.

Don't wash your hands in very hot water because it strips the skin of natural oils. Warm water and a gentle soap is just as effective. Always apply hand cream after you've got your hands wet.

▷▷ Legs & Feet

Give your feet a treat– a cup of baking soda or Epsom salts dissolved in a bowl of warm water makes a wonderful foot bath.

After having your legs waxed allow them to breathe. If you put tight trousers or stockings back on immediately you are encouraging infections.

Strengthen your ankles while watching television. Keep moving them in circular motions.

▷▷ All Over

A handful of dry sea salt rubbed over the body before a bath helps to slough off dead skin.

Oatmeal makes a good alternative to soap – put a handful in a muslin bag and use it in the bath as a body scrub.

Salt baths help to heal any wounds or scratches on the skin. Add a cup of salt to the bath water.

Milk baths soften skin – add 1 pint/600 ml of milk to your bath water and pretend you are Cleopatra.

Dry skin? Add a drop or two of good-quality olive oil to your bath.

Don't throw old fruit away. Pop any fruit that's gone too soft into the blender. Use the mixture as an all-over body mask and nutrient. Once you shower it off, your skin will feel really soft and you'll smell good enough to eat.

If you suffer from bad circulation try alternating hot and cold showers to get your system moving.

To stop flecks of toothpaste getting on your clothes while cleaning your teeth – wrap a towel around your shoulders to cover your front.

Face flannels can be thoroughly sterilised by 'cooking' them damp in a microwave oven for 5 minutes.

Avoid bubbles in your nail varnish by gently rolling the bottle to mix it, rather than shaking it as we all do.

Remove any stains left by nail varnish by dipping your nails into fresh lemon juice.

Remove dead skin and beat facial blackheads by adding a teaspoon of sugar to your soap.

To remove blackheads apply gentle pressure to the affected area with the rounded end of a hair grip.

To get rid of spots mix three teaspoons of honey with one teaspoon of cinnamon and dab the mixture on to your face nightly. In two weeks you'll have really clear skin.

For baby smooth skin add a cupful of milk granules to your bath and enjoy a long soak.

For a sensuous bath mix a few drops of your favourite perfume with some good olive oil.

Here's a fruity way to get rid of ugly verrucas: wrap a banana skin around your foot, with the inside of the banana skin against your foot. You could hold it in place with a sock over the top. Repeat nightly for four weeks and the offending verruca will disappear.

Don't waste money on expensive facial water sprays – just use a regular plant spray bottle filled with some mineral water. It's great for hot days and sets make-up a treat.

If your eyelids are sticky in the morning, dip a cotton bud in baby shampoo (which doesn't sting) and use it to clean the roots of your lashes. Then wash your eyes in clear, cool water.

If your eyes are puffy after washing, apply the pulp of a roasted apple to your eyelids.

To exfoliate and soften hands work a mixture of olive oil and granulated sugar into them, then rinse off.

To give yourself a good back scrub place a bar of soap inside a stocking or chopped off tights' leg, in the middle. Knot the stocking on each side of the soap, hold one end in each hand and with a see-sawing motion scrub your back. For a more vigorous scrub use grainy exfoliating soap.

For a cheap moisturiser blend a banana with a little milk and smooth on to your face for 20 minutes.

If you have excess moisturiser on your hands, don't rinse it off. Run your fingers through your hair – the cream will prevent frizz and makes a good conditioner.

There's no need to buy expensive make-up removers – baby oil does the job brilliantly.

Or try using cold milk.

Run out of toothpaste? A little bit of bicarbonate of soda does the trick.

Smelly feet? Try rubbing in a little eucalyptus oil.

Or sprinkle some talc inside your socks or shoes to keep them dry and smelling sweet.

Nobody likes bad breath . . . chew on a little garden mint.

Try cleansing your mouth with fennel or aniseed seeds available from health food shops. Chew after meals to get the best results.

To save water clean your teeth using a mug rather than have the water running constantly.

Also replace one bath with a shower each week.

Fingers that have become superglued together can be unstuck by rolling a pencil gently between them.

If you are unfortunate enough to have superglued your eyelids together, don't despair. A damp cotton-wool pad held over the eye should do the trick.

To keep spectacles clean rinse them in clear water every morning.

▶▶▶ Bird Breeders

Ron Willcocks

Make sure the cage is large enough. The bigger the cage, the better. By law, birds should be kept in cages that are wider than their wingspan. Shape is important – don't just go for tall and narrow. Budgies, for example, should be kept in a space at least $12 \times 24 \times 24$ in/$30 \times 60 \times 60$ cm.

Get the perfect perch. Don't just stick in a bit of dowelling and be done with it. Birds need different shapes and diameters of perch in order to exercise their feet. Sticks such as bamboo or willow that have varying diameters are best.

Never put sandpaper on the perch because the particles can get stuck in a bird's foot and cause infection.

For greenery that looks good all year, chop up fake Christmas trees.

Keep them amused. If you've got only one bird, you could give it a mirror for company. Birds like listening to the radio too – the choice of station is up to you.

If your bird is bored you could try introducing a mate. However, certain types of lovebirds won't accept a new mate after the old one dies.

Avoid accidents when clipping birds' claws – hold the bird up to the light so that you can see where the vein in the bird's claw ends and not cut into it.

It's easy to clean your bird's cage if you keep it lined with newspaper. Just take out each dirty sheet and replace it with a clean one.

Make provision in your will for your parrot – they often outlive their owners.

If a bird's egg is cracked, a thin layer of clear nail varnish will preserve it.

Spruce up your parrot – spray him once a week with lukewarm water, first thing in the morning.

If your parrot doesn't like being sprayed, place a container of water in the cage and let him bathe when he feels like it.

When you let birds out to fly round the house, make sure that you keep the toilet lid down, and cover any windows with an old bed sheet. Large expanses of glass can confuse birds and they may fly into a window and stun themselves.

If you can't get your bird back into the cage, darken the room as much as possible. Birds are more subdued in dark conditions.

Don't rush around after your bird. You can literally scare them to death. If you are approaching a bird, do so slowly and deliberately.

Make a cheap playstand – fill a bucket with sand and stand some branches in it.

Parrots enjoy climbing hardwoods such as beech or ash. Scrub with soap first to remove any dirt or parasites.

Put strips of willow bark in the nesting boxes of lovebirds.

Parrots like to dig, so place a pot filled with earth in their cage and let them root around to their heart's delight.

African Greys' perches should be placed low enough to stop the birds looking down on people. This stops them behaving in an aggressive manner.

Never cover a parrot's cage with a towel or knitted blanket. The bird might get its claws caught up in the material and end up hanging itself. Use an old sheet instead.

Parrots grow tired of bird seed. Spice up their diet with the occasional hot chilli as a treat.

Add a bit of variety to a parrot's diet. Hard dog chews with a small hole bored in the top are fun for them to peck at.

Collect berries in the autumn and then freeze them to keep for treats all year round.

Millet is a great treat for birds but be very sparing with it otherwise they'll end up eating it to the exclusion of everything else.

Birds need grit to help them digest seeds.

Two's company especially if you're out of the house a lot. Two cock birds get on better than two hens.

But canaries are not social birds. They are quite happy to be kept on their own. Two males will always fight, as will a male and female (except during the nesting season obviously!).

What's the difference between the sexes? Hens' plumage tends to be paler and not as bright as the males'.

When choosing a bird, check it for any signs of poor health. It should have bright eyes with no discharge, a good plump breast, no wheezy breathing, and no deformed bill or malformed claws.

Cock birds are usually easier to tame, teach to talk and so make better pets. Hens can be a bit destructive when the breeding season starts.

Be careful when handling the plumage of a water bird. It's a good idea to avoid touching it with your hands, especially if you're a bit sweaty. Wrap the bird in a clean cloth or bit of sacking to secure the wings.

To hold a small bird safely place your hand over the bird. Its neck should be between your first and second fingers, its wings safely tucked in the palm of your hand. Remember not to squeeze too hard.

Alternatively you can hold a small bird between your two hands, but this isn't as effective as the first method if your bird is a biter.

Parrots make good pets and can be great mimics, if taught from a young age. Mind you, they can also be extremely noisy and harbour vandalistic tendencies!

Budgerigars are popular pets and can be kept inside or as aviary birds.

You can tell the sex of a budgie by looking at the area above its beak (called the cere); purple or blue means it's a cock, brown means it's a hen.

Older budgies have a white iris, while younger birds (under 12 weeks) don't. Young budgies also have fine black bars on their foreheads, which disappear with their first moult.

Parakeets are quite happy in an aviary and will often nest successfully. Generally, they are better in a crowd than as sole pets.

Cockatiels can learn to talk and whistle. They make good pets because they're generally cheerful, gentle birds.

Finches enjoy life in an aviary, but may need a bit of extra heating in the winter. Grow plants in and around the aviary to act as a windbreak.

Bengalese finches make good foster parents.

Napoleon weavers are members of the finch family. To encourage them to nest, grow bamboo in their aviary.

Canaries are wonderful songsters and live quite happily in an
aviary with other birds.

Mynah birds are quite hardy, but aren't keen on damp weather
and so are happiest indoors.

▷ ▷ Cages & Aviaries

Cockatiels are ground feeders in the wild so spend a lot of time on
the cage floor. It's best to get a wide cage rather than a tall one (at
least 14 in square).

Square cages are better than round ones – birds like the security
of having a corner to hide in.

Bamboo cages may look pretty, but they are impossible to keep
clean and some birds can peck them to bits in minutes. Go for a
plain metal wire cage.

When you get a new metal wire cage for your bird, wipe it down
with vinegar and water to get rid of any excess zinc.

If your bird has a long tail, make sure you have a tall cage to
accommodate its shape.

When choosing a bird, decide what you want from such a pet. If
you want a pet to talk to and entertain you, you will probably want
to keep it indoors, so a cage is fine. If you want to breed and show
birds, you will need to build an aviary.

If you're going to build an aviary, check its position carefully.
Position it away from the road, so the birds won't be disturbed by
noise, passers-by or headlights. It should be near the house, where
you can see it, but not so that it will disturb your neighbours. Don't
position an aviary under trees or branches which could damage the
structure.

When building an aviary, make sure the floor is easy to clean. Concrete slabs or concrete are ideal.

Keep the cage away from draughts or too much sunlight. Make sure that other pets (such as cats) can't get to it.

Don't use cherry tree branches for perches – they are toxic, as are the resins in unmilled pine. Most hardwoods (not oak) and some fruitwoods (like apple) are safe.

Natural perches allow birds to chew on them, which is good for keeping beaks in tip-top condition.

Paper is the best medium to line the bottom of the cage because it is more difficult for bacteria to grow on it. It's also easy to keep an eye on the state of your bird's poo.

Birds will sleep better if their cages are covered. During the day it's a good idea to cover one corner of the cage so that the bird can retire there if it wants a rest in the middle of the day.

▷▷ At Play

A fir cone makes a cheap and effective toy.

When you let your bird fly around the house, cover up the fireplace – you don't want it disappearing up the chimney.

Don't leave hot drinks around while your bird is out of its cage.

Some plants are poisonous to birds so keep them out of the birds' way when they are flying around the house.

If you need to catch your bird, use a duster to cover him carefully before putting him back in his cage.

Some birds are great chatterboxes. If you want to teach your bird to talk, you will have to be patient – you won't get results overnight. Just keep repeating the lessons over and over again. Birds find it easier to mimic women's and children's voices. Keep the sentences short.

Cockatiels can be great screamers. Sometimes this is because of boredom or loneliness, or because the owner rewards the screaming with attention. Don't get into bad habits. If your bird is a screamer, try dropping a cover over the cage when it starts. Remove it as soon as the bird is quiet.

▷▷ Health and Cleanliness

If you're having difficulty getting your African Greys to nest, place a pair of smaller, quieter, prolific birds in sight. Cockatiels and lovebirds are the best choice.

An African Grey parrot benefits from a bit of rain and fresh air now and again.

Budgies are quite happy with a saucer of water for bathing. Always clean out the saucer and replace the water – birds are like us: they won't bathe in dirty water.

Some breeders add a dash of raspberry cordial to their budgies' water – they swear it kills bacteria and keeps their birds healthy.

The floor of a bird's cage must be cleaned each day. Once a week give the cage a thorough clean, remembering to take out the bird first.

You can change the colour of your canary by adding paprika, cayenne or red pepper to its food.

If your parrot is feather-picking too much, try a mixture of water and Aloe gel (1 tablespoon of Aloe to 1 quart of water). Spray the mixture on to him at bathtime.

Gaps in the wing feathers of young birds and dried blood on the feather shafts of older birds can be signs of French moult, which is a viral disease. Take your bird to the vet immediately.

To spot a sick bird look out for fluffed out feathers, closed eyes, dull and listless behaviour, and sleeping a lot.

If you think your bird is sick, turn the heating up. They can often lose a lot of body heat when they're not feeling well.

Birds can deteriorate rapidly when ill. Contact your vet straight away.

To examine a poorly bird wrap him quite firmly in a warm towel.

Parrots need their beauty sleep – around 10–12 hours a night.

During cold weather make sure that there is enough humidity for your parrots. When the central heating goes on, the air gets drier.

▷▷ Diet

Fruit is ideal for birds. The fruit shouldn't have any marks and must be washed thoroughly before being given to birds. Peel oranges and remove any large pips or stones. Give them a bit of fruit every day.

Another good source of vitamins is vegetables. Parrots go for cabbage leaves or stalks, sprouting seeds (like alfalfa) and sprouts. Freeze corn-on-the-cob so you've got some handy when it's out of season.

Food on the move. Some birds, like softbills and finches, rather enjoy eating live food. Mealworms are the most popular, but you could go into cricket or locust production to liven up your bird's diet.

Finches also enjoy dandelions and spinach. Chop them up finely before feeding your finch.

Budgerigars will tuck into the odd carrot now and again, but be prepared for some orange stains around their bills.

Canaries will enjoy a bit of hard–boiled egg as well as canned corn. Small pieces of whole-wheat bread are also greatly appreciated.

Cuttlefish bone is a good source of calcium. The softer side of the bone should be facing the bird.

Parrots also enjoy seeds with a high oil content.

Don't let your parrot out of its cage during mealtimes – they can be adept at stealing food from your plate, which is annoying, and they can get hold of food that is bad for them.

Soak seeds in hot water for 24 hours. This boosts the protein content and makes the seeds easier to eat if you're feeding chicks or sick birds.

Plastic containers are cheap and easy to keep clean; they will suit most birds. Parrots, however, need metal bowls.

Fresh water should always be available. Don't place the water beneath a perch. If your birds are in an aviary, check for ice during cold weather.

►►► Builders

Neil Harris, H. S. Hamilton & Sons; Tim Hobbs, H. S. Hamilton & Sons; Brian Harris, H. S. Hamilton & Sons; Godfrey Rawlings, Basement Construction; Phil Sheehan

▷▷ Banging About

Protect your fingers when hammering nails. Push the nail through a piece of stiff paper or cardboard and use this to hold the nail in place. Tear the paper away before the nail is hammered into place.

To prevent wood from splitting, blunt the end of the nail.

To mark a horizontal line on a wall for a shelf mark two points at either end of the shelf length. Rub chalk along a piece of string and then fix (or hold) the string at these points. Ping the string and the chalk is transferred onto the wall in a perfect straight line.

▷▷ A Screw Loose?

When screwing soft metal such as brass into hard wood there is a danger of snapping the head off the screw. Greasing the screw with a little tallow, soap or something similar will ease the friction and make it much easier to screw in.

Drill a pilot hole into wood (particularly MDF) so that it will accept a screw. A pilot hole is a smaller hole than the actual screw size.

Drill holes without leaving a mess behind by vacuuming up the dust as you drill.

If drilling above your head, push the drill bit through a yoghurt pot to stop the dust from falling into your face. It also saves you having to clear up afterwards.

To catch the dust when you are drilling, attach an envelope to the wall using masking tape, just beneath where you intend to drill. The dust will collect in the envelope and not on the floor.

Stop screws and nails rusting by storing them in an empty cold-cream jar.

Unscrew stubborn screws using a long-handled screwdriver.

▷▷ Sticking Together

Make a glue brush using the tube of an old ballpoint pen and some coarse string. Push the string all the way through the tube, then tease the ends out to make bristles. When you've finished the job, cut off the sticky end and pull a new bit through for the next job.

Broken a plate? Place one of the broken shards in a drawer and gently shut the drawer to use it like a vice. It leaves both hands free to stick the other pieces to it. You can also use the drawer to clamp objects together while the glue dries.

Unsticking a vinyl floor tile is easy. Cover the tile you want to remove with aluminium foil, put your iron on maximum and move it slowly over the tile. You should be able to lift the tile after a minute or so.

To keep bricks level place two bricks at each end of the wall you are building. Stretch a piece of string between them and anchor it with more bricks. Use the string as a guide while you put down the next layer of bricks.

To age new bricks brush them with milk.

To get stains off bricks rub or grate the marked brick with another similar brick.

Make your own spirit level – use a milk bottle with a little bit of water in it.

Concrete is easier to work with if you put some washing-up liquid into the mixture.

When hanging a door put a wedge under the end farthest away from the hinges to keep the whole door balanced upright.

▷▷ Getting Plastered

Plaster will set much quicker if mixed with warm water. Some plasterers find that weeing into their plaster has the same effect!

When plastering a brick wall, coat it first with a PVC-type glue. This prevents the surface from absorbing too much water and from drying out the plaster too quickly and making it crack.

Seal cracks effectively by wetting your finger and using it to spread the sealant.

If you need to fill a small hole in an emergency, use some toothpaste. Let it dry before painting the wall.

▷▷ Protection

Prevent birds from eating window putty – they're after the linseed oil – by mixing black pepper into the putty.

Store unused putty by rolling it tightly into a ball and wrapping it carefully in aluminium foil before replacing in a tub. The putty should keep for several months like this.

Put a damp–proof membrane between a new window or door frame where it meets the wall to stop moisture getting in and rotting the wood. Heavy-duty plastic works well.

▷▷ Clever Cutting

Measure twice and cut once – most people measure once and cut twice.

Stop plywood from splitting when you use a saw on it – apply masking tape to the area you intend to cut.

To cut wood in a straight line use another piece of wood to guide you.

▷▷ Finishing Off

When sanding floorboards knock the ends of nails down into the floor. Exposed nail heads wear down sandpaper much more quickly than a flat surface.

Stop stairs and floorboards from squeaking – use a wax-based furniture polish.

Stop hinges squeaking with petroleum jelly rather than oil, which will run and spoil the paintwork and floor.

Before varnishing a floor sweep all the debris up and then wipe it down with a damp cloth to pick up every last bit of dust.

Pick up metal objects with a magnet in a plastic bag. Then turn the bag inside out so that all the objects end up inside the bag.

Dirty hammers are actually dangerous – the head will keep slipping if it gets really grimy. Try banging it on a piece of wood covered with sandpaper a few times or, alternatively, rub the head over some coarse sand.

►►► Butchers

Frank Lee

Keep your wooden chopping block clean. Wash it down when you've finished butchering and then cover with sawdust. This soaks up the damp while the resin in the block kills off any bacteria.

To sharpen a serrated-edged knife use a steel on just the serrated side (not both sides).

Keep a carbon steel knife clean by dipping a cork in scouring powder and running it along the side of the blade. Rinse the knife, dry it and wipe it down with vegetable oil.

To make cocktail sausages, don't bother to buy the expensive ones in the shops. Just warm your hands and pinch a chipolata in the middle, forming two small cocktail sausages.

To make pork crackling, rub the fat with vinegar and then sprinkle with salt. The acidity will make the crackling. Pigs are much leaner nowadays so it's more difficult to get good crackling.

Score pork with a Stanley knife before putting it into the oven.

Gammon can be too salty; when boiling ham, put some lemon juice on it to reduce the saltiness. This also keeps the meat nice and pink.

Don't bother to pluck a pheasant ... skin it instead. The skin comes off like a sock!

If you get blood on a sheepskin coat, just sprinkle potting compost on it. It works like blotting paper. Leave it overnight and brush it off in the morning.

►►► Butlers

John Thomas, John Thomas International School of Butlers; Ivor Spencer; Don Weedon; Peter Greenhill; Boris Roberts; Robert Marshal

▷▷ Breakfast

Freshen bread rolls for breakfast by covering them with a damp towel and placing them in a hot oven for a short while.

▷▷ Dinner Is Served

For a truly professional-looking dinner table, use a ruler and line everything up 1 in/2.5 cm from the edge of the table.

Always lay the cutlery from the outside in, according to the sequence of courses.

Place the white-wine glass at the top of the first-course knife because that is usually what people will drink first.

Thirteen chairs and twelve guests can be unlucky so put a teddy bear on the thirteenth chair!

When seating someone at the dinner table, pull the chair back and manoeuvre your guest in front. Very gently tap the back of their knee with the edge of the seat; their knee will automatically buckle and they will sit down.

The correct way to eat caviare is not with a silver spoon but from the back of your hand. It's even better if you use somebody else's hand!

To tell the difference between Oscietra and Beluga caviare put a few eggs on a piece of paper and then crush them. If the oil is yellow, then it's Oscietra, but if it's grey then the caviare is Beluga.

Serve your best wine first. By the time you get to the cheaper stuff your guests will probably be incapable of noticing the drop in quality.

Don't wear strong aftershave when serving vintage wine because it will completely swamp the bouquet.

When picnicking, make an instant wine cooler by wrapping a wet newspaper around a bottle of wine. Hold the bottle out of the sunroof or window as you drive along to your chosen site.

When making coffee don't pour boiling water on to the granules as you will scald the coffee. Use water when it's just off the boil.

If you want the cream to float on your coffee rather than sink without trace, stir some sugar into the coffee first.

Always use boiling water when making tea – the air in the water helps the tea to brew properly.

Scald the teapot *and* **the cup** when you are making tea.

Don't use a gas lighter to light a cigar – it will ruin the taste. Always use a match but keep it away from the end of the cigar until the sulphur has burnt away.

When relighting a cigar, always get rid of the stale fumes by blowing through it first and then lighting it.

Keep cigars in cool, dark places. You could keep them in the fridge for a while to condition them.

▷▷ Home, James

When cleaning the limousine, use boot polish on the rubber trim in the interior.

Buff up the windows with newspaper and a mixture of water and vinegar.

When you have cleaned the Rolls, don't forget to wind the windows down slightly and wipe off any excess water and soap from the top.

Use a toothbrush to clean around the gear lever and in the switches on the dashboard.

▷▷ Silver Service

To keep silver clean use lemon and salt.

Be careful when washing silver cutlery. Take care it doesn't rub together too much. Silver is a soft metal and picks up scratches easily.

Remove wax easily from silver candlesticks. Place them in the fridge overnight and it's then easy to pick off the wax.

If you are packing silver away for any length of time, wrap it in a clean T-shirt away from the light.

Prevent tarnish by storing silver wrapped in clingfilm.

▷▷ Spit & Polish

Bone china should not be a museum piece. Take it out and clean it every year.

Rotate your best cutlery. Take it from the left-hand side of the drawer and put it back on the right-hand side.

For really clean glasses, wash in hot soapy water and then rinse in warm water with a couple of tablespoons of vinegar in it.

Polish glasses with a dry cloth. A damp cloth might grip the glass and break it.

Never store wine glasses upside down. They will absorb the smells of the cupboard they're in and this could affect the taste of the wine. Just clean glasses before use to get rid of any dust.

To dry a decanter use a hair-dryer.

If you don't have a bottle brush, fill the vase or bottle half full of warm soapy water and a handful of small pebbles. Shake vigorously. If the glass is delicate, replace the pebbles with split-peas or dried lentils.

To clean a smelly vase or glass, fill it half full of water and add a tablespoon of mustard. Shake the mixture and then leave for an hour.

▷▷ Keeping up Appearances

To iron silk ties, slip a piece of card inside the tie so that no creases come through.

Keep creases in your trousers for longer. Put soap on the inside of the crease when pressing your trouser leg.

To avoid creasing use tissue paper in between the folds when packing a case.

To avoid wrinkly trouser legs pack the top of the trousers first, followed by everything else. Then fold the trouser legs over the clothes.

Place shoes in plastic bags to prevent shoe polish getting all over your clothes.

Always pack silk inside out.

Hang a wet, clean white shirt outside on a cold morning and it will come up bright white.

►►► Cameramen

Justin Quinnell; Duncan Elson; Ray Lowe; Nik Mather; Maddie Attenborough

Warm your batteries in your hand before use – you'll get more power out of them.

Always get your nicad batteries to discharge fully before recharging them.

To save batteries don't keep zooming in and out while filming! And turn the camera off between shots.

Instead of zooming into a close-up of an object, stop recording and move physically closer to the object. Then film it in close-up. It will be a much more stable shot.

If you don't have a tripod, use a home-made monopod. Something along the lines of a ski-stick turned upside down would do.

Alternatively, lean on a wall, a gate, a car bonnet, anything that comes to hand that will give you a stable shot.

Make sure you get the colour right – always do a white balance, using some white paper, before filming.

If you're filming something on the move that's low to the ground (such as a cat or dog), take a plastic bag with handles and cut a lens-sized hole in it. Put the camera inside and carry the bag around in pursuit of your subject. This avoids you crouching down all the time.

Vary your camera angles – for example, if you're taking shots of children, get down to their level and take your shots in a kneeling position.

If you need to shoot through a window, shoot at an angle so you don't get your reflection in shot as well.

Protect your camera. Put clingfilm around it in wet or sandy conditions and put some insulating tape around the gap in the tape compartment so that dust or moisture won't get in.

Think sound as well as picture when shooting a home video. If you are 20 ft/6 m from your subject then so is the microphone.

Microphones don't select what they hear; they suck up every available bit of noise. So reduce ambient noise by closing curtains or windows to cut out interference caused by traffic, children playing, aeroplanes going overhead and so on.

Always wear headphones to monitor noise and to make sure you can hear the sound properly.

Tape down incoming leads and cables so that they don't get pulled. This reduces the risk of damaging your equipment.

To tidy up the cables running from your camera take two 4-in/10-cm Velcro strips and glue them back to back. Use them as a strap for wrapping your cables together.

If your recording is important to you, remember to snap off or close the recording tabs at the side of the tape. This will prevent you or anyone else from accidentally re-recording over it.

▶▶▶ Campers & Caravanners

CAMPERS Cynthia Simister, Outdoor Advisor, Midland Guide Association; Pat and Hazel Constance; David Wood; Jean Anthony; Mary Matthews; Christine Green; Robin Hamer

CARAVANNERS The Caravan Club; The Camping and Caravanning Club; Mr Chris Smith, Bedfordshire Centre of the Caravan Club; Mr B. Clarke; Mr B.E.J. Hall, Devon and Cornwall Caravan Club; Mrs Worsell, Dorset Caravan Club; Mrs Moore, Dorset Caravan Club

When camping for the first time, don't go miles away from home just in case you forget something important – or you discover you loathe the great outdoors.

Preparation is everything. Try putting your tent up in good conditions and in your own back garden in order to check that it all goes together smoothly and that all the pieces are there.

Weather your tent in preparation for all climates. Wet it before you leave or keep spraying it with water.

Don't camp in a hollow because cold air sinks and you will find the temperature drops substantially at night.

Avoid camping in a dried stream bed. If it rains, the stream may suddenly reappear!

When walking to the top of a steep or high hill, you will get very sweaty, so take a dry, clean T-shirt to change into for the journey down.

You can never have too many safety pins. They have lots of emergency uses and don't take up too much room.

When erecting your tent, use thick rubber bands to attach the guy ropes to the pegs. The bands will take up any slack that develops and will prevent your tent from sagging.

Sitting on the ground can be wet and cold. Make your own insulated cushion from a sheet of kitchen foil sandwiched between two pieces of foam.

When you pack up your tent make sure it's dry and clean. Any remaining grass or leaves will rot in the tent when it's stored away.

Keeping toilet paper dry can be difficult. Cut the end off a large plastic bottle and cut a thin slit down one side. Put the loo roll inside and thread the end of the roll through the slit; you can then tear off nice, dry sheets of loo paper at your convenience.

Toothbrushes quickly get mucky so cut one down and keep it in a film canister.

Keep your toothbrush clean by covering the head with some foil when not in use.

Keep your soap clean – store it in the foot of some tights slung over a nearby tree.

If you have a night out away from the campsite, tie a white plastic bag to the top of your tent so that you can find it when you get back later in the dark.

Keep your specs safe – use a safety pin to fasten the bridge of your glasses to the tent fabric when you're not wearing them.

No fly spray? Try hair-spray instead. Flies hate it because it sticks their wings together – they'll soon get the message and leave.

Avoid wearing too much yellow. Flies love the colour and can mistake you for a large flower.

Midges and flies can be a real problem. Cut a sock length off a pair of sheer tights and stretch over a baseball cap and down over your face for stylish protection!

Don't drink too much before you go to bed – there's nothing worse than having to wriggle out of your sleeping bag in the middle of the night to go to the loo.

When going to the loo in the great outdoors, you must dig a hole no deeper than 9 in/23 cm. Do your business and then bury it. All the bacteria that break down human waste are found in the top 9 in/ 23 cm of the soil.

If you need to evacuate from a hillside someone who cannot walk, lay a rucksack on the ground and sit the injured person down on it. Get two people to grasp the handles of the rucksack and carry the person down. Do not, however, attempt to move someone who has injured their back or neck

▷▷ Clothing

To keep warm wear lots of thin layers rather than a few bulky ones. You can take layers off as you wish.

It's more hygienic if the layer next to your skin is cotton.

Colour code your stuff sacks so you know which is dirty washing, where your clean clothes are, which bag holds your smalls or wet-weather gear and so on.

Make a snug neck loop out of a strip of fleece, secured by Velcro or poppers. It's better than having a scarf flapping around and much warmer, too.

Damp walking boots can be uncomfortable and cause blisters. Keep yours dry by banging a couple of sticks into the ground and then hanging the boots upside down on them.

Don't put wet boots in front of the fire because this makes them really stiff and they may even shrink. Stuff them with newspaper instead and leave them in a well-ventilated spot to dry out.

Don't take your shoes off in very hot weather. Your feet will expand and your shoes won't fit when you come to put them on again.

When packing your rucksack, work out what you will need last and put it in the bottom of the rucksack. Then keep packing things in the reverse order in which you will need them. There's nothing worse than having to unpack absolutely everything as soon as you arrive.

Keep clothes dry by packing them inside plastic carrier bags before putting them in your rucksack.

Bulky towels take up valuable room. Pack a square terry towel instead. They're pretty small but highly absorbent.

If you don't have a terry towel, a beer towel is good and compact, too.

J–cloths make good towels. They dry out quickly and can double up as flannels.

Leave clothes pegs behind. Just double up a long piece of rope and twist it. You can then tuck your wet clothes in between the twisted rope and leave them to dry.

Dry clothes on an old umbrella. Tear off the fabric and string fishing line between the spokes. Use the spokes to dry small items of clothing.

A wire shelf from a fridge makes an excellent clothes horse. Tie it between two branches and thread your wet clothes through the shelf to dry.

▷▷ Sleeping

Avoid washing your sleeping bag too often; make a liner for it out of a cotton sheet or duvet cover. You can wash that as often as you like.

No room to pack a pillow? Just button up your coat and stuff it with some clothes.

Make a comfy, emergency pillow by blowing up the bladder from a wine box.

Create a hot-water bottle: collect some warm stones from around the fire and pop them in a sock.

Alternatively, fill your metal water bottle with hot water and put that down your sleeping bag.

To keep warm during the night lay a piece of foam insulation roll under your air bed. One underneath is worth two on top! If you don't have any insulating foam, a length of old carpet underneath your sleeping bag will keep you snug too.

If you have cold feet, wear a hat – you lose most of your body heat through your head.

No one can sleep if they are cold so make a draught excluder by rolling up a towel and placing it in front of any cracks.

Does the zip on your sleeping bag stick? Try rubbing some petroleum jelly or vapour rub along the teeth and it will be as good as new.

Fill your kettle before going to bed. You'll be so pleased that you don't have to walk down to the toilet block for water first thing in the morning that you'll enjoy that cup of tea so much more.

▷▷ Cooking

To get the best use from your small camp stove, shove it up your jumper – before you've lit it, of course! This warms the gas up and it will last for longer.

Avoid as much washing-up as possible: take boil-in-the-bag food.

If you need a grate over your fire, a boot scraper is a useful alternative.

Make your own frying pan – a flat stone left in the embers will heat up and can be used to cook food on.

Don't give up the luxuries of life. Take some service station sachets of salt, pepper, mustard and ketchup to spice up your food.

Secure your gas stove by putting a couple of spare tent pegs through the base.

Forgotten the corkscrew? All you have to do is hit the bottom of the bottle sharply several times with a book or rubber-soled shoe. The cork will gradually rise up through the neck of the bottle.

Keep matches dry – store them in a film canister.

Waterproof your matches by dipping the heads in melted wax.

Make the washing-up easier – coat the base of your pan with diluted soapy liquid before you begin cooking. If you don't have soapy liquid, try a generous coating of mud.

For stubborn food deposits, try rubbing with a clump of grass.

Scrunched up kitchen foil makes a good pot scourer.

Take small, easily stored amounts of washing-up liquid in eye-drop containers or film canisters.

Make baking easy – if the urge takes you, simply line a biscuit tin with foil, put it on the fire and you've got an effective little oven.

You can cook eggs in their shells on an open fire – just prick the shells first.

Wrap eggs in orange peel and put them in the embers of the fire to bake.

Keep pans and bowls of food safe from insects by covering them with cheap plastic shower caps.

Create a fly-free larder – hang up a net curtain around the food.

Attract ants away from your food – put a white piece of paper on the ground. The ants will make a beeline for that instead.

The best instant food is a banana.

To get rid of stale, nasty smells from a water carrier fill it with water and drop a denture-cleaning tablet in to it. Leave for a couple of hours and then rinse out thoroughly.

To make thermos flask tea taste that little bit fresher, put half a teaspoon of lemon juice in the tea.

Get rid of smells from your thermos flask using a denture-cleaning tablet and some water. Leave to soak for 20 minutes.

Freshen your thermos flask by filling it with water and one tablespoon of bicarbonate of soda. Leave to soak. Rinse and drain.

Keep a thermos flask fresh by leaving a couple of sugar lumps in it when not in use.

Replace the stopper of your thermos flask so it's tilted to one side, allowing air to circulate. This will prevent it from smelling musty when you come to use it again.

▷▷ Children and Camping

Children love to draw but paper can quickly get damp outdoors. Try laminating a piece of paper and take some chinagraph pencils with you for happy children . . . and parents.

Don't bother with alarm clocks when camping with children. You'll never be up later than 6 am!

Keep your toddler (or dog!) away from the fire by attaching the child or animal to a length of guy rope which you then fix to the ground with a tent peg. Make sure the rope can't reach the fire.

►►► Car Mechanics

John Gleeson; Derek James; A. M. Carter; Douglas Coker; Mervyn Dove; Tim Shallcross; N. James; Jo Moss; David Shearman

Clean your windscreen with a mixture of warm water and a good dash of white vinegar.

When the car window steams up on a cold morning, smear a cut potato on the inside and then wipe off the excess moisture. This helps to stop condensation.

To avoid damp electrics park the car's front end away from the wind, up against a hedge or a wall.

If the lock has frozen, try heating the key with a flame before trying the lock; do this several times but never force the key – you could break it.

Alternatively, soak a cloth in some warm water and hold it to the outside of the lock. If it is really stuck, you can try holding your hand over the lock for a couple of minutes, but keep changing hands so you don't freeze yourself!

Screen wash bottles often freeze in the winter. Replace the bottle's hose with a longer length of hose and wrap this around something warm, such as the radiator. It won't freeze up again.

Antifreeze in your windscreen wash bottle will damage the paintwork. Dilute some methylated spirits in the water instead.

To check your antifreeze, take an egg cup of coolant from the car and put it in the freezer. If it freezes, you definitely need more antifreeze!

Remove ice from your windscreen with a phone card if you don't have a proper scraper.

Mop up oil spills with cat litter. Pour a thick layer over the spill and leave for about 24 hours. Just sweep it up when the oil has been absorbed.

If you have to jack up the car on a soft surface, such as grass, put the jack on a board to stop it sinking under the car's weight.

If your rear light gets smashed, cover it with some red plastic from a carrier bag until you can get it fixed.

If your indicator light goes, use the bulb from your fog light as an emergency bulb.

Patch up a leaking hose with insulating tape or a belt from a plastic raincoat. But you must remember to leave the cap off the radiator so that the pressure doesn't build up.

Radiators often spring a leak. Chew up a bit of gum and stick it over the hole to keep you going!

If the catch has gone on a door, secure it with a tie, or hook your seat belt through it until you reach a garage.

Replace a broken fan belt with a pair of stockings.

If your exhaust is blowing, stay calm. Just secure a baked bean tin or any old can over the pipe with some string, wire or jubilee clips.

To charge up a battery really quickly, just drive around in third gear for a while. The high revs will do the job for you.

Stuck in mud? Take the rubber foot mats out of the car and lay them down in front of the tyres. Gently rock the car backwards and forwards until it gets a grip on the mats. You should then be able to drive away.

If it's really muddy, don't forget to tie your mats to the bumper before you start rocking the car backwards and forwards. When you finally get the car going, you won't have to stop and go back for the mats.

Back tyres and brake locks wear down much more quickly than the front. When they start to wear, change the back to the front to get twice as much wear.

If you lose a set of bolts down a hole or drain whilst changing a tyre, don't panic. You can drive with three nuts on each wheel perfectly safely for a short while.

To free rusty bolts pour on a small amount of Coca-Cola. The acids in the drink eat away at the rust. Wait until the bolt is dry before trying to release it. You may have to repeat this several times.

Left your lights on? If the battery is likely to be flat, don't even try to start the car. Just be patient, turn the lights off and wait for 15 minutes. If the battery is any good, it will recharge itself.

If the wiper blade on the driver's side disintegrates, take the blade off the passenger's side or use the rear wiper blade until you can replace it.

You can make a good waterproof repair for almost anything that needs to be protected from the damp using just a bit of bin liner and a hair-dryer. Use the hair-dryer to melt a thin layer of bin liner across the hole or crack for a safe, interim measure.

If you need to do an emergency repair and your spanner is too big for the bolt, use a small coin or screwdriver to fill the gap.

Keep long hair, jewellery and clothing tucked away when doing any work on the engine. You don't want to get anything caught up in the moving parts.

To remove grease or oil stains, which tend to get on your clothes far too easily, coat the stain with lard. This will soften the stain and make it easier to treat.

If you don't use the ashtray for smoking, put your loose change in there. You'll always have something for parking meters and other emergencies.

An easy, accessible place to keep your rubbish is in a plastic bag hung over the gear stick.

Leaks in your engine are a lot easier to spot and fix if the engine is free of grease and grime.

While you're cleaning under your bonnet, it's a great time to look at all hoses, wires, belts etc. Check the hoses for cracks, or spongy or soft spots.

To clean your car windows partly roll them down, first clean the top edges and next to the rubber gaskets. As these are the dirtiest parts of the window, clean them with a separate cloth before you tackle the main part of the glass.

Spray glass cleaner on your cloth and not on the glass itself to avoid overspray on the vehicle's painted surfaces.

To avoid scratches on paintwork when cleaning car windows get rid of chunky belt buckles and don't wear jeans with rivets or studs.

Always wipe parallel to heated rear window lines. If you rub vigorously in the wrong direction, you risk snagging any cuts in the film and tearing it.

Clean one wheel at a time. Don't run around the vehicle trying to keep each wheel at the same stage of cleaning because cleaners shouldn't be allowed to dry or remain on the wheels any longer than the instructions state.

To avoid any overspray of cleaning products from tyre to wheel, cut out a cardboard disc the same size as the wheel with two horizontal slots for your finger and thumb. For extra strength cover the disc with tape to stop any liquid from seeping through the cardboard. Place the disc over the wheel to protect it when you're cleaning your tyres.

Use a nylon scrub brush to remove dirt from heavily grained vinyl soft tops. Be careful not to get the brush or the cleaner on the vehicle's paint.

Don't apply vinyl and rubber protectants to your windshield wiper blades. It stops their effectiveness.

Remember, cleaning your car is just like cleaning your home. Tidy up first, then vacuum, followed by carpet cleaning, upholstery cleaning, dashboard cleaning and any small interior detailing you care to do such as glass and chrome surfaces.

To speed up the drying process after cleaning your car leave the doors open, but make sure you shut off the interior lights by sticking something in the door jamb that keeps the buttons closed or by disconnecting the battery.

Before using shop-bought/home-made stain remover or upholstery or carpet shampoo on your vehicle's interior, first test it on an inconspicuous area, such as under the seat, to make sure it won't remove the colour from the material.

To remove sticky sweets or chocolate from car upholstery use a cloth soaked in lukewarm water, then blot and wipe until the stain is removed.

Crayon, oil or grease can be removed from car seats by scraping off any excess with a dull knife blade first, then blotting with a paper towel. If necessary, a stain remover can be used afterwards.

Coffee, fruit, ice-cream and milk stains can be rubbed with a cloth soaked in cold water, but don't use soap as this may set the stain.

Sponge urine stains with lukewarm mild soapsuds. Rinse with a cloth soaked in cold water, then soak a cloth in a solution of 1 part ammonia to 5 parts water. Hold it on the stain for 1 minute and then rinse with a clean, wet cloth.

Sponge vomit with a clean cloth dipped in cold water. Wash lightly with lukewarm water and mild soap. If odour persists, treat with a solution of 1 teaspoon baking soda in 1 cup warm water.

Don't use polish or cleaners on steering wheels and floor pedals. They'll make surfaces slippery, which could lead to accidents.

Take care of your chamois leather. Wash it in warm, soapy water and rinse it out after use. Let the leather dry away from direct heat so that the cloth keeps its natural oils.

When washing your car, don't use washing-up liquid because it contains salt, which can cause rust to form.

To remove rust spots from chrome bumpers dip kitchen foil in Coca-Cola and rub off the rust spots.

Always have a supply of hand wipes from fast-food outlets and plastic gloves from petrol stations to keep your hands clean when you have to do any minor repairs.

▶▶▶ Carpenters

Steven Powell

Always put a start-hole in the wood before you drill. This will stop the wood from splitting. Use a bradawl to make the hole.

Don't put screws in a row along the wood grain because this can split the wood.

To screw in awkward places, stick the screw to the screwdriver with a bit of wax.

Disguise small holes with a mixture of sawdust and glue.

If you want to disguise nail heads, use a second nail to drive the first nail a little deeper than the surface level. Remove the second nail and fill in the little hole with some sawdust and glue or a blob of paint.

When hammering, hold the hammer near the head, not at the other end. Make sure that you use several short sharp knocks rather than one almighty blow – this will prevent the nail from bending.

To make a nail go into hard wood more easily, run it through your hair before you hammer it in. The natural grease coats the nail, allowing it to slip into the wood easily.

To stop your hammer slipping off the head of a nail, rub some emery paper over the hammer head.

To avoid damaging a wooden surface, don't hammer a nail in all the way. Stop just above the surface and sink the nail in using a nail punch and hammer.

To remove a nail from a wooden surface, slip a piece of thin hardwood under the claw of the hammer to prevent it from damaging the wood.

People often make small holes bigger by fiddling around trying to find the right size of wall plug. Push some broken matchsticks into the hole until it's filled instead.

It's quite hard to drill into thin wood because the wood often splits. Put a thicker piece of wood behind the thin piece and let the drill go into this thicker piece as well.

If the head of a round-headed screw has become damaged, use a file to make a new slot for your screwdriver.

Don't be too forceful – if you use too much strength when driving a screw home you could end up splitting the wood.

If you want to remove a stubborn screw, try putting a little oil on the screw head and leaving it for a while before trying to release it.

For a smoother sawing action, rub the teeth of the saw with some candle wax.

Before you start to saw, make a small V-shaped cut with a knife and insert the saw. Start with a backward motion before pushing the saw forward.

When using a jigsaw, always put the 'good' side of the wood underneath and cut with the 'back' of the wood facing you. The jigsaw cuts on the upstroke so this won't spoil the surface of the wood.

It is much easier to use sandpaper if you glue a sheet onto a small block of wood.

Don't bother to take a sticking door off its hinges. Simply open and shut it several times over a piece of rough sandpaper.

If you have gaps left between doors when fitting units, cover the space with a length of thin beading.

Beading can give character to flat, boring doors. Arrange it in such a way as to give the impression of panels.

Tongue and groove panelling is attractive but expensive. Cut some grooves into hardboard and then paint it … no one will know the difference.

No plumb line? Just hang a bunch of keys from some string instead.

When hanging a dado rail, bang a nail into the middle and then let the rail even itself.

If you've mislaid your dustpan, wet the edge of a newspaper, brush the dirt over the edge and roll up the paper.

▶▶▶ Cat Breeders

Lyn Ingledew, Cat Naps; John Saxton, Towerwood Vet Group; Cath Chard, Bynkethyn Cat Protection League Shelter; Ann Cummins; Eileen Welsh; Dawn Teague

Female cats are generally more affectionate and playful than male cats.

Once a male cat is neutered, it becomes less territorial and won't wander as far as a tom.

Choose a pedigree cat if you are intending to show or breed from it. Like all pedigree animals, they take a lot of time and money. Go to a specialist breeder. If you are going to show your cat, you will have to register it with the correct cat authority.

Choose a moggy if you just want a pet. They're cheaper (often free) and usually friendlier than the pedigree breeds.

Animal sanctuaries are a good place to go to find a cat. Cats are only there because they are lost or unwanted.

Tortoiseshell cats are nearly always female. On the rare occasion that a male tortoiseshell appears in a litter he is invariably sterile. But it's a myth that gingers are always toms.

Tortoiseshell cats are sometimes called calico cats in this country.

▷▷ Kittens

When you bring your kitten home, you should make her feel secure. Make her a 'nest' out of a cardboard box. Wrap a jumper around a hot-water bottle and place it in the box with your kitten.

When choosing a kitten, watch its behaviour with its littermates. You will be able to get an idea of its personality from the way it interacts with the others.

Check your kitten for signs of good health before you take it home. Its rear end should be free of diarrhoea or discharge. Its ears should be clean and dry (excessive scratching and dark wax could mean mites). Its nose should be slightly moist and feel velvety. The gums should be pink and there shouldn't be any bad breath. Check its coat for signs of fleas.

Kittens are more of a handful than adult cats because of having to train them and keep an eye on them. However, they're more adaptable than older cats.

Don't separate kittens from their mothers until they are fully weaned. This is usually around 8 weeks of age.

Take your kitten to a vet as soon as you can. You will have to get it vaccinated against Feline Enteritis and Feline Influenza (both of which can be fatal).

When holding a kitten, make sure you are supporting its whole body.

When introducing your kitten to other pets, always be on hand to supervise the meeting. If you already have a dog, keep it on its lead or put your kitten in a travelling case while they get used to each other. Don't leave them alone until they've got to know each other.

▷▷ Cleanliness

Cats are naturally clean so toilet training isn't too much of a struggle. Start off with a litter tray; you can use an old baking tray if you don't want to buy a proper plastic one.

Mother cats teach kittens how to behave … even how to use a litter tray, so try not to separate them too early or you'll have your hands full trying to teach your kitten what she should have learnt from her mother.

If your cat keeps weeing in the same spot in the house, try feeding her in this place. She'll soon stop using it as a toilet.

If your kitten has a bit of an accident, transfer the puddle or poo to the litter tray. This should attract the cat to it next time she wants to go.

Clean a litter tray at least twice a day – some cats are fastidious and don't like to 'go' if the tray isn't clean. Well, would you go if the chain hadn't been pulled?

If you're busy, stack three clean litter trays on top of each other. You can simply lift off the top tray when it gets dirty and you have a clean one all ready and waiting to be used immediately.

Two cats? Two litter trays.

If your cat doesn't take to the cat litter try substituting it with soil.

Get cat hair off your furniture by rubbing the fabric with a scouring pad.

Kittens can start to be litter trained from the age of 4 weeks.

If you have to give your cat a bath (because its fur has got contaminated or you are going to be showing it), make sure you have an extra pair of hands to help you. Cats don't like having baths. Bathe it in a plastic bowl and use a proper cat shampoo.

Cats have a routine when cleaning themselves: with their paws they clean the face first and then the top of the head, followed by a good lick down of the shoulders and front legs, then the sides and lastly the tail.

▷▷ Behaviour

If you want a cat buy two because they will amuse each other.

If you have two cats, don't separate them when they get into a fight. They have to learn to live with each other and they need to establish who is top cat.

Cats get bored with their toys easily. Have two or three to hand and keep rotating them every month or so.

Make your own catnip ball. Just cut the ends off a pair of old tights and fill with catnip. Twist the tights and cover the ball several times and then knot the end.

Make mazes out of cardboard boxes to amuse your cats. They love it.

Keep a cat happy for ages – give her a cardboard box with a couple of holes in it. Brown paper bags are fun too.

Read a cat's mood by its tail and ears. An upright tail and pert ears means she likes you. If the tail is wagging or the ears lie flat then watch out!

A yawning cat is a happy cat – even lions and other big cats do it to show each other that they are relaxed. Try yawning at your cat to let her know how much you enjoy her company.

▷▷ Safety

Always put elasticated collars on your cats – this will let them slip out of trouble. They are always getting caught up in things and a rigid collar can be dangerous.

Don't stare directly at a cat – it's interpreted as a hostile gesture. Scrunch your eyes up and blink slowly and you'll get on fine. Best of all, wear sunglasses. You'll look cool and cats love it.

It's a myth that cats should be put out at night – most moggies are happy to stay indoors and sleep.

Make sure your cat can sit at a window so she can see what's going on. Cats love watching the outside world.

▷▷ Discipline

Cats behaving badly? Have a water pistol to hand. Then, if they do something wrong, they get soaked but don't associate you with the punishment. If only men were so easy to control!

Stop cats from using your lawn as a toilet – sprinkle some pepper on the grass. They hate the smell and won't go near it.

Keep cats off the lawn altogether by placing litre bottles full of water around the area you want to protect. Cats don't like reflections and will steer clear of them.

To stop a cat scratching wooden furniture use lemon-scented polish.

Alternatively – rub citrus soap on to chairs and sofas. The smell will put the cat off.

If your cat claws your curtains, dab a little peppermint oil on to the fabric to warn her off.

When moving out of a house, put the cat in the bathroom or where no one is likely to go. Put a sign on the door to make sure it isn't opened accidentally – otherwise, your cat will run off to get away from the pandemonium of moving.

When moving to a new house, keep your cat inside for at least a week. When you do let her out for the first time, make sure she goes out on an empty stomach so that she will return home to be fed.

If you have a new baby, tie a string of noisy rattles across the pram. Not only will the noise alert you if the cat jumps up but it will also scare the cat and put her off trying again.

To discipline your cat tap her on the nose, say 'no' in a loud voice. Then put the cat straight down and ignore her. Cats crave affection and respect and will hate the cold shoulder.

Stop cats from climbing up vinyl wallpaper. Keep a water spray to hand and give them a quick blast when they start their ascent.

Prevent cats from climbing over a fence by spraying the wood with surgical spirit.

Angling the top of the fence inwards prevents cats from getting out of the garden so easily.

If your cat continually jumps on to kitchen work surfaces, spray the surface with a little water and she will soon stop.

Create an effective scratching post with a carpet tile stuck to a wall 2 feet up from the floor. This should prevent your furniture from being reduced to shreds.

Orange and grapefruit peel scattered round the garden will stop cats coming in – they hate the smell of citrus fruits.

To preserve electricity and computer leads from being gnawed to bits – cover them with sturdy rubber tubing such as hosepipe. Just cut a section lengthwise and wrap it round the wires you want to protect.

Prepare your cat for the arrival of a baby by sprinkling baby powder and lotion on your skin so that the smells become familiar.

If your cat continually chews your houseplants, spray them with diluted lemon juice.

You can teach a cat to walk on a lead. Start by getting your cat used to wearing a harness before attaching the lead to it. Practise walking around the house and garden before you try using the lead outdoors.

Don't punish your cat if she brings home a dead bird or mouse. She's only trying to contribute to the family. Punishing her may indicate that you're not satisfied with her offering, so she'll go off and do it again. The best thing you can do is accept it gracefully and dispose of it as soon as possible.

▷▷ Health

Administering pills can be a bit of a tussle. Try wrapping the cat in a warm towel, keeping paws and claws out of the way while you slip the medicine down the throat.

Alternatively, put her in a pillow case or a terry towelling bag with a draw pull to keep her in one place without getting scratched.

If this doesn't work, crush the pill and mix it with some yoghurt. Put the solution into a pet syringe (available from your vet) and squirt it gently into the cat's mouth.

If getting medicine into the cat is proving a real struggle, gently pinch the nostrils. The cat will have to open her mouth to breathe and you can then pop the pill in.

After a cat has swallowed a pill she will usually lick her nose. If she doesn't, then be prepared for the pill to reappear!

White cats get sunburnt easily. On very hot days, try keeping them in the shade.

White cats are prone to deafness.

Toms that have not been neutered are prone to leukemia. It's also more responsible to have your cats neutered unless you intend to breed from them.

Hooded litter trays are best because cats prefer to pee up a wall rather than into the hole they have just dug.

Give your cats a glossy coat by dabbing a cotton-wool ball into some diluted vinegar and gently wiping it over their fur.

A great way to groom your cat is by wearing a rubber glove. They enjoy being stroked and you get rid of loose hairs while you are doing it.

To untangle knots in long-haired cats use a crochet hook.

Cut cats' claws with baby nail clippers.

Cats should be bathed twice a year. Put some cotton wool in their ears and hold their front paws while washing them. It's a good idea to get cats used to this while they are still kittens.

Cats are regularly sick. It's the best way to get rid of fur balls. Chewing grass helps them to throw up with greater ease. So, for cats who don't go outside, grow a tray of grass indoors.

Elderly cats find grooming difficult so they need extra help from their owners.

Cats can never be vegetarians. No matter what your beliefs are, cats need meat to survive.

Long-haired cats need to be brushed and have knots and tangles removed each day. Cats with long hair are often more docile than their short-haired cousins.

Get your cat used to being groomed. Always brush him at the same time each day. It's usually best to do this after you have fed him.

Short-haired cats don't need as much looking after as long-haired cats. They can groom themselves and it's easier to spot any problems such as wounds, parasites and bad skin conditions.

A compromise between a long- and a short-haired cat is one with semi-long hair. They have a long top coat and a thinner undercoat, so are easier to look after than the full blown long-hairs.

If you don't intend to breed from your cat, get it neutered. Female cats come into season several times a year, so you'll stop unwanted pregnancies (and antisocial sexual behaviour in males). Female cats should be neutered when they're 4 or 5 months old, while male cats should be done at 6 months.

Manx cats don't have tails – just a hollow at the base of the spine, but they do have very long hind legs, which give them great speed.

Cats sleep for around sixteen hours a day, so make sure they have somewhere comfortable to sleep.

A cat sleeping with its paws over its nose was believed to indicate that gales were on their way.

Make sure your cat's food bowl is always clean – cats are fussy eaters and won't eat from a dirty bowl.

If you have more than one cat, make sure each has its own feeding bowl.

Tinned cat food contains all the right nutrients for a cat's balanced diet. Now and again you can treat them to fresh food; scrambled egg, chicken, meat, pasta, canned tuna or even porridge are often popular.

Feed your cat regularly to discourage it from wandering from home and looking elsewhere for its meals.

Having a cat around can be a bit like having a child. They can poke their noses into all sorts of dangerous situations, so be aware of hazards: for example, don't leave small objects lying around which can be swallowed, keep plastic bags out of their reach and don't leave washing-machine doors open.

Cats regularly get into fights with other cats. Keep an eye out for bites and scratches; they can become infected. If this happens, try to bring the abcess to a head by bathing with salt water.

All cats have a third eyelid, which you shouldn't be able to see. If it does become visible, it's usually because your cat is unwell. Take it to the vet immediately.

Also be aware that the ears of white cats are prone to frostbite.

If a cat is affected by hypothermia, gently bathe the affected area in warm water. Then wrap the cat up in a towel and take her to the vet.

If your cat gets burnt, you must take her to the vet. You can help alleviate the pain by damping the scald with cold water (don't use butter on the area). Hold an ice-pack against the affected area and then put some petroleum jelly on to the wound to keep fur out of the wound.

Protect your cat's paws when they go outside by rubbing in some hair conditioner.

Keep eyes and ears clean by wiping carefully with a cotton bud dipped in warm water containing a little diluted baking soda.

If your cat suffers from a lot of hair balls, try rubbing in some hair conditioner. Check that it's not toxic, in case your cat tries to lick it off.

When grooming a cat, put him or her in a pillowcase or a terry towelling bag with a draw pull, so that you can keep them in one place and you don't get scratched. This is also useful if you have to give them tablets.

Most dental problems can be avoided if you get your cat used to having its teeth cleaned regularly.

Cats have a unique sense of taste. They aren't any good at detecting sweetness, but they can detect tiny variations in the taste of water.

To get rid of warts you could try this old wives' remedy: stroke the afflicted area with the tail of a tortoiseshell cat … but only in May.

Bad breath? Fish may be a feline favourite but it causes smelly breath afterwards.

Too much milk causes diarrhoea – cats were originally desert creatures used to water so don't give them too much milk.

You think your cat's got fleas? If you find black grains of dirt in your pet's fur, take a grain and place it on a damp piece of toilet paper. If it turns red, it's flea droppings.

Cat diarrhoea can be a problem. A bit of cereal crumbled into the food should help clear things up.

Dry food is an excellent diet for cats. Test the quality of the dried food by soaking a piece in water. The superior brands, with a high meat content, will only swell up a little bit.

Get your cat used to its travelling basket by feeding her inside the basket for a while. Your cat will then get used to the sensation of going inside the basket.

Feeding your cat in her travelling basket will make her associate it with nice things and not just vets and catteries.

Choose a top-loading cat basket so the cat doesn't feel as if it's entering a long, dark tunnel. Make sure it has open sides for all-round vision.

If your cat gets cat flu, leave her in a steamy shower room for a short while to help her breathing.

If your cat refuses to eat, try leaving the dish out with food in it, but make sure it's just out of reach for a while. Cats can't resist thieving and this might be just the challenge she needs to start eating again.

If you have two cats and one of them isn't eating, feed the other one first. Cats hate to be left out.

If your cat has lost her appetite, try heating the food for a few seconds in the microwave. Being natural hunters, cats prefer their food to come at blood temperature.

Cats are quite happy to spend time alone so they make good pets if you're out of the house for quite long stretches. They are also ideal if you live in a flat or a busy city centre because they can adapt to living inside. They make good pets for people who can't get about too easily because they'll exercise themselves.

▷▷ At Play

It can take a month for two cats to get used to each other.

Cats enjoy playing. Try to give them at least 10 to 15 minutes of your time each day.

A scared cat will crouch down with its tail held low and its fur fluffed out.

Rubbing their body against an object is a way of marking their territory … and that can include you.

If your cat rolls over on its back and shows you her tummy, she's demonstrating that she's completely at ease with you and trusts you. Don't try to tickle her tummy; cats are very sensitive there and you'll probably get clouted for your efforts.

A cat flap gives your cat freedom to come in and out of the house as she pleases. The best height to fit the cat flap is 6 inches from the floor.

▶▶▶ Caterers

Tiona Bowyer

If your tablecloth is stained and you've got guests arriving any minute, don't panic! Scatter some rose petals onto the cloth for an effective and pretty solution.

If you are worried about staining your table, put some clingfilm across the wood before placing the tablecloth on top. If you are concerned about hot dishes burning the wood, put a blanket underneath the tablecloth.

Don't be a stranger to your guests. The worst mistake people make is to throw a dinner party but spend all evening in the kitchen. Always choose menus that you can prepare in advance.

Provide contrast and variety – go for different flavours and textures. Meat, followed by fish or the other way round. Don't have too many spicy tastes in one meal.

Candles add atmosphere to a meal. Make sure yours are below eye-level, though, so that your guests can see each other.

When making soup put a crustless piece of bread in the blender with the other ingredients to give the soup a lovely texture.

To make soup go further add wine, cream or stock. This will enhance the taste as well.

If your hollandaise sauce curdles, gently stir in an ice cube.

You can disguise gravy made from instant gravy granules by stirring in one main flavour; for example, some apple juice for pork or a tin of chopped tomatoes for lamb.

Caramel sauces mustn't be allowed to boil. But if yours does, don't worry. Just stir in some milk or cream and turn it into toffee sauce.

Overcooked sauces will never improve so don't waste your time. Some melted butter will be a delicious alternative sauce for any dish.

When making stocks or gravy, put a chip basket inside the pan to hold bones, bay leaves and other chunky ingredients. This will make it easier to lift them all out when you have finished.

If your custard goes lumpy, quickly put the base of the pan into some cold water and keep whisking until things go smoothly again.

Has a vegetarian turned up without warning? Take a tin of baked beans, stir in some wine, pour the mixture over a selection of your vegetables, and bake it in the oven for 20 minutes while you recover from the shock with a glass of wine. Result – one tasty vegetable bake.

If an extra guest turns up, most things can be stretched by turning them into casseroles. Salmon steaks can be flaked and covered with a sauce, meat and vegetables can be put into a stewing dish.

If you're tight for oven space, all meats can be half cooked the day before, stored in the fridge and then finished off when needed.

To keep the kitchen smelling sweet put some orange peel in the oven (at 350 °F/180 °C/Gas Mark 4).

To disguise lingering cooking odours, boil some cloves in a mixture of 1 cup of water and 1 tablespoon of vinegar.

If your hands are stained from beetroot or red cabbage, rub them with a raw potato.

If you want whiter than white cauliflower, add some milk to the water when cooking it.

Carrots are easier to scrape if dunked in boiling water first.

Mushrooms won't shrink when cooked if you soak them in a little boiling water first.

To cook delicious broad beans add some chopped parsley to the water.

If a recipe calls for 'finely chopped onions', just grate or blend some of them to save you time.

To make onions brown more quickly when frying, add a pinch of sugar. They'll also taste delicious and be slightly caramelised.

To absorb the smell when frying onions, put a sheet of wet newspaper close to the hob.

If you want raw onions in your salad but are worried that they will taste too strong, soak them in some tepid water first.

If your lettuce has gone limp, put it in a bowl with a piece of rinsed coal and leave for several minutes.

If you only need to use the tomatoes from the tin and not the juice, pour the left-over juice into an ice-cube tray for use in gravy at a later date.

Soggy tomatoes will firm up if soaked in salty water for 10 minutes.

Rice is one of the most common culinary disasters. Cook yours well in advance if you're having a dinner party. Then, before it's quite done, turn off the heat. Leave the lid on and it will retain its heat whilst also losing some of its stodginess.

Presentation is everything. Some fresh herbs sprinkled on top of the most ordinary looking dish will turn it into something special.

Make sure your parsley stays green – only add it to a sauce once the liquid has boiled.

If you've overcooked your vegetables, put them in icy cold water for a few minutes then microwave them very briefly before serving.

Prepare your potatoes the night before. To stop them becoming discoloured, leave them in a pan of water along with a small lump of coal. They will stay looking fresh until the next day.

To clean up any spills in the oven sprinkle some salt and cinnamon over the spill. This stops the house from filling with that acrid smoky smell and the spill will be easy to lift of with a spatula.

If disaster strikes and you burn a pan, leave some cold tea to soak in the pan for a few hours. The black burnt-in crust will then come away quite easily.

To clean an aluminium pan, boil the peel of an apple in some water. This will make it much easier to clean the pan afterwards.

To clean a grater rub a hard crust of bread over it.

Keep your knives rust-free – plunge them into an onion and leave there for half an hour. Wash and then polish lightly with some vegetable oil.

Before plucking a chicken, soak the bird in boiling water for a minute or two. The feathers will come out more easily.

If sliced ham or tongue has dried out, soak it in a little milk for 5 minutes to restore its flavour and texture.

If you are marinating ingredients make sure you do so for long enough. Marinades only work if left for at least 24 hours.

If you're cooking a big casserole, put a sheet of tin foil between the pot and the lid to save having to wash up the grimy lid afterwards.

Does the meat seem a bit tough? Squirt a little lemon juice into it before carving.

If you've burnt your hand, make up a paste of baking soda and water and apply to the burnt area. This will take some of the pain away.

If you have run out of breadcrumbs, use some crushed cheese biscuits instead.

To bring out the taste of chocolate in most recipes add a few coffee granules.

To freeze fruit use the waxed paper from the inside of cereal packets to line the trays.

To serve beautiful drinks in no time at all, add pieces of sliced fruit to an ice tray and chill in the fridge beforehand. It's then easy to add the ice cubes without all the fiddly chopping when your guests arrive.

To add that certain something to drinks frost the edge of the glass. Just dip the rim in some egg white followed immediately by some castor sugar. For a jazzy look, mix some food colouring into the sugar.

Pour wine from a height to add air and flavour.

To prevent pieces of cork getting into wine glasses pour the wine through a coffee filter paper.

When holding a garden party, fill a child's paddling pool with ice to keep bottles cold.

To thicken home-made soup quickly just add some instant mashed potato before serving.

To get rid of congealed fat in a soup or stew drop in an ice cube. It should attract the excess grease to it, gathering it in one place for you to remove.

If you like adding yoghurt to soups and casseroles but find it separates, mix with a few spoonfuls of cooling stock beforehand.

Remember, when you're making a purée to decorate soup, make sure it's the same consistency – if it's heavier it will just sink to the bottom.

If you've got room in your fridge, save potato cooking water and use it for soups and sauces. It's more nutritious than plain water and adds flavour and body to your cooking. Potato water will keep in a fridge for three or four days.

Reserve the liquid used to soak dried mushrooms and freeze it. It will be a real boost to soups and sauces in the future.

Jazz up plain tinned soup by stirring in some sherry or port.

Pep up boring bean or vegetable soup with a large spoonful of balsamic vinegar.

A dash of lemon juice added to cream of mushroom soup just before serving will cut through the richness of the soup and bring out the full flavours.

Draw a slice of bread across soups or stews to soak up excess grease.

To avoid lumpy white sauce heat the milk before you start adding it in.

For handy ready-made portions of apple sauce freeze large quantities of stewed apples in an ice-cube tray and just defrost some when you need them.

Instead of using plain water as a base for gravies and sauces, save the water from boiling vegetables. It has more flavour, more goodness and it saves water.

To make mayonnaise more interesting add a pinch of curry powder or even some brown sauce.

Make your own chutney. Simply empty a packet of dates into a clean jam jar, cover with your favourite flavoured vinegar and leave for at least a week. It's cheap and delicious.

For a fresh-tasting home-made salad dressing mix a pinch of paprika and a squeeze of lemon juice into a carton of plain yoghurt.

To get really rich curry sauces add a little sugar to the butter or ghee while melting it.

To thicken gravy add instant mashed potato powder.

Create your own flavoured vinegars, oils and mustards using your favourite herbs and spices – place them into the bottles or jars and seal for at least a week.

Save left-over red wine in a screw-top bottle and keep for sauces and salad dressings.

Left-over chicken, beef bones or vegetables? Don't throw them out. If you've got room in your freezer put the whole lot in a sealed bag and freeze. You'll have all the ingredients to make a stock when required.

Try adding mustard or Marmite to your gravy for a special mixture that packs a punch.

For a yummy sandwich filling mix honey and mayonnaise.

To make better cheese on toast take the cheese out of the fridge 30 minutes before melting it. Cheese melts better and will not separate if you start off with it at room temperature.

Fancy some de luxe cheese on toast? Mix grated cheese with an egg for a scrummy bubbly topping. A pinch of chilli powder will give the mixture a bit of bite or try some chopped spring onion for a delicious extra flavour.

Store milk on fridge shelves, not in the door, as this usually isn't cold enough.

You can freeze milk for up to three weeks without doing too much harm to it nutritionally. Skimmed freezes better than whole fat milk. If you're off on holiday leave a carton in the freezer so you can make a cup of tea when you get back. Thaw in the fridge and beat it if it separates.

If your little ones aren't keen on milk, add it to food in place of water – they'll still get all the goodness.

Whipping cream calls for cool temperatures – refrigerate your utensils before you start.

Remember to remove the zest of oranges and lemons whenever you squeeze them. Pop the rinds into the freezer or store them in a jar and use them to flavour salads, stews and cakes.

The smoother a lemon skin is the juicier the lemon is.

To save money on lemons buy lots when they're on special offer. Squeeze the juice out and freeze it in ice-cube trays. When a recipe calls for lemon juice, just take out the required number of lemon ice cubes and add to the pot.

To make peeling grapefruit easier pour boiling water over the fruit and leave to stand for 5 minutes.

Bananas gone brown? Don't fancy eating them? Use them to make some delicious banana bread.

Ripen green bananas by leaving a red tomato next to them.

Banana trees (for hanging bananas from) are great because bananas kept in the fruit bowl make the other fruit go off. But what happens when you're down to your last banana? Make sure that the last one has a long stem and then poke the banana tree's hook through the stem.

An alternative use for brown bananas is in banana milkshakes where you don't see that they've gone brown.

To chop dried fruit wet the blade of the knife so the fruit doesn't stick to it.

If rhubarb is too acidic for you, try leaving it to soak in cold black tea for an hour before using.

Alternatively, before cooking, chop the rhubarb into 2-in pieces and soak it in a bowl of cold water containing a heaped teaspoon of bicarbonate of soda.

Peeling garlic can be fiddly. To peel it easily peel down the stem of the clove and soak in boiling water for a few minutes. The skin will then come straight off.

If you do have to keep your tomatoes in the fridge, take them out a couple of hours before eating, as they become juicier at room temperature.

Avocado pears make excellent face masks. Just mash them up and smear them on for that perfect complexion.

To tart up new potatoes or chips try a couple of teaspoons of mint jelly over the top instead of butter or ketchup.

To give cauliflower a bit more flavour substitute chicken stock for plain water – alternatively just add a stock cube to the water.

If your string beans have been around for a week and are starting to toughen, add some sugar to the water when cooking.

If your red cabbage turns blue or purple during boiling, add a tablespoon of vinegar to the water and the cabbage will turn red again.

To get the best out of slightly old vegetables while boiling add salt to the boiling water to help retain flavour and colour.

Raw carrots taste best if left in the fridge overnight in a pot of iced water with a little vinegar added to the water.

Left-over cucumber? Slice, sauté on both sides until brown and serve with cream cheese. Lovely!

To prevent potatoes sprouting before you have a chance to use them put an apple in the same bag as the spuds.

To get baked beans out of the can remove the tin from the shelf and turn the can upside down, open as normal and you'll find all of the beans shoot out – simple but very effective.

Or, to make really sure that every single bean comes out – use a can-opener to remove the top. Place a plate over the top and turn over quickly. Then, use the can-opener on the other end, but don't throw away the circle of metal. Instead, push it through the can at the same time as lifting up the can.

To make the best of left-over veggies – keep a plastic container in the fridge. Whenever you have left-over vegetables, put them in the container and when the container is full, make into a soup or stew.

To keep lettuce fresh for longer wrap it in a paper towel, put in a plastic bag and keep in the fridge.

For firm corn-on-the-cob add salt to the water while boiling.

To stop rice sticking together add a few drops of lemon juice to the boiling water.

Celery keeps longer if wrapped in foil.

Don't throw out the dark, outside leaves of cauliflowers. De-stalk and chop up finely, then add to soups.

To remove fat from tinned soup place the can in the fridge. When it's cold, open the tin and scoop the separated fat off from the top.

When serving wine at a dinner party – always give everyone some mineral water too. They'll quench their thirst with the water and sip the wine more slowly.

The simplest way to achieve a healthy diet is to eat more fruit and vegetables. You should ideally eat five different portions a day – remember, 'eat five to stay alive!'

Don't add oil to boiling pasta water because your sauce will slip off. A really good sauce should literally coat the pasta.

Raw spaghetti makes an excellent firelighter.

To check if your pasta is cooked try flinging a piece against the oven door or the fridge. If it sticks, it's cooked.

Never rinse your pasta – the starch helps the sauce stick to the pasta.

Children love coloured pasta – a bit of food colouring in the cooking water might make it even more fun.

Pasta bake is cheap and easy and an excellent way to use up leftovers. Simply pile any left-over vegetables in a dish with some cooked pasta, add a tin of tomatoes or some baked beans and cook.

Bored with rice? Go for great presentation by packing it into small shaped moulds (a small tea cup would do) – spray with a non-stick cooking spray, then turn it out like a jelly on to the plate.

Remember, rice triples its volume when cooked, so use a big enough pan.

Always fluff cooked rice with a fork – this allows the steam to escape and stops the grains sticking together.

Cooked rice keeps well in the freezer, so make plenty and freeze the extra.

To make rice bright white squeeze some lemon juice into the water while boiling.

Add toasted nuts to rice while boiling to enhance the nuttiness.

Love double cream, but you're cutting calories? Evaporated skimmed milk makes an excellent substitute when slightly frozen.

Substitute dessicated coconut for some of the sugar when making topping for fruit crumble.

For a healthy but tasty pudding add some low-calorie drinking chocolate powder to natural yoghurt and some dried fruit such as sultanas, apricots, raisons. Leave overnight to allow flavours to mingle.

A sugar-free way to enjoy a rhubarb tart is to add chopped dates instead.

Do you like fizzy drinks, but worry about tooth decay? Use a straw – it reduces the contact between your teeth and the drink.

Trying to get used to sugar-free drinks? Put a little sugar around the rim of the glass – just enough to taste on the lips.

If you take a lot of medication, lay off the grapefruit juice. It can reduce the body's ability to absorb some drugs.

Plain, low-fat yoghurt makes a healthier alternative to sour cream in recipes.

A frozen banana will stop hunger cravings – it's natural sweetness will give you energy without adding extra pounds. Peel, wrap in clingfilm and freeze. It will take ages to eat as well.

Do you love gingerbread, but could do without the fat? Try replacing the fat in the recipe with pumpkin. It's tasty, low in calories and cholesterol and extremely good for you.

Frozen sheets of filo pastry can be used as a low-fat alternative to shortcrust or puff.

Replace full-fat chocolate with cocoa powder in cakes and desserts for a low-calorie treat.

If you've been told to reduce your salt intake, try using dill seeds, crushed or ground, as a substitute.

Reduce the cooking smells from cabbage water by adding a few caraway seeds to the pan.

Pop a bayleaf into stored flour to deter weevils.

Remember, basil is one of the few herbs which increases in flavour when cooked, so always add it at the end of cooking unless you want a really strong flavour.

Sage is the ideal herb to use with meat as it aids digestion of fat and its antiseptic qualities help to kill off any bugs in the meat as it cooks.

People usually try too hard when entertaining. Stick to dishes you have made before rather than launching into an ambitious recipe plucked out of a book. And don't try to put together a really exotic menu – if the main course is rich, try some sliced melon for starters. Likewise, if fancy puds are your thing, serve a simple main course of grilled fish or steak and salad.

Use music to change the mood when entertaining. Something pacy will get you moving in the kitchen then slow things down with something relaxing so you can enjoy your meal with everyone else.

For comfortable guests remember to set your heating thermostat a few degrees lower than usual. All those bodies will create their own heat.

If you're having a party, set up drinks in a different corner to the food so that people aren't climbing on top of each other – it will also encourage guest to 'circulate'.

Don't feel you have to do all the cooking for a dinner party. If your guests ask if they can bring anything, suggest they bring a pudding – some lovely fresh cream cakes, Danish pastries or patisserie would go down a treat.

For a sweet treat at a barbecue bring out a couple of bags of marshmallows for toasting above the hot coals.

Warm plates for a dinner party in the drying cycle of your dishwasher.

Caviare must be served on cold toast – hot toast will make the eggs separate.

To stop dishes like lasagne and cottage pie sticking to the baking tin grease with butter and line with breadcrumbs.

If you always get in a mess with clingfilm, try storing it in the fridge. It's easier to use when cold.

To prevent scrambled eggs sticking to the pan add 2 tablespoons of cold water.

To stop honey or syrup sticking to your spoon grease it first with a little oil.

Also try dipping the spoon in boiling water before you dip it in the honey.

Clean old Pringles boxes and use to store biscuits. The smaller ones are ideal for children's school snacks.

Some foods like bacon or rhubarb can be difficult to chop – try using scissors instead of a knife.

If you need to cover a saucepan or wok, use kitchen foil as a lid. It can be used several times.

The waxed bags inside cereal boxes make excellent linings for your cake tins.

Line kitchen scales with clingfilm before weighing out ingredients, so you don't need to wash them afterwards. When weighing sticky butter, this means the correct amount goes into the mixture rather than staying in the scales.

To check whether the fat in your deep–fat fryer is hot enough to start cooking drop a popcorn kernel into the fat. When the kernel pops, the fat is hot enough to start cooking in.

Tomato ketchup has a clever second use – to clean the base of copper-bottomed pans. Pour some over the bottom of the pan and leave for a few minutes. Then rub the ketchup in and wash it off.

To stop the bottom of a pan scratching the inside of the one it is stacked on top of put the lid of a margarine tub inside the larger pan as a 'cushion'.

To stop you cutting the end of your fingers when grating cheese wear thimbles.

To make a more imaginative basting brush take the sprigs of fresh herbs and bind together so that they make a brush. When you use it to baste, the taste of the herbs will transfer to the meat.

To make filling piping bags easier stand the bag in a tall glass. Fold the edges of the bag over the top of the glass and fill.

To make cleaning a cheese-grater easier, after grating the cheese, grate a raw potato. The potato will clear the cheesy gunk from the holes.

Use different sides of the chopping board for different things – one for things with strong odours and one for things that you don't want to be affected by strong odours. Write on the board (with an indelible felt-tip pen) what each side is for.

Fill your testing spoon from your stirring spoon for reasons of hygiene.

If you've got no time for sifting, put all your dry ingredients in a bowl and stir briskly with a whisk.

An egg-slicer is perfect for slicing mushrooms.

Keep a spray bottle filled with water handy when grilling to douse any flare ups.

For really simple frozen yoghurt put a lollipop stick into a carton of yoghurt, freeze and remove the carton. Try different flavours and low fat yoghurts for a tasty slimming treat.

Try adding a layer of banana to apple pie.

To save cutting up a slab of toffee pour the mixture into greased ice-cube trays for ready-made bite-sized pieces.

If you love peanuts and ice-cream, try mixing them together for a yummy dessert.

If you are using baking recipes which call for liqueurs, rather than buy a whole bottle of one, buy a range of miniatures.

Instead of sugar, try golden syrup in your porridge or your favourite jam.

Had a bit too much to drink? A slice of toast with honey before you go to bed will avoid a hangover.

If you don't have a cocktail shaker, use a smaller glass inverted inside a pint glass.

Traditionally whisky should be served 2 parts whisky to 1 part water – the water brings out the flavour. Use mineral water instead of tap which can have too strong a taste and affect the flavour.

Ice makes whisky too cold and reduces its flavour.

Don't use soda in whisky – it ruins the taste.

Whisky evaporates very quickly so keep the cap tightly screwed on.

The Prairie Oyster is an ideal hangover cure. Rinse a glass with olive oil. Add tomato ketchup and a whole egg yolk. Season with Worcestershire sauce, vinegar, salt and pepper. Swallow the mixture in one gulp.

The best way to keep party punch cool is to freeze some of the punch in ice-cube trays or a ring mould. Float the frozen punch in your bowl to keep it chilled, but undiluted.

To decorate punch for a special occasion core and slice apples and cut shapes for the slices using pastry cutters or a sharp knife. Dip shapes in lemon juice and float on the punch.

Treat adult party guests to jelly made with a large dash of vodka. Enjoy experimenting with quantities at home.

For very special party nibbles inject cherry tomatoes with vodka and Worcestershire sauce – sprinkle with celery salt and black pepper for a very original take on the traditional Bloody Mary.

Store fresh ginger in vodka – it will improve the taste of the vodka and the ginger.

Flavoured vodka is all the rage in pubs and clubs so try making your own – cordials or crushed and puréed fruit can be added. Experiment with lighter and heavier cordials than the vodka itself for a pretty, layered drink.

Prevent hangovers by eating a spoonful of coleslaw before bed. (Honest!)

To prevent burnt fingers use ice tongs to remove tea-bags from cups.

Sloppy mashed potato? Fold in a stiffly beaten egg white and bake in the oven.

Always throw a can of food away if the can has an outward bulge – the contents will be bad.

Here's a handy tip to rescue brown sugar that has gone hard: put ½ cup of boiling water in a microwave. Next to it put your sugar in a microwave-proof container. Put the microwave on high until the sugar has gone soft. Allow 3 minutes for every pound of sugar.

If you burn your hands while handling chilli, rub a little vinegar over them.

To make a meal out of lettuce that has started to go brown, sauté it in a little olive oil with some garlic and salt.

If your cooking oil goes black while heating it, add a few drops of vinegar and cover with a saucepan lid. Continue heating like this for about 30 seconds and the oil should have returned to a lighter colour.

Too much garlic in a sauce or stew? Add some parsley to neutralise it.

To absorb the smell of frying fish whilst cooking add celery to the pan. It tastes good too.

If you run out of eggs while baking a cake, add a teaspoon of vinegar – one teaspoon per egg.

Run out of dishwasher powder? Try baking soda.

►►► Chauffeurs

Jane Fowler; Robert Gordon

To be on time is to be late. Always arrive 15 minutes early.

To get in to the most comfortable position for driving, wriggle your bottom into the seat. This way you give your back maximum support.

If you are very small, you can use a child's polystyrene car seat which should give you a bit of a boost for driving.

Stop yourself from falling asleep on long journeys. Always chew gum because it keeps you awake and alert.

Reduce tension when you're driving. Take a deep breath, draw your shoulders to your ears and then let your shoulders drop down again. Repeat this three or four times.

To ease tension in your back, especially if you've been cooped up for a long time, pull your stomach muscles in as you take a deep breath. Hold the breath for a short while, then release it.

To polish your car use a flunky (an imitation chamois), not a chamois leather. Keep it in a sealable plastic bag to stop it drying out.

To get the best shine on your windscreen, use newspaper to clean the glass.

To keep your windscreen clean always have a jar of baking soda and a soft cloth in the car. When it rains, dampen the cloth and put lots of baking soda on it; wipe the car windows and rinse off.

To clean your chrome wheels use lemonade. It works a treat.

Keep chrome bumpers looking as good as new – wipe them over with some petrol and then clean with black boot polish for a really shiny finish.

When buying an old car, take a bit of carpet with you to lie on so that you can check underneath. Take a torch with you as well so that you can see into all the nooks and crannies of an engine.

To check whether a handbrake is in good working order stop the car, apply the handbrake and try to move off in 1 second. If you can, the handbrake needs to be looked at.

To get into a low classic car put your bottom in first, then swing your legs around. It avoids twisting your back and shoulders and you look more elegant.

To lubricate stiff windows put a couple of drops of washing-up liquid into the tops of the window channels.

Help yourself when learning to reverse. Place little markers on the wing mirrors to learn the exact position of the car.

When cleaning the limousine, use boot polish on the interior rubber trim.

Buff the windows with newspaper and a mixture of water and vinegar.

When you have cleaned the Rolls, don't forget to wind down the windows slightly before wiping off any excess water and soap from the area at the top.

Use a toothbrush to clean round the gear lever and in the switches on the dashboard.

Car a bit smelly? Freshen it up with a fabric softener sheet placed beneath a seat.

▶▶▶ Chefs

Caroline Stokes, Beakerkent Park School; Sebastian Gougen, Michelle's; Paul Reed, Chester Grosvenor Hotel; Mohammed Ali Haydor, Kushi Restaurant; Enrico Maglifiore, San Carlo; Glen Chadwick

▷▷ Fabulous Fish & Meat

To cook delicious fish wrap in clingfilm and place in boiling water so that none of the natural flavours escapes.

To prevent fish skin from sticking to the frying pan rub with salt, leave for 15 minutes, rinse and rub dry. Then cook.

To ensure that meat is tender always carve across the grain.

To serve really thin slices of cold meat place the joint in the freezer for half an hour before carving – you'll find it much easier to carve thinly.

As an alternative to honey-roast ham, try emptying a can of Coca-Cola into the baking tray for really sweet-tasting meat.

To stop your gammon from curling over when frying simply snip the edges with a pair of scissors.

Marinating meat in distilled vinegar overnight tenderises it.

If you've overdone the chilli in your curry, squeeze half a lemon over it. Then place the half-lemon into the curry, stir for a few minutes, then remove it. The chilli taste will have disappeared.

To rescue a casserole that has been over-salted just add fizzy water. Or place a potato in the casserole for 10 minutes and then remove.

If there's too much fat on the top of your casserole or sauce, gently float a piece of kitchen paper across the top and it will soak up the excess.

▷▷ Soups & Sauces

To avoid lumpy white sauce heat the milk beforehand.

To thicken stews and soups, don't use flour – porridge oats are very effective and much tastier too.

To give your soup a beautiful golden colour add some of an onion's outer skin. Remember to remove it before serving.

To give soups a rich flavour and colour add a tablespoon of prune juice.

If you have some gravy left over and you don't want to throw it away, pour it into a small margarine tub, freeze it and keep it for stock.

▷▷ Preparation

When sieving, remove the top and bottom of a large tin and place over the mixing bowl as a rest for the sieve. Both your hands are then left free to pour and press.

To loosen a tight jar lid wind an elastic band around it to form a great grip.

If you're chopping an onion, place a small piece of bread under your top lip – no more tears!

Store onions and garlic in the foot of some sheer tights to keep them dry and fresh.

To peel garlic easily, peel down the stem of the clove and soak in boiling water for a few minutes. The skin will then come straight off.

You can bring water to the boil much more quickly if you place the lid on the pan and put a large scoop of salt on top of the lid.

To get the most juice out of a lemon cut it in half and warm both halves in the oven for a few minutes before use.

To get the best out of spices roast them before use.

To dry herbs instantly place them in the microwave for a few seconds. This works especially well with parsley.

To remove air from freezer bags use a bicycle pump.

To keep your fridge smelling nice stick some cloves in an orange and place it in your fridge.

Before boiling milk, dampen the bottom of the pan with water. When the milk boils, it won't burn the bottom.

Don't waste energy boiling eggs continuously – once the water's come to the boil, turn off the heat and leave the eggs in the pan for about 15 minutes.

To test whether an egg is properly hard-boiled try spinning it on a hard surface. If it doesn't spin easily, it isn't quite cooked.

To clean a rusty knife cut a potato in half and dip the cut surface in bicarbonate of soda. Rub the potato hard on both sides of the blade for a gleaming finish.

When chopping, put a damp tea towel under your chopping board to give it a firm grip on the table.

When cooking in a microwave, paper coffee filters make excellent lids for bowls and dishes.

To cut the perfect slice of pâté or gâteau, first run the knife blade under very hot water.

To cook rice soak in cold water for an hour or two first. This saves you time and fuel in the long run.

Remove fruit or berry stains from your hands by rubbing them with lemon juice.

▷▷ Clearing Up

To clean your microwave place half a lemon in a bowl of water and boil in the microwave for a few minutes. The lemony steam will vaporise all those greasy stains and clear nasty smells.

To get rid of the strong smell from new plastic containers wash, dry and put in the freezer for at least two days.

To clean a food-stained pan fill with distilled vinegar and soak for half an hour before washing in soapy water.

To clean burnt saucepans soak in Coca-Cola for a while.

If there are little bits of cork in your wine, give the bottle a really short, sharp flick over the sink and the cork should come flying out. It's all in the wrist action!

If you still have cork left in the bottle, try pouring it through a paper coffee filter.

Fill an ice-cube tray with left-over wine to use in cooking at a later date.

Always use the freshest ingredients for the best results.

To clean your hob try white vinegar. Not only does it bring up a nice shine, but it will eliminate persistent cooking smells too.

To keep the kitchen smelling sweet put some orange peel in the oven (at 350°F, 180°C, Gas Mark 4).

Alternatively, if the pong is really strong, boil some cloves in a mixture of 1 cup of water and ¼ cup of vinegar.

Clean a grotty roasting tin (not aluminium or non-stick) with a solution of washing soda and water boiled up in the tin. Rinse and then dry in a cool oven.

Cleaning a greasy grill pan is a horrible job. Line your grill pan with foil beneath the wire tray and simply lift the foil out – complete with dirt and fat – each time after use.

Don't try to keep your baking tins shining like new – once matt and dark they will actually retain the heat much better.

Keep your kitchen knives gleaming and rust-free – plunge them into an onion and leave there for half an hour. Wash and then polish lightly with some vegetable oil.

Also keep a good kitchen knife clean by dipping a cork in scouring powder and running it along the side of the blade. Rinse the knife, dry it and wipe it down with vegetable oil.

Boiled eggs will turn metal cutlery black if left on. Always clean your spoon after eating eggs.

To clean really baked-on food from a cooking pan put a sheet of fabric conditioner in the pan and fill with water. Leave overnight and the next day the food will just lift off with a sponge.

Clean cast-iron skillets on the outside with a commercial oven cleaner. Let stand for two hours. Then remove any accumulated black stains with vinegar and water.

To clean and deodorise wooden boards combine $1/2$ cup of baking soda with some warm water to make a paste. Rub the paste on to the wood. Rinse well with clear water and pat dry.

To restore the sheen on a wooden board rub in salad oil or linseed oil using a fine steel wool pad.

To remove hard–water lime deposits from your draining board soak in full strength white vinegar, then scrub.

To remove strong food smells from plastic chopping boards give them a rub down with a cut grapefruit.

Always dry wooden chopping boards upright to stop them warping.

After washing your baking trays put them back in the oven while it's still warm to prevent them from going rusty.

Wrap fish, poultry, veg and hot sandwiches, especially bacon, in white paper towels when you microwave them. It will keep the oven clean from grease and moisture; they also absorb excess fat from the food, so you don't eat it.

To get the best from vinaigrette make it at least an hour before dressing the salad to allow time for the flavours to mix together.

To dress a salad evenly pour the dressing down the sides of the bowl rather than directly on to the salad.

Also try putting your dressing in a spray bottle to coat salad lightly. This usually saves calories too.

Do your sauces stick to the spoon when serving them? Dip the spoon in cold water or cold milk (if a milk-based sauce) before serving and the sauce will run off it more easily.

To get the best from wine in sauces put it in a pan and bring to the boil beforehand. Then set light to it with a match. The flame will burn off the alcohol and any sharpness. Add a touch of sugar to sweeten and then add to the sauce.

Put too much salt in your sauce? Dip a sugar-cube into the sauce and swirl it around the surface for a minute or two.

If you're making a tomato sauce, but the tomatoes are a little tart, try adding finely diced carrots at the start of cooking. They'll mellow the flavour.

Thicken spicy sauces with unsweetened cocoa powder.

A spoonful of cream added to a sauce made with milk will give the impression that it's all made with cream.

For no fuss marinating pop the marinade and the meat into a self-seal bag. It takes up less room in the fridge than a bowl or plate and just needs a simple turn from time to time.

Remember that cold water brings out flavour and hot seals flavour in. Always start a stock with cold water.

If you have trouble peeling hard-boiled eggs, crack the shells and soak them in cold water for a minute – the shells will slip off beautifully.

Eggs will whip more easily if left for 10 minutes in cold water before breaking.

For perfect poached eggs without a poacher add white wine vinegar to the water, bring to the boil, crack in eggs and reduce to simmer.

You can freeze egg whites, but not egg yolks.

To open quails' eggs take a small knife. Towards the flat end of the egg, gently push the blade of the knife into the shell. Turn the egg, keeping the knife in place, taking a circle of shell from the top of the egg. Then carefully pour out the egg.

Here's a cracking tip for hard-boiling eggs. Boil ten or fifteen eggs at one time. While boiling, add food colouring to the water. The shells of the cooked eggs will take on the colour of the dye. You can then look in the fridge and tell which eggs are hard-boiled and which are raw.

If you've undercooked a boiled egg, just pop the top back on and wrap in clingfilm. Place gently back into the pan and finish off the cooking.

For extra fluffy scrambled eggs or omelettes pour all the ingredients into a large plastic milk container and give it a good shake.

To separate lots of eggs at the same time gently break them all into a bowl and with clean, careful hands scoop out the yolks.

Don't worry about keeping milk fresh while you're camping. Just mix muesli with milk powder, store in a sealable box until needed, and add water as required.

Toast parmesan cheese before serving for a better taste.

If a recipe calls for milk, for a change – try yoghurt instead.

If a recipe calls for buttermilk and you haven't got any, use ¼ cup milk and ¾ cup yoghurt instead of 1 cup of buttermilk.

To make delicious, creamy scrambled eggs beat in a tablespoon of mayonnaise for every two eggs.

To prevent blocks of cheese going mouldy before you have chance to use them, grate the cheese.

If you need softened butter, but have forgotten to take it out of

the fridge, try grating it on to a warm dish.

To test whether an egg is fresh or not hold it up to a burning candle. If there are black spots visible, the egg is bad.

If your cooked apples taste bland, grate some orange or lemon peel over the top and bake for a further 10 minutes.

Got a slightly discoloured apple slice? Rub a little lemon juice on it.

To ensure apples remain crisp and juicy store them in perforated plastic bags in the salad crisper of your fridge.

Keep fruit and veg longer by storing them in paper bags rather than plastic.

To check if a bunch of grapes is fresh shake the bunch gently. If any grapes fall off, they are not fresh.

For a tasty Bolognaise sauce try adding raisins, sliced apricots and apples to the mince.

Chopped fruit often goes brown. It's a good idea to keep some bottled lemon juice in a spray bottle in the fridge. Whenever you chop fruit just give it a quick squirt of lemon and that should stop it browning.

Test to see if a pineapple is ripe. You should be able to pull a leaf from the top easily.

To tell if a shelled nut is fresh or not shake it. If it rattles, it's not fresh.

For a nutty addition to dishes toast sesame seeds until brown and add.

Never buy artichokes if they have brown patches.

To keep artichokes fresh for a bit longer cut off the dry ends and put the stems in a jar of water, adding a teaspoon of sugar to the water.

For a perfectly chopped onion skin it and put it on the chopping board root-end down. Cut downwards, but don't cut all the way through the onion. Turn the onion round and slice across the cuts.

Here's the best way to skin tomatoes: cut a shallow 'x' in the bottom of the tomato. Put it into rapidly boiling water until the skin starts to split. Immediately pop the tomato into a bowl of ice water and leave until cool. The skin should now peel off like magic.

To stop broccoli smelling while cooking put a piece of red pepper in the pot with it while boiling.

To stop Brussels sprouts falling apart during boiling cut an 'x' into the stalk end (the bottom) of the sprout with a sharp knife before cooking.

Do stir-frys in vegetable broth rather than oil to cut down on the fat.

To remove the smell of onions from your hands after chopping turn on the cold tap and rub your hands up and down the neck of the tap. This only works with stainless steel taps. If you don't have stainless steel taps, try rubbing your hands with a stainless steel spoon instead.

To cut mushrooms easily and evenly use an egg slice.

To stop onions making you cry burn a candle near by while chopping them.

To keep olive oil fresh buy a large jar of olive oil, but pour the oil into a number of smaller jars. Air affects the quality of the oil, so if you leave it in a large jar, as the amount of oil decreases and the amount of air increases, the oil will diminish.

To prevent an unpleasant odour when boiling cauliflower or cabbage tear a slice of bread into small chunks and add it to the pot. The bread will absorb the smell. Rye bread works especially well.

When chopping up chilli peppers, avoid getting hot stuff on your skin by coating your hands with vegetable oil before handling them.

To keep potatoes firm while boiling add vinegar to the water. 1 part vinegar for every 2 parts water. Add a little salt too.

Be careful if wearing contact lenses when chopping shallots or chillies – the smells have been known to permeate the lens and harm the eyes.

To check the quality of raw beans put them in water. If they sink, they're good. If they float, throw them away.

Tight for time? Chop a quantity of onions, green peppers and celery at the beginning of the week and refrigerate in individual well-sealed containers. Dip into them as required.

If you have half an avocado left over, do not remove the stone. Store it in the fridge – leaving the stone in will stop the flesh browning so quickly.

A lot of people don't like the taste of olives in brine. Try putting them on to simmer with some fresh water for 10 minutes. Drain well.

You can have healthy roast potatoes! Parboil, then place on a baking tray lined with parchment paper. Roast in the top half of the oven.

Mushrooms can be fried in water as a low-fat alternative to butter or oil.

Dried beans are full of goodness, but they're also full of 'gas'. To reduce their gassy effect always dispose of the soaking water and cook them in fresh water.

Also, if you are prone to wind, rinse tinned beans such as kidney and flageolet in fresh water before using. This will also reduce your salt intake.

If you want to lose weight from your hips, avoid spicy foods because they over-stimulate the glands that cause fat storage in your hips and bum.

For a healthy pastry base that you can use in quiches and pizzas, substitute wholemeal breadcrumbs mixed with plain low-fat yoghurt for plain flour.

If you're watching your fat intake, but crave take–away curry, buy it, leave it to cool and place in the fridge. When the ghee or fat solidifies, skim it off – and presto, a low-fat curry that will taste delicious.

Eat vegetable soup as a starter to lose weight. The fibre causes the rest of the meal to pass through your digestive system more quickly.

To reduce the amount you eat turn out the lights. Dim lights make you want to eat less.

Also to reduce the amount you eat use smaller dishes. Large plates make you want to eat as much as you can fit on to them. It's all psychological.

Worried that you eat too quickly? Use chopsticks.

Eat eggs to clear up a cold – they're high in zinc, which helps cure colds.

To get rid of a filthy cold eat a strong curry – it will 'sweat' the cold out.

If cholesterol's a problem and you want to cut down on the number of eggs you eat, replace eggs in baking recipes with a tablespoon of soya flour mixed in with a tablespoon of water.

To persuade your kids to eat healthier cereal mix half a portion of healthy stuff with half a helping of something less wholesome.

A simple way to reduce calories and fat in your favourite pies: don't cover the top with pastry – just leave it off for a healthy open pie which is just as tasty.

Need a simple low-fat dip? Prick an aubergine all over and cook on high power in the microwave for 10 minutes.

Spice up corn-on-the-cob with a squeeze of lime and a pinch of chilli powder for the delicious flavour of South America without the usual indulgence of butter.

For mashed potato without the butter, cream or milk try beating in some of the hot cooking water. To make the spuds really light and fluffy you'll need lots of elbow grease but the exercise will help reduce those calories.

Alternatively try using low-fat buttermilk or yoghurt.

For spuds that are high on flavour, but low on calories try drizzling some balsamic vinegar over cooked potatoes.

To make thick broths without adding fat or flour just remove a portion of your soup, purée and put back in.

There's no need to fry French toast in oil or butter. Just pop it into a hot oven for 10 minutes, turning once.

Try using minced turkey instead of beef in mince dishes like chilli or spaghetti Bolognaise. It has less fat and calories and you can always 'beef' up the flavour using a beef stock cube.

To remove excess fat from soup and stock fill a plastic bag with ice and drag it right across the surface. The fat will cling to the ice-cold bag.

Alternatively pour your stock through a large funnel filled with ice cubes.

Fancy a vitamin–packed light dessert to finish off a meal? Try making fruit granita using freshly squeezed grapefruit or orange juice. Add a splash of your favourite liqueur and poor into a shallow plastic container. Freeze the mixture, whilst gently stirring occasionally. You should get a pretty, crystal-like consistency.

If you frequently use fresh herbs, save the measuring cups from medicine bottles. They can be used for measuring herbs and spices.

Try crumbling a vegetable stock cube into Welsh rarebit for a different taste.

Pep up dried stuffing mix. Use a dissolved vegetable stock cube instead of plain water.

To keep ground herbs fresh store them in a container that doesn't let in light.

Odds and ends of fresh root ginger can be preserved in rice wine.

For garlic popcorn just add a peeled clove to the popping oil.

When a recipe calls for you to fry onions and garlic, always add the garlic last to prevent burning.

If you don't have fresh herbs, mix dried with lemon juice and a chopped onion and allow to stand for about 15 minutes.

Don't throw away foil trays from take–aways – wash them and keep them to use as mini-baking trays.

To get rid of the starch that rises to the top of the pan when cooking rice rest a cold serving spoon on the surface of the water and most of the starch will stick to the bottom of the spoon.

Before lighting your barbecue, brush the grid with a dab of vegetable oil to bring out the taste.

Barbecue charcoal is ready for cooking when 80% is covered with grey ash.

Keep a scrapbook of recipes cut out of magazines, papers and from packets.

To restore whiteness to a plastic chopping board rub with half a lemon and wash in warm water.

To clean a coffeepot put in some ice cubes and some salt and swirl round.

To shine the bottom of copper pans rub with a lemon half and some salt.

When making pizzas or bread at home, create a brick-oven-baked flavour. Buy some terracotta tiles from a DIY store. Place a layer of the tiles on an oven shelf. Preheat the oven and place the pizza or bread directly on to the tiles to cook.

If your pan looks like it's about to boil over, put a whisk in and beat quickly. The bubbles will go down like magic.

When a recipe calls for a coating of oil, it's really hard to make that coating even. So try pouring some oil into a spray bottle. Hold it about a foot from the food and spray.

To remove burnt food from the bottom of pans without hassle leave for half an hour with a damp cloth stretched over the top of the pan. Wet the cloth in boiling water.

To save energy use the smallest pans you can – less metal, less energy needed to heat. (And less time to wash up afterwards.)

Save more pennies in the kitchen. If you have electric rings on your cooker, turn them off a minute or so before cooking is complete. The rings will stay hot enough to continue to cook the food.

Microwaves cook more efficiently if the inside is clean.

To prevent wooden kebab skewers charring in the oven soak them in water for 20 minutes before cooking.

To avoid frozen foods from a supermarket thawing out before you get them home pick them up last, so you don't carry them around the supermarket while you get your other shopping.

Try to draw up your shopping list in the order that you reach the appropriate aisles in the supermarket. That way, you're less likely to waste time criss-crossing the supermarket.

To remember what cans of food you need to replace when you go shopping put stickers on the walls by the shelf with the name of the food written on ('Canned tomatoes', 'Baked beans'). Put the appropriate can in front of its sticker. When you use the last can, it will reveal the sticker and remind you to get another one.

To avoid forgetting regular items when going shopping type a list on a computer and save. Then, each week, add one-off items and reprint.

When you're cooking from a recipe book, cover the open page with some clingfilm to stop it getting marked.

The bigger the pan you cook pasta in the better – the pieces won't stick together.

Rice slightly burnt and stuck to the bottom of the pan? Don't scrape it off – it can be salvaged. Place a layer of onion skins over the rice. Leave for quarter of an hour, throw away the onion skins and serve the rice.

Do your tortillas break when you roll them? Put them in a plastic bag and pop them in the microwave for 30 seconds and they'll be beautifully soft.

To restore the flavour to spices that have been sitting in your cupboard for months, roast them in the oven on a high heat until you start to smell the aroma.

To boil a cracked egg wrap it in foil, twisting the two ends into a cracker shape. Then boil as normal. When you take the foil and egg out of the water, plunge it into cold water for a moment to stop the egg cooking inside the foil.

▶▶▶ Children's Entertainers

Sue Harthill

When choosing an entertainer, get the prospective candidate to give you a step-by-step account of their act.

Make your own invitations – you can use lots of different things: white paper plates, photographs, folded paper shapes, for example.

Create an element of surprise – fill party bags for each child and give them out as the children arrive. Pop in hats, balloons, chocolate, or anything else that you fancy.

It's a good idea to hire somewhere to hold your party. Children can get very excited and cause a lot of mess, so this solution saves wear and tear on your home.

If you are having the party at a restaurant, check to see that they don't object to you bringing in an outside entertainer.

If you are having the party outside, get your children to decorate some old bed sheets and use them to sit on and have a picnic.

Instead of hiring a clown get your partner or a friend to dress up as a clown, a pirate, Darth Vader or Father Christmas (whatever is appropriate).

Themed parties always go down well. Pirates, cowboys and Indians, spacemen are just a few popular ideas. Don't be too ambitious though, or you'll find nobody will turn up in costume.

Goody bags can soon become very expensive so have a lucky dip barrel instead.

To make a lucky dip go to a pound shop and buy as many gifts as you want. Ask the children to decorate the lucky dip box while you wrap the presents.

Help the children get to know each other – make little name badges.

To avoid children getting upset during the party, it is a good idea to avoid elimination games, such as musical chairs. However, if you *do* want to play them, make sure that the children who are out can take on a different role (like playing the music or arranging the chairs).

If you don't have enough room to play musical chairs, play musical hats instead. Place the children in a circle so that each child is looking at the back of the next child's head. Give all the children, bar two, a home-made cardboard crown and away you go.

Children can get very competitive at parties and it can all end in tears, so make sure that some of the games are team games. Give everyone the chance to win something.

Organise all your running-around games before tea. You don't want children to be sick on those pretty party frocks!

To calm the children down just before home-time, try playing 'sleeping lions' or 'dead donkeys' (the children have to lie as still as possible; the winner is the one who moves the least).

Children love personalised games so get each of the parents to bring a baby photo of their child. The game is to recognise who the baby is in each photo.

Personalise 'pin the tail on the donkey'. Photocopy and enlarge a photo of the birthday girl or boy for the children to pin a red nose on to.

Make a fun jail – get some plywood and a couple of old sheets. Paint bars onto the sheets and use it as a 'detention centre'.

Save yourself a lot of hassle – make a lot of the party food beforehand and freeze it until you need it.

For a culinary delight, sprinkle multi-coloured jelly babies into your jelly mixture before it sets.

If you are no good at making cakes, buy a bag of ready-made fairy cakes, arrange them on a plate in the shape of the birthday child's initial and place a candle on each cake. It saves mess, too, because each guest can have their own little cake.

If you don't have a big enough table for everyone, just put a plastic throw-away cloth on the floor and have a 'picnic' indoors.

Hire a large screen projector from a camera shop and rent a video from your local video store.

Home-video your party then play it back to the children just before home-time. They'll love seeing themselves.

Save your puff! Balloons are easier to blow up if soaked in water.

Organise your little helpers afterwards. Don't be left to clear up on your own. Put sticky name tags on boxes and get the children to fill up the box with their name on it as quickly as they can.

▶▶▶ Chiropodists

Mrs Nickson; Mrs Hill; Liz Warburton; Society of Chiropodists; Chiropodist Association

You can sidestep a number of foot complaints just by wearing properly fitted shoes.

To get the most out of your everyday shoes, wear leather uppers and man-made soles.

If you want to avoid aching feet, lie or sit down with your feet higher than your hips for at least 15 minutes.

Aching feet can be caused by shoes with thin soles or rigid heels, so insert a foam insole to alleviate the problem.

You should wash your feet in water which is at a temperature of 140 °F/40 °C.

Bromidrosis can be a problem – that's smelly feet to you or me! Swab your feet with surgical spirit after washing and drying. Don't use too much talcum powder because this will only plug up your pores.

To avoid 'cheesy' feet only wear wool or cotton next to your feet. Never wear the same pair of shoes two days in a row.

Try not to wear wellies for any great length of time. Your feet won't benefit from it and they'll smell awful, too.

To cure anhydrosis (dry skin on the soles of your feet), try rubbing petroleum jelly into your feet every night without fail. Keep your feet covered overnight with a towelling sock. The dry skin will soon disappear.

Don't disrupt the circulation in your feet. Never wear tight-fitting socks or stockings.

Wear open-toed sandals instead of slippers.

Barefoot is best – give your feet a rest each day and walk about the house with no shoes on.

To avoid blisters don't wear new shoes for too long.

Blisters can be a pain on a long walk. To avoid them apply surgical spirit to the feet and then wear two pairs of thin socks. Make sure the outer pair is a size bigger.

To prevent toes chaffing together during a long walk put petroleum jelly between your toes.

To cure small verrucas cover them with a plaster.

To dissolve big verrucas get a match with a pink head, wet it in warm water and rub it into the verruca. Then cover with an ordinary waterproof plaster.

Stop your feet from sweating too much – wipe them with surgical spirit every morning.

To get rid of athlete's foot rub surgical spirit between the toes twice a day. Or get a jar of potash, and dissolve one or two crystals in a tub of warm water. Soak your feet in the tub for about quarter of an hour.

As a last resort, cure fungal infections on your feet by soaking them in a bucket of your own urine.

To heal sprains follow the ICE method – in other words, ice, compression and then elevation.

To prevent hangnails or ragged cuticles avoid soaking your feet in water, and apply a little olive oil to your cuticles.

To get rid of a recurring ingrowing toenail dab hydrogen peroxide (10 per cent) down the side of your nails. This should fizz for a bit and then you can wipe away any dead tissue.

Prevent hard skin on your feet – use a pumice stone regularly.

Shoes should be $^1/_2$ **in / 1 cm longer** than the longest toe.

The maximum heel height for everyday shoes is $1^1/_2$ in/4 cm.

Always buy shoes with a proper fastener that holds the foot in place. Laces are best.

When trying out new shoes, stand up and walk around to see how they feel. Or stand on tiptoe and ask a friend or the shop assistant to pull the back of the shoe. If it comes off, the shoe doesn't fit properly.

If the seams of new shoes rub, hammer them gently. This will soften them.

►►► Cleaners

Joan Burke, Lygon Arms; Wendy Croad, Wendy Ann Cleaners; Helen Bowley, Maid to Order; Susan Wooldridge, Molly Maid

To clean any spills in the oven sprinkle with automatic dish-washing powder, cover with wet paper towels, let stand for a few hours, then clean with a damp sponge.

Keep salt near the cooker to avoid a grease fire. Following a spill, immediately sprinkle with the salt. When the oven cools, brush off, then wipe with a damp sponge.

To rid white appliances of yellowing mix together ½ cup of bleach, ¼ cup of baking soda and 4 cups of warm water. Apply with a sponge and leave for 10 minutes. Rinse and dry thoroughly. Sparkling white!

Wipe large items like freezers and washing machines with car wax to make them shine and to remove small scratches.

Use rubbing alcohol instead of expensive commercial waxes on all white goods.

Dishwashers will work just as effectively if you use the cheapest brand of dish-washing detergent available, but add a few tablespoons of vinegar to the dish-water. The vinegar will cut the grease, leave your dishes sparkling and save you some money.

For a truly sweet-smelling fridge pour vanilla extract on to a piece of cotton wool and leave it on one of the shelves inside.

Keep the coils at the back of your fridge clean, unplug and pull out the fridge regularly, and use your vacuum to remove dust and dirt. The fridge will stay efficient and last longer too.

To clean beneath the refrigerator tie a sock around the end of a stick or broom handle.

To remove the sticky film on dishes and the inside of the dishwasher put a bowl with 1 cup of bleach in the bottom of the washer. Run through the wash cycle, but do not dry. Then fill the bowl with 1 cup white vinegar and run through an entire cycle.

To clean your dishwasher simply run a cup of white vinegar through the entire cycle of the empty dishwasher.

Plastic bread wrappers often melt on to the side of toasters – to remove this rub nail-varnish remover on to the melted bit and rub it off with a cloth.

Never put celery or other stringy matter in the waste disposal unit.

Drop fresh parsley into hot oil after use to absorb unwanted flavours from a pan. The oil can be reused without affecting the taste of the next food to be cooked.

Keep swing-bin liners in the bottom of your bin. When you take out a full bag, a new liner will always be at hand.

When you wash the kitchen floor, use your rubbish bin instead of a bucket to hold the water. This way you get a fresh bin without the extra job of washing it.

To get rid of unsightly build-up in the bottom of a vase add a few drops of automatic dishwasher detergent and fill with hot water. Soak overnight, then rinse.

To remove tea or coffee stains from fine china rub with a damp cloth dipped in baking soda.

▷▷ Windows

To remove the black mould that can grow in the corners of windows, use an old toothbrush dipped in a mixture of water and bleach.

Water down your glass cleaner to make it go further. It will work just as effectively.

Polish on a curtain rail will make curtains run smoothly.

Wipe one side of the window horizontally and the other vertically. That way you will know which side the smears are on.

Make invisible repairs in your net curtains by dabbing colourless nail-varnish on the torn edges and holding them together until the varnish is dry.

▷▷ Dusting & Polishing

To keep feathers clean sprinkle with talcum powder and then brush off.

Blow the dust off a pleated lampshade with a hair-dryer.

Clean a circular electric fan with an old sock over your hand.

Line the top of a tall bookcase with old newspaper. When you want to remove the dust, just throw away the paper and replace it. This works for the tops of kitchen cabinets as well.

Brush dust off shelves with a new paintbrush.

Make your own polishing pad by cutting up some old tights and putting them in a cotton bag.

Save wear and tear on your rubber gloves – put sticking plasters on the inside of each finger.

To ensure your new duster picks up dirt soak it in equal parts of vinegar and paraffin. When it's completely saturated, take it out of the mixture and store it in a screw top jar until you need it.

Make sure dirt stays in the dustpan – spray the inside with furniture polish so the dust has something to stick to.

Stop dried pampas grass from disintegrating by spraying it with hair-spray.

Take care of your chamois leather. Wash in warm, soapy water and rinse after use. Allow the leather to dry away from direct heat so that it retains its natural oils.

Keep pewter clean by rubbing with a cabbage leaf. Finish off by polishing with a soft cloth.

Alternatively, rub pewter with petrol and leave to dry. When it's dry, rub over with hot beer. Leave this to dry as well and then buff with a soft cloth.

Bring up the shine on silver with a piece of rhubarb.

▷▷ Floors

Move furniture with ease. Put foil pie dishes under each leg and the furniture will slide easily over the carpet.

Furniture can leave dents in the carpet. A cube of ice left on the dent will restore the pile of the carpet.

Make your own protective castor cups or mats with the lids of coffee jars. Just slide under the castor to protect the pile of the carpet.

Brush the dust away from the corners and edges of carpets with a hand brush and then vacuum it up.

Prevent your vacuum cleaner picking up metal pins and clips by taping a magnet to the front of the cleaner or the outside of the tube. This should stop anything metal getting into the dust bag and damaging it.

To clean a dirty mat put it in a bin bag and shake it around. The dust will stay in the bag rather than settling on the rest of your furniture.

Keep dust from flying around – empty the contents of your vacuum cleaner on to a damp newspaper.

If you've dropped a glass, use a piece of white bread to 'blot' up the tiny slivers of glass. Make sure you've cleared all the shards up.

Dropped an egg on the kitchen floor? Add some salt to the egg, leave it for 5 minutes and it will clean up more easily.

To neutralise odours and discourage pests liberally sprinkle bicarbonate of soda on your carpets and leave for 15 minutes before vacuuming up.

To clean a wooden floor scatter damp tea-leaves over it to keep the dust in one place when sweeping.

To refresh the colours of a carpet, sprinkle over a mixture of tea-leaves and salt over it and then vacuum.

Make your old linoleum floor look as good as new. Wipe it down with 1 part fresh milk mixed with 1 part turpentine. Rub into the floor and polish with a warm soft cloth.

Get your quarry tile floor shining – use sour milk to wash it down.

Stop your rugs from creeping away – put heavy-duty double-sided tape on the bottom of the rugs.

In icy weather clean the doorstep with a bucket of water to which you have added a crushed aspirin, 8 fl oz/250 ml of warm water and 1 tablespoon of methylated spirits. This will keep the step clean and stop ice from forming.

For heel marks on hard floors wipe with kerosene or turpentine or use a pencil eraser.

Nail polish spills can be left to solidify. When just barely pliable, peel off.

Be careful when cleaning quarry or ceramic tiles. Although the tiles are very tough, the grout surrounding them is not. Rinse thoroughly to avoid the grout deteriorating.

Dark coloured floors show up scuffs, dust and scratch marks, whilst black heel marks show up more easily on light coloured floors. Consider your options or face a lifetime on your knees scrubbing.

When choosing a mop, consider this: cotton mops need breaking in, but will dry a floor faster than other alternatives. Rayon mops require no breaking in and will immediately absorb water, often absorbing seven times the mop's weight. Blended mops can offer the best of both worlds: no breaking in, plus immediate absorbency.

To eliminate the re-depositing of dirt as you mop frequently flip the mophead as you work.

Top mop tips: always use cold water, not hot. Keep your back straight. Do not twist your spine. Bend at the knees, not your back. Use your arm muscles to move the mop in a figure eight pattern. (It's all good exercise too.)

Wipe your guests' feet for them! Most visitors don't wipe their feet. Their minds are focused on where they're going or they're keeping pace with the people behind them. Ensure you have a good width of matting at entrances.

To clean a varnished floor try adding instant tea granules to your bucket of water.

▷▷ Other Areas

For scratched woodwork you can minimise the damage by dabbing with cotton wool that's been dipped in diluted tea.

For a clean, sweet-smelling sponge just run it through the top rack of your dishwasher.

To clean your TV/video remote control unit first take the batteries out. Then with a paintbrush and a bit of meths give it a good scrub. Leave for half an hour and it will be as good as new.

Dusting your TV? Eliminate static electricity from the screen by wiping with a used sheet of fabric softener. It will help prevent dust re-settling.

To clean between computer keys use cotton buds.

Clean the ball of a computer mouse with a cotton bud dampened with alcohol.

To clean ink and ribbon fibre from typewriter keys roll Silly Putty into a ball and very carefully press into the keys.

To remove crayon marks from walls apply a thin coat of rubber cement glue and allow to dry thoroughly, then 'roll' it off. If a colour stain remains, try rubbing it with a little liquid detergent mixed with a few drops of ammonia.

To blow dust or cobwebs out of corners use a balloon pump or a bicycle pump.

Small, irritating marks on a ceiling can be blotted out with a little white shoe polish.

If a ceiling gets really grubby or smoke stained, it is often quicker to whitewash it than clean it. A pair of swimming goggles is a good idea to protect your eyes.

To whitewash a ceiling a new sponge mop is easier than perching up a ladder with a roller.

Don't try to clean unpainted bricks – water will make any marks worse.

Leave natural walls to acquire an attractive aged appearance.

Tiling all the wall space in a bathroom can look stunning, but it can be a pain to keep gleaming – a squeegee will do the trick in no time.

Embossed wallpapers often look grubby. A clean, soft bristled toothbrush solves the problem.

Mouldings and cornicing can be awkward to clean thoroughly. Put some detergent into a garden spray bottle to get into all the nooks and crannies. After wiping, spray again with clean water to make sure no detergent is left lingering.

A Terry nappy is good for wiping cornicing because the loops get into all the detail.

Vacuuming is hard work at the best of times. Change your vacuum bag before it gets too full – a full bag is less efficient and makes the task twice as difficult.

If your vacuum cleaner's hose gets clogged with dust you can knock out the clog with a broom handle threaded carefully through the hose.

Clean aluminium window frames with cream silver polish.

To keep the corners of windowpanes free of dust and moisture save the ends of white candles and rub on the corners of the wood.

Louvred windows and doors are easy to clean with a 2 in wide paintbrush dipped in a mild soap solution. Lightly towel dry.

Or dab lighter fluid on a cloth and rub gently.

Cure condensation by cleaning the affected area with bleach, then dry out with lots of warmth and ventilation.

If they are really filthy, soak Venetian blinds in the bath and, wearing a pair of fabric garden gloves, wipe each slat clean. Then hang over the bath to dry.

Dull net curtains can be transformed into gleaming white ones by putting a denture cleaning tablet into water and soaking the curtains.

Make life easier when cleaning: put some detergent on, say, a floor or a sink, then move on to the next job, leaving it to work for a while. By the time you return, the detergent will have really got into the dirt and your task will be half done for you.

Car wax makes an ideal cleanser and polish for ceramic tiles. Apply it generously and give it a wipe with a soft duster before it's completely dry. Not only will it clean your tiles a treat, but its natural waterproofing will keep them looking good for longer.

Sticky label marks can be stubborn to remove from glass. Try using a little peanut butter rubbed in on some soft cotton wool.

Dirty dishcloths cause germs. Always dry yours thoroughly before storing away – bacteria love nothing more than a nice, warm damp 'bed' …

Dustpans and brushes are always overlooked, but they get filthy – wash yours out thoroughly at least once a month. They will be much more effective at picking up dirt and more hygienic too.

▷▷ Bathrooms

Glass shower doors will stay cleaner longer if you spray them lightly with furniture polish and then shine.

To wash shower curtains put them in the washing machine along with warm water and two large bath towels. Add 1/2 cup each detergent and baking soda. Then wash, adding 1 cup white vinegar to the rinse cycle. Do not spin dry or wash the vinegar out. Hang immediately and wrinkles will disappear when completely dry.

To stop the bottom of your shower curtain from becoming discoloured or mouldy coat it with baby oil.

If your shower head is clogged, fill a plastic freezer bag with about 2 inches of vinegar and place the shower head in the bag. Place a tie wrap or elastic band around the neck of the shower head to hold the bag in place. Leave in soaking over night. In the morning remove the bag, and the head should be clean and function properly. Repeat if necessary.

Glass shower doors quickly look grubby, and limescale can be hard work to get rid of. Try using a squeegee – the sort motoring shops sell for car windscreens – for a sparkling look in minutes!

Safety first – never use two different commercial cleaners in the loo at the same time – they may combine to produce dangerous gases or even explode.

To clean a really grubby toilet tie a cloth around a toilet brush and push the water out of the bowl. Then soak the bowl in bleach for several hours before flushing again.

Alternatively, rub with a fine grade sandpaper (wet the sandpaper if the rings are very old).

When bleaching your toilet, don't forget to put some bleach into the toilet-brush holder to ensure the brush stays clean.

To clear blockages in sinks or basins cover the overflow holes with a damp cloth to build up the pressure while you are using a plunger.

For bad bathroom stains mix a paste of peroxide and cream of tartar. Scrub with a small brush and rinse thoroughly. If stains persist, re-apply paste and add a drop or two of ammonia. Let stand for 2 hours and scrub again.

Before you start to clean tiles, run the shower at its hottest water setting. The steam will help loosen the dirt and make for easier cleaning.

Lemon oil keeps tiles shinier longer and helps keep water stains from building up.

Dripping taps can cause a stain on the bath or sink enamel. Try rubbing the mark with a cut lemon to get rid of it.

If your acrylic bath gets scratched, try rubbing the scratches with silver polish.

For chrome taps or fixtures try rubbing them with alcohol for a super shine.

▷▷ After a Fire

Nothing causes more dirt and damage than a fire. If you're unfortunate enough to have needed the fire service to hose down your house, here are a few tips to get things back to normal:

If you must use your mattress temporarily, sun dry the mattress on both sides and cover with plastic sheeting. It is almost impossible to get the smell out of pillows as feathers and foam retain odours.

Let rugs and carpets dry out thoroughly. Clean with a wet/dry vacuum or water extractor carpet cleaning machine. They will remove the standing water and dirt. Rinse, using vinegar and water in the tank of the carpet cleaning machine. Dry the rugs as quickly as possible. A fan turned on the rug will speed the drying. Any moisture remaining at the base will quickly rot the rug, causing it to fall apart.

Most dishes can be washed in 1 tablespoon bleach to 1 gallon of lukewarm water for 30 minutes prior to washing. Wash in hot soapy water. Dishwashers are excellent for this purpose.

When water is underneath lino, it can cause odour and rot or warp a wood floor, which could become a major expense. If this happens, remove the entire sheet of lino. If glued, a heat lamp will soften it so you can roll it up without breaking it.

Walls may be washed down while still wet. Use a mild soap and rubber gloves. Work from the floor up, a small area at a time. Rinse with clear water. Work quickly when washing wallpaper, so paper does not become soaked. Wash ceilings last. Do not paint until dry.

Dry, heat and ventilate rooms for several days to dry plaster and paper. If mildewed, wipe with a cloth wrung with soap. Re-paste edges or loosened sections of paper.

▷▷ Lights

When light bulbs are cool, dab some of your favourite perfume on. When the light is on and the bulb heats up, the room will fill with the aroma.

▷▷ Protection

If your freezer is kept in the garage, polish the outside of the cabinet with wax. This prevents it being affected by damp, mould or rust.

To cut down on static put a few drops of fabric conditioner in some water and wipe down the front of your TV.

Wipe bathroom mirrors with some washing-up liquid on a cloth – this will reduce condensation.

Prevent rusty rings in your bathroom. Paint the bottom of aerosol cans with clear nail-varnish.

Spectacles need regular cleaning, but often go rather smeary. A little eau de Cologne or some astringent face toner wiped over the glass will prevent the problem.

To keep clean when you are doing dirty work wear an old dustbin liner. It's easy to throw away each day.

Make your life easier – put some washing-up liquid in the children's paints because it helps get them out of clothes when they're being washed.

To make non–dribbly paint mix it with wallpaper paste (but not one that has an anti-fungal agent in it) and it won't end up all over the place.

After cleaning cast iron, while the pan is still warm, wipe with a piece of wax paper to prevent rusting. Or, when clean, rub a small amount of vegetable oil on the inside to keep it seasoned.

Steel wool pads won't get rusty if you throw them in a plastic bag and store in the freezer.

▷▷ Smells

No time to clean but you want to give the impression that you've been busy? Spray furniture polish behind the radiators. The heat will dispel the scent round the room.

To prevent the smell of cigarettes from lingering put a small bowl of vinegar in the corner of the room. Cover the bowl with clingfilm and pierce it several times – then you won't get vinegar everywhere if the bowl is knocked over.

Prevent cigarette butts from smouldering. Line your ashtrays with bicarbonate of soda.

Keep your waste disposal unit smelling sweet by grinding citrus rind. Or use the discarded baking soda after it has finished absorbing odours in the refrigerator.

▷▷ Stains

To remove ink stains from all sorts of materials spray with hair-spray first and then clean.

To remove a cigarette stain from the carpet pour a little milk on the stain and leave it to soak in. This will dilute the colour and stop it browning. Then rub the stain with a raw potato and wash as normal.

Remove chocolate stains with a mixture of borax powder and glycerine. Stretch the fabric over a bowl, dab the mixture on, leave for a few minutes and then wash off.

To give a stainless steel sink a superb finish rub it down with a scrunched-up ball of newspaper after cleaning.

When descaling tap nozzles put a plastic bag filled with vinegar over the nozzle. Secure it with an elastic band and leave it for at least half an hour.

Save money – cut your steel wool pads in half so they go twice as far.

Preserve steel wool pads for longer by keeping them in soapy water. This will stop them from rusting.

The secret to removing bloodstains on white fabric is to use cold water and a little detergent. You can dab the stain with hydrogen peroxide, but be careful. Then rub on the secret weapon: unseasoned meat tenderiser. Rinse and wash. Do not use warm water – it will set the stain.

Remove oil marks from paper by covering with talcum powder, leave overnight and then brush off.

To get rid of ink stains from furniture soak a piece of cotton wool in water and cover the stain with it. The mark will be drawn out and into the cotton wool.

Remove lipstick stains from linen napkins by applying Vaseline petroleum jelly before washing.

▶▶▶ Cobblers

Bill Byrd, Blockley, Chipping Campden; Mark Beabey, Leeds; Guy Metcalf, Totnes; Alan Macdonald, Cheltenham; Su Randall; Guild of Master Craftsmen

When buying new shoes go shopping at the end of the day when your feet are at their 'largest'. If you buy shoes in the morning, they can become uncomfortable later on in the day.

Always try on both shoes because most people have one foot slightly smaller than the other.

New shoes often rub at the heel. Make sure yours are comfy from day one. Place the heel of the shoe over the arm of a wooden chair, cover with some cardboard and bash with a hammer ... it's a bit like tenderising meat!

The best way to soften leather is to wrap it in a soft cloth and then soak it in water overnight.

If your shoes are a bit tight, just poke a hairbrush handle down inside the toes to stretch them a little. Or stuff them with potato skins and leave overnight.

Give your shoes a rest. Try not to wear them day after day. They'll last longer and it's healthier for your feet to let the shoes dry out.

Stop your shoes losing their shape at the toes – keep your toenails short.

If you've got big feet, stick to dark or neutral colours. White or bright colours will only draw attention to them.

If you've got narrow feet, shoe flaps sometimes slip over each other. To prevent this happening, simply place a bit of felt under the flaps before you lace the shoes up.

Save your energy. Polish your shoes in the evening and then buff them up the next morning. This gives a better finish anyway.

To make leather shoes last longer try using some saddle soap in place of ordinary cleaning products.

To clean gents' shoes without damaging the stitching wrap a thin soft cloth around a knife and rub off any mud or dirt.

Keep your suede shoes looking pristine by removing any marks with an eraser.

Freshen up old suede shoes by giving them a good steam over the kettle.

Nubuck shoes quickly lose their downy roughness. To make them furry again rub gently with some fine sandpaper.

Get rid of salt marks during the winter by mixing 1 tablespoon of vinegar in 1 cup of water and then wiping over the marks.

To remove grease stains from leather rub in washing-up liquid. Leave to dry and then polish off.

Satin wedding shoes often get ruined because of water marks. Remove the stains by dipping some cotton wool in a little white spirit and dabbing it over the shoe. If the shoe is brightly dyed satin, test a little area inside first.

Wedding shoes come in such subtle colours that it can be hard to find a matching polish. Try rubbing oil pastels over the shoe; they come in a full spectrum of shades. When you find the perfect match, seal the shoe with a little neutral polish.

Dyed shoes often mark your feet when they get wet. Prevent this from happening by spraying the inside of the shoe with some Scotchguard.

Bring the shine back to patent leather – try rubbing a little vegetable or baby oil over the shoe and then buff with some kitchen paper towel.

Make patent leather sparkle, with furniture polish.

Scuff marks can be covered by gently building up layers of felt-tip pen until you reach the perfect colour match.

Even the grubbiest of trainers look fit for Centre Court if you give them a good clean with a baby wipe.

Keep new trainers looking white for longer – spray them with starch when you get them home from the shops. This makes them easier to clean as well.

If you've got marks on your white stilettos, try getting rid of them with nail-varnish remover. If you can't get them off, dab some correcting fluid over the marks.

Remove black marks from white leather shoes by gently rubbing with a damp Brillo pad.

White leather shoes appreciate a wipe down with beaten egg white instead of polish. Use cotton wool to clean them and then polish with a soft cloth.

Stiletto heels always get scuffed and marked. Try spraying them with some matching car paint as a durable solution.

Clean wooden heels with furniture polish.

To remove bad stains from leather use wood bleach.

To keep your football boots in good condition, avoid products that have paraffin in them because this will rot the leather.

Never wear new leather shoes in the rain. They need a bit of wear and tear to build up water resistance.

For an effective waterproof coating give your shoes a final polish with a coat of floor wax.

If you've run out of shoe polish you can use a little floor wax, furniture polish or window-cleaning spray.

For an alternative brown shoe polish, rub the inside of a banana skin along the leather. Leave to dry and don't buff them up.

Polish black shoes with the inside of the rind of a fresh orange.

To give shoes an instant antique look buy them one shade lighter than you really want but clean them with a slightly darker polish.

If your shoes get soaked, take them off as soon as you get home and stuff with newspaper. Leave them to dry naturally; don't try to speed the process up by putting them in front of a fire or in bright sunshine. When they are dry, use some saddle soap to condition them and then polish.

If flamenco dancing is your thing make sure your shoes last the distance. Hammer some carpet tacks into the heel. You'll sound the part too!

If your leather laces are a bit wide for the holes, dampen them first and then pull them through a small hole punched in some cardboard before trying to lace them up in the actual shoes.

To stop shoelaces coming undone wet them before you tie them. The knot will then remain in place. Or you could wax the laces with polish before doing them up.

The plastic tips often come off laces and once frayed they're very difficult to thread through shoe holes. Pull the plastic tips off and just burn the ends to seal them for a permanent solution.

If you're trying to sew stiff leather, first soak the cotton in melted wax.

Many leather-working tools have round wooden handles. Flatten one edge a little with some sandpaper to stop the tools rolling off tables and work surfaces.

Make your own shoe horn – use a large metal spoon or an old telephone card.

Make your Doc Martens last longer. Put a leather insole inside.

To dry wet wellies use a hair-dryer.

If your boots are really tight, put your foot into a small plastic bag and it will slip in more easily. Once you've got your boot on, you can tear the bag off your foot.

Never wear boots in hot weather – your feet will swell and get sticky. You'll find it really difficult to get your boots off – the more you tug, the hotter your feet get and the tighter the boots become!

When you get your sandals out of the wardrobe after a long winter they often feel really stiff and uncomfortable. Pop them in the oven for 3 or 4 minutes at 210 °F/100 °C and they will soon soften up.

If the bottoms of your shoes feel sticky, sprinkle a little talcum powder over the sole.

If your soles are slippery, rub a piece of sandpaper across them. Or stick a piece of sandpaper to each one.

To keep shoes smelling sweet fill a fine plant spray with water and some cologne and give the shoes a little shower.

If you have smelly feet sprinkle some bicarbonate of soda in your shoes overnight to cut down on the pong.

For a cheap pair of boot trees roll up some newspapers and stuff them down your boots. Or you could tie some kitchen towel cardboard tubes together.

To clean the white rubber areas (the 'bumpers') on training shoes, use toothpaste.

To clean white training shoes rub with bathroom cleaner, buff and then wipe off with a rag.

Alternatively, use cheap face cleansing milk.

Scuffs on high heels or shoes can be covered up using magic marker or felt-tip pen.

If you have smelly feet, place orange peel in a pair of smelly summer shoes overnight and they'll be much fresher next day.

Or you could try placing a fabric-softener sheet in them.

Alternatively, deodorise trainers by filling the feet of pop socks with unused cat litter, tie the ends, place inside and leave overnight.

Patent leather shoes come up a treat if rubbed over with petroleum jelly.

Canvas shoes often look grubby very quickly. Carpet shampoo, applied with a small brush, will make them look as good as new.

Prevent your shoes from scuffing by painting a layer of clear nail-varnish on the heel and toe of your shoes.

▶▶▶ Cyclists & Bikers

Simon Matthews, Freewheel; Sandra Barnett

Get more power out of your legs – make sure your leg is straight when you reach the six o'clock position on the pedals.

Don't have your seat at too much of an angle – it should be flat.

Keep your tyres pumped up properly; squishy tyres make cycling harder work and it's much less efficient.

If you have a mountain bike with thick, chunky tyres that you use mainly on the roads ... buy some road tyres!

When cycling long distances, wiggle your hands and fingers to avoid numbness.

If you get caught short when out cycling, use your cycle cape as an emergency portaloo.

If you're out in the wind and the rain without much protective gear, stick some newspaper, cardboard or even straw down your front and secure with a bungee cord round your middle. This should keep you nice and dry.

If it's raining, tuck a plastic bag under your saddle. When you reach your destination, you can use it to cover your seat. You'll have a dry bottom on your return journey.

Take some kitchen foil with you to cover the seat in case it rains.

When cycling in the hills you can stuff an old magazine up your shirt to stop the air flow cooling down the sweat on your body.

A cycling tip for men only – take a third sock with you when you go cycling in the winter to keep your crown jewels warm (impresses the girls as well).

Be noticed! Now is the time to wear that loud sweater or silly hat.

Covering your bike with stickers is a great anti-theft device; it makes your bike instantly recognisable and difficult for the thieves to strip down.

If people keep stealing the quick release on your bike when you remove the saddle; hit it with a hammer until the thread jams and then they won't be able to nick it!

For security, two locks are better than one.

Always lock your bike up at home – even if you keep it in a garage or shed.

Don't put the lock on your bike so that it is easy for you to remove … it makes it too easy for the thief as well.

Don't position the lock near the ground because a thief is less obvious to passers-by in this position.

If you are out touring, make sure you eat little and often, and drink liquid regularly.

When you're on a cycling holiday, take some dental floss for a washing line. You can also use it at night to tie between your leg and your bike – you'll soon know if anyone tries to nick your wheels.

Loading up panniers can be a pain, so take two guy ropes and peg one end to the ground and the other end to the bike. Secure both ropes so that the bike stands upright, keeping the panniers off the muddy, damp ground. You can then pack each pannier more easily.

To secure the bottom clip of your panniers put a key-ring through the main bolt.

For a cheap bike lever, use a spoon.

To check whether your valve is leaking get a small jar of water and submerge the tip of the valve in the water. If there are air bubbles, the valve is not working properly and should be changed.

Rather than carrying a puncture kit around with you, carry a spare inner tube. Then, if you get a puncture, you can replace the inner tube and repair the old one at home where it's nice and dry and the light is good.

A bike needs to be lubricated once a month if it is being used regularly. Don't be tempted to substitute vegetable oil for bike oil because it can muck up the chain.

Clean the chain and cog system regularly – it will cost a few pennies but will save a fortune in maintenance and repairs in the long run.

Polish any metal and painted surfaces with household wax to stop rust.

To get rid of rust from bicycle wheel rims put some emery paper between the brake blocks. Turn the pedals and lightly apply the brakes.

Keep chrome looking shiny – polish with a little bicarbonate of soda on a damp cloth. Rinse off and dry.

If you get bike oil on your clothes, rub the stain with washing-up liquid and then wash as normal.

Tar and oil stains can be removed with toothpaste.

Keep your visor wipe handy – cut a tennis ball in half and tie it around the handle. It makes a great place to store a damp sponge which you can use to keep your visor clean.

Protect your paintwork – put some sticky-back plastic on to the tank of your bike. It will stop the zips on your jacket and trousers from making scratches. The bike will be easier to sell if it isn't covered in marks.

▶▶▶ Dog Breeders

Helen Louise Johnston; Tracy St Clair Pearce; Lynn Bourne; Jude Simmons

When choosing the sex of your dog, remember that young unneutered males can wreak havoc when they go into sexual overdrive. Bitches go on heat twice a year so need to be watched carefully unless you don't mind the inevitable attention of all the neighbouring male dogs and subsequent pregnancies.

Pedigree dogs should be bought from a recognised breeder. Like cars, pedigree dogs come with documents that certify its breeding and confirm its vaccination record.

Cross breeds are cheaper than pedigree dogs and are often less likely to inherit the diseases and ailments that pure pedigree dogs can suffer from.

Show dogs require a lot of attention. They need to be groomed at all times and be incredibly well trained.

Working dogs need a lot of exercise and a larger diet than house dogs.

Lap dogs need a lot of exercise because they are usually active breeds but they won't eat you out of house and home.

Guard dogs give security and protection, but you must be an experienced dog handler and know what the legal requirements are for owning such a dog.

When fitting a dog with a collar, you should be able to slip two fingers under it.

Put the dog bed in a busy part of your home, such as the kitchen.

When introducing a child to your dog, make sure they stroke the dog on its side, not its front (dogs can interpret that as an aggressive gesture). Dogs and children should always be introduced to each other in the presence of an adult.

Explain to children that they must never rush up to a dog, shout at it or pat it on its head.

▷▷ Puppies

When you bring a puppy home, check that there are no holes or gaps in your fence where he can escape. Pick up all small items that could be swallowed. Have the puppy's bed ready because he will be tired after all the excitement.

Make him feel secure – this will be the first time he's been away from his mother. A quiet spot indoors, with a small pen that he can't escape from at night, is a good idea. Place a cardboard box inside, lined with an old jumper wrapped round a warm hot-water bottle. Put a good wad of newspaper nearby so he won't soil his bedding.

To keep a lonely puppy happy, especially at night, leave a ticking clock nearby. It will be like the beating of his mother's heart so he'll feel more secure.

Decide where the puppy's toilet is going to be in advance of his arrival. Take the puppy there as often as possible. Look for signs that he wants to go (whining, circling, snuffling) and praise him to the skies when he does it in the right place! Don't punish him or rub his nose in it if he makes a mistake – he won't understand.

Healthy puppies are happy to be picked up and should feel firm and heavy.

Watch a puppy interact with the rest of its litter; this should give you a good idea as to its temperament.

When choosing a puppy, check its ears – they should be pink inside with no crusty or waxy discharge (this indicates the presence of mites).

Also look at its eyes; they should be clear and bright, free from any discharge. If the puppy keeps pawing at its eyes, this could mean it has some sort of inflammation or irritation.

A puppy's teeth and gums should be pink (or black and pink) and not smelly.

Check your puppy's skin for oiliness or flakiness. There shouldn't be any sores or lumps. If you run your hand against the lie of the coat, you can check for any parasites.

A puppy's bottom should be clean and dry with no signs of discharge or diarrhoea. If the puppy keeps dragging its bottom along the floor, it could mean it's got blocked anal glands.

Get your puppy used to being picked up and carried. Don't pounce on it, but reassure it first before holding it firmly but comfortably. Put one hand under the puppy's chest and the other under its rump.

Tag your dog as soon as you get it home. More and more vets have the facility to place a microchip under the dog's skin.

Get your puppy used to wearing a collar. Put its first collar on for short periods each day. If you can't be around to keep an eye on your puppy, remove the collar.

Puppies need to eat three or four times a day. Once they are 6 months old, you can reduce that to two feeds a day. When they are between 6 and 9 months old, they can go on to adult dog food.

A crate makes a safe and secure home for a puppy especially if you keep it in a busy area of the home. It's somewhere for the dog to retreat to. Puppies are less likely to make a mess in their sleeping area, so it helps when it comes to house-training.

Never leave a dog in a crate for more than two or three hours a day.

A crate is for security, not for punishment. It's somewhere for your dog to want to go, not be afraid of.

▷▷ Cleanliness

Incontinent dogs can make your house smell awful. Put some bicarbonate of soda in their drinking water to reduce the smell of their urine.

If your dog wees on the carpet by accident don't apply disinfectant: it reacts badly with ammonia and could leave a mark. Instead, try using a soda siphon and keep blotting the stain until dry.

When your dog has rolled in something unpleasant, wash him with tomato ketchup instead of shampoo. It gets rid of the strongest smells.

Prevent your dog from walking clumps of mud into the house – keep his paws trimmed.

If your dog always jumps out of the tub at bathtime leave his collar and lead on. Hook the lead over the taps. He will know he can't escape and bathtime will be less of a struggle for both of you.

Stop your dog from scratching the bath – put a non-slip mat down so that he can keep his grip and your bath is protected at the same time.

To protect your clothes when bathing your dog wear a bin liner with three holes cut out for your arms and head.

Put dog shampoo in a squeezy bottle and dilute with 50 per cent water. Just squirt it out and the thinner mixture will spread evenly through his coat, avoiding great clumps of bubbles that can be difficult to rinse out.

Use baby shampoo if you don't have any dog shampoo.

To get rid of fleas start shampooing from both ends of your dog at the same time. The fleas get trapped in the middle and have nowhere to run to!

Discourage fleas with a dash of cider vinegar in the final rinse at bathtime.

Fleas hate garlic so drop a garlic capsule into your dog's feed to rid him of troublesome guests.

To dry your dog quickly use a chamois leather.

It's tricky to clean your dog's teeth. Make it easy by wrapping a fabric plaster around one finger and dabbing on some bicarbonate of soda. Use your finger as a toothbrush.

If your dog won't stand still while you groom him put something tasty on the door of your fridge or oven and let your dog lick it off while you get him looking smart.

Don't buy expensive pooper scoopers – plastic bags over your hand work just as well.

If your dog has weed where he shouldn't, damp the stain with soda water, sponge up the liquid and then let it dry. Sprinkle on some baking soda and leave for about quarter of an hour. Vacuum afterwards.

Don't use products which contain ammonia to clean up a dog's mess because it can remind a dog of the smell of its own urine. If a dog can smell its own odour, it will return to that spot and use it again.

Long-coated dogs need their hair brushing daily and to have regular trims.

Smooth-coated dogs are the easiest to look after and only require a weekly brushing.

Curly coats must be clipped every two months to keep under control.

Some dogs have the kind of faces which trap dirt and debris so the more wrinkly they are, the more they need keeping clean. Use damp cotton-wool balls to clean out the folds of skin.

Plug your dog's ears with cotton wool when you give him a bath.

Avoid getting shampoo in your dog's eyes and mouth.

After his bath, dry your dog's head first. This is the first thing he'll shake so it saves you from getting soaked.

You can use a hair-dryer to dry a wet dog, but only if it has healthy skin. Heat tends to aggravate sensitive skin.

Add a couple of drops of tea tree oil to some water and sponge your dog's coat. This will get rid of fleas.

The best time to trim a dog's nails is after his bath when they are softer than normal. Don't cut into the pink area of the nail because this is living tissue. If you're not sure where to cut, ask your vet to show you.

Over 75% of dogs require dental attention so keep your dog's teeth clean. Bad breath is often the first sign of a problem.

Use a non-slip mat to stand your dog on while you groom him.

Grooming is a great opportunity to check your dog for any parasites, sores, bumps and bruises.

A chamois leather will bring out the shine on a smooth-coated dog.

Some long-haired dogs with silky coats don't have a downy undercoat so need to be groomed carefully so that their skin isn't scratched.

Long-haired dogs should be groomed for at least 15 minutes in order to keep their coats in good condition and looking tidy. Pay attention to particular areas such as under their legs (where hair can get matted), between the toes and on the hind legs.

Dogs with a wiry coat have to be 'hand stripped' every month; you can pull the dead hair out with your fingers, always going in the direction of the hair's growth.

If your dog is in the habit of eating its own poo, try to break this bad habit by sprinkling his latest offering with a hot, peppery sauce.

▷▷ Discipline

Tone of voice is important – dogs will learn to associate your tone of voice with their behaviour. He'll soon learn that your stern tone after he's done something wrong isn't much fun. Be clear about the signals you're giving him.

Never hit a dog across the nose – instead, grab him on both sides of the head and growl at him. Mother dogs growl at their offspring and it works a treat.

To assert your authority never let a dog go through the door before you. He must know who's boss.

Don't force a puppy's training – 10 minutes at a time is about all they can take. Always make it fun for them.

Never train a well-fed puppy – a full tummy means a sleepy mind and the puppy won't be able to concentrate on learning.

If your puppy has the habit of running off, try hiding. Then call him to you. He won't be able to find you when he returns and it will worry him. He'll stay closer next time!

Reinforce a dog's respect for you by ensuring that he is never higher up than you are. Sofas and beds should always be out of bounds.

If your dog creeps up onto the sofa when he shouldn't, put a couple of whoopee cushions on the seat. The unexpected noise will deter him from doing it again.

If your dog steals food from kitchen surfaces, make a booby trap by tying a chicken carcass to a string of tin cans or similar noisy objects. When the dog steals the carcass, the shock of the noise that follows will soon teach him restraint.

Incessant barking can be hard to deal with. Squirt water in your dog's face whenever he barks and he'll soon stop.

To stop a small dog from yapping hold it up at arm's length.

If your dog keeps digging holes in your lawn or flowerbeds, fill a sock with pebbles. As your dog starts to dig, throw the sock out of an upstairs window so that it lands near the dog – not on him! He won't know where it came from but will associate the unwelcome shock with digging and soon give it up.

If your dog starts to chew the furniture, you can paint on anti-nail-biting fluid or oil of cloves to deter him. Better still, if you can catch him in the act, throw a cushion or something that makes a loud noise to startle him.

Stop your dog from chewing furniture by rubbing vapour rub on to the chewed places. The smell lasts for weeks and dogs hate it.

Catch your dog in the act and then punish him. It's no good punishing him a few minutes afterwards because he won't realise what he's being punished for and will just become confused.

If your dog gets too excited when you get his lead, put the lead back where you keep it and sit down. After a couple of times, he won't get so excited.

A dog that constantly pulls on his lead is a nuisance. Try filling a tin with pebbles to rattle next to his ear every time he pulls.

If your dog likes rummaging around rubbish bins, sprinkle the area with pepper to deter him.

Teach your dog to sit to command with a small titbit. Hold slightly below the line of vision and command 'Sit'. He will sit down automatically to get a better sight of the titbit.

If your dog won't let go of the TV remote control (or any other object), get up, ring the doorbell and the dog should drop whatever he has in his mouth and run to the door. Grab the remote (or whatever) before he comes back.

Keep food treats by the door. Visitors can then feed your dog if he's good and doesn't jump up at them when they enter the house.

If your dog keeps licking a wound try rubbing vapour rub near the sore (not on it).

A dog should obey you because you are in charge not because he's frightened of you. Punishment is OK as long as it doesn't terrify or hurt the dog.

Don't call a dog over to you to be punished because he will start to associate your call with punishment. Always go over to a dog to admonish him if he's done something wrong.

If your dog doesn't like travelling in the car, sit with him on the back seat, leave the engine running while you do so and just read the paper for a while. The dog will soon learn to relax.

When training a puppy or new dog, use a long training lead for outdoors and a long light houseline for indoors.

Never use a lead to punish a dog.

It's best to conduct training sessions in quiet places, away from people if that's possible. You don't want your dog to be distracted while he's learning.

Try to finish your training sessions on a positive note. Always encourage your dog.

After your dog has had a training session, follow up the hard work with a bit of play.

Don't allow your dog to play with old shoes or clothes because they'll assume it's OK for them to chew any shoe or item of clothing.

Enforce your training commands with praise, physical reassurance and an immediate reward.

Gradually reduce the reward treats as training progresses, so that your dog reacts to your voice and body language rather than bribes.

Don't bother with a training session if you or your dog is tired – it will just be a waste of time.

When using a choke or check chain, keep your dog on your left side.

The first thing a dog learns is usually the command 'sit' or 'come'. Start his training with him on the lead. Practice makes perfect.

If you are about to bring a new baby home, take something of the baby's back for the dog to smell, like a blanket or vest.

Introduce your dog to the baby and not the other way round; you are introducing a new member to the 'pack'. Hold the baby on your lap and let your dog have a good smell.

When the baby is home, try to keep the dog's routine the same, so you go for walks at the same time, he gets fed as normal and so on.

If your dog is a bit bold or too fearful, fit him with a head halter. Then if he pulls, his own momentum pulls the head down and the jaws shut. This is an alternative to a check chain.

A check or choke chain is ideal for bouncy dogs or ones with a rather short attention span. Make sure you don't put the collar on backwards because this can cause discomfort when it tightens. In the right position, the chain only tightens when tension is applied.

If your dog has to wear a muzzle, make sure that it can open its jaws and pant while the muzzle is on.

Fights usually happen between dogs of the same size, sex and age. When your dog meets another, keep the lead fairly loose (a taut lead encourages aggression) and praise him when he just sniffs the other dog.

Don't give in to begging. It can often become a habit with dogs, especially if they are bored. If you pander to their whims, you'll just reinforce the bad habit and get a fat dog.

Train your dog to eat always from its bowl, which should be kept well away from where you and the family eat.

Make sure you keep the lids on bins to deter your dog from having a poke around.

For dogs who suffer from travel sickness try children's travel sickness tablets. Half for puppies and a whole one for fully adult dogs.

Alternatively, try sitting your dog on newspaper during journeys.

Also sit the dog in a stationary car with the windows slightly open. Then travel a few yards so the dog gets used to the movement. Do this regularly over a fortnight, gradually increasing the speed and distance travelled until your dog is accustomed to the motion of the car.

If you don't have a car grille or special safety belt for dogs, tie its lead to the seat-belt anchor so that your dog can't move around too much while you're driving.

Sniffing the ground is a sign that a dog wants to relieve itself. If you're in the throes of house-training, you will have a very short time to get the dog or puppy on to the newspaper that you should always have at hand.

Keep some of the soiled newspaper around to show your dog or puppy, so it can smell where it's been and this will encourage it to use the same spot again.

Don't punish a dog for making a mess in the house – it will only make him more nervous and prone to more accidents.

Train a puppy to relieve itself outdoors as soon as possible. Use the garden first where you can easily remove any mess before moving out to a suitable public place where you can poop-scoop away the evidence.

Walking a dog helps to stimulate it to relieve itself. Always keep your dog on its lead until it has done its business; then let it off its lead to play. It will soon come to realise that it has to poo before playing.

While your dog is relieving itself, say 'Hurry up.' As soon as it's finished, praise him. Your dog will soon start to relieve itself on your 'hurry up'.

▷▷ Health

To get your dog to swallow a pill cover the tablet with butter. Your dog will love the taste and the pill will slip down easily. Or try hiding the pill in some cheese or meat.

If your dog has an upset tummy, feed him some bio-yoghurt mixed with a little honey to settle him.

When your dog is teething and about to lose a tooth give him an ice cube to chew. The tooth will fall out and the cold will ease any pain.

Spaying doesn't make a bitch fat – eating too much food is the only thing that will make her overweight.

For dogs with a sweet tooth cover a pill with melted chocolate.

When giving a pill to a dog, you should go to him rather than call him to you.

To feed a sick dog treat him as you would a puppy. Give him three or four small meals a day.

A good meal for a recuperating dog or very young puppy is a bowl of lightly scrambled eggs.

If your sick dog refuses to eat solid food, try him with some gravy broth in a saucer.

If your dog hasn't eaten for 24 hours, take him to the vet.

If your dog needs to go on a diet, try to give him around 60% of his normal calorie intake.

Also overweight dogs benefit from increased daily exercise.

Dogs cannot live on meat alone – make sure you vary their diet, mixing meat with cereals, vegetables, pasta and rice.

Dogs can eat their 'greens' as well as humans: cabbage, potatoes and carrots are all part of a well-balanced diet.

Want to go vegetarian? It can be done, but talk to your vet about getting the right balance at mealtimes.

Chicken is easy to digest and much lower in calories than other doggy meals.

Dried foods have four times as many calories as canned food, so always serve in small quantities. These foods shouldn't be confused with dog biscuits, which are mainly cereal.

For a high fat content try serving heart (it has double the calories of kidneys).

Always keep the water bowl clean and refill it each day.

The best kind of feeding bowl is made from stainless steel with a bottom rimmed with rubber to stop it from sliding all over the floor. Ceramic bowls can get chipped and harbour bacteria.

Don't treat your dog like a dustbin. Giving him food he's not used to can lead to stomach upsets. Stick to pet treats instead.

Small dogs have small stomachs so feed them small amounts twice a day.

Pregnant dogs need to eat up to 50% more food.

Old dogs should be fed little and often.

Dogs' food should contain protein for growth, fatty acids for a healthy coat and carbohydrates for bulk and bowel movements.

Don't be tempted to substitute cat food – it's too high in protein for a dog.

Pasta is a good carbohydrate source, but might need to be flavoured before you serve it up.

Serve dog food at room temperature.

If your dog hasn't eaten its canned or wet food after 15 minutes, remove the food and give it a new serving at the next mealtime.

A low-protein diet can help an incontinent dog. Feed him with cooked chicken, fish and vegetables.

If your dog suffers from incontinence, try fitting him with some disposable toddler training pants (with a hole cut for his tail).

Alternatively, you could try giving him cold boiled water.

Gnawing on bones is an ideal way to exercise jaw muscles and massage gums. Beef shin or knuckle bones are the best option because they are less likely to splinter.

Dog chews have fewer calories than bones and are often a more convenient (and pleasant) alternative.

When travelling, don't feed your dog just before a journey; you don't want to see the meal reappear.

During a long journey, stop every two to three hours to give your dog the chance to stretch its legs, relieve itself and have a drink.

A hot car – in summer or winter – can be a deathtrap. Never leave your dog unattended in warm weather or with the heater on.

Excessive panting and drooling can be a sign that your dog is overheated. If this happens, move your dog at once to a cooler spot. Get rid of any excess saliva to help it breathe. Sponge his face with cool water before giving him a drink. If things look really bad, wrap him in a cool, wet towel.

For sea dogs (or any dogs that are going by water) it's worth investing in a dog's life jacket. Dogs can swim, but may drown if they get exhausted.

▷▷ Games

Keep your dog occupied for hours – make a hole in a rubber dog toy and fill it with dog treats.

Having a dog takes commitment – work out how much time you can give a dog, where to exercise him and how to clean up after him. What shape and size of dog will suit your family? Dogs cost money – the bigger the dog, the more money! All dog owners have to pay for visits to the vet, inoculations and food; some will pay for insurance and kennel fees, too.

Make your own chewy toy – take a hollow bone, sterilise it and then fill it with cheese spread. Show it to your dog and leave him to get on with it; he'll have a busy, happy time trying to reach the food.

A bored dog can often indulge in destructive behaviour so it's a good idea to channel his frustration into something such as playing tug of war. Make sure you always win though, you are the dominant one in this partnership, so don't start to play until you've taught him to drop an object on your command.

Train your dog to run to heel so you both get a bit of exercise.

It is illegal to deny a blind person guided by a dog access to any public place. These dogs are usually better behaved than most people.

Labradors, Golden Retrievers and German Shepherds are the most popular breeds for guide dogs. They are generally intelligent, hard workers, large enough to fit a harness and small enough to be controlled.

Hearing dogs are used to alert their owner to a variety of sounds, such as the doorbell, smoke alarms, crying babies and so on.

▶▶▶ Dressers

Duncan Newman; Claire Hartley; Jimmy Flockhart; Joe Hobbs; Nujma Yousaf

▷▷ Washing

Stop tights and stockings from getting in a tangle during washing. Place them in an old pillow case or cushion cover. This works for delicate items as well.

Make a 'delicates' bag for the washing machine out of old net curtains.

To stop ladders in tights starch the tights lightly before you wash them.

To make tights and stockings last longer wet them thoroughly, wring out the excess water and then freeze them in a plastic bag.

When you want to wear them, thaw them out and dry thoroughly.

Put your woollies in a pillow case when you spin dry them to prevent them losing their shape.

Wash teddy bears with carpet shampoo and then just fluff them up afterwards.

For the best wash results, mix small and large items of clothing together so that they can move more freely during the wash.

Too many suds when hand washing? Sprinkle talcum powder on them and they will subside.

To remove rust stains cover with salt. Rinse, then put some lemon juice over the stain. Leave for an hour and then wash.

One way to get bloodstains out of clothes is to get the person whose blood it is to suck it off. Their own saliva should dissolve the blood. Tell that to Dracula!

To remove grass stains place a clean cloth under the fabric and dab another cloth in methylated spirits. Clean the stain with a small circular movement, working from the centre outwards.

Use wet wipes to clean patent leather or bring a shine to your PVC trousers!

To clean white training shoes rub with bathroom cleaner, buff and then wipe off with a rag.

▷▷ Drying

Turn white T-shirts and shirts inside out and, if possible, dry in the shade so that direct sunlight doesn't turn them yellow.

To ensure that the pleats stay in a pleated skirt while it's drying on a washing line, hang by the waistband and clip clothes pegs to the bottom of the pleats. Dry all skirts by the waistband.

Save space on the washing line, peg your socks and tights to a hanger and hang it on the line.

When drying socks on a line, they should be pegged by the heels because this keeps the stretch in the right direction.

▷▷ Ironing

Start your ironing with items that need a cool iron. Gradually work through the ironing, finishing with items that need a hotter setting.

If your pile of ironing has become bone dry, pop it back into the tumble dryer with a wet towel for a minute. This will get the items slightly damp again and they will be easier to iron. If you don't have a tumble dryer, wrap them in a wet towel instead.

To remove fabric shine, dampen a cloth and wring out the excess water. Put this cloth on top of the shiny fabric and steam press. Do this several times, pressing the area until it is almost dry.

When ironing velvet fold a thick towel in two and place over the reverse side of the velvet while using the iron.

To put a good, lasting crease in trousers apply a thin line of paper glue along the inside of the crease and then iron it.

When ironing the collar of a shirt, go from one tip to the middle and then repeat. Never iron straight across the collar because this pushes the fibre across to one end and makes the collar uneven.

Ironing on the reverse side of clothes keeps the colour longer.

Protect delicate buttons when ironing – place a metal spoon over them.

Avoid ironing altogether – silk and velvet will lose their creases if hung in a steamy bathroom.

Clean the bottom of your iron with wet wipes.

▷▷ Storing

A great way to keep trousers looking good is to do as sailors do, roll them up when you're not wearing them.

If you hang trousers on a wire coat–hanger, put sheets of newspaper over the hanger first to avoid creasing.

Avoid creases – don't fold trousers over a hanger, peg them to the hanger by the ends of the legs.

If clothes keep falling off their hangers, put a rubber band around each end of the hanger.

Keep jackets in good shape by stuffing the arms with tissue paper or newspaper.

Roll up silk scarves inside loo-roll or kitchen-roll cardboard tubes.

Linen should be rolled up rather than folded otherwise it will crease too much.

Skirts will keep their pleats if you pack them lengthways in a pair of old tights.

If you're worried about damp in your cupboards, tie a handful of sticks of chalk together and hang them inside. They will absorb any moisture.

Moths don't like bay leaves, allspice berries or cedar chip so put some in your wardrobe.

Make your own pomander by sticking whole cloves into the skin of an orange. Then place a teaspoon of ground cinnamon and a teaspoon of orris root in a plastic bag along with the studded orange. Shake until the orange is coated all over. Store it in tissue paper for at least two weeks before hanging in your wardrobe.

▷▷ Mending

Scuffs on high heels or shoes can be covered up using magic marker or felt-tip pen.

Clear nail-varnish stops ladders in tights from running.

If buttons have a habit of popping off, dab a bit of clear nail-varnish over the button thread to strengthen the fibres.

To mend a dropped hem in an emergency, use a stapler.

A fishing tackle box makes a good sewing box.

Use wax on ordinary thread to stop it sticking.

When threading a needle don't use the end you have just cut from the reel because it will twirl and knot. Use the other end.

If your needle keeps sticking rub some talcum powder over it.

Emergency mending kits should always include double-sided tape and safety pins.

When you cut a button off a jacket, slip a comb underneath to protect the jacket.

If a button is to take a lot of weight, stitch another smaller one on the inside of the jacket to anchor the main button.

White line down your jeans? Mix some permanent blue ink with water until you've got the right shade. Paint down the line with a small brush and leave the jeans to dry.

To stop your jeans fading soak them in a mixture of 4 tablespoons of vinegar and 8 pints/4.5 litres of water for about 30 minutes.

▷▷ Wearing

To prevent the fluff from your angora jumper getting all over the inside of a jacket, put the jumper in the freezer before wearing it.

Alternatively, give your mohair and angora woollies the occasional squirt of hair-spray to stop them from moulting.

Get rid of static electricity by running a wire coat-hanger over the offending garment.

To get a jacket to hang straight put pennies (or spare foreign coins) into the bottom of the hem.

To look after a jacket when driving turn it inside out and place on the back seat of your car so that it doesn't get covered in fluff and muck.

If your shirt collar is too tight, move the button over. It won't be seen behind your tie.

To get rid of the shine from black trousers brush them with black coffee and then press with a damp cloth.

When buying socks, wrap them round your clenched fist. If the heel just meets the toe, they will fit you perfectly.

If shoes are too tight put damp newspaper in them or spray them with water and leave to stretch.

For extra emergency heat insulation cut out a polystyrene shape to fit in the bottom of your shoes or boots.

To stretch canvas shoes dampen them and then wear them. They will dry to fit your feet.

Stop bras from rubbing by soaking them regularly in hair conditioner.

You can treat wigs with fabric conditioner. This also works on your own hair.

Stop blouses and shirts from escaping from the waistband of skirts and trousers. Sew the elastic from the top of some old stay-up stockings into the waistband.

Stop the end of a ribbon from fraying – put a drop of clear nail-varnish on the end.

Wash your make-up brushes and sponges regularly in washing-up liquid.

▷▷ A New Look

To dye satin or fabric shoes use ordinary hand dye but add methylated spirits to the mixture.

Give leather shoes a radical new colour – paint them with acrylic paint.

Don't throw out unwanted shoulder pads from that 1980s power suit – they make great shoe stuffers, polishing pads and pin cushions.

Get extra life from your roll-on deodorant – store it upside down and it will last much longer.

For a rusty iron tie a piece of beeswax inside a rag and rub the iron when hot. Then rub with another rag sprinkled with salt.

Milk-stained clothes should be rinsed in cool water. Then washed in cold water using liquid detergent.

Remove fresh coffee stains by applying a mixture of egg yolk and glycerin to the area. Wash out with warm water.

Minimise the amount of detergent you use – always place it in a detergent ball so that it gets right into the wash and isn't wasted in the system.

Don't ruin your best clothes in the wash. Zips, buttons, hooks and eyes, and poppers may cause damage to other items, so do them up first.

Left-over detergent in fabric will attract dirt. Use slightly less than the manufacturer's recommended amount and if you think there's some left in the clothes after rinsing, give them an extra rinse.

If you're pushed for time and don't have a chance to mend tears and sew loose buttons, put garments in a pillow case so they don't tear further in the wash.

Too many suds when hand-washing? Sprinkle talcum powder on them.

Wash silk garments after every wear, otherwise perspiration stains may be impossible to remove and will actually weaken the fabric.

To prevent soap scum add a tablespoon of white vinegar to the rinsing water .

Really grimy work clothes? Empty a can of cola into them, add detergent and run through your regular wash cycle.

Dirty rings on shirt collars can be removed with oily hair shampoo – the principle is the same.

For sweaty stains spray with vinegar before washing.

As an extra measure on ground-in sweat you can also add a couple of crushed aspirin tablets to the washing water.

White cotton socks gone a bit grey? Add a slice of lemon to the water and boil them for 5 minutes to restore whiteness.

For really clean clothes make sure your washing machine is clean. Fill the washer with warm water and pour in a gallon of distilled vinegar. Run through an entire cycle. The vinegar cleans the hoses and cleans away soap scum.

If your machine overflows from too many suds, adding some fabric softener will get rid of the suds.

To eliminate lint add 1 cup of white vinegar to the final rinse cycle.

Rinse washable wool garments in lukewarm water and add a few tablespoons of glycerin to keep them soft. It also helps prevent itching.

When washing silk, a couple of lumps of sugar added to the final rinse will give the silk more body and make life all the sweeter.

If your jumper cuffs go baggy after washing, try dipping them in cold water then drying them with a very hot hair-dryer – they should shrink back to shape.

Wash your clothes pegs once in a while by putting them inside a pillow case in the machine to make sure your pegs don't leave dirty marks on clean washing.

When soaking an item of clothing to remove a stain, always immerse the whole garment to avoid patchiness even if the stain itself is only small.

If you're unsure whether a coloured garment will run, pop a white hanky in with the load to pick up any dye. When the hanky stays white, you're safe to wash these clothes with your whites.

Alternatively, to check whether an item is colour fast when dry, iron a corner of it between two white cloths. If any dye runs, you'll know it needs to be washed separately.

To remove rain spots from suede rub lightly with an emery board.

To remove grease spots from suede dip a cloth in vinegar and blot out the stain. Brush with a suede brush to restore the nap.

Instead of bleach, leave newly washed clothes out in the sun to dry because the sun acts as a natural bleach.

Keep tough stains away from hot water or steam. Lots of foods contain albumen, a protein which is fixed by heat. So tackle the stain first, before putting in a hot wash, for instance.

As soon as dirt appears on your treasured sheepskin coat or suede jacket, get it cleaned. Ground in dirt will never come out.

Ballpoint pen on your best suede jacket or bag? Very carefully, try gently rubbing an emery board or fine sandpaper on the offending mark.

►►► Dressmakers

Paula Carpenter; Julia Dee

Make things easy for yourself – put all your bits and bobs on a trolley so you can wheel it round with you and you have everything to hand.

Keep different sized scissors in order – hang them from a row of hooks.

When choosing a pattern, it's more important to get the right measurement for the bust than for the hips. The hip measurements are normally much easier to adjust.

When drawing patterns, especially tricky curves, be bold and draw quickly. You'll achieve a much smoother line than if you go at it more cautiously.

To achieve the best possible fit start making adjustments at the neckline and shoulders as these will affect the whole hang and style of a garment.

When trying a garment on, make it easier by putting it on inside out. Adjust it accordingly, tack it up and then try it on again the right way round.

A waistline will be much more flattering if it dips slightly at the back.

To make a small bust look fuller use long darts round the chest area.

To prevent bra straps from showing fix Velcro strips to your bra and on the inside of the dress strap.

Fabrics like tartan and complicated checks will fray badly. Cut them with pinking shears to reduce the problem.

Fabric tape-measures often stretch. This can leave you with inaccurate measurements. For accuracy, buy a fibreglass or coated one.

Don't make your thread too long. The longer the thread, the more it gets weakened as it's drawn through the fabric. Shorter threads are less work – your arm doesn't have to move as much!

Put synthetic thread in the fridge for a couple of hours before you use it. This will stop it clinging to the fabric.

Always cut thread at an angle.

To keep loose embroidery threads tidy, cut strips off a cereal box, punch holes along one edge and put the threads through the holes. Use bulldog clips to hold the strips together.

Pins can damage delicate fabric. Use sticky tape instead.

To avoid messy or ragged edges scissors must always be razor-sharp.

To choose a practical fabric try squashing it in your hand to see how easily it will crease.

Don't ruin beautiful chintz. Always iron the reverse side to protect the special glaze.

Protect your fabrics (such as velvet or silk) by wrapping them around a tube rather than folding them. This will prevent creases.

If you're finding it hard to push the needle through a fabric, rub some soap over the cloth on the wrong side.

Use an old tailor's trick and rub your needle along the side of your nose. It picks up just enough grease to 'oil' its passage through the fabric.

Keep your sewing machine needle sharp – stitch it through some fine sandpaper for a few inches.

When mending a small tear in very fine fabric tape on some stiff paper behind the tear to stop the fabric from slipping.

Always keep a spool of clear thread for emergency repairs when you can't match any of your threads with a fabric.

Silk slips and slides, making pattern cutting a problem. Try putting an old cotton sheet underneath the silk to give it a firmer grip.

To make fur cuffs and collars neater, use a lightweight material for the inner layer.

To recycle your old dresses, cut off the skirt below the hip line, sew a hem, and wear it as a blouse.

If your knitting needles stick, just run them through your hair to oil them lightly.

Keep track of where you are on your knitting pattern. Use a hair grip as a guide. Slide it down the pattern as you work your way through.

Check if you've got enough wool to finish a row – the wool has to be three times the width of the piece you're knitting.

▶▶▶ Environmentalists

Chris Crean; Friends of the Earth; Wastewatch

Never ignore a skip! When you pass one in the street, always have a look for old pieces of wood and a host of other useful things. One man's rubbish is another's salvation!

To help developing countries don't throw your old spectacles away. Take them round to your nearest Oxfam shop.

Save the rainforest! Avoid buying hardwoods like mahogany.

Avoid excess packaging. Buy in bulk . . . it's much cheaper, too.

Save space in your dustbin. When a plastic milk bottle is empty, pour in the left-over boiling water from the kettle. Swill it round the plastic bottle several times and then pour it away. The plastic will have become pliable and can be rolled up like a sausage.

Recycle milk cartons for planting seedlings. Cut them in half and use the bottom half as a planter.

Better still, make friends with your local milkman. He recycles the bottles for you.

Put plastic shopping bags in your car, not under the kitchen sink. Then you can reuse them for any shopping trips.

If you have your own canvas shopping bag or basket you won't need so many plastic carrier bags.

Don't buy soap. Use natural oatmeal – it works just as well.

To soften your lips use a little almond oil.

When disinfecting your sink, don't bother with strong chemical solutions. Just use ordinary household salt.

Don't put kitchen fat down the sink – let it solidify in a container, such as a yoghurt pot, and then put in the bin.

Make your kitchen utensils last longer. Always buy items made for the professional catering trade. They are more durable than domestic ranges and often have less of a mark-up.

There's no need to buy kitchen paper towels. Drain food on brown paper bags instead.

Put lids on your pots when cooking – it will save time and energy.

Line up the bottoms of your pans with the rings on the hob so that you don't lose too much heat.

When cooking vegetables, steam fast-cooking vegetables over slow-cooking ones. It saves energy, preserves the goodness in the food and makes a wonderful meal.

To stop ants going into your kitchen cupboards you don't have to buy pesticides. Just sprinkle around some dried tansy.

Avoid using toxic oven cleaners. Sprinkle the oven with water and bicarbonate of soda then start scrubbing. This also works well on baths.

Check that you're not wasting electricity – make sure that your fridge and freezer door seals are still effective. Place a piece of paper in between the seal and the door. If it falls out or slides down easily, you are losing energy, the food isn't being stored safely and you need new door seals.

Fill your freezer compartment so that it doesn't waste energy trying to keep a large space cold. You can always fill it with loaves of bread or even newspaper.

To conserve energy avoid placing your freezer next to a cooker or a window that gets direct sunlight.

A cheap and natural alternative to bleach is to put freshly washed clothes outside in the direct sunlight.

For home-made furniture polish, mix up 1 part lemon juice to 2 parts olive oil.

Save money! Put your washing machine on after midnight and before 7 am so that you're using off-peak electricity.

Minimise the amount of detergent you use. Always place it in a detergent ball so that it gets right into the wash and isn't wasted in the system.

Tumble drying can use a lot of electricity. Put a dry towel in with the wet clothes to absorb the excess moisture.

Roll clothes in a towel before putting into the dryer. This will soak up excess moisture.

Keep the electricity bill down by using energy-efficient light bulbs. They use 80 per cent less energy than normal bulbs.

Don't throw away empty washing–powder boxes. Use them to keep magazines or files in. Just cut a large corner away and cover the box with left-over wallpaper or wrapping paper.

Keep your toilet bowl looking clean – put 5 fl oz/150 ml white wine vinegar in the bowl, leave for about 5 minutes and then flush.

To save water clean your teeth using a mug rather than having the water running constantly. Also replace one bath with a shower each week.

To save water in the cistern, place a $3^{1}/_{2}$ pint/2-litre plastic bottle filled with water in the cistern; position it away from the handle.

To insulate your house hang heavy drapes from the ceiling to the floor. It's much cheaper than double glazing.

Keep warmth in – don't hang long curtains over radiators because you'll just lose the heat behind them. Make sure your curtains hang just above the radiators.

Close curtains at north–facing windows in winter so that they don't let any heat out during the day.

Fix cracks in windows – seal with some tape.

Make your own draught excluders – roll up a towel and fix with rubber bands at either end.

Save money during the winter – put a pan of water near a radiator to humidify the room. A warm and humid atmosphere feels warmer so you will be less inclined to turn the thermostat up.

Clean your radiators as well as the furniture. Dust can insulate a radiator, keeping down the amount of heat that it gives off.

Get rid of tobacco fumes – leave a bowl of cider vinegar in the room overnight.

Avoid shiny fruit. It's probably been coated in pesticides.

There's no need to use a sticky plaster when you cut yourself. Press the inside of a clear onion skin onto the cut. Leave it there for as long as you can. Onion is a natural antiseptic.

To absorb chemicals from the air, try planting azaleas (to counteract formaldehyde), English ivy (for Benzene) and Peace Lily (for Trichloroethylene). Such chemicals are found in paints and varnishes.

Get a water butt – rain water is soft and much better for your plants. It will save water as well.

Don't waste time and energy watering lawns – they can be left for longer than you think.

Speed up the composting process – put some fresh horse manure inside and you'll soon be rewarded with wonderful organic compost.

To construct your own composter, put some holes in the side and base of an old dustbin and stand on some bricks for drainage.

Make sure you put some carbon in your compost – cereal packets, egg boxes and so on will give the compost some bulk.

Create a cheap mulch for the garden by shredding any left-over bits of wood.

Using peat is not environmentally friendly so investigate the alternatives.

To make your hot-water bottle last longer, put a couple of drops of glycerine inside the first time you use it.

Keep your engine properly tuned – it will save petrol in the long run.

Braking sharply and accelerating uses up more fuel … so don't!

Don't sit for ages letting the car warm up – an engine will warm up quickly when the car is moving and it uses up less fuel doing so.

If you're stuck in a bad traffic jam, turn off your engine.

Take out any unnecessary items from the car – the heavier the car, the more fuel you use.

Don't just throw your old car oil away. Take it to your local garage so it can be reused.

To save on petrol consumption slow down! Going at 70 mph/ 110 kph uses 30 per cent more energy than driving at 50 mph/ 80 kph. Better still …

Leave the car at home and go to work on a bike.

Forget specialist oven cleaners. For an inexpensive alternative that will remove even hard, baked-on grease put your oven on warm for about 2 minutes, then turn it off. Place a small dish of full-strength ammonia on the top shelf and put a large pan of boiling water on the bottom shelf and leave overnight. In the morning, open and air for a while before washing down with soapy water.

If you've mislaid your dustpan, wet the edge of a newspaper, brush the dirt over the edge and roll up the paper.

Preserve steel wool pads for longer by keeping them in soapy water. This will stop them from rusting.

If your steel wool scourers are rusting, wrap them in kitchen foil after use.

Save those soap slivers. Mix them in the blender with some water and make your own liquid soap.

Or collect them in an old nylon stocking and hang near an outside tap for a fast outdoors clean-up.

Make your own ceramic tile cleaner by mixing 1/4 cup of baking soda, 1/2 cup of white vinegar, 1 cup of ammonia and 1 gallon of warm water in a bucket. Stir and apply with a sponge or brush. This will not keep between cleaning, so you'll need to make a fresh batch each time, and always wear rubber gloves as the solution is quite harsh. But the tiles will be 'mirror clean'.

▶▶▶ Equestrians

Eric Mackechnie, Mark Phillips Equestrian Centre; Lucy Henderson; PC Mark Wood, Mounted Horse Division; Delia Cunningham; Shona Kinnear, Warwick Equestrian Centre; Sharon Burt, Warwick Equestrian Centre

When buying a new pony, ask to ride him away from the stables or house, rather than just back again. If he swishes his tail or is stubborn, you know he's likely to be trouble.

Help children to look up when jumping. Stand the other side of the jump and ask them to shout out how many fingers you're holding up.

Persuade children to keep their hands up while riding – ask them to hold a cup of water and see how much they spill.

Teach children to relax and breathe while they're riding – encourage them to sing a song when doing rising trotting.

Horses are sensitive souls so don't shout at them. Tone of voice is important. Speak calmly and with authority.

And they have sensitive spots . . . well, ticklish ones anyway. Be careful around the stomach, flanks and inside thighs.

Always warn a horse if you are going to walk behind him. Horses don't like surprises. Run your hand along his back and quarters as you move behind him so he knows where you are all the time. You're harder to kick if you're close.

Keep an eye on the ears. They are a good barometer of mood. Pricked forward, they mean that a horse is alert. Ears back could mean the horse has heard something behind him or that he's unhappy about something. Ears flattened back is a sure sign of anger.

Signs of distress (due to fear or pain) are showing the whites of the eyes, snorting a lot, sweating and increased breathing.

Horses are creatures of habit; they love routine, so make sure you feed, clean and exercise them regularly.

A 'cob' horse is known for its dependability and strength.

When buying a horse, ask the owner to ride it first and then get a friend to ride it for you. You can thus see what its action and temperament are like before you have a go yourself.

Always ask to see a horse being ridden in traffic before you buy. A traffic-shy horse can be a liability if you enjoy hacking out. Don't try to ride a strange horse yourself in traffic.

When tacking up, talk to your horse. Approach him so he can see you and keep talking to him to reassure him.

To check that the stirrups are at the right length adjust the leathers so that your fingertips rest on the stirrup bar and the base of the stirrup reaches your armpit.

To check the length of the stirrup leathers once you are on the horse see if the base of the stirrup reaches your ankles when you let your leg dangle.

When you are about to mount, make sure the horse is standing still and squarely. You don't want to catch him or yourself off balance.

As you mount your horse try to avoid digging your toes into his side. This will only make him move away from you and it will be harder to mount properly.

When turning your horse, make sure you haven't gone so far into a corner that his hind quarters can't follow properly.

Keep your shoulders parallel with your horse's shoulders.

When trotting, your hands should remain still and you should absorb the rise and fall motion through the ankles, knees and hips. Lean slightly forward and stay relaxed.

If you are going out in the country for a ride for the first time, plan your route carefully in advance. Let someone know that you are going out, what your route is and what time you plan to return.

When riding out in the countryside, if in doubt, walk. Keep an eye open for potential hazards such as boggy ground, low branches or slippery surfaces.

As you ride uphill, lean forward and let your horse stretch his neck out. This allows your horse to use his hind quarters and legs more effectively.

Always walk through water unless it is very shallow. Galloping at full tilt through water may look great on the movies, but you want to be sure that the footing is safe and secure for both you and your horse.

▷▷ Clothes & Equipment

Don't make your saddle too slippery when polishing it; clean the straps and underneath but never the top part where you actually sit.

Don't wear one stirrup out faster than the other. Although you always mount from the right, you can cut down wear on stirrups by regularly swapping them around every couple of weeks.

Saddle racks can quickly mark saddles, so glue a couple of pieces of foam on to the racks to protect expensive tack.

Make saddle soap go further – melt it down in some milk before using.

Soak a new pair of boots in manure overnight. It will draw out any excess grease and they'll stay easier to clean.

Get a great shine on your boots without too much elbow grease. Polish them with washing-up liquid and leave overnight.

Shine boots with furniture polish. For extra sparkle, try a final rub down with some nylon tights.

For a really rich shine on boots, the penultimate layer of polish on black boots should be brown.

To harden up new boots, add a few drops of methylated spirits to the water when first cleaning.

Tight-fitting boots can be hard to pull on. Wear a pair of pop socks over the tops of your jodhpurs and the boots should slip on more easily.

To keep boots in pristine condition don't go to the expense of buying inner woods. Old nut bags scrunched up inside a soft pillow case and stuffed inside the boots will work just as well.

Keep your grip when riding – don't polish the insteps of your boots.

Avoid unnecessary discomfort when riding – don't wear skimpy underwear that can rub. Really big pants may not feel glamorous but they will be far more comfortable and won't show under tight-fitting jodhpurs either.

Buff up your velvet hat by leaving it in the bathroom when you take a hot, steamy shower.

Keep your hoof pick clean – just ask your vet for an old syringe holder to keep it in.

To muck out you don't really need an expensive shovel and broom. The side of your foot and an old washing basket is just as good.

Soak hay overnight in a wheelie bin. Just pierce a hole or two in the bottom to let the water drain out. Once soaked, it will be much easier to move the hay around.

Don't saddle soap the seat of your saddle (try saying that quickly after a few drinks!) or you'll end up with a black bottom.

To stop your saddle drying out try putting some hair conditioner on it. Rub it in as you would polish.

Put oil on your tack to make is soft and supple – especially when new.

Always run up both stirrup irons after dismounting. This avoids them hitting the horse when it moves and it's easier for you to carry the saddle this way.

If you have to leave a horse when you've tacked up, loop the reins under the stirrups so that they don't get in the way.

For extra grip wear jodhpurs with a suede bottom or chaps.

When learning to ride, wear fitted clothing so your teacher can correct your position.

To stop your horse becoming cast (stuck against the wall), always bed him down with big bales of straw.

To open a bale of hay or straw use another piece of twine to cut it open. Slip the piece of twine under where you want to cut and then saw it backwards and forwards. The twine holding the hay together will always come apart first.

Always tie haynets up high so your horse doesn't get tangled in it.

▷▷ **Horse Care**

When washing greys, use a blue rinse shampoo for that whiter than white tail.

Plaiting a mane can be difficult, but a little hair gel rubbed through before you start will make all the difference.

When plaiting your horse's tail before travelling, cut one leg off some tights and stretch it over the plait to stop it falling out.

For showing, set the mane to one side of your horse's neck with a little egg white.

When pulling a mane, a little oil of cloves rubbed into the hair will prevent it from hurting your horse.

To keep a horse's tail shiny and tangle-free put a little baby oil in some water and spray on to the tail. Run your fingers through to the tips.

To take the sweat off a horse try winding some bale twine around your hand; it makes a great scraper and you'll be able to get into all the curves of a horse's body.

If your horse gets really greasy he can be difficult to clean. Dip a towel in some methylated spirits and hot water and wipe over the coat; this will draw out the grease from his coat.

Don't frighten your horse by throwing the whole rug over him, fold the rug in half before placing it over the horse and then gently unfold it once it's on his back.

If loudspeakers or low-flying planes distract your horse, just put a little cotton wool in both his ears, being careful not to push it too far down.

When a foal is first born, push the mane neatly to one side while it is still damp and it will stay like that.

To calm a young foal scratch his neck.

If your foal won't suckle, try tickling his bottom; it stimulates the sucking reflex.

If your horse is difficult to catch, always approach him from a 45° angle; it's much less threatening than head on.

Mounting a horse can be tricky if you've had a hip replacement or are arthritic. Always use a mounting block. Climb on with very short stirrups and lengthen them once you're seated.

Try not to throttle your horse. When fitting the bridle, put your hand beneath the throatleash to check that there is enough room to allow him to breathe.

Strengthen your horse's shoulder muscles by holding a carrot to one side of his head, let him take a bite and then move the carrot to the other side. Make sure you exercise each side equally.

You can use a carrot to strengthen a horse's legs. Place the carrot between his front and back legs and he will reach down to eat it. Again, always make sure you repeat this exercise equally on each side of the horse.

To make your horse's features stand out rub a little Vaseline round his muzzle and eyes.

To keep the flowing locks under control use some egg white.

To get a horse's mane to lie over comb it the way you want it to lie and then dampen it down every day.

For a shiny, tangle-free tail try washing it with some fabric conditioner.

If his tail is in a tangle, comb some hair conditioner through it to get rid of the knots.

If your horse or pony lives out during the winter, don't groom him. The mud that they get themselves covered in acts as a second coat and insulates them against the cold. They may look scruffy, but they'll be warm too.

If you need to get your horse looking clean in a hurry, damp a cloth (an old dishcloth will do) and wipe it over his coat to produce a clean looking shine.

Keep two sponges handy for cleaning your horse: one for the eyes, nose and mouth area and the other for the dock area. It's a good idea to have them in different colours so you won't confuse the two.

To give a shine to a horse's hooves rub in some hair conditioner.

Pick your horse's feet out at least twice a day and after exercise. Horses should be shod every four to six weeks.

Never dice carrots – always chop lengthwise otherwise you run the risk of your horse choking.

Feed little and often. Horses have small stomachs, digest food slowly and can't take a huge meal in one go.

Don't feed a horse if he's hot and tired.

When feeding a horse titbits, keep your hand flat. You don't want your fingers to become part of the snack.

To make bran mash put 2-3lb (900-1350g) of bran in a bucket and pour boiling water over it. Stir, adding some salt and a handful of oats to taste. Place a sack over the bucket and let the mixture steep until it is cool. You can add chopped carrots and apples as extra treats.

If you must change his diet, do it gradually. Horses don't like sudden changes and it could lead to colic.

For fussy feeders add molasses to their feed.

After exercising during the winter, give your horse warm water to drink rather than straight from the tap. Cold water could give him colic.

Never feed or water a horse straight before or after heavy work – otherwise you could give him colic.

If your horse is allergic to dust or spores, use shredded paper as bedding rather than sawdust, straw, shavings or peat.

Try looking a gift horse in the mouth. You can tell the age of a horse by looking at his teeth. The more angular they are, the older the horse is.

A piggy eye, where too much white is showing, is often thought to indicate a mean nature.

▷▷ Donkeys

Donkeys have a strong sense of self-preservation; if they think something is dangerous, they won't do it . . . so don't make them.

Like horses, donkeys are sociable creatures – it's best to keep them with another donkey or horse.

Donkeys were originally desert creatures so they don't handle the cold as well as some other animals. Make sure they have adequate shelter.

A dirty donkey is a happy donkey. They use dust and grit like shampoo to keep their coats in good condition.

Donkeys can live to a ripe old age, sometimes over forty years so you will be taking on a long-term commitment.

▶▶▶ Estate Agents

Steve Daly

▷▷ Selling

Check whether an estate agent is the right one for you. Look at their adverts in the local paper. Are they clearly laid out? Do they feature good photographs and do they sell properties in a similar bracket to your own?

To judge the sort of efficiency you're likely to get from your selling agent, register with them first as a would-be buyer and see what sort of service you get.

To check your agent is doing everything necessary to sell your property, ask a friend to register as a buyer looking for a similar type of property to your own and see how well your home is being marketed.

To calculate the approximate value of your property, find the average asking price of four properties in your area, then deduct 5% from it for the average difference between the asking price and actual selling price.

Avoid a low valuation – never admit to wanting a quick sale.

To sell an empty house arrange for someone to clear away mail regularly and open the windows from time to time.

Present your property at its best – make sure any photos the agent takes are in colour and not black and white.

Find out what sort of impression your house makes on a potential buyer. Ask a friend to come round, show them the house and then ask them to be brutally honest. Don't be offended at what they say … you did ask for honesty!

Make your house more appealing to potential buyers. Take down any net curtains and let as much light as possible flood into the rooms.

Keep your windows clean – it makes a huge difference.

Be tidy. Keep kitchens and bathrooms tidy, clear up hallways and stairs and make sure the garden looks neat.

Deal with any potential problems such as sticking doors or dripping taps.

Make potential buyers feel welcome. Turn off the television, offer them a drink and be friendly.

… but don't be too friendly! Traditional clichés like brewing coffee can make people nervous. What are you trying to hide?

Many people don't like pets. Make sure yours are well out of the way.

Don't have too many people in the house. It can be offputting for potential buyers.

Look efficient. Have an information pack with guarantees, plans and local information ready to show prospective buyers. Have an idea how much your last electricity, gas and water bills are.

Speed things up. Chase your agent regularly and find out how things are progressing.

When choosing a solicitor, don't go to the one suggested by the agents. Personal recommendations are much better.

If you are in a hurry to sell, appoint a solicitor when you first put your house on the market and not at completion. When the time for completion comes, your solicitor will have had plenty of time to find all the deeds and relevant information.

Keep track of all dealings with your solicitor – just in case things do go wrong.

Unusual properties can be hard to price but often do well at auctions.

▷▷ Buying

Avoid the mad rush and over-competitive markets. Try looking for a home over Christmas or during the summer holidays which are traditionally quiet times for buying and selling houses. You'll get more of the estate agent's attention, too.

Don't get carried away at an auction. Ask a friend to bid on your behalf with clear instructions not to go over your affordable price.

Try to assess what a house will look like all year round. For example, once the trees don't have leaves on them will the house be overlooked?

Check that nearby roots haven't caused any damage by looking for bulges in the main wall.

Underground streams or a damp environment can cause structural problems. See if there are any willow trees nearby because they are often a good indicator for these conditions.

Check whether a house gets good television reception. Do neighbouring houses have over-sized aerials?

To see how good the water pressure is in a house, turn on the highest tap in the building. Water should still come pouring out at a good rate.

To check for woodworm, look round the base of a toilet. The grubs are attracted to the protein found in urine-soaked floorboards.

To discover whether a house has wet rot, slide a pen knife into the wood at right angles to the grain. If the blade slips in, then there's rot about.

Dry rot shows itself by cube-shaped cracks in timbers.

If you buy a house with plans to extend it, check what building regulations are relevant before exchange of contract to avoid disappointment.

To find a redundant church to buy up and convert, contact the local diocese to see if there are any available properties that haven't come on to the market yet.

For security reasons, always change the locks in a house as soon as you move in.

To calculate the insurance for a thatched cottage, allow four times as much premium as normal insurance to cover the potential fire hazard.

To get the most from your survey let your surveyor know of any plans you may have so that he can check out the suitability of the house and plot.

►►► Explorers

Simon Tarver, Raleigh International; Rebecca Drury, Raleigh International; Hilary Bradt; Paul Cammack; Major Anrezej Frank; Peter Hill, Highlander Mountaineering

▷▷ Made for Walking

Keep blisters at bay – wear thin liner socks under thick outer socks.

Buying boots should take place during the afternoon when you've been walking around for a while. Your feet can be up to half a size smaller in the morning.

For the perfect fit, take along the socks you would normally wear when you go to buy a new pair of boots.

The best way to dry socks is to stuff them under your armpits.

For sea-level traversing (or coasteering), wear sturdy, supportive shoes to deal with all kinds of terrain, from seaweed to sand dunes, rocks to boulder-hopping. Modern climbing shoes are tight, lightweight and close-fitting and aren't really suitable for this activity.

▷▷ Dressed for the Occasion

Don't wear gaiters over the top of your outdoor trousers because water will dribble down into your boots. It's better to wear them under your outdoor trousers.

Secure your gaiters to plastic boots with a strong glue to stop snow or mud getting inside.

Waterproof overtrousers often fall down – spare your blushes and wear braces to keep them up.

Wear layers of clothes. Cotton T-shirts get wet and clammy from sweat. Wearing a thermal T-shirt not only keeps you warm but also draws sweat off the body and out through the clothes.

Make sure your clothes can 'breathe' – this goes for inner and outer layers. The more layers you have, the more you can draw the sweat away from your body. Putting another layer on once you've worked up a sweat may warm you up for a minute or so but it will cool you down in the long run.

For coasteering, you need to be amphibious and you should dress accordingly. Wear modern, tight-fitting synthetics such as Lycra or polyester. They'll keep you warm in the water by trapping a layer of water underneath, but they will also dry out very quickly.

Wear a hat – 70 per cent of your body heat is lost through the head.

Mittens are warmer than gloves because fingers preserve heat next to each other. Mittens also allow you to wiggle your fingers around to generate more heat.

If you don't have any gloves, use socks.

When putting on a jacket on a windy day, face away from the wind to put your arm in the first sleeve. Then turn and let the wind wrap the jacket round the rest of your body.

▷▷ Bending & Stretching

Warm up before a climb by hanging from rocks. This will help to prevent any injury and stop you becoming stiff and inflexible in dangerous situations.

Give your knees a bit of help – use two trekking poles, setting them so that there is a slight bend in your arms as you walk. This can take up to 200 tons of pressure off your knees in a single day!

Improve your grip when climbing – take a bag full of chalk to dust on your hands and sprinkle in handholds.

Always carry non-stretch strapping tape (3/4 in/2 cm wide and easy to tear). It's useful for plastering over cuts, acting as a bandage support for any weak joints and wrapping around the back of hands and fingers to make them more effective for jamming into rocks.

Sticking plaster is a versatile piece of equipment – for example, it is excellent for binding up tent poles.

Panty liners make wonderful first-aid dressings because they are sterile on one side and waterproof on the other. The padding won't allow blood to soak through and they are just the right size.

To light fires in wet weather – be prepared in advance. Dip a tampon in methylated spirits and wrap in a plastic bag until needed.

Belly-button fluff makes great kindling for fires.

Stop your meths-fuelled stove from smelling or sooting and clogging; put a few drops of water into the methylated spirits.

Always try to turn a fall into a jump to give you a chance of choosing where you land.

If you fall off rocks into deep water, fill your lungs with air before you hit the water. Streamline your body shape to get you through the surface of the water with the least impact. Then immediately spread your limbs and start to swim up in order to slow your descent.

Line your rucksack with a bin liner to make it waterproof in case it falls into a river.

To traverse a zawn (a crevice cut in a cliff), make a giant lasso, hook over a jutting rock on the opposite side and secure the other end to your side. You should now have two lengths of rope stretched across the crevice. Lie on the rope, hang one leg down as ballast and crook the other one over the rope. Keeping the rope in the bend of your ankle, shuffle across. This is called the Tyrolean Traverse.

Always carry your pickaxe in the arrest position (facing up and out) so you can dig it in to a slope quickly if you fall.

When climbing, 'jam' rather than grip – insert a hand, foot, knee or arm into a crack and expand it to hold you up. This puts less strain on fingers.

Stop snow sticking to your crampons – snow can quickly form large lumps making it difficult to walk. Fix a plastic bag over the crampons to stop snow sticking, leaving the crampons free to grip.

Keep an eye out for thin ice – it is grey rather than white. Avoid thin ice whenever possible, but as ice cracks are constantly opening and closing, you have to take risks at times.

If you've lost your sunglasses and you find yourself on a glacier or elsewhere where there is a strong glare, use a long piece of cardboard with a slit in it to see through. Wrap it round your head – like wrap-around sunglasses!

Use the sun to navigate – make sure you know in advance where it should be in the sky and at what time of day.

Use pace counting when visibility is poor – count in advance how many of your paces make up 110 yd/100 m. Then, when you have walked that number of paces put a little pebble in one pocket to mark each 110 yd/100 m.

Protect your maps – cover them with sticky-back plastic.

If you get hopelessly lost in the jungle (or forest) follow a river and it will lead you out. Sometimes turning back takes more courage than going on.

Keep precious items waterproof – use a condom. They are ideal for keeping matches dry or protecting specimens such as insects or plants.

Condoms make great water carriers – they expand, and are strong and sealable.

Make your own buoyancy aids – when crossing rivers, blow up condoms and put them in your rucksack and clothing to stop that sinking feeling.

Always carry an ID card on you no matter how remote the area. If you are found by a rescue party they will know who you are!

Don't be confrontational – always preserve the self-esteem of border guards, soldiers and potentially hostile strangers. Don't be either aggressive or too submissive.

Don't just read books by travel writers before leaving home. Read accounts by anthropologists and naturalists. Know the culture of the people so that you don't end up giving offence (for example, in some parts of Africa a firm handshake and direct eye contact is offensive).

To avoid hypothermia in the snow, dig a bivouac as an emergency shelter. Wind is the greatest cooling factor, even in summer, and the bivouac will protect you from the wind chill.

If you've got frostbite, ease the pain by gently dabbing on some warmed olive oil.

Use a down-filled sleeping bag rather than a synthetic one. It will be much more expensive but it is lighter to carry and much warmer.

Always use a tent with a sewn-in ground sheet. Use a mosquito net in hot climates and always hang your pack above ground.

The easy way to put up a tent on a windy day is to lay it out on the ground with the tip folded and into the wind. Hammer in pegs or snow stakes upwind. Lift the top of the tent up and the wind will take the fabric and erect the tent for you.

To sleep on a mountain climb where there are no ledges, attach your hammock to the rock face and abseil into it.

Avoid dehydration – if you are tired and have a headache, you're probably not getting enough water. You should drink about 3 1/2 pints/2 litres a day.

Drink fluids in snowy regions – the climate is as dry as the Sahara because cold air carries less moisture. When breathing out, your breath is full of water vapour, but in a snowy climate, you don't breathe any in. Also, you are using up a lot of energy and sweating a lot so you need to replenish your water levels.

Carry a pipe to suck snow through when you are in snowy regions.

When shipwrecked or stranded on pack ice you can break off ice from the highest point because the brine will already have drained out making it drinkable.

Purify water – put a couple of drops of iodine in it.

Save water – wash steel or enamel plates in sand. They come up a treat. Just wipe over with a damp cloth when you've finished.

Keep water cool – dig a hole and put your water bottle in it or float it in water.

Make instant hot-water bottles – fill your standard, large, metal drinking bottles with boiled water at night. Pop the bottles straight into your sleeping bag to warm it up. The water cools overnight and will be ready to drink.

Carry dehydrated powdered food – 96 per cent of food is made up of water so lighten your pack and save energy.

Culinary tip – stir in a lump of lard to thicken low-fat yoghurt.

Never take plain chocolate to cold regions – it freezes so hard you'll probably break your teeth on it. Rather, take milk chocolate because this won't freeze as hard.

Stop chocolate from melting – put it in some water and keep it in the shade.

Observe the social etiquette of the bathroom ... even in the wilds – either dig a hole or cover it up with a stone.

Never use a leaf to wipe your bottom because any insects and larva living on the leaf may decide that your bottom makes a more attractive habitat.

If you run out of food in Arctic regions, eat the dog food first and then the dogs (dogs are now banned from the Antarctic in case they infect the seals so don't run out of food there).

When you run out of food in the jungle, don't eat any old insect you come across. Insects protect themselves against predators with warning colours. If they're brightly coloured (such as red or yellow), then you should avoid them because they will probably be poisonous.

In the jungle, rainwater collects in air plants called Bromeliads. They grow low down on trees and are an easily accessible source of water and food (insects often live, or drown, in them).

Always look before you touch – danger comes from small creatures as well as large. For example, scorpions seek out dark places during the day so check out your rucksack before plunging your hand inside.

Worried about inquisitive polar bears?
Make your own early warning system.
Place ski poles around your campsite and
thread a string between them. Hang
anything that rattles or makes a noise on
the string.

To frighten off polar bears shout as loud
as you can and wave your arms about.
Look as big and aggressive as possible!

If you get stung by an insect, put some bleach on the afflicted area – the ammonia will help lessen the pain. If you don't have any bleach, just pee on the stung spot.

Llamas are intelligent and easy to train.

Become the best friend of weavers and knitters – give them llama hair to spin or knit into warm, luxurious garments.

If a llama spits at you, take notice. He's telling you to push off.

Generally, llamas are gentle and easy to get along with. They are extremely sociable and therefore shouldn't be kept on their own.

Llamas are multi-functional: they can carry heavy loads (up to 100lbs) and travel between 20 to 30km a day. Some exclusive golf courses use them as caddies. They can be trained to pull a cart and they make great guard dogs (they're very territorial and protective).

Owing to their efficient digestive system, llamas can polish off hay, grass, weeds, shrubs and trees.

If you want to keep a monkey as a pet, be warned – they can't be toilet-trained.

Never keep a monkey on its own – it needs companions of its own kind.

Capuchin monkeys like strong smells. They have been known to rub food such as onions or orange peel over their bodies.

A cage can never be strong enough for a monkey – don't ever underestimate the escape power of them.

Some monkeys scent mark their cage so don't sterilise it when you clean it. Always clean the nestbox and the cage at different times so a familiar smell remains at all times.

Gorillas are great bluffers – all that rushing about and chest-beating are usually just to try to scare away intruders, while the rest of the gorilla band slope off quietly into the forest.

Gorillas and chimps love termites and ants, but hate getting bitten, so they slap the ground to stun the insects before eating them.

If you come across a beached whale or dolphin, make sure its blowhole is clear so it can breathe. Try to keep it upright (don't drag it by its tail). The skin should be kept cool and wet; you can use damp cloths and seaweed to cover it, if necessary. Call the Fire Brigade for assistance.

If you are bitten by a venomous snake, forget what you saw in the old Western movies. Don't try to suck the poison out with your mouth or try to cut into the bite. Let the bite bleed freely for 15–30 seconds. Cleanse and disinfect the area quickly with iodine. Apply hard, direct pressure over the bite and tape an adhesive bandage in place (tightly, as if it were a sprain), and then get to a hospital as quickly as possible.

If you come across a snake in the field and don't know what it is, don't approach it, try to examine it or take a photo (unless you've got a zoom lens).

▶▶▶ Farmers

Simon Bowyer

To keep your cattle troughs clear put goldfish in them.

One way to keep deer away is to hang bars of soap around your crops.

If you are worried about hedgehogs getting trapped in cattle grids, put a brick or little ramp on the inside so that they have an escape route.

To stay warm in winter wear lots of light layers, making sure you've got wool next to your skin.

To reuse an old jacket, cut the sleeves off and wear it under your boiler suit for extra warmth.

Don't throw old string away. Use it again. It's ideal for tying up kidney beans or trees laden with apples.

For the optimum shelter for your animals, keep your hedges at a minimum 6 1/2 ft/2 m high.

To make your fencing last longer soak the wood in creosote first. When you see it change colour, you can take it out and put it in the ground. Then paint it with creosote as normal.

Fences provide the ideal site for bird boxes or standing posts for birds of prey. Just put in the occasional tall pole and fix a bird box or perch on to the pole.

To attract wildlife on to your land, plant mountain ash or alder. They are fast-growing trees and produce lots of fruit for the birds.

Make sure newly planted trees have a good start in life by providing shelter for them as they grow and by keeping them clear of weeds.

Give the birds a treat – place small piles of wood and branches around your land. These 'islands' will soon fill up with insects, providing a welcome source of food for the birds.

Ensure that your hedges are stocked with fruits for birds and mammals – trim the hedges in the winter.

Minimise the threat to wildlife when getting rid of rats. Put bait down intensively for one week and then remove it.

To avoid disturbing birds that may be nesting around your pond, try mowing towards the end of August.

Keep your ducks happy while they are moulting. They can't fly at this time so check on them regularly during the summer.

If you are worried that a fox might eat your duck eggs, don't go looking for the nest. Your scent will lead the fox straight to the clutch of eggs.

Owls can be fatally attracted to water troughs so float a piece of wood on the surface which will allow the bird to get itself out of danger.

Never trust a bull even if you know him really well. Bulls respond to dominant behaviour; twist the nose ring slightly to let him know who is boss.

To keep a cow from fidgeting hold her tail near the base and lift it up. This will keep her still.

Raising your own chickens means you have your own supply of fresh eggs and meat. Gardeners like them because they keep pests and weeds down and are a good source of nitrogen-rich manure.

Choose the right breed for your purpose. Some chickens are better layers while others are best for eating. Some, like Rhode Island Reds, serve both purposes.

If you want your hens to lay eggs, provide them with nesting boxes. These should feel enclosed and secure. A laying hen will produce an egg every one or two days.

Try to keep your poultry yard in two halves. The chickens can be kept in one half while the grass grows in the other half. Once there is enough grass there, the chickens can be moved into the second half.

Like other birds, chickens need grit to help with digestion.

If a goose tries to attack you, call its bluff and advance towards it rather than retreat. It will usually turn tail and run, unless it's protecting a nest.

Always stand behind the head of a billy goat to avoid being thumped.

Pigs are intelligent animals. They respond well to being talked to quietly.

Only pick up a piglet if the sow is restrained. Piglets tend to make an almighty row when handled and this could alarm the mother.

Sheep have a blind spot so, if you want to catch one, approach it from behind.

Some sheep have a habit of falling over onto their backs and being unable to right themselves. If this happens, you must get them on their feet as soon as possible. They can develop acute indigestion in this position and may even die.

Sheep hate being on their own. They're happiest in a group and are then much easier to handle.

Sheep are great ones for panicking. If they are going to make a run for it, they tend to aim uphill or towards the light.

If you are shepherding sheep, make sure they can see an opening in front of them. They hate entering dark places, walking into their own shadows or going into water.

To examine a sheep get it into a 'docile' position. This involves sitting it on its back legs. One way to do this is to lift its front end, then walk the sheep backwards until it sits down.

If an animal is suffering badly from bloat (when one of its stomachs blows up with gas), you may need to resort to emergency remedies such as peanut oil (a pint in warm water for cattle), liquid paraffin (50ml for a goat), washing soda crystals (for cattle, 1/4 lb dissolved in hot water then diluted to about a pint with cold). These remedies should be administered as a drench by somebody who knows what they're doing.

►►► Fashion Designers

Serafina Grafton-Beaves, Kensington & Chelsea College, London; Julia Dee, Designer Alterations, London; Karen Spurgin, London; Raj Mairs, Exclusively Mairs, Birmingham

▷▷ Keeping Clean

Remove a water stain from silk by placing a dry cloth underneath and dabbing the spot with a damp cloth.

Cut down on creases when washing your sari – fold it up and place it in a pillow case before putting it in to the wash.

To get an old black grease stain off fabric, rub gently with margarine and then wash as normal.

Get rid of black spots on white shoes and handbags with nail-varnish remover.

Dirty marks on white material can be covered up with white chalk.

Remove pencil marks from embroidery material by rubbing the fabric with kneaded white bread.

Clean a felt hat by wrapping sticky tape round your hand and gently dabbing the fluff away.

Alternatively, brush a felt hat vigorously with a nail brush and then steam over a kettle to bring the pile back up.

Remove stubborn stains from a felt hat by brushing with sandpaper. If that fails, colour in the mark with an appropriately coloured felt-tip pen.

▷▷ Ironing

Iron your sleeves by hanging the jacket on the door and placing the sleeve board vertically up the sleeve.

To iron a shoulder pad, wrap your hand in a towel and place under the shoulder.

Remove creases from silk after a long journey with a hair-dryer. If you're on the road, you can use a hot-air hand dryer in a service station.

When ironing delicate fabrics place tissue paper over the top.

▷▷ Sewing

To get a good hem on chiffon or silk, fold an inch of the material over and sew as close as possible to the edge. Cut the excess, fold over again and then sew.

Make a thimble from an old elbow patch.

To thread a needle easily put a piece of white paper behind the eye of the needle.

Never put pins in your mouth if you wear lipstick because it will stain the material. Instead, use a small pin cushion attached to your wrist by a band.

Stop your embroidery thread ending up like a rat's nest – simply tie it into a braid and the threads will come away easily.

▷▷ Getting Dressed

Make zips run more efficiently by running a lead pencil along the metal teeth.

To stop the pleats in your sari from coming undone, use two safety pins to hold them in place.

If you want to reuse your bindi, just place a little bit of Blu tack on the back.

Remove the shine from velvet, wool or viscose by spraying the affected area with water and then leaving to dry. Give the material a good brush when it's completely dry.

Get rid of fluff and cat hairs by wrapping sticky tape around your hand and rubbing up and down the item of clothing.

▷▷ Creating 'The Look'

To give you good luck on your wedding day, whoever sews your dress should place a lock of their hair in the hem.

To look slimmer tuck the flaps of your pockets into your jacket to create a smoother line.

Wear a V-neck for a slimmer-looking neckline.

To make your bust look larger dust a little bit of blusher on your cleavage.

To draw attention away from a large bust, wear a very simple, plain white shirt.

To draw attention away from your hips, wear a scarf around your neck.

To give an old jacket a new lease of life simply sew on a velvet collar.

To really jazz up an old jacket put it on a hanger in the garage and throw a large tin of fabric paint all over it.

Stop the hem of your silk skirt or sari from flying away – sew a 2p piece into the hem.

To make a hat smaller, line it with draft excluder.

▷▷ Keeping Clothes

Protect your wedding dress – sew two cotton sheets together as a protective cover.

Clothes keep their shape longer if you do up all the buttons when you hang them in the wardrobe.

Prevent your shoes from scuffing by painting a layer of clear nail-varnish on to the heel and toe of your shoes.

To stop a new pair of shoes rubbing on your heel, rub some candle wax along the edge to soften the leather.

►►► Fish Breeders

Mary Bailey; Nick Fletcherl; Richard Mills, Slough; Ben Helm, Brooksby College, Warwick; John Mulvana, Aquatica, Wakefield

A healthy fish always has an erect dorsal fin.

When transporting koi in a car, make sure the fish is in a container that doesn't allow it to turn round. Then place the container so that the fish is lying across the car and not back to front. This stops the fish from banging his nose every time you brake.

When transporting very small fish, twist the corners of the plastic bag and secure with an elastic band. This stops the fish from getting crushed in the corners.

When bringing new fish home, put their plastic bags or containers inside brown paper bags. This stops them from getting too stressed on the journey.

Imported fish can suffer from jet lag, so it's not always a good idea to take them straight home from the shop. A good breeder will allow you to reserve fish.

When choosing fish, check what size they will grow to. You could end up with a very large fish in a very small aquarium. Piranhas can grow up to 12 inches long while some Angelfishes can reach 16 inches.

If you've never kept fish before, start with freshwater species rather than the more demanding marine fishes. Tropical freshwater fishes can be just as colourful and attractive to look at as their marine counterparts.

Cold freshwater systems don't need as many bits of technology as the tropical systems but they are more difficult to maintain. Coldwater fish consume more oxygen than tropical fish; therefore you will need a larger tank with aquatic plants to oxygenate the water.

Tropical marine fish are more expensive than freshwater ones so it's worth getting a bit of experience with other (cheaper) fish before you move into this area.

Some fish need more expert care and handling than others: for example, the Moray Eel, sea horses and the venomous Tailbar Lionfish are really only for the more experienced fish keeper.

Make sure your fish will get along together. Some fish can't stand the company of their own species but will happily share a tank with others. This might be a bit 'obvious' but don't put carnivorous fish into an aquarium with small fish ... you might start to notice numbers dwindling. Carnivorous fish should be kept on their own or with fish of a similar size to themselves.

A mix of species is a good idea because different fish tend to have different habits, live in different parts of the aquarium and move around during different parts of the day. For example, Catfish feed at the bottom of a tank, while Tetras move happily around all areas.

Koi and goldfish can live for over twenty years, while Killifish only last for a year. A good rule of thumb is: the larger the fish, the longer it will live.

You don't need to buy a net for catching fish – a plastic bag will do just as well.

▷▷ Health

If your male fish refuses to mate, make him jealous. Introduce a bit of competition by making a false fish out of paper. Wriggle it about in the tank for a while. It should hopefully make your male get his act together.

A healthy fish should have a good strong colour with no blurring and it should be eating.

An unhealthy fish can swim with its fins held flat against its body. Avoid fish covered in spots, lumps, wounds or split fins. Don't buy a fish if the tank also contains dead fish.

Feed fish little and often. Like all animals, fish thrive on a balanced diet.

Nominate one member of the family as the fish feeder or have set feeding times so you don't run the risk of the whole family dropping meals into the water and overfeeding the fish.

Grow your own whiteworms. Buy a few to start off with from a fish dealer. Put the worms in a box of earth and cover with a slice of wet bread. This should give you a continuous supply of worms for your fish.

▷▷ Aquariums & Tanks

A tropical freshwater aquarium should be kept at a temperature of around 25°C (77°F).

Rainwater is ideal for aquariums, but not if it comes from a dirty roof or metal containers.

Think carefully where you are going to place your aquarium. Try not to put it in a window; the sun can cause too much algae to grow and the water to overheat. You need to be near an electrical point to run the filter, air pumps and heaters.

You will need a heater if you intend to keep tropical fish. Allow 10 watts of power per 5 litres of water for a tank in a normally heated room. If you have a large tank (over 36 inches), install two heaters.

Filling your tank with plants and rocks makes it look more attractive but don't go overboard. Your aim is to try to copy the natural habitat of the fish as well as make it look good.

Plants are a good way of absorbing carbon dioxide and producing oxygen; they also remove nitrate from the water, while some plants are part of a fish's diet.

Plants are also an ideal way of hiding the technical bits and pieces which you need to run your aquarium.

When planting up your aquarium, put the taller plants at the back, but don't place them too densely together. The odd gap here and there will give an illusion of distance and space.

You can't keep live plants in a marine aquarium, but you can use synthetic plants and corals to liven things up.

Purify the water in a tank by putting watercress in the filter chamber. Buy it ready-prepared from a supermarket or grocer. If you introduce it from the wild, you run the risk of introducing diseases into the water.

Don't overcrowd your aquarium. You should keep three fish for every 2 gall/9 ltr of water. If you've got more fish than that, you should get an air pump.

Don't tip your new fish into their aquarium straight away. You have to let the temperature of the water in the bag equalise with the aquarium water. The easiest solution is to float the bag in the tank for a couple of hours before letting the fish into the water.

If you are planning to introduce new fish to an established tank, keep them in quarantine for a couple of weeks. Keep expensive fish in quarantine for longer (at least a couple of months).

When you set up a new aquarium, let it 'settle' for at least a week before you start introducing fish. The first fish to go in should just be a couple of goldfish. If something's wrong with the tank and the fish die, you won't have wasted lots of money on expensive fish.

When setting up a new tank, use the filter from an old tank to establish beneficial bacteria into the new water immediately.

If you have to take your fish out of the water, place it on a baby-changing mat. The raised edges will stop it sliding off. Also, cover the fish with a soft, damp cloth.

If you want to dispose of a terminally ill fish, don't flush it down the loo. Fish can survive for some time in the warm water of the sewers. The humane way is to put water in a jam jar, put the fish in the jar and place in the freezer.

Rocks in tanks shouldn't contain calcium – test them by dabbing them with a bit of vinegar. If they fizz, don't put them in the tank.

For fish that like caves, use terracotta plant pots in tanks. They make great breeding grounds.

A good alternative plant fertiliser for tanks is rabbit or guinea pig droppings. They won't harm the fish and they do a lot for the plants.

If your fish like alkaline conditions, sprinkle a bit of baking powder into the water.

For fish that like more acidic water, put a tea-bag in the tank. This will also encourage plants to grow.

To stop fish getting cold during a power cut, put a plastic bottle filled with hot water inside their tank. Replace it as necessary.

When cleaning out your fish tank, don't throw away the water. Put it on your garden instead. It's full of nitrates that will do your plants a lot of good.

To clean a tank remove one-third of the water every fortnight, replacing it with clean water.

Bring out the exotic colours of your fish by exchanging the gravel in your tank with coal.

Get fish used to shows – place their tank in a busy part of the house.

To make male fish display themselves effectively for competitions, place them in adjacent tanks so they can show off to each other.

To encourage egg laying, cut nylon wool into strips. Tie one end to the bottom of the tank then secure the other end to a piece of cork so that it floats. Your fish will lay their eggs along the small pieces of wool.

A great way to catch flies for your fish is to attach a piece of fine net to the side of your car in the summer.

To feed your fish using a timer drill three holes into a clock face at the times you want the fish to be fed. Remove the minute hand and place some food over the holes. Suspend the clock face over the tank. When it's dinner time, the big hand will knock the food into the tank.

Fishy food treats are pieces of cucumber, lettuce or orange.

Don't overfeed your fish. They should have finished eating within 2 minutes. Anything left over just mucks up the water.

A good way to hatch brine shrimps is to place them in a milk bottle.

Feeding fish with fresh fish is nutritionally very good for them. Always feed freshwater fish to salt-water fish and vice versa.

To stop big fish eating small eggs, put some net curtain or glass marbles into the tank. The eggs will drop between the holes and cracks to safety.

To feed fry fish (and stop the bigger fish from getting more than their share), use a gravy baster to squirt the fry food in the right direction.

▷▷ Ponds

If you're planning to build a fish pond, don't make it too involved. Awkward shapes can cause water to stagnate in odd nooks and crannies.

Don't situate your pond underneath trees because you'll have your hands full keeping the surface clear of falling leaves.

To remove blanket weed from the side of a pond, use a windscreen ice scraper.

During a frost, make sure you leave an air hole for your fish to breathe. Float a rubber ball on the surface overnight. During the day, you can take the ball away and, if possible, draw off some of the water so that oxygen can reach the surface. Never break the ice with a hammer – it's like a bomb going off at close quarters and the shock waves can kill the fish.

If you've forgotten to leave an air hole, heat a pan of water and hold it on top of the ice so that it melts, leaving a perfect hole.

▶▶▶ Fishmongers

Ralph Easton, Blackburn Fishmarket; Peter Preece, Queensgate Market

▷▷ Fresh Is Best

To ensure that you get the best range and quality of fish, choose a fishmonger that supplies local restaurants.

The most important thing when buying fish is to ensure that it's really fresh.

Fresh fish should have a firm texture. Push your fingers into the flesh; if your indentation stays there, the fish is not really fresh.

To tell if a fish is fresh, check the brightness of the scales and the pinkness of the gills. The eyes must be clear, bright and not sunken.

Fresh sea fish should be bright and not noticeably dry.

Fresh trout should be slightly slimy to the touch.

When buying white fish fillets, look for neat, trim fillets and a white, translucent appearance.

Smoked fish should have a fresh smoky aroma and a glossy appearance.

Frozen fish should be frozen hard with no signs of partial thawing and the packaging should be undamaged.

Don't buy plaice that has roe in it because it will be absolutely tasteless.

To tell if a salmon is wild or farmed, hold the tail between your thumb and forefinger. Farmed fish have far fewer scales and are more slippery. If it slips through your fingers, the fish is farmed.

Fresh fish should be used as soon as possible. However, it can be stored in the fridge overnight.

Keep fish cool. Remove from the packaging and rinse in cold water. Pat dry, cover and store near the bottom of the fridge.

Store fresh fish and smoked fish separately so that the flavours don't get mixed up.

Store cooked, ready-to-eat fish (such as smoked mackerel, prawns and crab) separately from raw fish.

Before freezing your fish, rinse it in water to create a protective glaze around the fish when it's frozen.

Soak fish such as shark, ray and skate in salt water for 20 minutes beforehand to remove the smell of ammonia.

Choose mussels with undamaged shells. To make sure that all the mussels open when cooking, stir them regularly in the saucepan. The sheer bulk of numbers may prevent some mussels from opening.

Crab and lobster should feel heavier than you would expect. This means that they will be meaty and juicy.

▷▷ Gutting & Filleting

When preparing fish always use a sharp knife.

Before filleting and skinning fish, dip your fingers in salt. You'll get a much better grip.

Cut the fish from the bottom to the neck and then chop off the head. The innards will pull out easily.

Use a spoon to scrape out the guts, especially of larger fish.

When filleting a plaice, start with the white side first. The head is on this side; it's quite knobbly so it's easier to grip.

In trout and salmon, there is a line along the spine of the fish (a black kidney shape in a trout and a red blood patch in a salmon) which doesn't taste very nice. You can remove it easily by running your fingernail along the spine.

The head-end third of cod contains all the large, noticeable bones. Run your thumb along the top of the fish. Where the bumps stop marks the end of these bones (the tail-end of cod only has small bones). If you cut a V-shape in the back of the fish up to where the bumps end, you will have a boneless piece of fish.

When preparing monkfish, cut the head off and pull the skin off from the tail. Then remove the membrane that covers the flesh of the fish before cooking, otherwise the fish will have a chewy texture.

To clear fish guts and scales from your chopping board, use a window squeegee.

Clean fish on newspaper. This keeps your board clean and means you can wrap the waste up and put it straight into the bin.

Mustard removes fishy smells from wooden boards.

Clean wooden chopping boards with half a lemon dipped in salt. This also prevents the surface from staining.

To remove strong food smells from plastic chopping boards, give them a rub down with a cut lemon.

Stop wooden chopping boards from warping by drying them upright and not flat.

Prevent that lingering fish smell on plates and in pots and pans, by putting a tablespoon of vinegar in the washing-up water.

To clean a pan after cooking and to remove the fishy smell, leave some cold tea in the pan for 10 minutes before you come to wash it.

Always pick a hake up by its eyes so you don't cut your hands.

▷▷ Fishy Dishes

Crab should be placed alive in cold water over a low heat. If you place it in hot water, its membrane will let water in and parts of it will fall off! Always heat it up slowly to make sure your presentation is perfect.

When crab has been cooked, get the shell off and remove the 'dead man's fingers'; these are the gills and taste nasty. There are five on either side of the inner body.

Don't crush crab and lobster claws – use the handle of a teaspoon to get the meat out instead.

A clean and easy way to coat fish in batter or breadcrumbs is to place the fish in a freezer bag with the batter or crumbs and shake gently until it is covered.

Before shallow-frying fish, first dip it into well-seasoned flour. This will create a protective layer which helps to form a good crust and keep the fish moist.

Always mix the pre-mixed batter from supermarkets with chilled water (46 °F/8 °C). If the water is too warm, the batter will ferment. Whisk the batter so it's light and fluffy, then drop the batter-covered fish into hot fat (375 °F/190 °C). If your fat isn't hot enough, the fish absorbs the fat and the batter won't be crispy. Hot fat instantly seals the batter.

To make an unusual and delicious batter replace the milk in the batter with the same quantity of beer. Allow to stand in the fridge for half an hour before using. The starch grains in the flour absorb liquid and swell, producing a lighter mixture.

When keeping fried fish warm don't stack it or cover it up because this will make it soggy.

To stop fish from falling apart after it's been fried, dip it in boiling water before you fry it.

To test whether fish is cooked, look for flesh that is opaque and feels firm to the touch. You should be able to insert a knife easily and peel the skin away.

Fish can be cooked straight from the freezer – just add a couple of extra minutes to the cooking time.

Pieces of bacon laid over skinned white fish fillets will keep them moist while cooking.

Cook fish in foil parcels to give delicious, moist morsels of fish.

You don't need an expensive steamer for fish, just put a colander over a pan of boiling water and cover the colander with a large lid.

To remove a fishy smell, rinse your hands in lemon juice.

Remove fiddly bones from salmon fillets with tweezers.

If grilling a whole fish (mackerel, for example), slash the skin three or four times on the diagonal on both sides. This prevents the skin from breaking open when cooked.

Skinning a fish is fiddly. Flash grill the fish first under a very hot grill and the crispy, scorched skin will lift off effortlessly.

If you need only a couple of drops of lemon juice for fish, simply pierce the lemon with a cocktail stick and it will then stay fresh after use.

Fish cooks quickly and the golden rule is *never* to overcook it.

To cook delicious juicy fish wrap it in clingfilm and place in boiling water so that none of the natural flavour escapes.

To prevent fish skin from sticking to the frying pan rub with salt, leave for 15 minutes, rinse and rub dry. Then cook.

For a tasty, crunchy coating for fish or potato croquettes first dip in egg and then roll in crushed crisps – just choose your favourite flavour.

It's easy to cook trout in the microwave – try brushing each side with some balsamic vinegar for a lovely flavour.

To slice tuna thinly pop it in the freezer for an hour before use to make the task easier.

To stop fish going soggy during cooking sprinkle it with salt and leave for half an hour before cooking.

To store lobster for longer soak some sheets of newspaper in cold water. Roll up the lobster in the newspaper and put in the fridge. The lobster will keep fresh for a couple of days longer.

To remove the bones from raw fish use a vegetable peeler. Run the peeler along the flesh, catching bones in the centre slit. Twist the peeler and pull the bones out.

Never buy a fresh fish if it has dull eyes – it's not fresh.

To reduce the unpleasant fishy smell when poaching fish, add some celery leaves to the pot.

The tail of a truly fresh fish will be stiff.

To make batter stick properly to fish or whatever else you're battering, add 1/2 teaspoon sugar to the mix.

To make haddock less salty poach it in milk.

To make opening sardine tins easy don't even try to use the troublesome key. Just turn the tin upside down and use a tin opener.

▶▶▶ Fitness Instructors

Anne-Marie Millard

Start off moderately – you don't have to go at things like a bull at a gate.

Warm up and cool down every time.

Always do your least favourite exercise first so you can get it over with and enjoy the rest of your workout.

Exercise can become addictive so be careful that you don't overdo things.

Get a partner – exercising with someone is more interesting. You'll be more likely to turn up at the gym or exercise class if you have to meet your partner there.

Listen to your body – if it hurts then don't do it. Gone are the days of Jane Fonda's 'going for the burn'.

Don't weigh yourself when training. You'll get despondent because muscle weighs more than fat and you'll think you're getting fatter! Measure yourself instead and you'll realise the good you're achieving as your body changes shape.

Smile from time to time while you're exercising. It stops you getting cramps in your cheeks!

If you are running out of steam, it is psychologically easier to count backwards when exercising. So ... 5, 4, 3, 2, 1!

To keep your muscles warm when exercising, rub some fat over your body before you begin.

For real energy, eat a banana before exercising.

To firm up your bum walk up the stairs backwards.

To improve the front of your thighs and your bum muscles, walk up the stairs two at a time.

To strengthen your thighs, sit against a wall without a chair and build up the time you can hold this position. Always remember to stretch out before and after the exercise.

Increase your leg strength by exercising with a small child. Let them sit on the bottom of your legs, ankles together, and raise your legs up and down. They'll enjoy the ride and you'll feel the benefit.

You don't need to buy expensive dumbbells for basic work – use large plastic bottles of water.

You can make your own cheap weights by using baked-bean cans.

If you don't have an exercise bike, sit on an ordinary cycle propped against a wall and cycle backwards.

Make your own body liniment for strains and sprains. Mix two drops of lavender oil with two tablespoons of grapeseed oil.

A wonderful home–made isotonic drink is to mix 1/2 pint/300 ml each of filtered water and orange juice. Add two pinches of salt and two pinches of glucose to the mixture.

For a great energy shake, blend old bananas, honey, brown sugar, two or three ice cubes and one small pot of plain yoghurt together.

To make your legs work harder when swimming, tie some sponges to your calves. Because they absorb so much water, you'll really feel the difference.

Keep yourself motivated when out walking or running – aim for visual reference points. You can alternate between fast and slow.

For a cheap pair of training shorts, cut the legs off some old tights or leggings.

To keep trainers smelling sweet, splash them with a shot of Dettox.

Don't get despondent on a diet. Think of all the positive points rather than the negative ones – like that size 12 you're going to get into, rather than all the cream cakes you're not eating.

Boredom can kill a diet stone dead so experiment with low-fat recipes. Low-fat foods don't have to be boring.

If you get stressed before a competition, try juggling. The sheer concentration will stop you feeling anxious.

If you are too nervous to eat before a big event, one healthy helping of rice pudding will give you enough energy for the whole day.

Losing weight is all about good diet and healthy exercise.

▶▶▶ Florists

Paula Pryke; Linda Trompetto, Society of Floristry; Hilary West; Jinnie McCabe; Sandy Martin, Branching Out, Glasgow

Store oasis in a bucket of water – it should never be allowed to dry out.

Oasis should stand higher than the edge of the vase so you can have flowers and foliage hanging down rather than all standing to attention.

Stop oasis from floating around in a vase or bowl – secure it to the bottom with double-sided tape or Blu tack.

To reuse oasis just turn it over and start again.

If you don't have any oasis put sticky tape across the top of the vase in a criss-cross pattern to form a grid to hold the flowers upright.

Use pebbles from the garden (make sure they are clean first) instead of oasis in the bottom of the vase.

Marbles hold flowers in place. If used in a glass vase, they look attractive too.

To make flower arranging easy put a wire scouring pad in the bottom of the vase and push the flower stems into the wire. The pad will last longer than oasis and, unlike oasis, can be used again even after it dries out.

Use polystyrene for drainage instead of stones.

If your vase has a small crack in it, seal the leak with a piece of soft candle wax.

If your vase is too big for the number of flowers you have, put a smaller tumbler inside the vase, fill it with water and put the flowers in that. The flowers will stand upright in the vase and won't look overwhelmed and droopy.

Never buy roses or spray carnations in tight bud but make sure the petals are unfurling. Very tight buds may never open.

Use lukewarm water when arranging flowers; it has less oxygen in it and so you don't get so many air bubbles up the stems of flowers.

When arranging flowers, strip off all leaves below the water line to prevent them rotting.

When buying foliage with flowers avoid dowdy, yellow leaves. Foliage dies before flowers so make sure it's healthy and vibrant.

Smash hard woody stems but cut soft stems before placing them in your arrangement.

Don't place flowers in direct sunlight, near central heating or on top of the television. Make sure they are in a well-ventilated part of the room.

If your flower arrangement is going to be in a warm room, keep the blooms looking lovely by popping some ice cubes into the water each morning.

Don't put flowers next to fruit because the fruit produces ethylene gas which increases the maturity rate of flowers, so they die more quickly. Equally, remove dying flowers from a bunch or arrangement because they produce the same gas.

Don't mix daffodils with other blooms – they release a poison which kills off other flowers.

Cut wide-stemmed flowers under water and then, keeping your finger over the cut end to stop air from getting into the stem, transfer to the vase.

Cut poppies will loose sap quickly and therefore won't last long unless you carefully singe the ends in a candle flame to create a seal.

Rubber plants leak sap when cut so use cigarette ash to stem the sap.

Gardenias leak white sap that can cause a rash if it comes into contact with your skin. Seal the cut stem over a naked flame.

Remove the stamens from lilies to prevent the pollen from staining clothes and furnishing fabrics. Wipe up any pollen that falls onto polished wood surfaces because, if left, it will eat into the wood.

If the stem of a lily splits, wrap it in sticky tape.

To water plants while you are away, stick one end of a pipe cleaner into a bowl of water and place the other end into the plant pot. The plant will then suck up the water when required.

Alternatively, fill your bath with about an inch of water and place a thick bath towel on top. Stand your plants on the towel so that they can take up water when they require it.

To give plants a really good watering have them in the shower with you. A verse of 'Everything's coming up roses' goes down well too.

Revive droopy tulips and roses – wrap them tightly in wet newspaper and put them in a deep bucket of water overnight.

Alternatively, revive droopy flowers with a soluble aspirin in their vase – it's a great pick-me-up.

Perk up woody-stemmed flowers (such as roses) by putting the stems in boiling water for 10 seconds, and then immediately plunging them into deep, cold water. This will move the air lock that has formed in the stem up to the flower.

To keep your posy of roses fresh, punch holes in a raw potato and insert each stem into a hole separately. Your flowers will stay fresh and pretty for a considerable time.

Devon violets drink water through their leaves so always dunk them right under water.

To revive a bone-dry plant plunge it in a bucket of water and then drain. Don't pour water over it: this will just wash out the soil.

Scented flowers don't last as long as non-scented varieties because they use up extra energy creating the smell.

To keep fresh tulips closed paint them with unbeaten egg white.

Preserve dried flowers by spraying with hair-spray. It acts like an adhesive and prevents them from falling apart.

Revitalise dried roses by holding them over a kettle of boiling water.

Make your own dried flowers – use the microwave. A rose, for example, will take 3 minutes on medium power.

If you don't have a microwave, hang the flowers upside down in the airing cupboard for a couple of days.

To crystallise flowers mix 1 part sugar to 1 part water, simmer until the sugar has dissolved. Then put the flowers in the syrup and simmer gently for a short while. Remove and leave to dry.

Clean vases regularly with bleach – not washing-up liquid – to kill the bacteria residue. Flowers are dirty things!

Repot a plant without making a mess. Simply place the old pot inside the new larger pot and fill the gap with soil. Then remove the smaller pot, take the plant out of the old pot and place into the hole in the new pot.

To repot cacti use old carpet scraps to hold the plant so you don't damage your hands.

Sharpen scissors by cutting tin foil.

Don't waste your money on expensive leaf shine – give your potted plants a good wipe down with milk.

If the pollen from flowers has fallen on to your carpet or furnishing fabrics, lift it off gently with sticky tape so that you don't rub it in and leave an indelible stain.

House plants are used to being warm so, when you take them home, keep them in the plastic sleeves the shops put them in. If it's really quite cold, add an extra layer of insulation by putting the plants in a cardboard box.

Cut flowers in the late evening and they'll last longer.

Lily bulbs can rot in damp weather, so put a layer of gravel in the planting hole to encourage the water to drain away.

Alternatively, plant lily bulbs on their side so that water doesn't gather round the crown of the bulb and cause it to rot.

Always keep one set of tools for house plants and another for the garden so you don't run the risk of introducing damaging diseases or pests.

House plants grow towards the source of light so turn them regularly to encourage even growth.

Many house plants benefit from a humid atmosphere. Grouping them together is one way to increase humidity.

To clean a large plant with small leaves put it in the bath and spray it with tepid water using the shower attachment.

Keep plants with hairy leaves clean by brushing away dust using a small, soft paintbrush.

Golden barrel cactus likes a dry atmosphere. Don't water it during its rest period in the winter.

To repot cacti fold a length of brown paper into a wide band, wrap it round the cactus and hold both ends in one hand. Pull the pot away with the other hand.

Spotted dumb crane likes shady conditions, but keep it away from children because its sap is poisonous.

Herringbone plant is another one that likes shady conditions. Don't leave it in too bright a light because the bright colours of its leaves will fade.

To clean a smelly vase fill it half full of water and add a tablespoon of mustard. Shake the mixture and then leave for an hour.

Create a tower of flowers. Stack pots one on top of the other to create a dramatic display.

Add a shot of vodka to the water in your vases – it will keep your flowers fresh for longer.

Protect roses from frost by piling the soil up into a mound round the stems. Remove once the weather improves.

Put marigold flowers in your bath water to soften the water.

Love-in-a-mist (*Nigella damascena*) produces spice-scented seeds which can be used in cooking.

Heartsease can be added to salads, sundaes and drinks.

Use rose petals in cream, ice-cream, cordials and salads.

Try adding the flowers of pinks to salads or vinegar, or even use them to decorate cakes.

Nasturtiums have a strong, peppery flavour which works well in salads and sandwiches.

Keep flowers fresh for longer – add a splash of lemonade to their water.

When deadheading long-stemmed plants, cut back to the next growth point or set of leaves.

As rhododendron flowers fade, remove them, but be careful not to damage the plant as you do so.

Deadhead soft-stemmed plants by hand. You get better access to the flower heads and it's easier than using secateurs.

▶▶▶ Football Players

Andrew Collins; Erroll Hibbert

When you have brought your new football boots home, soak them in water, then stuff with newspaper. Allow them to dry naturally. When they are fully dry, rub them with petroleum jelly.

To get your new boots to fit perfectly, sit in the bath with them on – as practised by the professionals!

After the game fill your boots with scrunched-up newspaper to keep them dry and in shape.

For your own home-made isotonic drink, mix together some glucose powder, salt and water.

After any exercise, stretch your muscles out, keeping each one tense for 30 seconds, to keep them free from aches and pains.

If you have sprained yourself, stick a bag of frozen peas on the affected area.

To practise heading, use balloons. This is particularly useful in building confidence when heading the ball at the same time as another player. Throw the balloon between two people; they have to go for the balloon carefully and slowly.

To build confidence in dribbling, place several kit bags on top of each other and dribble around them. Don't use anything small, like a cone or disc on the ground, until later.

Keep in touch with the rest of the team – improve your communication with your team members. Give everyone a number from one to ten. Then, in a confined area, pass the ball from one to two to three and so on. Each person has to shout out their number to get the ball.

Improve your thinking and sharpen your reactions – get someone to shout out the points of the compass. React as quickly as you can by diving in the correct direction: left for west, for example.

Speed up reaction time by throwing the ball at a player and shouting 'Head it' … except they must catch it. Likewise, when you shout 'Catch it', they have to head it.

To bend the ball in flight, hit the ball on the outside and point your foot in the direction you want the ball to go. Follow through with the kick.

When throwing the ball in, stand sideways and turn like a javelin player, dragging your foot on the ground as you turn (don't let your foot come away from the floor).

To improve your goalkeeping skills, make sure you keep your arms up as you dive to save the ball. People normally dive with their arms down, bringing them up as they move towards the ball . . . by which time it can often be too late.

The proper stance for a goalie comes straight from a gunslinger's book. Stand with your hands spread out by the side of your body – as if you are about to go for your gun, cowboy!

When in goal, never cross your feet: sidestep along the goal line.

Every time goalies catch or hold the ball, they should spread their fingers, making sure that their thumbs are touching (so that there is a W-shape at the back of the ball).

A fun way to get your team warmed up is to put your players in a confined area with their shirts tucked into their shorts. One player starts out trying to pull the back of the shirts out of the shorts. Once you've 'lost your shirt', you grab others' shirts.

To get children to control the ball, set out a 6 ft/1.8 m square. Keep throwing the ball into and through the square; the child has to stop and control it and, in doing so, they will learn how to trap, stop and control the ball naturally.

When playing with small children, don't use small goals because they'll never score! Use a large adult goal and then the scoring opportunities increase and they remain interested.

To stop studs rusting into the soles of football boots unscrew them and rub Vaseline on to the screw before screwing back in.

Never tumble dry football shirts with names and numbers on the back – you'll melt the transfers.

Hang football shirts on your wall between washing and wearing – they make great posters.

Don't knock mud off the soles of football boots by banging them against a wall – you'll damage both the wall and the studs. Instead, leave the mud to dry and peel.

Many football boots – despite appearances – aren't actually made of leather, but are synthetic. Avoid the hassle of polishing – synthetic boots can be cleaned with soapy water.

Contrary to popular belief, use shoe polish on leather football boots rather than dubbin. Dubbin stops the leather breathing.

Leave boots to dry naturally – drying them under a radiator or in an airing cupboard will dry out the oils in the leather and it'll crack.

When folding up football shirts after washing, avoid folding along the line of the sponsor's name on the front of the shirt – you'll crack the print.

If your team has two kits, wear them alternately to get the life back into them between matches.

The best thing to clean white stripes on football boots is a bit of kitchen cleaner cream. Second best is toothpaste.

And the best way to touch up trendy coloured boots is with a simple crayon of the right colour.

To air sweaty, smelly goalkeepers' gloves turn them inside out and attach them to the handle-bars of a bike with rubber bands. Then ride round on the bike.

►►► Gamekeepers

Leslie Ferguson, Representative of BASC; Country Landowners Association; Game Conservancy

Give your dog a good rub down after a wet day's shooting. Use discarded newspapers instead of towels.

Get the most out of your trap or snare. Bury it in the ground for several weeks to remove all traces of manufactured smells.

Stop foxes from eating your pheasants. Place mirrors or plastic bags round the pen and it should help to deter them.

Encourage pheasant chicks to peck at their food by mixing the corn with chocolate 'hundreds and thousands'.

Make wheat more palatable to young pheasants. Soak it in water first.

For an indestructible beater's flag, use old plastic fertiliser sacks. As well as being completely waterproof, they have the added advantage of 'cracking' when used for driving partridges and grouse.

Prevent your shot game from turning green and deteriorating within a matter of hours. Never leave it in a heap. The body heat must be allowed to disperse as quickly as possible.

▶▶▶ Gardeners

Ken Hollingsworth; Andy Flitney; Mary Griffin; Michael Walker; David Parker

Shift stains from plastic garden furniture with a paste made from bicarbonate of soda and water. Leave the paste on the stain for about 2 minutes and then wipe off.

To preserve aluminium garden furniture over winter, lightly wipe down with cooking oil. Remember to wipe it off when you want to use the furniture again.

To remove rust from garden tools, mix 2 tablespoons of salt with 1 tablespoon of lemon juice. Apply this mixture to the rust and rub hard.

To store garden tools over winter grease lightly with cooking oil.

To prevent your tools from rusting store them in buckets of sand and oil.

Prevent rust by using left-over engine oil. Leave the bottle to drain into a jar, then brush the oil on to your garden tools or furniture to keep them in good condition. Wipe off before using.

▷▷ Seeds and Young Plants

When storing seeds, make sure moisture doesn't ruin them. Keep them in an airtight tin. As an added precaution, wrap some milk powder in tissue, seal with a rubber band and leave it in the tin.

Sow seeds evenly. Punch holes in the top of a jam jar or coffee jar and screw the top on; use this to shake out the seeds.

The smaller the seed, the shallower it should be sown.

Mix small seeds with sand for easy planting.

Plant seedlings in bits of old guttering – they are easy to slide off the end for repotting.

For an alternative seed starter use tea-bags.

Thin delicate seedlings with a pair of tweezers. This doesn't disturb the roots of the remaining seedlings.

Make a mini-greenhouse – cut the top off a plastic drinks bottle and place it over your seedlings.

Make a temporary greenhouse from a clear plastic bag; support it with sticks and secure with a rubber band.

Tie up delicate climbers with old tights cut into strips.

To support your herbaceous plants pull a wire coat-hanger into a square and hook on to supporting canes.

To support small plants remove the inner part of a ballpoint pen and use the transparent outer skin as a support.

When planting a shrub in dry soil, put a pot of gravel next to the roots. When you water it, the water should go straight through to the roots.

In hot weather, line a pot with damp paper before potting up a plant. This conserves moisture.

To make a self-watering plant pot, cut a plastic bottle in half, remove the lid and pull a piece of fabric partly through the spout end. Then place the plant in the top, on the fabric. Fill the bottom half of the bottle with water and place the spout end, complete with 'wick' and plant, on top. The fabric will soak up the water from below.

using a plastic bottle   using a jam jar

Alternatively, fill an old jam jar or container with water, cut a hole in the lid and thread through one end of a long strip from an old pair of tights so that it reaches the bottom of the jar. Put the other end of the strip through the hole in the bottom of the plant pot. Stand the pot on top of the container.

To kick-start woody cuttings, slit the end of the stem and put a grain of wheat into the cut. As the wheat germinates, it encourages the root of the cutting to form.

Don't throw banana skins away; place them round the bottom of your roses for a great fertiliser.

Fertilise your azaleas and camellias by placing used tea-bags around their roots.

Give azaleas the odd drink of 2 pints/1.2 litres of water mixed with 2 tablespoons of white vinegar.

To encourage geranium growth, keep all your eggshells in a bucket of water. After a few weeks, remove the eggshells and water your geraniums with this liquid.

To collect seeds put the ripe seed head in a paper bag and shake.

Seeds in pods should not be stored in airtight containers. They need a flow of air round them. When the pods are dry, you can remove the seeds and put in a paper bag.

Small seeds can stick to your hands when you're sowing. Keep your hands cool by running cold water over your wrists and then drying your hands thoroughly before you start.

Dry seeds by putting on a piece of kitchen paper and leave to dry thoroughly. If seeds are still damp, they may start to rot or germinate.

The best place to store seeds is in the fridge.

Always label your seeds; some will keep for ages, while others only last a year.

Use your linen cupboard to propagate seeds that don't need much light. Cover seed trays with clingfilm and check daily. As soon as the first seedlings appear, remove the trays.

Conserve moisture – cover seedling pots with clingfilm; this keeps out draughts and ensures that the temperature remains constant. Take the clingfilm off from time to time to prevent too much moisture building up.

Make sure you have a ready supply of plants for next year – pot cuttings from perennials in late summer.

Use a clear plastic bag as a temporary greenhouse. Support it with sticks and secure with a rubber band.

If you use a propagator for seedlings, make sure you wipe the inside surface regularly to remove any condensation. Too much condensation cuts down the amount of light reaching the seedlings.

If the light levels are low where your seeds are growing, stand the pots of seedlings on kitchen foil so that they benefit from the reflected light.

To separate very small seedlings use an old fork to lift them and divide them carefully.

Settle small seeds into the compost by wetting them with a plant mister.

To test if the soil is warm enough for sowing gardeners of old would remove their trousers and sit on it. If you don't want to bare all, test the ground with your elbow as you would a baby's bath water.

To avoid disturbing the roots of plants roll newspaper strips into tubes. Fill with compost and moisten before sowing seeds into each one. Plant out the tubes and the roots will go down through the newspaper.

Sow lawn seeds using a plant pot with holes in the bottom as a shaker.

Once you've sown grass seed, gently rake over some soil to protect it from birds. This will help to give it a good start.

If you are planning to plant seeds with hard coats, soak them in water overnight. This will give them a head start when you plant them.

Always dry seeds before storing them; use paper towels or newspaper.

To avoid damping off in seed boxes always use seedling compost and never garden soil. Don't reuse compost either.

Collect seeds from flowers – it's a lot cheaper than going out and buying them in packets.

Cut up old magazines and make seed packets.

Empty film canisters make excellent containers for storing seeds.

Cover seed trays with clingfilm to prevent the compost from drying out while the seeds germinate.

Seed vegetables in the clean plastic containers from ready-cooked meals.

Instead of using pots or boxes to grow your seedlings, plant them in soil blocks. The advantage is that you can plant them straight out as soon as the roots emerge. Take a short length of plastic piping, 2–3 in wide. Find a glass bottle that fits inside snugly. Stand the tube on a flat surface and fill with compost mixture. Pound down with the bottle several times. Lift off with a twisting motion. You are left with a solid soil block.

Cover a piece of cardboard with silver foil and place it behind a seedling. The foil reflects light from the window onto the plants, helping them to grow.

Swap cuttings with other gardeners.

Nobody likes getting into a cold bed and seeds are no different. Warm the soil before you plant by putting a dustbin liner over the soil and holding it in place with stones.

Avoid sowing in cold, damp conditions – you don't want the seeds to rot before they've had a chance to start growing. Delay sowing until conditions improve.

▷▷ Planting

When you have divided your perennials, you may be left with spare sections of plants; use them in containers as well as other parts of the garden.

Always check the roots of a plant. If they are all knotted up and congested, soak the rootball in water for a few hours, tease the roots out and then plant it.

Before moving a plant, water the ground thoroughly for several days.

When moving a plant, tie up any loose stems or branches. This makes it easier to carry and reduces the risk of bits and pieces snapping off.

After moving a plant, cut back the foliage to reduce stress from moisture loss.

If there is a delay before replanting, wrap the roots in a plastic bag to retain moisture.

After transplanting an evergreen shrub, spray the foliage every day for two weeks.

Don't stick too rigidly to a planting timetable. Try sowing spring-sown annuals in the autumn. If it works, you can often get a much longer flowering period out of them.

Use annual climbers to cover a bare trellis while the slower growing plants get a chance to establish themselves.

Try growing a cutting from a shrub by bending a low branch over and pegging it into the ground. Within a few weeks, you can often find you've got a new plant growing apace.

Protect tender perennials from frost by lining a hanging basket with straw and placing it over the top of the plants.

Planting bulbs in baskets means you can easily lift them when they start to fade and leave them out of sight while the foliage dies down.

Plant bulbs under deciduous shrubs. They will flower and fill the bare patch of earth. When the shrub's in leaf, it will hide the dying plants.

A container for bulbs should have lots of holes for drainage. A pond basket is a good alternative.

New water plants often contain tiny duckweed plants which, once *in situ*, can multiply at an alarming rate. Always rinse all new pond plants under the tap before planting.

Always line the baskets of pond plants to keep soil round the roots. A bit of old sacking is just fine.

Adding floating plants to a pond not only makes it look attractive but will also help prevent the water getting too warm and give shelter to the pond's inhabitants.

Protect a young clematis by planting it several inches deeper than it was in its container and surround the base with a cylinder of cardboard or plastic to prevent slugs from nibbling at it. Put some grease round the top of the cylinder to stop slugs and snails from climbing over it.

You can give a new lease of life to a hawthorn hedge by bending some of the pliable stems down into the soil. Secure them using metal hooks. In time, they will take root and start to fill out the bottom of the hedge.

When planting against a brick wall, remember that the wall will take moisture from the soil so choose your plants accordingly (*aquifolium*, *Euonymus*, *Alchemilla mollis* are good choices).

Removing flowers and large leaves from a perennial when planting helps give it a good start in life and prevents moisture loss.

Check your insurance policy if you have window boxes or hanging baskets. Are you covered if they fall and damage someone or something?

Always push – never pull – your wheelbarrow; you have more control this way.

The best time to buy plants is in the spring because you can get a good idea of their health by checking their foliage.

When buying a plant, there's nothing wrong with taking the plant out of its pot and checking its root system.

Try not to buy plants that have moss, algae or weeds growing in their compost. This could mean that the plant's been in its pot too long.

When buying shrubs, look for young, small plants. They will grow more rapidly and establish themselves more successfully than larger shrubs … and they'll probably be cheaper too.

If you come across a shrub for sale that's been pruned in an odd fashion, don't touch it. It probably means that the plant was damaged in some way.

Don't buy new heather plants; just place a heap of cuttings compost in the centre of your old heather plant and moisten. New heather roots will start to form in about six months' time.

Bubble wrap is an effective way to insulate your greenhouse. With an aluminium frame use clips to attach the wrap and in a wooden greenhouse pin the wrap to the frame. Cover the ventilators separately so they can be opened.

To keep an eye on your greenhouse in winter place a small dish of water inside and you'll know when the temperature reaches freezing.

When sweeping up the leaves in autumn, first check which way the wind is blowing and then sweep with the wind.

When growing azaleas and rhododendrons, plant some foxgloves next to them. They help to keep the other plants healthy.

Cover yourself before moving a plant – take some cuttings just in case the move doesn't work.

When taking cuttings, put them in a plastic bag until you're ready to plant them up.

To stimulate a cutting and encourage root formation, cut a sliver of bark from one side of the cutting's base.

After trimming your garden hedge, leave the cuttings and then when you mow the lawn, the twigs and leaves can be collected with the grass cuttings.

Don't be too tidy – leave some areas for helpful garden animals to hide in.

If you have a piece of lawn that isn't doing too well, why not turn it into a wildflower area? Wildflowers love poor soils.

If you plant a wildflower area, don't fertilise the ground. Always wait until the flowers have set seed before cutting.

Don't replace a sick or dying plant with something similar. If you put the new shrub in the same spot, it may pick up the same disease.

Pinch out the tips of ivy to encourage bushiness.

Box is often used to edge lawns and paths. One problem is that, after trimming, it can smell a bit 'catty'. One remedy is to leave hard limestones in some water for three to four hours and then water the box with this water.

When storing bulbs, make sure they are kept dry. Put them on dry sand or newspaper so that they're not touching each other.

To check if a bulb is healthy give it a squeeze. It should be firm to the touch.

Some people are allergic to the scales on bulbs so wear gloves when handling hyacinth, iris, narcissus, bluebell and tulip bulbs.

Don't do too much digging and moving of plants in winter – you'll only run the risk of damaging their roots and your back. Wait until spring.

You can store a plant for a while before planting it. Evergreen shrubs and conifers can stay in a sheltered spot to protect them from extreme temperatures.

Bare root plants can be left in an unheated shed or garage for a few days before planting. Cover the roots loosely with an old sack or polythene bag so they don't dry out.

If you are planning to store a plant for a while, don't feed it. You want it to rest, not get all stimulated.

Transporting young plants can be difficult. Try using cereal boxes. Cut the box in half lengthwise. Punch a few holes in the bottom and then slip over the top of the seedling tray.

Protect a small plant from the sun by covering it with a large empty flowerpot before the temperature starts to rise.

▷▷ Gardening

Put soap under your fingernails before gardening. They'll be much easier to clean afterwards.

Get hands clean after a hard day's gardening with soap, water and sugar.

Stop your wooden water butt from splitting during a freeze – place a piece of wood in the barrel.

Age a new statue or pot by rubbing over with natural yoghurt. Within a few weeks algae and bacteria will have begun to 'age' it.

Don't blast dry compost out of hanging baskets when you water them in the summer. Place half a dozen ice cubes in a perforated food bag and place overnight in the hanging basket. By the morning, the plants will have been watered.

To make sure the soil in hanging baskets is properly watered, punch holes in empty yoghurt cartons and bury in the middle of the hanging baskets. The soil gets watered and doesn't run off the top.

Protect your arms when pruning old brambles or holly. Cut the top and bottom off a couple of old, plastic sweet jars and use as arm protectors.

When growing leeks, give them some stout to drink to stimulate their growth.

Encourage leeks to grow by applying soot to the soil.

▷▷ Weeds

Use an old potato peeler to dig up weeds from your lawn.

To slaughter stubborn weeds blast them with a mixture of gin and detergent.

To make your own funnel to administer weedkiller more easily, cut off the top of a plastic drinks bottle. You can then just throw it away after you've used it.

Make your own kneeling pad. Use your children's plastic sledge.

Alternatively, sew old shoulder pads inside your gardening trousers.

Use an old colander to remove algae from ponds.

A good way to prevent algae from growing in your pond is to stuff the leg of a pair of old tights with barley straw. Tie both ends securely, attach a weight to one end and then submerge in the pond.

Keep pond surfaces clear of fallen leaves. If you leave them, they can cause a build-up of toxic gases, which can kill fish and wildlife.

Use an old net curtain to cover your pond in winter. This will catch falling leaves for you. Shake it out regularly and then replace.

Blanket weed is best removed from your pond using a stick. Wind it round and round as if it were candyfloss.

To remove duckweed from a pond draw a plank vertically across the surface and then remove using an old colander or sieve.

Always bury duckweed in a hole, or put it in the dustbin or on the compost heap. It's a tough little plant and can spread easily.

Keep weeds down by planting up the gaps and cracks between pavingstones with seeds of hardy annuals.

Alternatively, ensure that the grouting between paving stones is done properly in the first place.

▷▷ Garden Pests

Protect your vegetable patch with an 'instant snake'. Take an old piece of garden hose, about the length of a snake and wind it on the ground around your plants. Cats and birds will stay away at the sight of a 'snake'.

Orange and grapefruit peel scattered around the garden will stop cats coming in – they hate the smell of citrus fruits.

Keep cats off your garden with a judicious sprinkling of pepper.

Keep pests out of the shed and house – spray insect repellent across the edge of the door and along the window-sill.

When the birds have flown, take down their nest and either throw it away or burn it. Nests are great places for insects to live.

Stop slugs and snails in their tracks. Smear petroleum jelly on the rim of a flowerpot to stop your plants getting attacked.

Half a grapefruit left upside down, with the cut surface on the ground, makes a great slug trap.

Deter slugs by scattering crushed eggshells around your tender plants. Slugs hate to crawl over such a rough surface.

Slug pubs are a great bait. Cut slug-sized holes in the lid of a cottage cheese tub, fill it with beer and sink it into the ground. Slugs will be attracted to the beer, and drown in it.

Mix up your own insect spray from a mixture of water and a little washing-up liquid.

To get rid of pests from plants, spray with garlic tea. To make the tea, infuse garlic cloves in hot water and leave to stand for half an hour before using.

Clear flying insects and their eggs from your greenhouse – use a vacuum cleaner.

Rhubarb leaves help to deter pests.

Protect your carrots by sprinkling coffee granules around them.

Leave your rose prunings on the ground; rabbits and cats don't like a prickly surface.

Keep greenfly down – put on some rubber gloves and go and squash them.

Sink empty bottles up to their necks in the garden. Moles don't like the sound of the wind across the empty tops.

Stick a child's windmill in the ground near a mole's run; it causes vibrations to run down the stem and into the run which disturbs the mole.

Deter moles by lining the bottom of their run with gorse. Moles hate having their noses pricked.

A 5 in/13 cm square of carpet underlay placed around your cabbages protects them from the root fly maggot.

Grow carnivorous plants in the greenhouse – it's one way to keep pests at bay!

Wave goodbye to slugs by smearing lettuce or cabbage leaves with lard and leave dotted around the garden. When they are covered with slugs, pick them up and throw them away.

Slugs don't like strands of horse hair rope laid across the soil surface.

Holly twigs are also a slug deterrent.

Encourage frogs and toads into the garden; they love slugs. Victorian gardeners used to keep a couple of toads in the green-house to keep down the slug population.

Protect delicate seedlings from slugs by surrounding them with the cardboard centres of loo rolls or milk cartons with the top and bottom cut off.

Garden pests can be controlled using Jeyes fluid. Pop some in your spray bottle and use on blackfly and greenfly.

Alternatively, use Jeyes fluid in your watering can to combat slugs and snails.

If you are plagued by blackfly, just sprinkle some soil from the base of the plant over the pests.

When using weedkiller, be careful not to get any on your boots or gardening shoes. You don't want to tramp it all over the garden.

To catch codling moths wrap a piece of old sacking round the trunk of an apple tree in the summer. The moths crawl into the sacking and you can then take it down and burn it.

A bruised garlic clove left at the entrance of a wasp's nest will clear it.

Protect carrot plants from carrot flies by surrounding them with a fence, 2 ft high, made of polythene or old bin liners. Carrot flies aren't high flyers and so won't be able to clear the fence.

Exposed colonies of mealy bugs can be treated by touching them with a cottonwool bud dipped in methylated spirits. Repeat when necessary.

To control clubroot insert a small stick of rhubarb into the planting hole.

To avoid Phlox eelworm take root cuttings – this pest doesn't enter by the roots.

Alternatively place eggshells in the hole.

A handful of soot should also do the trick.

Protect the bark of young trees from rabbits by wrapping a 'skirt' of chicken wire round the tree. Check that it doesn't restrict the tree as it grows.

To keep rabbits out of your garden remember:

> R   *Rosemary*
>
> A   *Azaleas*
>
> B   *Bluebells*
>
> B   *Box*
>
> I   *Iris*
>
> T   *Tulips*
>
> B   *Bay*
>
> A   *Asters*
>
> N   *Nasturtiums*

The red spider mite loves hot, dry conditions so make sure you wet the floor of your greenhouse several times a day. This increases the humidity and lowers the overall temperature.

Get rid of wire worms which can attack root vegetables by making traps. Cut potatoes into pieces and put on a wooden skewer. Bury the chunks in the ground, leaving enough of the skewer above ground to act as a marker.

To prevent aphids from attacking your apple trees, grow nasturtiums up the trunk.

Aphids can wreck plants in hanging baskets. Spray the baskets with soapy water to kill off the aphids.

Flea beetles can cause a lot of damage. To get rid of them smear a piece of bright yellow card (flea beetles *love* yellow) with grease and leave by the threatened plants.

Not all creepy crawlies are pests. Many insects will help you wage war against pests so encourage them. Ladybirds, spiders, lacewings, hoverflies, centipedes, ground beetles, many birds and wasps are friends of the gardener.

Insects hate the smell of lemongrass, melissa, eucalyptus, tea tree and citronella. Use them (in the form of essential oils) when eating outside in the summer.

Pots of basil will keep whitefly at bay in the greenhouse.

Stop twigs, leaves and other bits and pieces from getting into your water butt by securely fixing a pair of old tights to the end of the downpipe. Clear out regularly, especially after heavy rainfall.

A water butt should be kept clear of algae. Scrub it out with a stiff, long-handled brush and soapy water.

Make sure you can get a watering can under the tap of a water butt. Raise the butt off the ground using some old bricks if necessary.

Tap water is fine for most plants. However, if you live in an area with a high lime content, boil the water first, particularly if you have a lot of lime-hating plants (like azaleas).

Don't use water that has been put through a water filter because the chemicals in the filter can damage your plants.

For drainage in window boxes use small pine cones. They are great lightweight drainage material.

Poke four holes into the bottom of a plastic milk bottle and bury it half way. Plant your cucumber seeds around the outside. When you need to water or fertilise, fill up the jug. The moisture will go straight to the roots without wetting the foliage.

Watering is required every five to seven days during a period of drought in summer. There's no need to water every day or two just because the plants droop or are not growing.

Don't waste time and energy watering lawns. They can be left for longer.

When you do water a dry lawn, spike it with a fork to ensure the water runs down to the roots rather than evaporates on the surface.

A sign of overwatering is if moss starts to grow on top of the potting compost.

If you have overwatered a potted plant, take it out of its pot and repot it using fresh potting mixture. Mix in some sand to help with drainage.

To rescue a parched potted plant break up the potting mixture slightly with a fork (being careful not to damage the roots). Put the pot in a bowl of water until bubbles stop rising to the surface. Spray the leaves with a plant spray. Drain and leave in a cool place.

Be careful when watering plants in a greenhouse or on a window-sill. A drop of water on a leaf can act like a magnifying glass and cause damage to the plant. Try to water in the early morning or avoid getting water on the leaves.

Never pour water directly into the tuber of a Florist's cyclamen; just immerse the pot in water for 15 minutes.

Keep moisture in a hanging basket by placing an old saucer in the base of the basket when planting up.

If the compost in a hanging basket has dried out so much that water just runs off it, add a few drops of washing-up liquid to the water. The water will then be able to penetrate the surface.

Alternatively, take down the hanging basket and put it in a bowl of water until the compost becomes moist.

To avoid lifting heavy watering cans up to hanging baskets use a 1-litre plastic bottle – it contains just about the right amount of water for the task.

Save water. Put pots under hanging baskets to catch any overspill of water.

To check if you've had the sprinkler on long enough put an empty jam jar by the sprinkler. When there's an inch of water in the bottom, it's time to move the sprinkler.

▷▷ Flowers and House Plants

Cut, hollow–stemmed flowers last longer if you turn them upside down and fill the stem with water.

Bring the shine back to dusty house plants by wiping the leaves with a mixture of milk and water.

To keep cacti dust-free, brush gently every week with a pastry brush.

If you've bought decorative plant pots with no drainage holes line the base with a lot of gravel.

To stop soil from leaking out of pots, line the base with some coffee filter paper.

▷▷ Compost and Fertiliser

Urine is a great fertiliser if you dilute it 10 to 1.

When you clean your coffee-maker, sprinkle a thin layer of coffee grounds on to the soil surfaces of your potted plants. As the coffee grounds are high in nitrogen and other nutrients, they will decompose into a slightly acid-forming nutrient source.

Pigeon poo, rabbit and goat droppings all make good compost activators.

If you're friendly with a brewery, try getting some of their spent hops to use as a soil conditioner. Use them as mulch or compost.

Gardeners living near the sea have a ready source of rich fertiliser. Seaweed can be used straight away or put into the compost heap.

Collect sheep droppings in a hessian sack, then suspend the sack in a barrel of water. Use the water as liquid fertiliser.

To improve the texture of the soil add a handful of chopped bracken when planting. Bracken is slightly acidic, so don't use with lime-loving plants.

Leaf mould, cocoa fibre and organic matter will all improve the soil's moisture retention, drainage and texture.

Make your own leaf mould. Collect the leaves and put them in a large bin bag. Make some holes in the side of the bag and fold the top over. Weigh down with a brick and leave for six to twelve months.

Apply humus mulch at the right time – when the soil is warm and moist. May is ideal.

Keep grass cuttings. Throw them on to the compost heap (or into a black bag) and cover with a piece of carpet until they've mulched down.

To preserve nutrients in grass only cut the top third of the grass and leave the other two-thirds; that way, the grass keeps its nutrients and doesn't die.

An inexpensive alternative to mulch is to lay wet newspaper on to wet soil round a shrub. Cover with soil to disguise it.

Use hedge trimmings in compost, but don't put them into a compost heap if you know that the hedge is diseased.

Don't feed a plant if it's been suffering from lack of water. It won't be able to absorb the fertiliser properly.

Alternatively, use chicken wire held in place by wooden stakes. Cover it with a piece of old carpet.

Natural fibre knitted items such as jumpers and cardigans can be cut up and added to your compost. Don't use your Mum's cashmere sweater though.

Old carpet can be used in compost as well as an effective lid on your compost heap. Chop it up into small squares.

Alternatively, old feather pillows make a good compost ingredient.

Always layer your compost. Try not to add too much of any ingredient at one time and try to alternate a moist ingredient (like grass clippings) with something drier.

Accelerate your compost by mixing green manure into it.

Alternatively, put some fresh horse manure in your compost and you'll soon be rewarded with wonderful organic compost.

If the weather gets hot, give your compost a drink of water. This encourages the ingredients to break down.

When it's cold, make sure your compost wraps up nice and warm. If it gets too cold, it won't rot down.

To construct your own composter put some holes in the side and base of an old dustbin, and stand it on some bricks for drainage.

Make sure you put some carbon in your compost such as cereal packets, egg boxes and so on which will give the compost some bulk.

Create a cheap mulch for the garden by shredding any left-over bits of wood.

Using peat is not environmentally friendly, so investigate the alternatives.

To encourage geranium growth keep all your eggshells in a bucket of water. After a few weeks remove the eggshells and water your geraniums with this liquid.

Put crushed eggshells in the bottom of a planting hole for extra calcium. Eggshells are alkaline, so don't use for plants that like acid soil.

Make your own liquid fertiliser from nettles. Put freshly picked nettles into a large bucket. Cover with water (around 18 pints of water to 2lbs of nettles) and seal with clingfilm. Leave for a few weeks, stirring now and again. When the nettles have rotted down, strain the mixture into a bucket. Dilute the liquid with water about ten times before using.

Alternatively, soak nettles together with thistles for a few months and use that as a fertiliser.

If you can't be bothered to dig in organic matter, spread it over the soil in the autumn and leave the winter weather to break it down for you.

Improve the texture of your soil by digging in coarse sand and gravel. Avoid using builder's sand because it can contain harmful contaminants.

If you want to improve the alkalinity of your soil, use mushroom compost.

Try not to walk on frost-covered grass because you can damage the blades which make it vulnerable to disease.

▷▷ Fruit

Don't plant potatoes too near your apple trees – they just don't get on together.

Peeing on your apple trees (especially if old men are doing the watering) is said to encourage fruiting.

Plum trees thrive on a mixture of urine, left-over wine and some water.

Beating a tree is a sure fire way to encourage fruit growth.

To grow an apple tree from a pip half fill a plastic food container with damp compost and put several pips in it. Put the lid on, place somewhere warm (like an airing cupboard) and leave for several weeks.

Alternatively, drop all your apple cores in a chosen spot in the garden. Cover them with compost occasionally and eventually one will start to grow.

To protect peach trees from leaf curl grow garlic at the base of the trunk.

Put saucers of water under gooseberry bushes to keep the atmosphere moist.

Gooseberries grow well from hardwood cuttings.

Remove fruit or berry stains from your hands by rubbing them with lemon juice.

Melon seeds should be kept in a warm place for 6–8 hours before sowing.

To freeze fruit use the waxed paper from the inside of cereal packets to line the trays.

To get rid of freckles follow this old recipe. Take a pint of white wine vinegar and put it into a glass with 6 oak apples and a few elder leaves. Set it in the sun and wash your face with the mixture.

▷▷ Vegetables

When sowing vegetable seeds, put two seeds in each hole to allow for poor germination. Thin if more than one seed starts to grow.

To kick-start parsnip, early carrots, onions and parsley sow the seeds on damp kitchen paper. Leave somewhere warm until they germinate. When the roots emerge, wash the seeds in a sieve and then mix into wallpaper paste. Prepare a small trench in your vegetable plot. Fill a plastic bag with the wallpaper mix and cut the corner off. Go along the trench, squeezing out the paste and seeds as if you were icing a cake.

You can save space by sowing two different crops in a single row. Mix a slow-growing crop such as parsnips or carrots with something faster such as lettuces and radishes.

In addition, you can save space by growing trailing varieties of marrow and squash up an arch or pergola.

Use newspapers to line a bean trench before filling up with compost and soil. This helps retain moisture, especially if there's a dry spell, while the rotting paper will feed the roots.

Pigeon or poultry dung in your asparagus beds will help the vegetables grow to a larger than average size.

Keep onions away from runner beans.

Peas and beans will increase the nitrogen levels in the soil, so include them in your planting scheme.

Remember to cut peas and beans down to ground level once they have finished cropping. Leave the roots to add nourishment to the soil.

Peas and beans don't like garlic (maybe they're closet vampires), so never plant them next to each other.

A pair of old tights slipped over a marrow will protect it from the birds.

Make a trench alongside your rows of vegetables. Water into the trench so that the moisture gets down to the roots.

To water long rows of vegetables lay plastic guttering between the rows. Make small holes along its length. Pour water into the guttering.

Always water vegetables in the evening.

Don't grow large areas of vegetables. It's like hanging up a neon sign to pests saying, 'Come and eat me.' Grow small areas, interspersed with other plants and vegetables.

The simplest way of storing carrots, beetroot and swedes is to leave them in the ground. Lay some straw down for frost protection in the colder months.

When you've harvested your cabbages, leave the stumps to grow again. Cut them at an angle so that the rain and snow won't settle and start to rot what's left.

Cabbage can stink when it's being cooked. A bay leaf added to the boiling water will stop the smell without affecting the taste of the vegetables.

Carrots are easier to scrape if dunked in boiling water first.

To cook delicious broad beans add some chopped parsley to the water.

If your hands smell of onions, soak them in some milk.

There's no need to use a sticking plaster when you cut yourself. Press the inside of a clear onion skin onto the cut. Leave it there for as long as you can. Onion is a natural antiseptic.

Store onions and garlic in the foot of some sheer tights to keep them dry and fresh.

▷▷ Tools of the Trade

Make a kneeling mat out of an old hot waterbottle stuffed with bits of material.

Put a couple of drops of food colouring into your rain gauge to make it easier to read.

Turn your electric drill into a bulb planter with extra large drill bits. Use a 2 1/4 in wide bit for small bulbs, try a 2 1/2 in for medium bulbs, and a 3 in wide bit for larger bulbs.

To make the handle of your spade or fork more comfortable to hold, put a small section of pipe-insulating foam over the handle. Hold it in place with some insulating tape.

Make your own dibber. Use a broken fork handle or a couple of bits of wood screwed together in the shape of a T.

To make a cheap cold frame get a wooden apple box and cover with a rigid piece of plastic held in place with twine or a strong elastic band. To shade the contents, use a piece of greenhouse shade netting or an old onion bag.

If you have an external tap, make sure it doesn't drip. The water can encourage algae growth which can cause unattractive green marks and dangerous slippery patches.

Keep the tyres of your wheelbarrow free of mud. If you allow mud to build up, it could conceal sharp stones that may cause a puncture.

If your soil is heavy, stand on a board when digging it to avoid compacting it further.

If you have clay soil, use a fork, not a spade. A spade can seal the edges and make it hard for water to drain through.

Use a staple gun to fix climbing plants to a fence.

The best support for clematis is nylon wire wrapped round sheds, posts and tree trunks.

Hang an old curtain over the shed door to keep out draughts.

To keep warm while you're working in the garden, wear lots of thin layers rather than a few bulky ones. You can take layers off as you wish.

It's more hygienic if the layer next to your skin is cotton.

Add a drop of brandy to your watering can so that you can be sure your lawn comes up half cut.

Clean grubby nails with minty toothpaste (this is especially effective for smokers).

Always protect your hands – wear gloves.

Salt baths help to heal any wounds or scratches on the skin. Add a cup of salt to the bath water.

Don't wash your hands in very hot water because it strips the skin of its natural oils. Warm water and a gentle soap are just as effective. Always apply hand cream after you've got your hands wet.

If your hands become stained or discoloured, rub the skin with half a lemon. Rinse off and dry your hands carefully, then massage in some hand cream, because lemon has a drying effect on the skin.

For heavy duty hand cream, mix virgin olive oil and petroleum jelly together. Rub the mixture into your hands and then put them in freezer bags. Sit and have a cuppa or read the paper while your hands absorb this perfect conditioner.

If you've been on your feet all day, give them a treat. A cup of baking soda or Epsom salts dissolved in a bowl of warm water makes a wonderful foot bath.

Try not to wear wellies for any great length of time. Your feet won't benefit from it and they'll smell awful as well.

An old American recipe for waterproofing gardener's boots:
1 pint of boiled linseed oil, 1/2lb mutton suet, 6 oz clean beeswax,
4 oz resin. Melt them down and mix together. While the mixture
is still warm, brush on to new boots or shoes which are dry and
clean.

Sitting on the ground or stone can be wet and cold. Make your
own insulated cushion from a sheet of kitchen foil sandwiched
between two pieces of foam.

▷ See also **Landscape Gardeners**

▶▶▶ Golfers

Dennis Sheehy; Martin Tyson, Dainton Park Golf Club; Jamie Waugh, Dartmouth
Golf Club; Simon Lloyd, Bigbury Golf Club; Owen Mckenna, Elsenham Golf Club,
Stansted; Joan Walsh, Finham Golf Club; Pam Dick, Finham Golf Club

▷▷ Clothing

Your gloves should be kept in mint condition at all times. Golf
gloves are made from first-class leather and cost a lot of money so
keep them in a small plastic bag when not in use.

Retain the shape of your gloves – store them with a golf ball
inside.

Keep a grip in wet weather, try wearing rubber gloves! The other
players will soon stop laughing once they see you beating them.

Jewellery can get in the way while you're playing. Put a loop on
your golf bag to thread your jewellery on so you don't lose it.

Use different-coloured balls for practising chipping. This helps you to keep track of which ball is which . . . remember, you should be keeping your head down all the time!

Pick up your metal markers using a magnet stuck to the end of a club. Put the markers at the top of your bag so you know where they are when you need one.

▷▷ Clubs

To clean the grooves in your clubs, use an old toothbrush.

Smart wooden clubs can soon look shoddy when the paint becomes chipped. Instead of buying expensive paints, try applying two layers of permanent marker pen – first black, then red – which together make a lovely deep brown. Seal with a varnish and your clubs will look the part for ages.

A left-handed club is a useful addition to your golf bag. Use it when you're up against an object and can't use your right-handed clubs. If you're left-handed, read this trade secret back to front!

▷▷ Playing

Bunker shots aren't really difficult! It's all psychological. Here's a cracking idea to overcome those bunker fears: just imagine the ball is a fried egg and you're trying to scoop it out without breaking the yolk.

Improve the pressure of your golf swing by driving a heavy piece of wood along the floor. The resistance will build muscle.

Perfect your swing – stand in front of patio doors. Put masking tape in a V-shape on the window; it should have a 45° angle in the point of the V. Your swing should begin and end parallel to the V-shape.

Practise chipping at home – just invert a tee on the carpet and try to chip it up.

To get your putt straight, practise putting along the skirting board at home.

It's important not to let your legs collapse when hitting a golf ball – try practising with a beach ball between your knees. You mustn't let it go when you hit the ball.

To stop yourself bending your arm at the elbow during shots take a 2-litre Coca-Cola bottle and cut the top and bottom off. Slice down the side of the remaining middle section and place it over your elbow. This will prevent you from bending your arm.

Don't bend your wrists when putting. Pop a comb or ruler under your wrist-watch and you won't be able to.

Teach yourself to stand up straight and still. Place your golf bag on the side you have a tendency to sway towards. Then if you do sway that way, you will knock the bag over.

Keep your balance when driving off – stand on concrete while wearing spiked golfing shoes. This will force you to keep upright and well-balanced.

To make sure you stand on the balls of your feet and don't move around, practise standing on two bricks.

If you want to mark your ball when you are out on the course, scratch some of the paint off the ball with a wooden tee-peg.

Make your own tee that will stand up in the windiest weather – snip off a 2-in/5-cm length of hosepipe.

If you wear your glove on your left hand, put your tees in your right-hand pocket. They will be easier to get out.

When the ground is frozen, use a plastic bottle top as a tee.

Professionals never play with their arms too close to their body. Practise swinging wearing a couple of blow-up arm bands and you'll soon look like a pro – at least you will once you've taken the arm bands off!

Keep your head down. It's disastrous to look up when putting, even after you've hit the ball. Try perfecting your putting on a carpet. Put a coin under the ball and, even after you've made your stroke, keep staring at the coin.

Save your lawn from ugly divots – practise on a door mat.

To keep your score use a knitting counter. This is especially useful for beginners.

It's never too early to start – ask a pro to cut down a club for toddlers to practise swinging with.

►►► Graphic Designers

Gary Beard; David Mason

To look after your computer – keep it out of direct sunlight.

For security reasons, keep your computer, printer and scanner away from the window. You don't want people to see all the equipment you've got.

When travelling, always protect your work. Make sure you carry it in a waterproof container.

To ensure that you are always relaxed when working, arrange your desk and chair so that you have easy access to everything you need.

To remove glue from a piece of artwork, you don't need to buy expensive art-shop equipment. Lighter fuel does just as well.

To remember where and what colour your ink pens are, stain MDF boxes the appropriate colour and fill with your pens.

To blank out a mark between two pieces of white paper, place a bit of black paper in the gap and the mark disappears.

▶▶▶ Greengrocers

Robin Blair, J. J. Blair; Connie Lucas

To find out if a Cox's apple is ready to eat, shake it. If the pips rattle, it's perfect.

When buying Golden Delicious apples, choose the ones with more brown spots on the skin. The more spots, the more flavour.

To peel apples in half the time, blanch them first in boiling water.

Make great teethers for babies using dried apple rings.

Stop cut apples from going brown – sprinkle with lemon juice.

Don't lose all the filling when cooking baked apples – before you put them in the oven, plug the top of the hole with a little piece of marzipan.

To stop fruit in a bowl going mouldy, place a piece of kitchen roll in the bottom. It absorbs all the moisture.

Bounce your cranberries to find out if they are fresh or not. If they bounce, they are!

To trim gooseberries, use baby nail clippers.

When choosing lemons and oranges, always go for the fruit that feels too heavy for its size.

If you need to keep lemons fresh for a long time, store them covered in cold water.

Old, wrinkly lemons can be restored to their former glory by boiling them in water for a few minutes, then leaving to cool.

If your lemons are overripe, squeeze the juice into hot water and use this to clean your windows.

Before you grate citrus fruit, rinse the grater in cold water. After use, the peel will come away from the grater much more easily.

Citrus peel makes a barbecue smell great and helps to get it going.

Oranges look much prettier in fruit salad if you can remove the white pith. To make it easy, soak the fruit in boiling water before you peel off the skin and the pith should come away, too.

For fruit salad with a difference, use lemonade instead of fruit juices. For a celebration, try Champagne instead.

To chop dried fruit wet the blade of the knife so the fruit doesn't stick to it.

Dry orange peel in the oven to make useful firelighters.

If you suffer from constipation, a couple of drops of linseed oil in orange juice will help get things moving.

To stop bananas from turning black in a fruit salad, cover the unpeeled fruit with cold water for 10 or 15 minutes before peeling.

Rhubarb is a great blood purifier.

Don't always buy with your eyes – the more crinkly the skin on a honeydew melon, the sweeter it will be inside.

To ripen tomatoes quickly, place them in a brown paper bag along with one ripe tomato.

Don't store tomatoes in a fridge because they will blister.

Make your lettuce last longer by cutting out the core and sprinkling sugar into the cavity.

Tear lettuce instead of cutting it to avoid the leaves turning brown.

It doesn't have to end in tears. Store an onion in the fridge for several hours before using and you won't cry when you peel it.

The more wrinkled a red pepper is, the sweeter and riper the taste.

Store mushrooms in a paper bag to stop them sweating.

Freeze parsley on its stem in a clear plastic bag. When you need it, remove it from the freezer and rub it between your fingers. Your parsley is automatically chopped.

To keep watercress fresh for longer, immerse the leaves – but not the roots – in a jug of water.

Freshen up bad breath instantly by chewing two or three sprigs of watercress and a couple of grapes.

To keep water fresh, put a watercress leaf into a jug before filling with water.

To get rid of garlic breath, chew some parsley.

Keep flies away – place fresh mint on the kitchen window-sill.

Avocado pears make excellent face masks. Just mash them up and smear them on for that perfect complexion.

When buying cabbage, check its bottom. If it's too white, don't buy it – it's a sign that the leaves and root have been trimmed off.

Always buy broccoli with tight heads – this way they won't drop off when you cook them.

Look out for really purple turnips – the more purple the turnip, the better it will taste.

Aubergines can be either male or female – both taste equally good.

Add herbs to your barbecue for even sweeter aromas.

Prevent car sickness – chew some crystallised ginger.

If you smoke but want to kick the habit, try chewing on liquorice root.

Ease painful indigestion – drop cardamom pods into your coffee.

►►► Hairdressers & Barbers

Errol Douglas; Paula Jerem, Mad P; Daniel Field, Organic & Mineral Hairdresser;
Dominic Flynn, Capelli; Ian Matthews, Geo F. Trumper

If you usually don't have time to blow dry your hair at home, don't let your hairdresser do it after a cut either. Let it dry on its own to test whether you're happy with the basic cut.

If your funds are limited, spend all you have on one really good cut rather than all the fancy (and overpriced) products on the market.

If your hair is thinning, have a shorter, blunter cut to give the illusion of thickness.

Body shampoo is just as good as hair shampoo – and half the price.

If you run out of hair conditioner, fabric conditioner will do just as well.

Detangle knotty hair – just comb some lemonade through it.

If you have long, lank hair, try drying it with your head upside down to get more lift and body.

To straighten out your curls, spread your hair between some brown paper and get a friend to smooth it down using a cool iron.

Make your own styling wax – use petroleum jelly.

For an alternative setting lotion, use pale ale.

To give your hair a firm hold use sugared water.

For the ultimate beehive, nothing works better than egg white.

Fancy hairstyles can be held in place with a little discreet sticky tape.

After a dye job, you can remove stains from your skin by rubbing with cotton wool dipped in milk.

Dyed blonde hair often turns slightly green after swimming. Retrieve your bombshell glory by rubbing in some tomato ketchup and then rinsing your hair.

When colouring with henna, you could add some coffee, tea or red wine to enhance and deepen the colour.

If you are getting the odd grey hair, don't bother to dye your whole head, just cover up the offending hairs with a mascara wand.

To ease itching caused by dandruff or a dry scalp, soak some dried thyme and sage in warm water and use it as a final rinse.

Don't buy expensive dandruff shampoos – just add some olive oil to your conditioner.

To stop dandruff proliferating, soak your comb in vinegar.

Hair is more fragile when wet, so be careful when brushing after washing. Using a wide-toothed comb helps to minimise the damage.

Heal and prevent split ends by rubbing corn oil into your hair, making sure the ends are covered. Leave on for several minutes, then rinse your hair.

Reduce split ends by using a pure bristle brush.

Give your hair a really deep condition by massaging in lots of mayonnaise and then leaving it on for 10 minutes before rinsing off.

If your hair is brittle, mix two eggs with a dash of warm oil and massage in. Leave for about 10 minutes and then rinse out.

Most conditioners work better if left on for a 20-minute soak.

To make your own conditioner mash up an avocado and smear over your hair and scalp. Leave for at least 10 to 15 minutes and then wash off.

For extra shine, add a spoonful of honey to your conditioner. Or you could try a teaspoonful of vinegar mixed in with your conditioner.

To give your hair a treat, warm a couple of tablespoons of olive or almond oil in a cup (more if your hair is very long). Rub into your hair and then wrap your head in clingfilm. Cover with a warm towel and leave for at least half an hour, but much longer if you can manage it – try not to answer the door! Shampoo and rinse.

To cut children's hair without tears or mistakes, trim the ends while they're asleep.

If cutting children's hair when they're awake, try putting them in front of a fish tank – it should hold their attention.

Alternatively, draw a blank face on a piece of paper. As you cut your child's hair, get them to stick the cut pieces around the face on the paper.

Use an old tie to hold hair ornaments and scrunchies.

Make your own hair curlers – use old toilet roll tubes for big curls.

Make your own egg shampoo by mixing two eggs and half an eggshell of olive oil. Just massage into your scalp and rinse thoroughly.

Don't pile long hair on top of your head when washing. It will cause it to tangle. Instead wash hair hanging straight down.

Olive oil makes a fabulous conditioner. Rub some through your hair, then wrap a warm towel around. Put your feet up and relax for 10 minutes, then shampoo out.

If you suffer from dandruff, place one teaspoon of parsley and an egg in a cup and beat together. Massage into your hair and leave for 5 minutes, then rinse out thoroughly.

Another good cure for dandruff is to put about ten or twelve stinging nettle heads into a bowl. Pour boiling water over them and leave to cool. Strain so that any bits are removed. The left-over liquid can be used as a final rinse after shampooing.

▷▷ Shaving

No shaving foam? Use peanut butter if you don't have anything else. Or you could smear on some olive oil.

Take your shower or bath before you shave to soften up the bristles. If you don't have time for full ablutions, try pressing a warm flannel against your stubble instead.

Don't put shaving foam all over your brush because you'll end up with far too much. Instead, separate the bristles and put a little foam inside and then close the bristles round the foam. This way, you'll get the amount you need gently released as you apply the foam.

If you have a rather broad face, shave a concave line under the chin to make your face look thinner.

To sharpen razor blades press the blade flat against the inside of a glass and move it firmly backwards and forwards. The glass will sharpen the metal edges so you'll always have a perfect blade.

For a silky-smooth, kissable chin, first shave down with the grain, then a second time against the grain.

After shaving, rinse thoroughly in cold water to close up your pores.

▶▶▶ Herbalists

Christopher Robbins

For a bath-time treat, make your own herbal infusion. Put dried herbs in a muslin bag (you can use fresh herbs but these are not as concentrated as dried ones), tie it to the hot-water tap so that the water flows over and through the bag. When the bath is ready, put the bag in the water and leave it to float around while you bathe.

For a reviving bath, use herbs such as mint, thyme, nettles (to boost circulation), and pine (which is refreshing).

For a relaxing bath, use lavender, marjoram (a great natural tranquilliser), sage (an antidote for stress) and lemon balm (which relieves tension).

To make your own herb tea, put one small handful of the fresh herb or one heaped teaspoon of the dried herb in a cup of boiling water. Leave to stand for about 5–10 minutes. Strain and then drink the tea while it's still hot.

Soothe a nasty sore throat – try gargling with tea made from sage leaves (you can buy them from most supermarkets).

To fight the onslaught of a cold, use rose-hip berries. Crush the berries and then pour on boiling water. It makes delicious tea.

To make your own poultice it's best to use powdered herbs. Mix them up into a paste with hot water. Put the mixture on to some muslin or a sterile dressing and place on the affected area.

For a restful night, drink some camomile tea before bed. It's a good idea to make a hop pillow, too; just get some dried hops and sew into a muslin bag.

To reduce travel sickness or morning sickness, try camomile, fennel or ginger tea.

To get rid of warts, rub them with the milky sap from the stalk of a dandelion.

Combat acne with some comfrey or marigold ointment. Dabbing on lemon juice and garlic also helps to dry up spots.

Feeling bruised and battered? A comfrey or arnica poultice will help keep bruises down (don't apply arnica to broken skin).

For indigestion, make up some camomile or marigold tea. If your indigestion is of a 'windy' nature, try fennel or peppermint tea. Meadowsweet tea will bring quick relief.

If you are suffering from toothache, try sucking on a clove next to the bad tooth (or put a drop of clove oil on to the tooth). Take sage tea as a mouthwash if your gums are bleeding; if they become infected, suck a clove of garlic. Sage tea is also good dabbed on to mouth ulcers.

Colds and flu don't like peppermint and elderflower tea. If you have a headache as well, add some limeflowers.

When you have a really bad cough eat loads of garlic. Elderflower and thyme tea will also help ease the cough and make breathing easier.

If you're bunged up with a bad cold, try inhaling the steam from thyme and peppermint tea. Put your head over a bowl of the tea, cover your head with a towel and breathe deeply.

If you're really blocked solid, try sniffing some salt water or beetroot juice up your nose through a straw. It sounds disgusting, but it can move the blockage and bring relief.

Bunged up at the other end? Try dandelion root tea to get things moving again. Increase your intake of fibre as well.

An alternative antiseptic cream can be made from thyme leaves, scraped off the stem and then crushed on a board. Apply this paste to the affected area.

For sore breasts make up a camomile poultice. Put 2 tablespoons of camomile flowers into a mug of boiling water and leave it to stand for about 10 minutes. Soak a flannel in the tea, then hold it gently on the affected area. Leave until the flannel has cooled.

If your nipples are sore from breastfeeding, you can put on marigold ointment, but you should wipe it off carefully before feeding your baby.

If you suffer from hay fever, try drinking a mixture of equal parts of elderflower and nettle tea.

When your chilblains get really bad, squeeze fresh root ginger or lemon juice over the unbroken skin. If you eat a lot of garlic, you will help to improve your circulation as well.

To get rid of nasty splinters, mash up some bread and mix with water to make a gooey paste. Apply to the splinter which should then be drawn out by the paste.

After a bee sting, crush some marigold petals on the affected area.

To soothe a bite or sting, rub some fresh sage leaves on it.

To speed up the repair of broken bones, take comfrey.

Make your own toothpaste. Take some juniper twigs and leaves that are full of sap. Dry them in the airing cupboard. Place them on a large metal tray and set fire to them. The resulting ash can be used to clean your teeth.

A good cure for dandruff is to put 10 to 12 stinging nettle heads into a bowl. Pour boiling water over them and leave to cool. Strain, and use the left-over liquid as a final rinse after shampooing.

A natural way of darkening one's hair is to get a large handful of sage leaves, cover with a teaspoon of borax and half a pint of boiling water. Leave until cold, then apply carefully to your hair with a brush.

If you run out of starch and you've got bluebells in your garden, you can use the juice from the white part of the stems as a substitute.

For a natural dye, use elderberry leaves for green, the flowers for yellow and the berries for purple.

Put marigold flowers into your bath water to soften the water.

When planting herbs in a container, plant frost-tender herbs in their own pot so you can easily replace them if they succumb to the bad weather.

To cut lavender for drying, trim the stalks as the buds open or cut back after flowers have faded. Lightly prune the whole bush at the same time.

Rosemary needs regular trimming.

Mint can run amok if not kept under control. Plant it in its own container.

Camomile lawns are wonderful and give off a fabulous scent when crushed under foot. They need weeding by hand and like an open, sunny space.

Thyme lawns are a good idea if you want to cover an uneven, sunny area.

Use the flowers of chives and pansies in salads to give colour.

Presentation is everything. Some fresh herbs sprinkled on top of the most ordinary looking dish will turn it into something special.

Make sure your parsley stays green – only add it to a sauce once the liquid has boiled.

To clean up any spills in the oven sprinkle some salt and cinnamon over the spill. This stops the house from filling with that acrid, smoky smell and the spill will be easy to lift off with a spatula.

If you get a bit too much sun, dab some sage tea on to your skin.

Sage helps to relieve sore throats.

For a soothing hand lotion soak marigold petals in almond oil for a couple of weeks.

Plant camomile next to sickly plants to perk them up.

Combat acne with some comfrey or marigold ointment. Dabbing on lemon juice and garlic also helps to dry up spots.

Fennel seeds are good at combating excessive flatulence.

Feverfew can help to reduce migraine attacks. Pop a few young leaves into a sandwich on a regular basis. Feverfew should not be taken by pregnant women.

▶▶▶ Home Safety Officers

Helen Richardson, Child Accident Prevention Trust; Cindy Allen; Linda Milne; James Black; Jo Downie; Philip Davies

Make sure your house *looks* secure. During an evening when the family is in, go outside and see how the house looks (which curtains are open, what lights are on and so on). This is how the house should look when you are out for the evening. Just leaving the hall light on isn't enough.

Take the back–door keys with you when you go out. A burglar may be able to break a small window to get in but he will need to be able to open a door to get your stuff out. Going out of the back door will be less risky for him than the front.

When going on holiday, make sure that curtains aren't caught behind a chair or hanging in an unusual way. People will notice that this hasn't changed for a while. Make sure they are straight or get a neighbour to rearrange them every few days.

Taking children on holiday? Dress them in a similar fashion for the journey so that if one gets lost, you can give an accurate idea of what they look like by showing what their sibling is wearing.

Plant hedges and build walls so the entrance to your house can always be seen from the road.

Save yourself from a scalding. Turn your thermostat down to 130 °F/54 °C so that water never comes out of the tap boiling hot (and it saves you money, too).

Sharp knives can be dangerous. Never leave them in the bottom of a washing-up bowl. Always wash and dry them straight away and put them back where they belong.

Use a wipe-clean board or blackboard at child-eye level near the phone for emergency numbers and numbers where you can be contacted if needed.

Stop children from getting into cupboards and drawers. Elastic bands make ideal safety catches. Just stretch them across adjacent doorknobs and the doors can only open an inch or two.

Children have a habit of running into glass patio doors, thinking that they're open when they're not. Avoid a nasty accident by putting a few stickers on any glass door.

Before storing carrier bags, tie them in a knot. It will then be much more difficult for a child to put one over his head without thinking.

Lots of accidents happen on or near stairs. Make sure this is one area that you have clearly lit and keep the stairs clear of objects.

To prevent people falling downstairs, replace 60-watt light bulbs in hallways with 100-watt bulbs.

Throw away novelty slippers. They cause people to slip and fall all the time. And they look really stupid.

Put a box or bag near the stairs, so toys can be quickly tidied away rather than lying around where they could cause an accident.

Don't store newspapers for recycling under the stairs. If they catch fire you won't be able to use the stairs to get out of the house.

Don't store bottles by the kitchen door. People can trip over them and cut themselves. You can put them under the stairs: they're not flammable.

If a frying pan catches fire, turn off the heat immediately and cover with a lid or damp towel. Don't move the pan or throw water on it. Leave it covered for at least half an hour to allow any flames to die away.

If your TV or computer catches fire, pull the plug out or turn off the main fuse box. Cover the TV with a blanket or rug. Don't throw water over it because there could be a danger from the residual electricity.

To stop little fingers getting trapped in slamming doors, glue a small cork to the door frame so that the doors cannot actually slam shut.

Alternatively, make a sausage out of old tights and bend it round the edge of door, attaching the ends to the door handles.

To test the safety of folding toys, insert a pencil in any nooks or crannies where little fingers could go and see if you can snap the pencil. If you can, then don't let your child play with the toy.

Make windows safe for children. Instead of child bars, fix garden trellis across the bottom of the window.

Keep an eye on children but stop them from getting under your feet. Fix a garden gate, which you can lock, across your kitchen doorway. You can still see them but they won't get in your way.

If your house opens on to a busy road, a sensible precaution with toddlers about is to fix a baby gate across your porch or front doorway.

▶▶▶ Hoteliers

Judy and David Green, Teviotdale Lodge Country Hotel; Steven Morris, Grafton Manor Hotel

To reduce the need for artificial lights in your hotel, make sure you clean the windows. Dirty windows can reduce the natural light by around 20 per cent.

To serve white wine immediately without having to put it in an ice cooler, just store it at a temperature of 50–55 °F/10–12.8 °C.

If you haven't got a corkscrew, put a long screw into the top of the cork and pull it out with a piece of string.

Breakfast cereals taste horrid if stale. Freshen them up by putting them in a bowl lined with kitchen towel and heat in a microwave for 30 seconds.

Freshen stale peanuts in the same way as the cereals above, but sprinkle the paper with a little coarse salt first.

When grilling lots of sausages, thread them onto skewers so that it's easier to keep turning them.

Your bacon will be really crispy if you trim the rind with pinking shears before cooking it.

If you get a little bit of yolk in the white when you are separating eggs, take a bit of tightly rolled kitchen towel that you have heated up in some boiling water and hold it near the yolk. The heat will draw the yolk towards the towel.

Scramble eggs in a heatproof glass bowl placed in a pan of boiling water. This way, you don't have to scrub lots of eggy saucepans afterwards.

For really fluffy omelettes, add a squirt of soda water to the egg mixture before cooking.

To stop oil from spitting in a frying pan, add a pinch of salt when melting the butter.

To help your fridge last that bit longer don't open and close it unnecessarily. Otherwise, you will make the fridge motor work twice as hard and it will wear out twice as fast.

Brazil nuts are easier to crack when frozen in the freezer.

To keep salad really fresh, put a saucer upside down in the bottom of the bowl to collect any spare moisture.

Make consommé look more appetising – drop a lump of sugar into the soup before serving.

If your hands smell of onions, soak them in some milk.

If your hands are stained, rub with a piece of raw potato. This works on kitchen worktops, too.

Cabbage can stink when it's being cooked. A bay leaf added to the boiling water will stop the smell without affecting the taste of the vegetable.

To keep cheese fresh for longer, wrap it in a cloth that you have dampened with white wine vinegar.

A sugar cube in the cheese box will keep cheese fresh for longer.

To stop your bins from smelling unpleasant, throw in a few fresh herbs each time you throw something away.

Keep teapots smelling fresh – put a sugar lump or dry tea-bag inside until you want to use it.

▶▶▶ Housekeepers

Maureen Cummins; Liz Foley; Jill Wright; Janet Reaney

▷▷ Stains, Smells and General Nastiness

Leave your wastebaskets smelling sweet – put a fabric conditioner sheet in the bottom.

Keep moths away! Place conkers or bay leaves in your wardrobes and drawers.

To leave the air fresh in wardrobes and cupboards, use a fabric conditioner sheet in among the clothes.

Make your clothes smell nice by placing empty perfume bottles in your wardrobes and drawers.

Absorb smells in any closed closet – use charcoal bricks placed in a small muslin sack – ideal for families with teenage boys!

Stop the smell of dirty clothes from becoming too overpowering – an empty perfume bottle at the bottom of a laundry bag keeps things sweet.

Remove unwanted blobs of chewing gum by placing a bag of ice cubes over the gum to freeze it. Tap the frozen gum with a hammer to break it up and then pick off as much as you can. Any remaining bits can be removed using a cloth dipped in methylated spirits.

Remove tannin stains from your teapot – put a tablespoon of bicarbonate of soda into the teapot, add boiling water and leave to soak overnight. Rinse out and wash thoroughly.

To shift tea and coffee stains from china cups, mix equal amounts of salt and vinegar, put in the cups and leave to soak, then rinse thoroughly.

Get rid of limescale from your kettle – just put a cup of vinegar in the kettle and boil it up. Rinse out thoroughly afterwards.

To shift limescale from a steam iron, simply fill the water tank with cider vinegar, turn the iron to 'steam' and run it over a soft cloth for several minutes. You'll need to rinse out the inside of your iron thoroughly afterwards.

Starch can get stuck to the sole plate of an iron – to remove it, run the iron over a piece of kitchen foil.

Tarnish can be removed from silver cutlery by placing the knives, forks and spoons in a saucepan with some scrunched-up kitchen foil and water and boiling for about 10 minutes.

Alternatively, put a strip of kitchen foil in a plastic bowl and place the silver cutlery on top. Cover with hot water and add a handful of washing soda. Rinse the cutlery thoroughly afterwards.

Get rid of those awkward stubborn black spots from silver salt cellars – immerse in a solution of 1 tablespoon of salt to 1 pint/ 600 ml of hot water for 5 minutes. Remove and wash the salt cellar; the spots will disappear.

To clean small glass and china ornaments put them in a sink and spray with liquid window cleaner. Dry them on a towel.

When cleaning a chandelier, you should always wear cotton gloves. This stops you from leaving greasy fingermarks on the crystal. If you have to dry a chandelier *in situ*, use a hair-dryer.

To clean delicate porcelain or china figurines hold the base and work from top to bottom. Brush off the dirt with a long-haired, soft make-up brush dipped in a warm solution of washing-up liquid (or soap flakes if the finish is matt). Rinse in the same way and leave to dry on a paper towel.

Store valuable china without it chipping. Place a paper coffee filter between each plate or bowl.

Clean porcelain or china figures by placing them on a cloth in a plastic bowl. Put a solution of warm water and washing-up liquid in a spray bottle. Wash and then rinse the figure. Empty the water as it accumulates. Leave to dry on a towel.

To remove a stubborn stain from the bottom of a glass vase just fill the vase with water and put in one denture-cleaning tablet. Leave for 20 minutes and then rinse out.

To shine badly tarnished brass use a mixture of salt and vinegar and rub the tarnish off with a soft cloth.

Tarnished copper benefits from a rub down with lemon juice (neat or mixed with water). For very dirty areas, dip half a lemon in salt and rub it over the offending part.

Bronze is improved by regularly cleaning the surface with dark brown shoe polish and buffing vigorously with a soft cloth.

To clean pewter, mix wood ash with some water into a paste. Rub this over the pewter and then polish off.

Remove rust and stains from plastic worktops with lemon juice (neat or mixed with water).

Wooden work surfaces can be cleaned using a nylon scouring pad dipped in hot water. Rub in the direction of the grain.

Ballpoint-ink stains need to be removed quickly – dab them with a cotton-wool bud dipped in methylated spirits.

To remove children's crayon marks from walls, brush with toothpaste using an old toothbrush. Wipe the excess off afterwards – for minty, clean walls!

Has Blu tack marked your walls? Dab a little toothpaste on to the stain and leave to harden. Wash it off afterwards, taking the mark with it.

Remove light stains from marble using lemon juice or white wine vinegar. Don't leave the juice or vinegar on the marble for longer than 2 minutes. Rinse off and repeat if necessary. Marble stains easily so get to work as quickly as possible.

For stubborn stains on marble, use a solution of 1 part hydrogen peroxide (which you can get from a chemist) to 2 parts water. Put a teaspoon of this solution on to the stain and then add a few drops of ammonia. When the solution stops bubbling, rinse with lots of cold water. Great fun for budding Dr Frankensteins.

Ivory should never be washed because it can discolour. Clean ivory only when absolutely necessary by using a cotton-wool bud dampened in methylated spirits.

If your sponge has become slimy, soak it in 1 tablespoon of vinegar to 1 pint/600 ml of water for an hour, then wash thoroughly.

To get rid of sticky-label adhesive, wipe the surface with methylated spirits.

Alternatively, sprinkle talcum powder on to the adhesive and rub with your finger to remove.

Rubber spatula ready for the bin? Trim off the tattered edges and keep trimming until there's nothing left.

Spray vegetable oil on a grater before use for a fast clean-up.

Graters are impossible to clean without losing a bit of your own finger . . . an old toothbrush does the trick and is ideal for sieves as well.

Use baking soda to remove coffee and tea stains from plastic cups and dishes.

To get rid of odours from plastic containers fill with crumpled black-and-white newspaper. Cover tightly and leave overnight. Next day the smell is gone.

To get rid of the strong plastic smell from new containers wash, dry and put in the freezer for at least two days.

To remove unpleasant odours in your waste disposal unit grind orange rinds or a half lemon.

If your waste disposal still has bad breath, try feeding it a handful of ice cubes, a splash of vinegar, a lemon and a pinch of allspice.

When disinfecting your sink, don't bother with strong chemical solutions. Just use ordinary household salt.

Baking soda is excellent for cleaning stainless steel sinks.

To give a stainless steel sink a superb finish rub it down with a scrunched up ball of newspaper after cleaning.

To remove water spots from a stainless steel sink use a cloth dampened with rubbing alcohol or white vinegar.

Rub stainless sinks with lighter fluid if rust marks appear. After the rust disappears, wipe with your regular kitchen cleaner.

For a sparkling white sink bleach is best. But it is expensive to fill a sink with bleach. Instead, line it first with kitchen paper then soak the paper in bleach. Leave for an hour or so before throwing the paper away.

Never use bleach in coloured porcelain sinks because it will fade the colour. Instead, clean with mild liquid detergents, vinegar or baking soda.

To rid your sink of soap suds after washing up wipe around the sink with a bar of soap with the tap running.

To pack glassware for a move wrap wet newspaper around the glass and let it dry. It will act like a cast around the glass.

Scratches in glassware will disappear if polished with toothpaste.

A good hallway mat should be four lazy steps in length or about 15 feet. By the time the average visitor has taken those steps, most of the grit and dirt is off their shoes and on the mat where you can collect it regularly.

Brooms can be cleaned with a mild detergent and warm water.

Storing your broom on its head will damage the bristles. Bang a couple of cotton reels into a cupboard door or wall to hang the head on, with the handle hanging down, to preserve the life of your broom.

Check your broom handle is the right length for you. Held upright, it should reach the bridge of your nose.

Always use a mop for one job only – mark the handle or use a different colour mop to indicate its purpose.

For really mucky floors a squeegee is perfect for scraping up the mud and grime before you give it a wash.

When you are applying polish, wrap an old towel around a broom head to buff up afterwards. The towel will ensure there isn't too much excess polish left on the wood and also bring up a wonderful shine.

Or bring up a shine by rubbing the floor with a bundle of old nylon tights.

Linoleum and vinyl are often used in children's rooms in place of carpets. If little fingers mark it with wax crayons, there's no need for tears. A little bit of silver polish will remove the damage.

Remove grease marks from vinyl by holding an ice cube on the stain before washing it with some soapy water.

Scratched floors look messy, but the scratches are often caused by old mops. Change the sponge on your mop before it gets too worn down and make sure your floor stays looking as good as new.

To clean a dirty mat put it in a bin bag and shake it around. The dust will stay in the bag rather than on the rest of your furniture.

Keep dust from flying around – empty the contents of your vacuum onto a damp newspaper.

To clean a wooden floor scatter damp tea-leaves over it to keep the dust in one place when sweeping.

Lambskin rugs can be brushed with lots of dry, powdered magnesia. Leave for a day, shake well and brush thoroughly.

The average small doormat is fairly useless for trapping dirt. Fit the first few feet of your hall with coconut matting, instead of carpet, to capture dust and mud. Edge it with some simple brass tread and it will look stylish too.

Always vacuum your carpet as you would mow your lawn, in neat rows, back and forth so that you don't miss a spot. Each section needs two or three passes at least.

Sooty footprints: sprinkle with salt, let stand for 30 minutes, then vacuum. On light-coloured carpets try an art gum eraser.

Ugly insect or fly spots on windows can be removed with cold tea.

Never clean windows on a very cold or frosty day – the glass will be brittle and liable to break.

When you've cleaned your windows, for a really fine shine, after the windows are dry, rub a clean blackboard eraser over them.

Here's a pithy tip … for sparkling glass, if your lemons are over ripe, squeeze them into hot water and use them to clean your windows.

When the artificial coal in an electric fire becomes faded and grey, soak a cloth in blackcurrant jelly and rub over the coals. Leave to dry and they'll come up really glossy.

To clean in the tiniest nooks and crannies use a camera lens-cleaning brush, the sort with an air-sac attached.

For difficult areas such as stair railings, chairs, etc., use old socks as mitts to clean. (Just make sure they're clean before you start.)

Dust louvred doors by wrapping a cloth around a ruler. Spray the cloth with polish and run the flat end across each slat.

To remove sticky–back shelf paper use your hair-dryer to 'warm' the adhesive. Use the lowest setting first, holding the dryer over a small area. When it is warmed enough, it should just lift away from the shelf. Continue warming and lifting small sections until the job is done.

To clean a room quickly of cigarette smoke odour soak a towel in equal parts of hot water and vinegar, wring it out completely and wave it like a flag over your head several times around the room (you'll feel very silly but your room will smell wonderful).

When cleaning light bulbs, rub a little vanilla essence around the bulb with a soft cloth. When the light is switched back on, a lovely smell will be gently released.

Cleaning behind radiators is tricky and often gets overlooked altogether. A sock placed over a broom handle will reach the parts other cleaners cannot.

Clean a circular fan with an old sock over your hand.

Line the top of a tall bookcase with old newspaper. When you want to remove the dust, just throw away the paper and replace it. This works for the tops of kitchen cabinets as well.

Alternatively, use a new paintbrush to brush off the dust.

Tapestry work can be sprinkled with powdered magnesia. Work in well with fingertips covered with a clean cloth. Leave for several hours at least, then brush out gently.

To clean the inside of a clock soak a small piece of cotton wool in kerosene or paraffin and place in the base of the clock. Leave for a few days. This will draw down all the dust and leave the clock clean.

Some fluffy toys can't be washed. When teddy needs a clean shake him in a plastic bag with some bicarbonate of soda, then brush him well afterwards (and there'll be no tearful nights waiting for him to dry either).

Fountain pens are fiddly things to clean – they're best soaked in some neat vinegar for 10 minutes or so, then left to dry on some blotting paper.

To clean glass shower doors try using left-over white wine.

To deep clean shower surrounds use a sponge mop dipped in a solution of 1/2 a cup of vinegar, 1 cup of ammonia, a 1/4 cup of baking soda in 1 gallon of warm water. After cleaning, rinse with warm water.

Make your own spray cleaner by filling a spray bottle with 3 tablespoons of ammonia, 1 tablespoon of vinegar and some cool water.

Bathroom tile grout a bit grotty? Simply camouflage with some Liquid Paper.

Always wipe the bath down after use. Some essential oils can mark plastic baths if they are left on the surface.

Avoid hard-to-remove tide marks on the bath – don't use concentrated bath oils.

When descaling tap nozzles, put a plastic bag filled with vinegar over the nozzle. Secure it with an elastic band and leave it for at least half an hour.

Shift hard water deposits from around the base of taps with an old toothbrush dipped in vinegar. Rinse well afterwards.

To remove toilet rings flush first to wet sides and apply a paste of borax and lemon juice. Let sit for two hours, then scrub.

▷▷ Dusting and Cleaning

Damp dusters pick up dust more effectively.

If your steel wool scourers are rusting, wrap them in kitchen foil after use.

Pin a plastic bag to your clothes as you work your way around the house. You can empty bins as you go, without constantly running up and down the stairs.

Blow dust off dried or artificial flowers using a hair-dryer (on its lowest setting).

To clean silk flowers – put them into a large paper bag with a generous scoop of salt. Shake vigorously until all the dust is removed from the flowers.

To remove difficult, dried-on stains sew a button on to the corner of the cloth you use for wiping down surfaces. Use the edge of the button to scrape off any stubborn crusty stains you come across.

Changing duvet covers needn't end up as a wrestling match. Put one corner of the duvet into its cover and hold it in position with a clothes peg. Repeat with the other corner and shake the duvet down into the cover.

▷▷ Light a Candle

Candle wax can be removed from a surface by warming a knife over a candle flame. Use the heated knife to gently lift the wax from the surface. If the candle wax has left a stain, dab it with a cotton-wool bud dipped in methylated spirits.

You can get rid of candle wax by covering it with brown paper and running a warm iron (switched off) over it. Change the position of the paper as the wax is absorbed. This works well with other grease stains, too.

To shift wax from metal candlesticks, carefully pour boiling water over the candlestick; this will melt the wax.

Alternatively, to remove wax from a candlestick, use a hair-dryer on a low setting to blow hot air over the surface until the wax has melted.

Keep night–light candles burning for ages. Put a pinch of salt in each one.

To stop candles dripping, sharpen the ends like a pencil. This stops the wax from collecting in a pool and then suddenly spilling over.

Candles burn more evenly and won't drip if you pop them in a freezer before use.

Strong cooking smells will be minimised by lighting a candle in the kitchen while you're cooking – useful in the loo, too!

Spray candles with your favourite perfume. As they burn down, they release the smell into the room. Ideal for candle-lit dinners!

Recycle candles by melting down all the left-over stubs in a heat-proof bowl in a warm oven. Take a yoghurt pot and make a small hole in the bottom, thread some string through the hole, and tie to a pencil balanced horizontally on the rim of the pot. Pour in the melted wax and leave to set.

Creaking door hinges and stiff zips can be miraculously transformed by rubbing a candle along the offending hinge or zip.

Sash windows will run more smoothly if you rub a candle on all the sliding surfaces.

Sticking doors can be unstuck by rubbing the sticky edge with a candle.

If your furniture drawers keep sticking, try rubbing vegetable soap on the runners.

▷▷ Bathrooms

Prevent the bottom of a bathroom pull cord getting discoloured – place the casing from a clear ballpoint pen over the 'pulling' end.

To clean a toilet bowl, pour a can of Coca-Cola around the rim. Leave it for one hour and then brush and flush!

Alternatively, drop several denture-cleaning tablets into the toilet bowl.

Dripping taps can cause a stain on the bath or sink enamel. Remove such stains by rubbing with a cut lemon.

Mould spots on bath sealant should be tackled with domestic bleach and a toothbrush. Rinse thoroughly.

To prevent mildew from forming in your bathroom, fill a small, flat box with cat litter and place in the bottom of the bath. This is especially important if you're going to be away for a long time – but remember to keep the door shut if you've got cats!

Shower curtains (plastic or polyester) with mildew spots should be soaked in a solution of 1 part domestic bleach to 4 parts water. Then rinse thoroughly or machine-wash if possible.

Grimy shower curtains should be wiped with distilled vinegar then rinsed with water.

Get rid of soap scum from shower doors by rubbing with a used fabric-conditioner strip.

Reduce steam in the bathroom by running cold water into the bath before turning the hot water on. The less steam you get, the fewer mould spots there will be.

To clean a bath use an old net curtain. It's mildly abrasive and gets the marks off brilliantly.

To clean delicate bathroom surfaces, sheer tights make an excellent, non-abrasive scouring pad.

For clogged shower heads, unscrew and place in a bowl of vinegar for 20 minutes – remove the rubber washer but don't lose it! Brush out any sediment with an old toothbrush before reassembling.

Clean soap splashes from tiles with a solution of 1 part white vinegar to 4 parts water. Rinse and wipe down.

If hard water has caused splashes on tiles or glass that are hard to remove, rub malt vinegar over the surface. Leave for 10 minutes before rinsing off.

▷▷ Furniture

To get rid of dog or cat hair on furniture, use a damp rubber glove.

Collect cat or dog hairs from furniture with a fabric-conditioner sheet.

Saggy cane seats can be re-tightened by wetting the top and bottom of the seat with hot, soapy water. Leave the chair to dry in the open air. As the cane dries, it shrinks and tightens. Unfortunately, this method doesn't work on saggy bottoms!

If you've lost a castor off the bottom of a chair, place a cotton bobbin there instead. If it shows too much, colour it first with dark felt-tip pen.

Remove water marks by mixing a paste of butter and cigarette ash, and buff with a damp cloth, then polish. If you don't have any cigarette ash, try rubbing the mark with some mayonnaise on a soft cloth.

Or try toothpaste applied to the water mark on a damp cloth.

Children's stickers can be removed from wood by 'painting' the sticker with white vinegar, letting it soak in and then scraping off.

Scratches on wood can be concealed by rubbing in a little cod liver oil.

To get rid of rings or minor scratches on wood cover with petroleum jelly and leave for 24 hours. Rub it into the wood, wipe off the excess and then polish as normal.

Polish wood with metal polish instead of the normal woody kind and it should come up a treat.

Laminated playing cards can be effectively cleaned by rubbing with some white bread.

Valuable embossed or gilded china should be cleaned with a small eyebrow brush kept specifically for the purpose.

Bone china should not be a museum piece. Take it out and clean it every year.

For crayon stains rub lightly with a dry, soap-filled steel wool pad.

Or use a damp cloth sprinkled with baking soda.

Catch a carpet stain within the first few days. The longer a stain chemically reacts with the carpet the harder it will be to remove it.

To remove curry stains from carpets use a little lemon juice with water.

To remove a cigarette stain from the carpet pour a small amount of milk on the stain and leave it to soak in. This will dilute the colour and stops it browning. Then rub the stain with a raw potato and wash as normal.

Beer stains can be removed from carpets with soda water.

Don't use chemical cleaners on stains caused by drinks with chemicals in them (e.g. orange squash or cola) because the chemicals in the cleaner may react with the chemicals in the drink.

Light stains can be rubbed with a cut lemon.

For dark stains or rust rub with a paste of borax and lemon juice.

For a yellowing bath rub with a solution of salt and turpentine. Rinse well.

To remove dark stains from well water in a toilet or sink sprinkle some citrus drink powder and swirl around. Let stand for a few minutes, then rinse.

For glue stains saturate the spot with a vinegar soaked cloth.

To clean engraved silver napkin rings or intricate handles on silver cutlery rub in a little minty toothpaste with a soft cloth then wipe off.

Chrome taps come up a treat if you rub them with some plain flour, then wash off.

If you want to get Biro marks off a photograph, rub the mark with some silver polish wadding. Then rub the same spot with some cotton wool and the mark vanishes.

▷▷ Windows

Wash windows on a dull day. Too much sun can dry a window too quickly and leave the glass all streaky.

Windows can be made to sparkle using a bit of vinegar and water mixed together (methylated spirits works just as well). Work the mixture around the glass with a piece of chamois leather or newspaper.

Alternatively, to make windows and mirrors sparkle rub them with scrunched-up paper coffee filters.

Windows can be buffed using crumpled newspaper – the printer's ink gives added sparkle.

Stop windows steaming up by putting glycerine or a little washing-up liquid in some water and wiping over the glass.

To clean venetian blinds, wear thick cotton gloves and wipe along the slats with your fingers. Reverse the slats and repeat to clean the other side.

Dull net curtains can be transformed back to gleaming white by putting a denture-cleaning tablet into water and soaking the curtains in the solution.

▷▷ Walls

When washing walls, start off at the bottom and work upwards so that any dirty trickles are absorbed by the already wet surface. Skirting boards are usually the dirtiest part of the room so leave cleaning them until last.

To clean wallpaper, use stale but still slightly moist bread. This gets the marks off without the need for soap and water.

Tobacco stains on walls can be removed by lightly scrubbing them with a soft brush dipped in a weak solution of washing-up liquid.

Dirty marks around light switches can be removed using a soft india rubber.

To protect the wall while you clean light switches, make a cardboard template.

▷▷ Breakages

If a bulb breaks while you are removing it, press an old cork on to the broken glass and twist.

▷▷ Floors and Carpets

Freshen carpets by sprinkling liberally with salt, oatmeal or cornflour. Leave for a couple of hours and then vacuum.

Revive the colour in a faded carpet using a mix of 1 part vinegar to 2 parts boiling water. Soak a cloth in this solution, rub into the carpet and watch the colours come back.

Fountain-pen ink should be blotted up with absorbent paper and sponged with cold water until the stain lifts. Use carpet shampoo to finish off.

For bloodstains on the carpet, sponge with cold water and blot firmly with a towel as often as you need. Finish off with carpet shampoo.

Pet puddles needn't be a problem. To get rid of stains from a carpet, mix equal parts of white vinegar and cool water, blot up the stain, rinse and allow to dry.

Remove shoe marks from linoleum by scrubbing gently with fine steel wool dipped in white spirit or turpentine.

Raise dents in carpets made by heavy furniture by rubbing the dent with the edge of a coin.

Alternatively, remove dents in carpet pile by covering with a damp cloth and then quickly placing a hot iron on top. The steam lifts the pile.

To clean up muddy paw– or footprints, resist the temptation to remove them straight away. Leave the mud to dry completely before vacuuming it up. Sponge off any marks that are left with carpet shampoo.

To vacuum the fringes on rugs, slip an old stocking over the end of the hose attachment.

To retrieve a contact lens from the floor, cover the end of the vacuum hose with a stocking, as above, and vacuum the area. The stocking will stop the lens disappearing into the bowels of the cleaner.

Prevent rugs getting worn and bald too quickly. Turn them regularly so that they get even wear.

To clean scorch marks on rugs or carpets, use the edge of a coin to loosen the burn fibres and then sweep them up. Really bad scorch marks are impossible to get rid of but you can minimise the effect of light marks by trimming with a pair of scissors.

Wooden floors can be given a wonderful shine by buffing them with nylon stockings.

To clean a varnished floor try adding instant tea granules to your bucket of water.

For scratched woodwork, you can minimise the damage by dabbing with cotton wool that has been dipped in diluted tea.

Scratches on dark woods can be disguised by rubbing with the cut edge of a Brazil nut. For light woods, use a wax crayon or shoe polish.

Water marks on wooden surfaces (left by a glass or made by spirits) can be removed by rubbing dampened cigarette or cigar ash into the mark with a soft cloth (you can make it into a paste using a little vegetable oil). Make sure you rub with the grain of the wood. Wipe with a damp cloth, then a dry cloth, and repolish. Buff with a soft duster.

White rings on waxed surfaces can be removed using a paste made from salt and olive oil. Leave the stain covered with the paste overnight and then wipe off. The surface can then be rewaxed.

Remove greasy marks from wood veneers by sprinkling the surface with talcum powder. Cover with a couple of sheets of tissue paper and, using the tip of a warm iron, gently press on to the surface to draw out the grease.

You can raise dents in wood by placing a damp cloth over the dent and holding a warm iron (don't get it too hot) over the cloth for a few minutes. The moisture from the cloth swells the grain. Allow the wood to dry before polishing.

Repair a dent in wood by filling with a few drops of clear nail-varnish.

Messy ovens needn't take hours to clean. A sheet of aluminium foil on the bottom will catch all the drips and spills. Replace as necessary.

▷▷ Pianos

Protect an unused piano from damp by covering the working parts and keyboard with sheets of brown paper.

To clean ivory piano keys, squeeze a little fluoride toothpaste on to a damp cloth. Rub the keys quite hard and buff with a soft dry cloth.

Alternatively, you can try the Victorian way and clean the keys with milk.

▷▷ Fires & Fireplaces

When cleaning away ashes from a fireplace, sprinkle damp tea-leaves over them to keep the dust down.

Remove soot from bricks around a fireplace by scrubbing with neat malt vinegar. Rinse well and then blot the surface with a sponge.

▷▷ Ironing

If your iron sticks to your clothes, wrap a bar of soap in a hanky and rub it over the hot face of the iron – it will be as smooth as new.

When ironing, put a drop of essential oil into your steam iron water to make clothes smell nice.

When ironing bed linen, spray it with water infused with lavender oil. The smell will help you sleep.

After ironing, fold matching sheets and duvet covers and place inside matching pillow-case covers. This way sets will be much easier to find.

In icy weather clean the doorstep with a bucket of water to which you have added a crushed aspirin, 8 fl ounces of warm water and 1 tablespoon of methylated spirits. This will keep the step clean and stop ice from forming.

Remove dirt, sand, small rock particles and debris from your entrance way so it can't be tracked into the home. A simple solution that will save you time in the long run.

Unclog grease from your drains: pour a cup of salt water and a cup of fizzy soda into the drain followed by a pan of boiling water. The grease will usually dissolve immediately and open the drain.

Take a water hose and spray the outside of your house. This will remove the dust and cobwebs. On textured walls attach a car-washing brush to the hose to remove dirt.

For outside windows dip a long-handled mop in your cleaning solution, wash, then hose off. Throw a clean towel over the mop to dry.

To keep frost off windows add antifreeze to your cleaning water. Rub the inside of windows with a sponge dipped in the solution. Polish with newspapers or paper towels.

To clean perspex and get rid of scratches rub with toothpaste and then buff up with a cloth.

When shampooing carpet, put small plastic bags or glass jars around furniture legs to prevent rust stains from forming.

Wooden floors needn't be hard to maintain. The trick is not to use too much polish – it just traps more dirt. So only use polish every few months.

The bristles on your new broom will last much longer if you dip the broom head in salted water before you use it. (This will only work on real bristles though.)

Prevent cigarette butts from smouldering. Line your ashtrays with bicarbonate of soda.

▶▶▶ Insect Owners

Most insects are easier to handle if they're cool. Pop them in the fridge for a few minutes to slow down their metabolism.

If you have a wounded arthropod (that includes spiders, millipedes, centipedes, crustaceans, insects) with a damaged outer body casing, you can stick them back together with glue.

▷▷ Spiders

Tarantulas make great pets, but they're not ideal to 'play' with. You can enjoy the look of them rather than expect them to play 'fetch'.

When buying a tarantula, avoid one that is huddled up in the corner with its legs tucked under it. If it doesn't react quickly (or at all) to touch, don't buy it. It's probably dying.

A male tarantula will have little hooks on the undersides of its front legs. Mature males live from a couple of months to two or three years, depending on the species. Adult females can live for decades; again, it depends on the species.

Different species of tarantulas need different living conditions. Arboreals live in trees and make their homes in holes in the bark. Burrowers live in holes. You will need to reflect this when you put them in their cage.

Some tarantulas require very little attention and are therefore easy to keep. Generally, the ground-dwelling tarantulas from arid climates are the easiest. Arboreals and spiders from wet regions need a lot more care. A good choice for the beginner is the Chilean Rose tarantula.

A home for a tarantula can be a 5-gallon aquarium, a large plastic jar, plastic shoebox or custom-made cage. The top should be covered with screen, mesh or cheesecloth so that there is enough ventilation and secured tightly so there are no escapes.

Tarantulas are the Victor Meldrews of the creepy-crawly world: they don't really enjoy company and are best kept in solitary confinement.

Ground-dwelling tarantulas can easily be killed by a fall, even a short one. So don't let them climb too high.

Tarantulas love crickets. Larger spiders will also eat baby mice and bits of meat.

When a tarantula is about to moult, it will stop feeding, so remove food from the cage. For a small spider, this can be a few days before it moults; for adults, it can be up to several months before they moult.

Spiders which are upside down with their legs in the air are almost certainly moulting. Just leave them to get on with it.

Don't feed a spider which has just moulted. Leave it for a week until the new exoskeleton has hardened (usually when the fangs turn from white to black).

Tarantulas are venomous – that doesn't mean that they are lethal, but bites from some species can be extremely painful and cause unpleasant symptoms. Some people can be allergic to the venom. If you are bitten and experience difficulty breathing, see a doctor.

▷▷ Stick Insects

Always handle gently – the limbs of a stick insect are easily snapped in two.

Overcrowding can lead to cannibalism so give them enough space.

Make sure there is enough ventilation for your insects – damp conditions can harm eggs as well as adult insects.

Size is important when it comes to housing your stick insect – some species require more space than others. As a general rule, the height of the tank must be at least twice as great as the insect's length.

You can use newspaper to line the floor of your insect's home. Some species, like the Giant Spiny, also like to rest on the floor, so they will need a layer of peat to sit on or cork bark to hide under.

Sphagnum moss in the corner of the tank sprayed regularly can keep the atmosphere humid.

A good temporary home can be made from an empty sweet jar. Make sure you put some air holes in the lid.

Some stick insects need extra heat in order to thrive. You can use a screened light bulb with a low wattage bulb. A tungsten light bulb gives a very concentrated heat but make sure your insects don't dehydrate.

Stick insects are masters of camouflage – some use shape and colour to blend into the background. Others will rock back and forward like leaves or twigs in a breeze.

Food isn't a problem especially if you have access to bramble leaves throughout the year. Avoid leaves with brown edges or other insects eggs planted on the underside. Leave the leaves on the stem.

To keep food supplies fresh make a cut in the base of the stem and then set it in a heavy, narrow-necked water container (some stick insects are quite large and could knock over a container). Plug the top of the container with some cotton wool or tissue paper.

Try to vary the diet now and again. The Javanese and Green stick insects are quite partial to rhododendron leaves. Some species will also take privet leaves as well as rose leaves, oak and pyracantha.

Stick insects tend to prefer large leaves to smaller ones.

If you want to experiment with your insect's diet, do so after their moult when new food is more likely to be accepted.

Moults occur several times before the insect reaches adulthood. The higher the temperature, the greater the tendency for the insect to moult. Before a moult your pet will become less active, even losing its appetite for a day or two.

Once a moult is complete, the insect will stay still for several hours while its 'new' skin hardens. Don't handle it during this stage.

Help your stick insect to exercise – put some dried twigs in his cage.

A rose by any other name – some stick insects give off a chemical secretion which smells like rather pleasant perfume.

Don't let your stick insects escape into the wild in case they manage to establish themselves. There are at least two species of New Zealand stick insects living wild in parts of south-western England.

If you want to encourage your stick insects to mate take them on a car journey. Apparently this can arouse their romantic inclinations, especially with the Giant Spiny stick insect.

Mantids are distant relatives of stick insects, but don't be tempted to keep them together. For many mantids a stick insect is a tasty snack.

▶▶▶ Interior Designers

Jenny Hooper, J.H.D.; Claire Shread, Inardec Art Decor; Karen Mae Birch

Brighten up a dark room. Yellow will make it feel sunny, pink will create a dramatic, warm effect and orange will give it a warm and welcoming feel.

If a room feels claustrophobic, remove any picture rails and paper the walls with vertical stripes.

If a room feels too tall, make a feature of a picture rail or create the same effect with a paper border. Or try painting the ceiling to match the floor.

If a room feels very large, break up the expanse with scattered rugs or pretty screens.

For north-facing rooms, you need to create a feeling of warmth. Try shades of terracotta or sunny, warm yellow.

Natural materials such as wood or brick give a warm feeling.

Test out colour combinations on the back of an old cereal packet.

Get free advice. Many paint and wallpaper companies offer free advice about colour schemes.

Decorative paint effects needn't be hard to achieve. Try scrunching up a plastic bag, dipping it lightly in paint and dabbing it on to a wall for a stunning, dappled effect.

Create an interesting paint effect by dipping a toothbrush in paint and flicking the paint onto a wall.

Transform a wall by cutting a simple design into a potato, dipping it in paint and stamping it on to the wall in a regular pattern.

Want to know where to put a dado rail? Remember that they were originally there to protect the wall from chairs so they should generally be fixed at the height of the back of a chair.

Cover a wall cheaply by stapling large pieces of fabric to it.

Save money on expensive wallpapers – use old sheet music, maps, newspaper cuttings or comics.

When choosing wallpaper, check how it looks by standing back away from it. You never really stand up close to the wall in your own room.

Paint your radiators to match your walls – it looks better than just leaving them plain white.

Paint shelves and storage units the same colour as skirting boards and picture rails to tie them in to the room and make them an integral part of the overall theme.

After painting the walls, mix up the left-over paint with some clear varnish and use it on the woodwork for a cohesive effect.

You can create an illusion of loads of floor space by painting the skirting boards the same colour as the floor.

If your woodwork is less than perfect, use eggshell paint rather than gloss; its semi-matt finish will hide imperfections.

To brighten up a dark hallway, paint the wall or door at the far end a sunny, bright colour. This has the effect of shortening the long corridor. A wall of mirror also lightens and brightens the space.

To plan a child's room, get down on the floor and view things from a child's perspective.

Brighten up a child's room by making fun borders. Get long strips of paper and let the children walk up and down them with painted feet.

Yes, your children can scribble on walls! Just paint a section with matt black paint and have a tub of chalks to hand.

If storage is a problem in a toddler's room, double up the rails in their wardrobe. Their clothes aren't long enough to need the extra hanging space.

Paint or decorate a plastic bin for a child's room. You can use it as a toy 'box'.

Don't put pegs at an adult height in a child's room. This won't encourage kids to clear their own mess up. Put pegs where they can reach them.

When hanging a picture, mark your holes on to masking tape rather than the wall.

Never get a tall person to hang your pictures – you'll always be craning your neck to see them.

When shopping for curtains, take a cushion off your sofa to help you match the exact shade you want.

To change the colour of an old light fitting, spray it with car paint (ordinary paint can be flammable).

Jazz up old light cords by threading them with beads.

Tablecloths can look elegant if trimmed with braid or tassels. However, it can be expensive to trim all the way round a piece of fabric. Instead, decorate the edges of a much smaller top cloth.

Fire surrounds can be expensive. For an effective but cheaper alternative, fix some wall brackets and a shelf over the fireplace.

Give old chairs a new look by covering them with fabric paint.

Transform ordinary-looking boxes or storage cases by covering them in black-and-white photocopies of interesting images. Finish off with a layer of varnish for extra protection.

Make a feature of storage – hang baskets and bags from the kitchen ceiling.

To age pictures, stain with a used tea-bag.

Make cheap and cheerful curtains by hanging colourful sheets on to a broom handle.

The more fabric you can use for curtains, the more effective they will look.

To block out an unattractive view, use stained or etched glass in the window.

Alternatively, make your own mini greenhouse using double glazing. Put glass shelves with plants on them between two sheets of double glazing glass. The plants will thrive in this atmosphere.

Keep an eye out for second-hand sheets. If they are in good condition, you can dye them and use them as curtains, throws, tablecloths or cushion covers.

For inexpensive curtains, clip key-rings to the top of a blanket and thread on to a curtain rail.

For the ultimate snappy shower curtain, use a sheet of bubble wrap.

Make a splash! Decorate the side of your bath with images cut out of wrapping paper or postcards which you can laminate with sticky-back plastic. Alternatively, get a printer to do it for you – it's very inexpensive.

Refitting a bathroom can be an expensive business. To save money, stick with a basic theme and colour. Try picking up different fittings from end-of-range models.

Old kitchen doors can be transformed by putting new fittings (door handles, beading, etc.) on them.

If your kitchen is very small, simply rehang the door so that it swings outwards.

Bring more light into your home – replace the upper panels in your doors with glass.

Light the object and not yourself. To see where you could do with more lighting use a table lamp on an extension lead to experiment with light in different sections of your rooms.

Create the illusion of extra space by hanging a really large mirror on one wall (try to fill the wall space if possible).

Transform a cheap plastic garden container into a sophisticated jardinière with a few coats of emulsion.

Take photos of features or buildings that you like and want to duplicate at home.

Spend most money on the things that you use or touch the most – a chair rather than a poster, for example.

Keep it simple. People often put too much into a room.

►►► Jewellers

Louise Callow

For security when going on holiday, use eggcups as jewellery cases and store them in the fridge.

To create a lovely antique effect, paint egg yolk on to silver bracelets and necklaces.

To stop silver jewellery from tarnishing, wrap in black tissue.

You can clean your silver jewellery in toothpaste. Rinse thoroughly in warm water afterwards.

For a good, general jewellery cleaner try a weak solution of washing-up liquid in warm water with a drop of household ammonia.

Useful cleaning tools are old toothbrushes and mascara wands.

Some stones shouldn't be put in cleaning solution: jade, coral and lapis lazuli only need a gentle polish. Opals and turquoise are fragile so polish carefully with a cloth.

Clean amber in some warm milk, dry, and polish with a soft silk cloth.

Jet can be cleaned with soft breadcrumbs.

Cameos should never be immersed in water. Use a brush dipped in the cleaner and brush the surface gently. Rinse in the same way with clean water. Blot off excess water and rub with a chamois leather.

You can wash jade from time to time in soapy warm water. Jade should be handled as much as possible.

Gold chains need careful handling. Soapy water is the best thing to clean them with but try rubbing the gold gently in a chamois leather afterwards to make them really sparkle.

When washing up, attach your precious rings to a safetypin and pin them to your clothing.

To prevent your gold rings from getting misshapen, dented or scratched cover your car steering-wheel with some soft foam or fabric (apparently gripping the wheel too tight is the most common cause of damage).

Don't be conned into buying expensive gold cleaners: most are just variations on common household bleach.

For really sparkling gold soak it for several minutes in gin.

The best way to bring up a nine-carat shine is with a soft bristled toothbrush.

The best thing to buff up gold jewellery is a spectacle cleaning cloth.

To store your gold and silver without damage line your jewellery box with an empty egg tray, so you can keep each piece of jewellery in a separate compartment.

To stop jewellery becoming tarnished place a piece of chalk in your trinket box.

To maintain a gleam remove all gold before bathing. The soapy water simply builds up a film and your precious jewellery will soon look dull.

Make sure you don't lose your valuables – hang a few hooks inside your bathroom cabinet. Not only will your jewellery be safely away from plugholes but also away from the damaging steam.

A good general cleaner is a weak solution of washing-up liquid in warm water with a little drop of household ammonia.

Emeralds are naturally fragile – always get them cleaned professionally.

Never put your emeralds in hot water: the gems will absorb the liquid and crack.

Opals are very porous so avoid washing altogether. Instead buff up with a soft chamois leather.

Shine pearls with a dab of olive oil and wipe dry with a chamois.

Clean artificial pearls with a chamois leather. Just rub it carefully over the beads.

▷▷ A Girl's Best Friend

If your diamonds have lost their sparkle, drop them into a glass of water, add one denture-cleaning tablet and leave them to soak for a couple of minutes.

▷▷ Pearls

To test whether pearls are real or not, simply place them between your teeth. Real pearls have a gritty surface; fake pearls are smooth.

Real pearls should be worn regularly so that they can absorb the moisture from your body that will keep them looking lustrous. They should be the first thing to go on in the morning and the last thing to come off at night.

Don't wear your pearls in the shower – the silk thread will become damaged and rot.

If your string of pearls breaks, pick up all the pearls and put them on a round tea tray. You can then use the curve to sort the pearls out so that they are in the right order for restringing.

Wash real pearls in very salty water. Let them dry and then polish with a piece of velvet.

▷▷ Green Stones

If your emeralds dry out, pour a little almond oil on the stones, wrap them in a towel and leave them on the radiator overnight.

▷▷ Gold Finger

If you've lost a lot of weight, get your wedding ring altered.

If your family heirloom is too large for your finger, use the ring as a scarf clasp or as a pendant.

If a ring becomes stuck on your finger, use Windowlene rather than soap to unstick it.

▷▷ Ear, Ear

Fishing flies make great earrings.

Use table-football figures as earrings and support your team at the same time.

Store earrings by poking them through a piece of fabric.

Something different? Aluminium wire that has been wound around a small paintbrush or pencil makes effective earrings.

Lost the butterfly from the back of your earring? Use a piece of pencil rubber as a temporary measure.

▷▷ Arms & Necks

Make a great bracelet from the inside of a vacuum-cleaner belt.

Can't find your cufflinks? Buff up a couple of nuts and bolts and use them instead.

To untangle your chains simply use a drop of almond oil, some needles and a lot of patience.

Alternatively, dust lightly with talcum powder.

Make a necklace from electrical wire.

To store necklaces, hang them on tiny nails or a key-ring holder in your wardrobe.

If you are getting a rash from a piece of jewellery but can't bear to get rid of it, try cleaning it first, then apply a coat of clear nail-varnish to all the parts that touch your skin.

To stop stones falling out of your costume jewellery, paint them with clear nail-varnish.

Prolong the life of your umbrella – rub petroleum jelly on the hinges to stop them rusting.

►►► Landscape Gardeners

Jane Williams-Thomas, Pershore; Glyn Jones, Cambridge; Gordon MacVity, Coventry; Richard Thomas, Bath; Peter Philips, Bristol; Stephen Welch, Doncaster; Karen Cole, Cambridge

Feeling generous? Donate a plant to the neighbours to create a visual link between small gardens.

If you've inherited an overgrown, neglected garden and don't know where to start, begin by clearing away the rubbish and cutting the lawn. Things will start to look better immediately.

Never look at your garden at midday because flowers will rarely look their best. As the angle of light changes, the flowers will come into their own.

Tall plants give focus. Plants such as cardoons, angelica or globe artichokes provide a wonderful background. Artichokes are notorious for smothering smaller neighbours, so give them at least a square metre each to expand.

Not sure about plants, but can't resist them? Pot them up in tubs, if you really must have something. Don't rush to put it into the ground if you're not sure what your final plan will be.

Save money and create a stunning effect. Buy annuals in bulk and only use two or three colours.

Don't use just herbaceous and annual plants. Vegetables and fruit look attractive in flowerbeds as well. Rhubarb, runner beans, strawberries and chard, for example, all look good *and* produce fresh food for the table.

Green glass wine bottles make good edging for your beds.

In a short garden surrounded by hedge cut the top of the hedge slightly lower towards the back of the garden to give the illusion that the end of the garden is further away than it actually is.

Alternatively, lay a path which tapers to a point away from the house. Plant trees and shrubs along it which get gradually shorter as you move away from the house.

Planting two pots in a similar way, but one larger than the other will give the feeling of space. Put the larger one in the foreground and the smaller one to the rear.

Secret nooks and crannies add a sense of mystery to a garden.

Plant a quick-growing climber next to your newly erected trellis or screen. Make sure you choose a plant which won't outgrow the trellis.

Clumps of bamboo make an effective screen and can hide unsightly objects such as compost heaps, dustbins and so on.

If screening something in your garden is difficult, you could make a feature of it or highlight it in some way, rather than trying to hide it.

If you've got a post or an old tree stump that you don't like but can't get rid of, grow a climber up it.

Pergolas are a useful way of adding shelter and giving an element of privacy if your garden is overlooked.

If your garden is overlooked, add a section of trellis to the top of your fence and plant some evergreen climbers.

If you want to create a bog garden, think big. A larger bog garden won't dry out as quickly as a small one.

When planning a water feature, make sure any container you use is frost proof.

If you are building a pond, make sure animals can get in and out easily – incorporate shallow, sloping sides and rocks for them to use.

Don't situate your pond beneath trees because you'll have your hands full keeping the surface clear of falling leaves.

When laying paths through the garden, you should ensure that they are wide enough for one person to walk along with ease.

If your garden is full of curves, make sure your paths follow the curves rather than cut right through them.

A path should lead somewhere, even if it's just to a shed, greenhouse, different part of the garden, a seat or a statue. Paths that don't go anywhere look odd.

If you have a dark path running through your garden, lighten it up by planting the borders with evergreens which have brightly variegated leaves.

To make a border look longer plant brightly coloured flowers and plants in the foreground. Put pale colours at the back of the garden.

Grey plants will make a border seem longer.

Hot, fiery-coloured flowers shorten the distance.

Glossy foliage perks up dull, dark corners.

Grow copper maples, dark red roses and pink camellias in the west of your garden to catch the rays of the setting sun.

If your patio is too small, you can extend it by simply laying some gravel and surrounding it with brick.

If your patio doesn't get enough sun, consider pruning, even moving, a tree or painting the surrounding walls white.

Use mirrors to enlarge a small garden.

Old baler twine makes a bright and cheap way to mark out your garden.

Get rid of boring stretches of grass. Alter the shape by adding curves or making an island bed.

Alternatively, create a focal point by planting a specimen tree.

To make curves in the edge of the lawn drive a small stake into the ground and attach some string to it. Attach a funnel filled with sand to the other end, pull the string taut and use it to make an even curve.

When planting a tree in a lawn, leave a circle three to four times the diameter of the rootball. You can feed a tree more easily this way and it prevents direct competition from the grass.

If you want something screening from spring to autumn, plant a deciduous tree.

Bulbs which flower in the spring are a nice feature to plant under a tree. They don't have to worry about not getting enough sun because the tree doesn't cast much shade at this time.

If you want to put a bench or seat round a tree, make sure you leave enough room for the trunk to expand.

Island beds break up big expanses of grass, but make sure the proportions are in keeping with the size of the lawn.

A trellis arch can divide a garden in two. Plant two evergreen shrubs either side to mark the boundary.

A curved lawn gives the garden a more casual look while straight edges are suitable for a formal look.

An ornamental divider breaks up a long lawn.

When building an archway, make sure it's wide enough for two people to walk through and tall enough to take into account the kind of plants you're going to grow up it.

Make a quick and easy arch for a lightweight plant. Get a length of old hosepipe and stop up the ends. Push both ends into the ground and you have an instant arch.

Fast growing climbers such as *Ipomea*, *Eccremocarpus scaber* and *Thunbergia alta* will cover an archway really quickly.

Alternatively, runner beans make an attractive edible arch.

If you want to cover an archway with roses, choose a rambler rather than a climber. Ramblers are more flexible.

When putting up a shed or greenhouse, choose your site carefully. You don't want to create a wind tunnel and damage your plants.

Where wind is a problem, a hedge is better than a wall. Hedges disrupt the wind, creating calm, whereas wind simply rushes over and around walls.

Noise is a nuisance in built-up areas. A solid hedge will block quite a lot of noise. Even a fairly big tree will reduce road noise.

Well-planted pergolas will reduce overhead aircraft noise.

Alternatively, rustling trees, water and birds will detract from other more unpleasant noises.

Perk up a dull brick wall by painting it, growing fruit trees or climbers against it, adding a mirror or be really creative and paint a mural.

Autumn and spring are the best times to lay a new lawn because the grass will re-establish itself quickly. Always water a new lawn regularly.

For lawns which suffer from heavy use add finely chopped car tyres to the top dressing.

If your lawn has too many dips and hollows, it might be due to poor drainage (check for moss; this is a good indicator of poor drainage). Use a lot of grit in the soil you use to fill out the hollows.

Uneven areas can also be caused by buried tree roots or lumps of debris. Dig out whatever is causing the problem and replace it with topsoil.

When sinking slabs into the lawn, make sure they are deep enough so that the lawnmower runs over them easily.

Stepping stones make an ideal alternative pathway across a lawn.

To break up a long flight of steps place terracotta pots along the edge.

Alternatively, soften the line of steps by growing plants along the treads. Make sure you use plants which aren't going to take over too much.

You can make a flight of steps look more formal by placing two matching containers with plants in either side of the bottom or top step. Plants such as rose trees, bay trees, box plants or spiralling wire with ivy growing up it are ideal.

If your garden slopes away from the house, put progressively taller shrubs down the slope – an effective way of seeing more garden.

Direct night–lights away from your garden and towards nearby trees for a magical green backdrop.

Use yoghurt or liquid manure to age your patio. Just paint it on and leave for a while.

Use old car tyres to make simple, cheap plant holders for your patio.

You don't have to put plants in containers. If they are interesting shapes, they can be a focal point in their own right.

Group several plants together in a container, especially ones with interesting foliage or when they're in full flower. Choose plants which need similar growing conditions.

When grouping container grown plants together, choose pots which are of a similar shape or size. If you don't have the same sort of containers, make sure that you put similar plants in them in order to link the group together.

Raised beds are a good way of adding interest to a patio. If you are using bricks, make sure they are frost proof and that they blend into their surroundings.

Alternatively, use concrete blocks to make a raised bed. If you want to grow lime-hating plants, line the sides of the bed with heavy-duty polythene.

Always put drainage holes in the bottom of raised beds.

Fences need to be checked regularly and patched up. If a post rots at its base, sink a new one beside it and bolt the two together.

If your fence leans, large wooden struts wedged against the posts at angles will bring it back upright. Once plants grow, they'll be hidden.

Got a garden with a slope like the side of Everest? Cut terraces into the slope and build retaining walls to keep the soil in place.

To keep soil in place on a slope use netting pegged into the ground.

Grow a variety of climbers up a wall. If they have different flowering times, you will always have something attractive to look at.

Hide hanging basket chains by growing trailing plants up them.

If you've got a pile of unwanted rubble, don't bother to move it. Plant a climber next to it to disguise it, such as a rose or clematis. If the rubble includes concrete, don't use lime-hating plants.

Combine different materials for a more interesting effect: slabs, bricks, paving stones, gravel and cobble stones can all be mixed and matched.

To achieve an even pointing finish use a piece of old garden hose. Push it against the mortar to get the desired result.

Plant compact annuals between patio slabs to soften the look of your patio.

Don't use plants in a patio which have a vigorous root system because they may start to displace the slabs in the future.

Remove broken slabs or whole sections of your patio and plant directly into the soil. Make sure that you prepare the soil carefully; it won't have had many nutrients and will probably be severely compacted.

To age new bricks brush them with milk.

A wooden frame will support a trellis more effectively than a plastic one – it will look better and last longer. Use pressure-treated timber for your support.

Use galvanised nails and screws when fitting a trellis to prevent rust from forming.

Drill a pilot hole into wood so that it will accept a screw. A pilot hole is a hole smaller than the actual screw size.

Don't be a square when it comes to choosing the shape of your trellis. They come in all sorts of shapes and sizes nowadays so you don't have to go for the more traditional look.

For a dramatic effect paint your trellis with coloured wood preservative. You can choose something which either complements your colour scheme or strongly contrasts with it.

You don't have to scatter seeds randomly. If you sow them in straight lines, you will be able to distinguish between them and weeds as they grow.

When planting out, make sure that the stem base isn't any deeper than it was before.

When tying canes, secure them temporarily with an elastic band. Now your hands are free to tie the canes in position.

Remember to water plants 10 minutes before you dig the holes for them.

If your shrubs are getting too leggy, grow climbers like clematis over them.

Never plant roses in soil where other roses have previously been grown for five years or more. Roses can't thrive in poor soil.

Don't plant roses under trees – they need air to be healthy.

Before planting small alpines, wrap the roots in moist tissue, then place in a crevice. This will protect the roots and give the plant a good start in life.

Weigh a new pond plant down with several large stones. This will keep the roots beneath the soil and the plant in position.

Deep water plants, such as waterlilies, can be planted up in old washing-up bowls. Use a heavy soil and cover with gravel to keep in place. Put the bowl in a shallow part of the pond to start with and then move it into deeper water in a couple of weeks.

Spring-flowering bulbs like Narcissi are ideal to fill in the gaps in a newly planted border. They look at their most effective just at the time when all the other plants aren't doing much.

Planting a climber at an angle will encourage it to grow towards its support. It will also prevent the roots from being too sheltered and away from rain.

Don't buy plants after a very cold spell – their roots may have been badly affected.

Annuals, perennials and bulbs are great for filling gaps in borders.

Grow fragrant flowers, such as honeysuckle, jasmine and roses round the area where you keep your dustbins. They'll not only make the area look more attractive but it will smell better too.

Dense planting round the bin area in the summer will help cut down any strong pong.

Containers don't have to sit on patios or walls. They are useful when it comes to filling in gaps in your borders as well.

When planting up a terracotta or stone container, water both it and the plants before planting to stop the compost from drying out.

If your container is quite tall, make sure you stabilise it by putting large stones or rubble in the bottom before planting up.

When planting up a tall container, save compost by planting up a smaller pot which will fit into the top of the container.

Don't put a plant which will grow a lot into a barrel or urn-shaped container. You will only be able to remove it by smashing the pot.

When planting up hanging baskets, wrap plants in pieces of polythene shaped into a cone. This will protect the rootball when you pull it through the basket. Once the plant is in position, remove the polythene.

Alternative linings for hanging baskets are newspaper, knitwear or blanket weed.

Make your own hanging basket – use an old colander or large sieve with some chains attached.

Alternatively, large catering containers may not look attractive but plant them up with trailing plants to hide the sides and you have a handy pot.

For a different hanging basket transform unwanted lampshades by turning them upside down and planting them up.

Bulbs should be planted at a depth of between three and five times their height.

When choosing bulbs, 'big is best'.

Most bulbs look best planted in informal groups of odd numbers.

Save yourself time and effort – plant several bulbs in one large hole rather than having lots of little holes with one bulb in them.

If you like a sloping garden, make sure you use plants which don't need much looking after. They can be difficult to get to.

It can often be damper at the bottom of a slope so make sure you plant moisture-loving plants there.

Plant annuals on cool days or in a shady area. Avoid extreme temperatures. The best time to plant is in early evening, which gives the plants time to settle before the midday heat.

Autumn is the time to divide congested water plants. Remove any weak or damaged sections before replanting.

Check the growing habits of a tree before planting it. Some roots can undermine large structural foundations (especially if you have a clay-based soil).

To avoid tree roots damaging drains find out the ultimate height of the tree you want. Then plant it at least one and a half times this distance from your buildings and drains.

If your garden is dominated by trees, use plants which like woodland conditions.

For a natural woodland look go for plants which are self-seeding, have small flowers and simple foliage.

Don't forget to water plants under trees. The leaves and branches act like an umbrella and keep most of the rain off them.

The further away from a tree you go the more light the plants on the ground will receive so plant accordingly.

When planting under trees, be careful not to damage the tree roots.

Make sure newly planted trees have a good start in life by providing shelter for them as they grow and by keeping them clear of weeds.

▷▷ Design

If you're taking over an established garden, leave things for at least a year to see what the garden looks like at different times.

Draw a plan out on paper first. Take photographs of your garden from lots of different viewpoints (winter is usually a good time for this). With a felt-tip pen, you can then sketch in the features that you are thinking of adding.

Take note of which part of the garden the sun reaches and for how long to help your planting plan.

Allow for growth. Plants are like children ... they grow up, so leave them enough room. Check with the nursery if you're not sure.

Can't resist a new plant, but you've not yet made a final plan for the garden? Plant it in a tub for now – don't rush to put it in the ground.

Divide a long, narrow garden into a series of 'rooms' using screens, hedges and trellis.

If you want a patio, you will need a space at least 8 ft/2.4 m by 8 ft/2.4 m to accommodate a standard garden table and four chairs.

▷▷ Weeding & Pests

Don't throw away the salted boiling water that you've cooked your potatoes in. Use it as a weedkiller on paths and drives.

To deter weeds sprinkle sand on garden paths.

Wear an old woolly glove over a rubber glove. Dip your hand into weedkiller and then stroke the weeds you want to destroy.

Use old carpets as mulch to kill weeds.

Use Epsom salts to kill weeds.

Slugs hate seaweed so use it on your beds. It makes a great fertiliser as well.

Rake up the moss from your lawn and keep it in a damp place to use in hanging baskets.

To stop mice and birds eating your peas, soak the packet of peas in paraffin and leave for 24 hours. Cut off the end of the packet, drain the peas and then plant when needed.

For a cheap and effective bird scarer, cut flaps in a plastic bottle, put it over the top of a cane and secure with a nail. The wind will spin the bottle around, which will scare the birds away.

Cut nettles down to the ground the moment they appear. Under constant persecution, they will eventually give up.

Cover garden beds with pine bark to prevent weeds.

Leaving soil uncovered will only encourage weeds. Use some form of ground cover, either a mulch or ground-cover plants.

When tackling bindweed, grow it up a cane before applying weedkiller. This way you won't damage other garden plants.

Remember this rhyme:
Thistles cut in May return next day
Thistles cut in June come up soon
But cut them in July
And they are sure to die

When weeding, attach your rings to a safety pin and pin them to your clothing so you don't lose them.

Use an old kitchen knife to dig up dandelions and daisies from a lawn. Keep the blade vertical and cut in a circle round the weed. Pull out with the root intact.

If you're using a weedkiller, protect your plants with a sheet of cardboard or bin liner while you are spraying.

To make your own funnel to administer weedkiller more easily cut off the top of a plastic bottle. You can then throw it away after you've used it.

Some weeds will absorb chemicals more easily if you crush their foliage before applying the weedkiller. So stamp your feet.

To get rid of green slime from your patio scrub with a stiff brush and soapy water.

Weeds like water too so remove them regularly and make sure your plants get the moisture instead.

In hot weather leave uprooted weeds on the soil surface. They'll act as a layer of mulch and help retain moisture in the soil.

Stop your neighbour's weeds from creeping into your garden. Dig a trench 1 foot deep alongside the fence. Line on one side with dustbin bags, then replace the soil.

When the birds have flown, take down their nest and either throw it away or burn it. Nests are great places for insects to live in.

Make your own bird scarers by sticking feathers in the ground amongst the vegetables. Being territorial creatures, they'll keep off another bird's patch.

Make your own insect spray by soaking 3oz of chopped onion or garlic in 2 tsp of liquid paraffin for 24 hours. Strain the liquid. Mix with a solution of 1/4 oz soft soap in 1 pint of warm water. Shake well. Dilute 2 tbsp to a pint of water and fill your spray bottle. Go get 'em!

To control aphids soak nettle and wormwood leaves in a bucket of water for a week and then spray.

To control flea beetle soak elder leaves in a bucket of water for a week and spray.

To control caterpillar damage to cabbages soak tomato leaves in a bucket of water for a week and spray.

Deter rose pests by planting marigolds round the base of a rose bush.

Alternatively, growing alliums and catmint next to your roses will help combat aphids.

To protect your dahlias from earwigs dip a piece of cottonwool in machine oil and tie it round the stem of the plant (about 1ft from the ground). Tie some round any canes as well to stop them climbing up to reach the flowers.

To stop earwigs nibbling your fruit and veg place an empty matchbox, half open, at the top of the plant canes.

If earwigs are causing a problem on your fruit trees, tie some cloths round the branches. Once a week take the cloths off the branches and shake them out – well away from your garden.

Marigolds attract hoverflies, which control pests as well as repel whitefly. Grow some in your hanging baskets, grow bags and vegetable plots.

Marigolds, nasturtiums and flax will help protect potatoes from pests.

Alternatively, growing peas next to your potatoes is thought to deter pests.

Plant caper spurge near a mole run. Some people consider it a weed, but moles hate the smell.

Moles also don't get along with cats.

Try putting sweet chewing-gum into mole holes. Some say the moles eat the gum and it clogs their digestive system.

Daisy-like flowering plants are very attractive to insects which will help you combat pests and aid in pollination. Plants such as alyssum, campanula, geranium, gypsophila and salvia are ideal.

Get rid of ants by placing half a squeezed orange where the ants will find it. Soon the peel will be full of ants and you can then dispose of them suitably. Placing the peel where the birds will find them and eat the ants is a good idea.

Place banana skins around plants and rose bushes outside the house to stop ants from coming in.

If you have an infestation of ants in your wall-grown fruit, make a small trench under the wall and pour in a mixture of brine and soot.

To clear areas infested with red ants try a sprinkling of whole cloves or oil of cloves.

To keep ants away scatter spearmint leaves.

Prevent ants from coming into the house by planting mint beside the kitchen door.

Wherever you see ants sprinkle equal parts of borax and icing sugar.

To destroy ants' eggs pour boiling water on the nest.

If you want to treat mildew without resorting to modern fungicides, try a simple solution of soapy water instead.

Don't want your garden used as a cat's loo? Keep the soil moist and use a moisture retentive mulch to keep the cats away.

Alternatively, burying prickly leaves just under the surface of the soil will deter a cat when it starts to dig.

Prevent cats from climbing over a fence by spraying the wood with surgical spirit.

Keep dogs away from fence posts by spraying the posts with unwanted perfume or aftershave.

If your dog has peed on the lawn, pour a couple of buckets of water over the spot straight away. This will dilute the urine, making it harmless, and avoid unsightly brown patches of grass.

A prickly hedge such as pyracanthus will stop a neighbour's dog from digging through into your garden.

If your dog likes rummaging around rubbish bins, sprinkle the area with pepper to deter him.

Tree stumps can encourage fungus if left, so always try to remove them.

If your lawn is suffering from a rash of toadstools, sweep them away with a stiff brush before the caps open and release the spores.

If your hedge is prone to silver leaf disease, only give it its annual trim during the summer months.

Keep your garden tidy to reduce the risk of pests and diseases. Remove any rubbish, old plants and bits and bobs – these are the natural habitats for many of your garden's enemies.

Do a regular spot check for pests and diseased leaves. If you find any, pick them off and dispose of carefully.

No fly spray? Try hair-spray instead. Flies hate it because it sticks their wings together – they'll soon get the message and leave you alone.

Always clean out seedling trays and pots. This will cut down the risk of disease.

Use plastic pots and trays for young plants and seedlings. They are easier to keep clean and so are free of pests and diseases.

If you live near a busy road, your plants can be affected. A laurel hedge is more able to cope with high levels of pollution than other plants.

Marrow seeds are a most effective bait in a mousetrap.

▷▷ Sowing & Planting

An old sieve is ideal for putting compost for seeds into trays.

Use white sand to mark out the areas where you are going to sow your seeds.

Split the contents of a grow bag into four pots rather than using the three holes. This will give you room for one extra plant and they will all be much healthier because the soil is looser.

Make planting holes for small bulbs with an apple corer.

Cut up old margarine tubs and use them to label plants.

The bottom of an old washing-up-liquid bottle makes a very effective scoop.

Use the black plastic bases of drinks bottles as seed trays – they already have drainage holes cut in them and are ideal for the task.

Digging a new bed? Use your hosepipe as a guide to give you a great curve.

Make a kneeling mat out of an old hot-water bottle stuffed with bits of material.

Collect seeds from flowers – it's a lot cheaper than going out and buying them in packets.

Cut up old magazines to make seed packets.

Swap cuttings with other gardeners.

Try growing a cutting from a shrub by bending a low branch over and pegging it into the ground. Within a few weeks, you will often find you've got a new plant growing apace.

Create a herb garden using old bricks laid out in the shape of the spokes of a wheel.

Sew vegetable seeds in the clean plastic containers from ready-cooked meals.

Before planting parsley seeds, pour boiling water into the trench. This speeds up germination.

Can't bend down to sow seeds? Use a drainpipe or hose and drop the seeds down through it.

Put a used gun cartridge over the ends of your canes to avoid blinding yourself!

Alternatively, cover the ends of canes with ping-pong balls.

To stop larger seedlings from wilting in the sun, make them little hats out of newspaper. Weigh down the rim with stones to stop them blowing away.

Plants with a blue, silver or grey leaf generally like to go in the warm part of the garden.

Don't plant plants that are in flower. No one wants to move while they're making love … and it's the same for a plant!

Perk up your plants by feeding them with half a can of non-diet Coca-Cola.

Grow house plants from the green tops of fresh pineapples and carrots. Just cut off the bit you intend to eat and push the green end into some compost. When your plant starts to grow, cover the pot with a clear plastic bag, secured by a rubber band, to give it a kick-start.

To help your carnation cutting to take root, place a grain of rice alongside the cutting when planting up.

Acidic plants *can* be grown in alkaline soil. Collect leaves from your garden and place them in plastic bags. In the spring, dig a large hole, line with the dead leaves and place the plant (now cocooned by the leaves) into the hole. Fill and water as normal.

When planting a tree, cut off a bit of old hose and place one end next to the roots. When you fill in the hole, leave the other end poking out of the soil. Then when you water, it will go directly to the roots.

To encourage young trees to grow, spank them!

Don't throw away your old tights – use them as hanging baskets.

Put plastic pots in the legs of old tights, hang them in the shed and cut off the toes. The pots are then easily accessible and can be taken out (rather like cups from a vending machine).

Use old car tyres to make simple, cheap plant holders for your patio.

▷▷ Growing

Make your own fertiliser – boil nettle leaves and leave to steep for 24 hours.

Horse manure, cow dung and compost make good fertilisers.

Wood ash is also a useful fertiliser and a good way of getting rid of what's left of a bonfire. It also deters beetles and other insects if spread around your plants.

Comfrey leaves are potassium-rich. You can harvest the leaves, put them to soak in some water or let them rot down before putting them on the garden.

Keep grass cuttings. Throw them on to the compost heap (or into a black bag) and cover with a piece of carpet until they've mulched down.

Make your own mini compost heap – use plastic bin bags (heavy duty ones if possible) and put all your kitchen waste, garden trimmings and old newspapers in them. Bodge a few holes in the side and turn the contents over every now and again. Use when everything has rotted down.

Alternatively, bury small amounts of rubbish and clippings around the garden. The worms will then take over and do the composting for you.

Accelerate your compost by mixing green manure into it.

Prune climbing roses in September – they bend more easily.

To bring out really deep colours in your roses, scatter crushed eggshells around their roots.

To get a strong blue colour in your hydrangeas, plant something made from iron underneath.

Train young plants – use a bit of exhaust putty or Blu tack.

The best support for clematis is nylon wire wrapped around sheds, posts and tree trunks.

Moved into a new house and don't know what to put in the garden? Have a peek over the fence and see what's thriving next door.

▷▷ Lawns

If the edge of your lawn starts to look a bit tired, cut the edge of the turf off, turn it over and place it back on the ground where it came from.

If you're starting a new lawn, cut old car tyres in half and place them under the soil (at least 12 in/30 cm below) to act as reservoirs.

Gaps in the lawn? If you can't be bothered to start all over again, simply fill in the gaps with tea-bags.

During a drought, use bath water to water the grass. Avoid using the water though if it has bath foam or oil in it.

Water plants in the evening so that the moisture has time to soak in overnight and not get burnt off by the sun.

▷▷ Fencing

Stain your fences a variety of colours for a stunning effect.

A cheap way to preserve your fence is to paint it with engine oil from your car.

A dense trellis is more beneficial to plants than fencing because it creates an air flow through the garden.

When fixing a trellis to a wall, always set it slightly away from the wall so that air can circulate around the plants. Use small wooden blocks or old cotton reels to make a space between the trellis and the wall.

Fill old pairs of tights with compost to make 'bricks' that can be used to build a retaining wall.

Don't creosote a fence if you want to grow climbers up it because it takes time for the fumes to die away.

Don't put plants too near a wall – a climber should be about 12 in/30 cm from the wall while shrubs can be up to 3 ft/90 cm away.

▷▷ Tools of the Trade

Pick fruit using an old sieve attached to a broom handle.

Put your tools in a bucket and carry it around the garden with you; you'll have everything to hand.

Stop cast–iron furniture rusting by wiping with olive oil or sunflower oil.

To restore a saggy cane or wicker chair seat scrub with soapy water and then rinse. Leave the chair outside in the sun to dry.

Put each leg of wooden furniture on a brick to stop any rot setting in over winter.

If you are worried about staining your wooden table, put some clingfilm across the wood before placing a cloth over it. If you are concerned about hot dishes burning the wood, put a blanket underneath the tablecloth.

Save the rainforest! Avoid buying hardwoods such as mahogany.

Never leave tools standing on soil. If you can't hang them up, rest them on a wooden board wrapped in a bin bag.

Always keep your tools clean; use an old kitchen knife to scrape lumps of soil away.

Alternatively, use any left-over engine oil. Leave the bottle to drain into a jar, then brush the oil on to your garden tools or furniture to keep them in good condition. Wipe off before using.

Don't throw away broken terracotta pots – they can still be planted up. Plants such as Sempervivum grow well in dry conditions.

Conceal broken or chipped edges on containers by growing trailing plants such as Lobelia or Aubretia.

Keep drainpipes clear – stick a ball of galvanised wire wool into the opening of the drainpipe. This acts as a filter and stops debris from bunging up the pipe.

Don't have the blades of your mower set too low. If you do, you could weaken the grass and make it more vulnerable to weeds and moss.

If you've just had a new bathroom put in and find yourself with an old bath you don't need, put it in the garden. It's ideal for large plants which need a big growing space.

If you're planting up a bottomless container (like an old chimney pot), put a piece of old net curtain across the bottom to keep pests out.

Little plastic crates available from supermarkets and DIY stores make an ideal alternative to special pond baskets.

Old watering cans, chamber pots, vegetable crates, metal drums and so on make ideal plant containers. Always make sure there are enough drainage holes in the bottom.

To ensure that you get a level edge when trimming a hedge tie a piece of string to two points along the top.

When pruning a hedge for the first time, only cut one side right back to encourage new growth. In the second year, trim the new growth lightly and cut back the other side hard.

Protect plants from overnight frost by covering with old net curtains.

Alternatively, cover plants with a couple of sheets of newspaper held in place by some stones.

When painting wood, make sure you get rid of any algae and other growth. Scrub it down, allow it to dry and then paint it with preservative.

If you are putting up a wooden trellis, make sure the base is at least 2–3 in above the soil to avoid damp and wood rot.

You can make a cheap fence from old floorboards.

Make your own screen using chicken wire. You can shape it into columns or stretch it across a space.

Alternatively, use willow or hazel as a screen.

Clean the upper and roof sections of your greenhouse using a long-handled floor mop.

To remove stubborn marks from greenhouse glass put some methylated spirits on a cloth and rub hard.

Buff up the windows of a greenhouse with newspaper and a mixture of water and vinegar.

Always build a barbecue a little larger than you think you'll need. You'll be glad you did when you hold a big party.

Don't build a barbecue too near the house – you want to cook food, not smoke out your home.

Don't put it too near your neighbour's fence either – you want to remain on good terms with them!

When building your own barbecue, make sure you can fit standard-sized metal grilling racks so that they can be easily replaced.

Avoid placing a barbecue under trees – they may be badly scorched by the heat.

Make your barbecue double up as an incinerator in the winter. Just lift of the metal grilling rack and secure it to the front of the barbecue so that it will hold in the leaves and rubbish you're going to burn.

Snow can damage trees. Protect conifers and similar densely branched trees by tying together with wire or rope.

If a climber has grown in too symmetrical a fashion, trim it back unevenly to give it a more informal outline.

Keep container grown plants warm over winter – line the pot with sheets of bubble wrap before planting up.

To stop thieves walking off with your planters and tubs put several stones in the bottom of each tub before filling and planting. They will be then too heavy to lift.

If you want to create a garden on a balcony or roof, always check that it can take the added weight.

On a balcony or roof-garden use large containers which can take as many plants as lots of small pots but won't dry out as quickly.

If you live in a high-rise flat, only put low-growing plants in your window box. Make sure they are anchored firmly in the soil to protect them from the wind.

Twigs make good supports for multi-stemmed plants.

Avoid clipping or trimming your hedge during the nesting season. Wait for at least two weeks until the birds have flown the nest. The hedge can wait that little bit longer and you're doing your bit for wildlife.

Always clip hedges so that the upper surface slopes. This will stop snow from collecting on top and damaging the shape of the hedge.

Prune a pyrocanthus in stages and you will have berries in the autumn. Cut some stems in early spring and others after flowering.

A newly planted pond will invariably turn bright green with algae at first. Be patient. Allow the natural balance to establish itself before you rush in with drastic solutions.

If you want fish in your pond, introduce them to the idea gently. Float the plastic bag that they've been transported in on the surface of the pond water for an hour. The water temperature in the bag will equalise gradually; you can then release the fish into their new home.

Always handle plants by the soil or leaves, never by the stems.

If you have to replace or treat a section of fence, do so in the autumn or winter so that you don't damage plants.

If you suffer from hay fever, try avoiding pollen-rich flowers and go for something else – hostas are a good alternative.

In winter, put an old plate on top of your hanging basket and use it as a bird table. At this height, it should also be cat-proof.

▷▷ Heavy Work

Make your own paving slabs from concrete. Create the shape you want using two semi-rigid pieces of metal or plastic held together by string. Put this on a wooden base and pour your concrete mix in, making sure there are no gaps for it to seep out. Leave it for 48 hours and then untie the mould. Protect from frost until completely dry.

When making your own paving slabs, add concrete dye to make different colours.

When laying out slabs for a patio, dab the cement out in the shape of a number five on a dice. It's more economical and a lot easier to handle because there's less of it.

If you can't find a replacement for a cracked slab, move the offending piece to a less noticeable area and swap it with a better one.

Make sure your wheelbarrow is facing the direction you want to go before you fill it up. It will be a lot easier to manoeuvre.

When building a wall, always spray the bricks with water to keep the mortar wet.

▷▷ Watering

Get a water butt. Rain water is soft and much better for your plants. It will save water as well.

Old bin bags surrounding a plant will help retain moisture. Just cover with soil to disguise it.

Before planting a shrub, soak the roots in tap water. This way they get a really good drink and it's easier for you to unravel any knotted roots.

During a drought, use bath water to water the garden. Try not to use the water though if it has bath foam or oil in it.

Water from a dishwasher or washing machine isn't suitable for the garden.

During drought, leave grass clippings on the lawn to act as mulch.

Choose drought-tolerant plants such as yarrow, cotoneaster, broom, euonymous, lavender and lamb's ears.

Water plants in the evening so that the moisture has time to soak in overnight and not get burnt off by the sun.

Prevent bacteria from building up in your garden hose – don't leave it lying around in the sun. The bacteria can breed really quickly in those conditions.

To prevent a hose from being dragged across flowerbeds drive small stakes of wood into the corners and edges of beds so the hose runs round these rather than damaging plants.

To ensure water gets to the roots of plants in a grow bag plant a plastic bottle. Cut the bottom off the bottle, make sure the cap is off and put the top end into the compost. Water through the bottle.

Hedges need to be fed and watered regularly because they are constantly being clipped and trimmed so they tend to use up a lot of energy replacing the lost growth.

If your hedge is situated next to a road, make sure you screen it with polythene. This will prevent the roots from taking up de-icing salt during the winter.

If you're planting a shrub in a dry spot, make sure there's a bit of a depression in the soil round the shrub so that the water soaks down through the soil rather than running off.

Alternatively, if your soil is wet and heavy, don't put anything round the plant which might retain moisture. Too much water will damage the roots.

Regular watering will prevent fruit from cracking and developing any disorders.

Water plants under a cloche with a leaky hose. Block one end of a section of hose and make some small holes along its length. Lay the hose along a row of plants and attach the other end to a tap. Turn on the tap very gently when you need to water.

Plants which need a lot of water are house plants that are actively growing, have budding leaves and flowers, have delicate thin leaves, are housed in fairly small pots, live in a fairly dry atmosphere (like a centrally heated house) or come from marshy areas.

To water house plants use tepid water. Fill your watering can the night before so you don't give your plants a nasty cold shock.

If you are going away for a short time and are worried about your house plants, water them thoroughly, leave them to drain and then seal them in large plastic bags. Put some small canes or twigs in the compost to stop the plastic from touching the leaves if necessary.

▷▷ Fruit

A good choice for fan-training a fruit tree against a shady wall is a Morello cherry tree.

Fruit can be grown in containers – such as strawberries, apples, pears, plums, nectarines and any tree fruit on developing rootstock.

Make sure your strawberries get enough water. Put some holes in a length of hose and place this in your strawberry pot before planting up. Then just water through the hose.

Putting your strawberries under cloches will bring the crop on earlier.

Edging a bed with neat plants such as alpine strawberries gives a sense of unity.

Once you've picked your strawberries, don't get them near water – they'll turn soggy and tasteless.

Strawberries are a good way to clean your teeth – they remove plaque and leave your mouth feeling fresh.

For a reviving face mask mash some strawberries and spread them over your face.

Never pull stalks out of fruit – infection may spread in the resulting wound.

Always store fruit separately.

To store apples put a dozen in old shopping bags; punch a few holes for ventilation.

Alternatively, use a cabbage leaf in the bottom of the fruit bowl.

Pears should be stored individually on slatted trays. An old wooden shoe rack or plate rack is ideal as long as it's thoroughly scrubbed.

A dab of sealing wax on the end of a pear stalk will help keep the fruit fresh while you're storing it.

Don't throw away old fruit. Pop any fruit that's gone too soft into the blender. Use the mixture as an all-over body mask and nutrient. Once you shower it off, your skin will feel really soft and you'll smell good enough to eat.

▷▷ Vegetables

Sunflowers, with runner beans growing up their stems, make an attractive and effective screen.

Mix runner beans with sweet peas on the same support. Pollinating insects will be attracted to the sweet peas which will help your runner beans.

Vegetables can be grown in containers – suitable ones are French beans, beetroot, radishes, tomatoes, aubergines, peppers, spring onions, lettuce and carrots.

If growing vegetables in containers – make sure you choose large pots. They're easier to look after and water than small ones.

Tomatoes will grow well in a window box.

Plant African marigolds alongside your tomatoes to keep greenfly away.

Try planting vegetables for effect as well as food. Oak-leafed lettuce next to purple basil or spring onions between curly, red-leafed lettuce look stunning.

Plant flowers like poppies and love-in-a-mist between vegetable beds. They can survive in fairly poor soil so won't mind if the vegetables get most of the nutrients and the flowers will look pretty between the foliage.

If you are bothered by slugs, but don't want to use slug pellets, plant a ring of cheap lettuce around your more prized varieties. Once they've found some food, they won't bother looking elsewhere.

If you want easy care vegetables, stick to dwarf varieties.

►►► Midwives

Chris Warren; Su Down, Derby General Hospital; Association of Radical Midwives; Midwife Information and Resource Service; Independent Midwives Association

▷▷ Conception

If you want a girl, make love a couple of days before ovulation – female sperm survive for much longer than male sperm.

For a female baby, make love a lot! This will lower the proportion of male to female sperm in your partner's semen.

Eat lots of bananas if you want a girl – apparently, a potassium-rich diet will increase the chances of a daughter.

If all else fails, go and train as a fighter pilot. They seem to father a greater number of girls!

If you want a boy, only make love on the day of or immediately after ovulation because male sperm swim faster than female sperm and will reach the ovum first.

For a son, make love infrequently as this increases the proportion of male sperm.

▷▷ Before the Baby Comes …

Eat sensibly … three-quarters of mums remain at least 2 lb/1 kg heavier after the birth! However, you do need to increase your intake by 500 calories a day.

Little and often is best. Try five or six small snacks instead of one or two blow-outs.

To accommodate your bump without splashing out on lots of special clothes, wear your usual leggings back to front.

Don't buy dungarees. You'll want to go to the loo a lot more often when pregnant so skirts and dresses are much less fiddly.

If you can't face eating anything, wear a travel-sick bangle on both wrists.

Sick or nauseous? Try sucking on some ginger. If that doesn't work, vitamin B6 is good, so tuck into some Marmite.

Travel sickness is a common complaint during pregnancy. Driving yourself will help rather than being the passenger.

Have some glucose tablets to hand if you suffer from travel sickness, as it is often caused by low blood sugar.

If you are laid low by morning sickness, cut out caffeine which triggers nausea.

Backache is common in pregnancy. When washing up, rest the bowl on another inverted bowl to make it higher – it will be much more comfortable for your back.

Cramp in your legs, especially first thing in the morning, can be another pregnancy ailment. It is caused by calcium deficiency, so drink a large glass of milk before bedtime or eat more yoghurt.

Thrush can often irritate mums-to-be. If you haven't eaten all the yoghurt to help your cramps, try spreading it on the infected area to soothe and heal.

Constipated? It's very common in pregnancy. Prevent it by doubling your intake of water.

If you are suffering from heartburn, a glass of milk will help to neutralise stomach acid.

To tone up your uterus for labour, drink lots of raspberry-leaf tea in the later stages of pregnancy (but never in the first six months because it might bring on premature labour).

Most heavily pregnant women get insomnia. Make sure you get a good night's sleep. First, try a long, relaxing, warm bath. Then enjoy a warm, milky drink and a plain biscuit. Finally, put a couple of drops of lavender oil on your pillow – it's wonderfully relaxing and will ensure sweet dreams.

If you simply can't get comfortable, lie curled up on your side around a soft pillow. Put the pillow between your knees and rest your bump against it.

If you have given birth prematurely in the past, eating oil-rich fish, such as mackerel and sardines, will help reduce the risk of pre-term birth.

If you've gone past your due date you'll be desperate for the baby to come. To avoid a hospital induction, try nipple stimulation to help the uterus to contract. Sex also helps to bring on contractions.

Kick-start a late baby, by eating certain foods. Curry, chilli and other strong foods are believed to trigger things off.

Bring on labour, by rubbing a little jasmine oil on to your abdomen or adding a couple of drops of clary sage oil to your bath.

To get your baby into a good position for delivery, try cleaning the skirting boards – being on all fours will shift things about.

▷▷ **The Labour ...**

First-time mums often arrive at hospital far too early. To avoid boredom and nerves, take lots of coins with you so you can have a good natter to some friends on the phone.

Avoid being in hospital too early. Once contractions begin, try setting yourself a little task to finish before you leave. Tidying a drawer or writing a letter not only kills time but will also help to distract you from the discomfort of early labour.

To help you relax and prepare you for labour, try running a warm bath. You'll enjoy it far more at home than in a hospital bathroom.

Labour has been compared to running a marathon. Prepare yourself for the big event by eating lots of carbohydrates – potatoes, pasta, bread and vegetables.

Many women can't face eating or drinking during labour. Your mouth gets very dry so take a damp sponge to suck on for when you get dry.

Back pain can be a real problem in labour. Try making a simple back rub by filling a sock with some uncooked rice mixed in with a little massage oil, and knotting the open end. When you need it, ask the midwife to pop the sock in the microwave (most hospitals have them) and then get your partner or anyone else who's with you to rub it over the painful part of your back.

To help ease back pain, take the weight off your spine – kneel on all fours with your bottom in the air and your head on a pillow.

For sheer reassurance and comfort, take a hot-water bottle with you into hospital.

Women in labour often get very hot – ask your partner or someone else with you to have a plant spray filled with cool water to hand so you can have a quick burst of cool spray when things start to heat up.

If you have long hair, take a hair band. There's nothing worse when you're hot and sticky than having your hair flop all over your face.

Women often feel a burning sensation in labour. Try holding a hot or cold pad against the skin to ease the pain.

▷▷ After the Birth ...

You are likely to be starving. Be prepared and have some high-energy food ready, such as a chocolate bar or a banana.

If you're left sore after stitches, try holding a bag of finely crushed ice wrapped in a soft cloth against the painful area.

Soothe sore stiches with a bag of frozen peas or sweetcorn.

To speed up healing after stitches, add some salt to the bath or, even better, some good-quality lavender oil.

Drying with a towel can be painful, but it's important to keep stitches clean and dry. Try a quick blast with the hair-dryer.

Weeing can really sting if you've had stitches. When nature calls, try standing up in a cool shower – the running water will dilute the acid that causes the burning sensation.

Having stitches makes it painful to sit down. Try sitting on a child's rubber ring – you may feel a little silly but it's a great way to reduce painful pressure on the sore area.

To stop your breasts feeling sore, pop a couple of cabbage leaves inside your bra.

If your nipples become sore, try sleeping topless at night (put a towel under you to stop any leaks). It will help if you can let air circulate around your boobs.

Go to the doctor if you get sudden pains, a rash or feel as if you're coming down with flu. It could be mastitis, which must be treated straight away.

Feed your baby last thing at night before you go to bed so you can get as much sleep as possible before it's time for the next feed. Prepare a thermos so that you can have a nice warm drink while you do the feed in the middle of the night.

Lots of new mums suffer hair loss. Add some powdered gelatine to your shampoo and leave it on for 10 minutes to encourage the return of glossy locks.

Start building up a mental map of where all the mother-and-baby rooms are in your area so that you won't panic if you get caught short.

Try to make some time for yourself. When the baby is asleep or someone is looking after it for you, try to do something that you enjoy – read a magazine, have a hot soak, listen to some music.

Be kind to yourself after the birth. Don't go on a strict diet because you will be tired and need all the energy you can get. There isn't a prize for getting back into your jeans within a fortnight.

▷▷ Your New Bundle of Joy ...

... will cry more than you think. Don't worry. The average baby will cry for at least two hours a day, and up to four is not unusual. If you accept it's normal, you'll find it less stressful.

New-born babies may appear to be very fragile but will be much happier if you handle them firmly – they're used to being contained in a very confined space so try wrapping them quite tightly in a blanket.

Babies are born without any bacteria in their mouths. Nearly all children under three catch tooth-decaying germs from their mother's saliva, so avoid 'cleaning' your baby's dummy or teething ring by sucking on it yourself.

Reassure your child. While you are out of the room, play them a tape of familiar sounds, such as the vacuum cleaner or the hair-dryer, so that they don't feel isolated.

If your baby gets colic, try lying him face down across your lap with his tummy resting on a hot-water bottle filled with warm water.

Babies hate having tight things pulled over the heads so choose clothes with wide, envelope necks.

However pretty they may be (the clothes, not the baby!), don't choose knitwear with lacy patterns. Babies will only get their fingers caught up in them.

Jaundice is common in babies. Lying in natural sunlight for a short time, while adequately dressed to avoid either cold or sunburn, clears it up quickly.

When bottle-feeding your baby, you must keep the bottle at such an angle that the teat is always full of milk. Swallowing air while feeding is the most common cause of colic.

You can get pregnant when breast-feeding – most accidental pregnancies happen within nine months of giving birth! So perhaps we should learn from the women of Papua New Guinea who avoid resuming sex until their first-born can walk, or the African Masai who abstain until the little one has cut its teeth!

▶▶▶ Milliners

Geoff Bates; Paul Pleass; Locks the Hatters; Katherine Franklin-Adams

To measure the size of a head correctly, take your tape-measure around from the centre of the forehead, behind the ear, over the bump at the back of the head, behind the other ear and back to the front.

If the final hat is going to be made from a thick fabric such as velvet, add 1 in/2.5 cm to the measurements.

If you're making your first hat, a lightweight fabric is easier to work with.

Create your own hat stand – use a bottle of champagne.

Don't mess up expensive ribbon by practising how to tie it. Play around with some muslin instead until you are sure where and how you want the bow.

To avoid a lop-sided look, the front brim of a hat should always be wider than the back.

If you have a long neck, a wide-brimmed hat will suit you best.

Big shoulders can be made to look smaller by wearing smaller, neater hats.

The best hat for heart-shaped faces is one with a medium brim worn at an angle.

For those with square faces, choose a wide-brimmed hat.

For those with long faces, hats that have curved brims with some decoration look best.

Those with round faces should choose hats that are deep-crowned and worn low on the head. If you can't find this sort of hat, tilt any other sort of hat at an angle.

Always try a hat on standing up and walking about so that you can assess the whole outline and not just the 'head and shoulders'.

Never iron a hat backward and forward because this will stretch the fabric. Instead, place an iron straight down on the fabric and lift it off.

To avoid marking a hat when ironing it always use a chromium-plated iron.

To prevent your hats becoming discoloured, use acid-free tissue paper to store them.

To clean a Panama hat, wipe it with a mixture of water and lemon juice, and use a soft, clean cloth.

To get marks off your Panama hat, rub them with stale bread.

Store your Panama hat in the bathroom – they love the humidity.

Only real Panama hats should be rolled so don't be tempted to try it on your cheap holiday bargain. The best way to carry a Panama is to hold it gently by the brim and not the crown.

After wearing your felt hat, brush it gently with a soft brush. Do this each time you take it off. Keep it in a plastic bag.

To check for weak spots in a length of felt, hold it up to the light to see if there are any uneven or thin patches.

If you get caught in the rain wearing a felt hat, use tissue paper to blot the raindrops away and then get a handful of tissue paper and run it over the hat with a smooth, circular action.

If your felt hat has become droopy, steam it for a few seconds and then brush it gently, making sure you are brushing in the direction of the nap.

To bring up the colour on a white or cream felt hat, sprinkle with talcum powder.

Sprinkle a white or cream felt hat with bran. Leave it overnight, then brush it off in the morning. This works like an exfoliator.

When steaming a hat, use a kettle with a short spout, not a jug kettle. You'll have more control over the direction of the steam.

To revive flowers on a hat, shake them over a steaming kettle and they'll blossom back into life.

Always buy a flat cap one size too large. You're most likely to be wearing it in damp or really wet weather and it will probably end up shrinking.

To clean a flat cap, wash it in mild soapy liquid.

If you get your beret wet, slip it over a plate that is the same size to stop it from shrinking.

To change the size and fitting of a top hat, heat it up on top of an Aga or in front of a fire then put it on your head. It should mould to the shape of your head while it is still warm and give you a perfect fit.

Make sure you are wearing your hat the right way round. A woman should wear the bow or feather to her right, the man to his left.

If you're making a bobble hat (do people still do that?), crochet it to give it more body and shape rather than knitting it.

To pack crushable hats in a suitcase, fill them with underwear.

Remove stubborn stains from a felt hat by brushing with sandpaper. If that fails, colour in the mark with an appropriately coloured felt-tip pen.

▶▶▶ Models

Caitlin Powell

Make sure you give the agent the best shots of you. Take in holiday pictures of you looking relaxed and natural and, no doubt, wearing a swimming costume.

When visiting an agent for the first time, let them judge how you really look. Don't wear make-up, high heels or do your hair in an elaborate style.

Keep your portfolio up to date by asking for test Polaroids at a shoot. They may be as good as the finished product and you won't have to wait months for them to be ready.

To improve your portfolio, include pictures of any special skills you may have, such as horse riding, wind surfing, skiing and so on.

For a child's portfolio, don't pay more than £60.

Don't let an amateur photographer take shots for your portfolio – they may just 'click' six times for six photos.

When placing your child with an agency, find out as much information as possible before parting with any money.

Accentuate your cheekbones – say the word 'poor', while keeping your lips soft, and hold for a couple of seconds.

Perfect your catwalk technique – practise walking towards a mirror, keeping your toes directly ahead, brushing your knees together and taking steps no longer than 12 in/30 cm.

To test whether you need to wear a bra or not, place a pencil underneath your breast. If it falls, you don't need to wear one!

Avoid blemishes – always have your body waxed a couple of days in advance of a shoot.

To be prepared for a shoot, you should take a pair of black shoes, your own make-up and beauty products, just in case the stylists and make-up artists don't have anything suitable for you.

Create a good impression on a shoot. Write down the names and job descriptions of each member of the crew. You never know when you'll meet them again.

For free information on what to look for in a modelling agency contact the Model Information Bureau (Body's House, 25–27 Queens Road, Southend, Essex, SS1 1LT. Telephone: 01702 435328).

▶▶▶ Musicians

Nicholas Korth, Birmingham Royal Ballet Orchestra

Keep ahead of the game when playing. Check what's over the page!

To help your music books last just that bit longer, laminate them and store them in a flat box.

Encourage children to practise their instruments by getting them into a routine. They should play at the same time every day. It sounds simple but it's very effective.

To play any instrument effectively (apart from the guitar), you should keep your nails relatively short. If you can see the ends of your fingers above your nails, then so much the better.

To clean the inside of your guitar – fill it with uncooked rice, give it a really good shake and then empty.

You'll know when it's time to change the strings on your guitar when the sound goes.

Keep an eye on the strings of your violin bow – if little hairs are beginning to come off the bow then it's time for a change.

To avoid making too much noise when moving between your percussion instruments, don't wear shoes. Put on some thick slipper socks.

Don't trip over your microphone wire – it doesn't look too cool. Tuck it into your belt at the back.

If you want to be a pianist and get the best out of your fingers, don't play racket games.

To start playing the piano after the age of 16 is not a good idea. Go for something a little easier.

To play the piano effectively during a concert, avoid wearing long sleeves and take off your bangles.

Make sure you get a good sound from your piano – once it is in the room, leave it where it is.

To polish your piano keys properly, never spray directly on to them. Spray on to a cloth and work from the top of the key to the bottom. Don't polish sideways.

You can clean your brass instrument cheaply and effectively with warm soapy water.

Avoid valve problems during a concert – keep a small bottle of valve oil with you at all times.

To get a good strong sound out of your horn you should not clean it on the inside. All the dirt and bacteria add to the beautiful sound. If you clean the horn, it sounds too clinical.

To play your horn well for a long period of time, pace yourself. Don't use all your strength up in the first few pages of music.

Get the most out of your wind instrument by cleaning it as soon as you have finished with it.

Clean your clarinet properly by attaching a piece of flannelette sheet to a knitting needle and pushing that down your instrument.

Ensure that your clarinet produces a good tone – change the reeds quite often.

Make a halter for your saxophone from an old silk scarf.

▶▶▶ Nannies

Marianne Bell; Catherine Wilson; Linda Elderkin; Alison Tweedale

▷▷ Babies

Don't be too fastidious about constantly washing and changing the cot sheets – babies like the smell of familiar surroundings.

To reassure the baby and encourage good sleeping habits, place something in the cot that the baby's mum has worn during the day.

Leave a babysitter some extra pieces of a parent's clothing to wrap the baby in if they wake up fretful.

Leave a babysitter a tape of a parent either singing or, for older children, telling a story.

Don't hush everything up when you put the baby to sleep. Teach your child to sleep through normal noise levels.

Young babies don't need expensive toys. They will love to watch a washing machine going round or listen to a vacuum cleaner. Many new mothers try to keep all noises down – but babies find them fascinating and it's good to get them used to normal domestic surroundings.

Make your own changing table from the top of a chest of drawers. Place the chest against a wall and add a 4-in/10-cm-high lip to the front to stop the baby rolling off. Definitely don't ever leave the baby unattended, though.

Bathing tiny babies can be a bit tricky. You may find it easier to bath them in a sink rather than bending down over a large tub.

If your baby dislikes having a bath, it may be because the bathroom is too cold. Make sure the room is warm before you start the bath, or bathe the baby in another, warmer room.

Babies can be bathed every day or every other day. You can 'top and tail' them – wipe their faces and bottoms – at least twice a day.

New babies (up to a month old) can be washed in a washing-up bowl. Cover the taps with a towel so that you don't bang your baby's head against them. Remove dirty pots and pans first!

To prevent babies from slipping in a big bath, use a terry nappy as a non-slip mat.

Never leave a baby or child alone in the bath. It only takes a few inches of water to drown a child so always supervise them.

Babies quickly get cold after a bath. Make sure you have everything you'll need before you put your baby in the water.

Feed babies after their bath and not before. Babies often decide to throw up if they've been jiggled around, so wait until after they've been cleaned before feeding.

Keep all your equipment together – use a hanging shoe container which you can fill with cotton wool, ointment, creams, terry towels … in fact, anything that you need for changing or cleaning your baby. It can be hung on a wall or door for easy access.

Use plastic stacking boxes from DIY stores for storage. They are cheaper than specially designed baby equipment.

When babies are young, put them in nighties rather than playsuits at night. It will make night changes easier and less disruptive, and begin to teach them the difference between night and day.

Lay out a clean set of night clothes before you go to bed so that you're not stumbling around in the gloom if you have to do a complete change in the wee small hours.

Make your own baby wipes – they're cheaper and less synthetic. Simply soak some cotton-wool roll in an old ice-cream carton filled with water and a little baby oil. Tear off strips as you need it.

Make your own nappy–rash cream. Whip up an egg white until it has soft peaks. Apply it to the affected area with cotton wool.

Treat nappy rash with a soft paste of fuller's earth and water. Gently apply to the affected area.

Cradle cap looks horrid – a little almond oil should clear it up in no time.

When you wash children's hair, draw a thin line of petroleum jelly above their eyes; it will stop the shampoo running down into their eyes and stinging them.

To keep shampoo out of children's eyes, get them to wear a golf visor.

Teething can be a major problem. Cut some slightly stale bread into fingers, dip into milk and then bake for a couple of minutes until brown for excellent teething strips.

To soothe hot, painful gums, put some fresh fruit flesh into the middle of a muslin square and twist the cloth into a tight sausage. Chill it in the fridge for a couple of hours then let your baby gnash away at it.

Always have lots of muslin squares around – they have lots of uses. Try placing one over a pillow to save laundry if your baby keeps posseting; or use one tied to the cot with a little vapour rub on it to help a sniffly baby. Take the chill off a baby-changing mat by laying a muslin square across it first.

Cleaning first milk teeth is a fiddly job and many babies hate toothbrushes. Instead, wrap a little muslin around your finger – it makes it much easier to get at little gnashers.

To wind a baby, try holding him over your shoulder and walk up and down the stairs – the natural up-and-down movement works much better than trying to bounce him and the rhythm will relax him, too.

When you first wean a baby on to solids, they'll only want a bit each time. Avoid waste and make life more convenient by making up large batches of fresh vegetables or fruit then puréeing them into ice trays to use as needed.

Be patient when introducing solids. Start off with one or two teaspoons of food a day. If your baby isn't interested, go back to milk for a day or so and then try again.

Introduce new foods one after the other. You can then detect more easily if your child is allergic to anything.

Save time by cooking for the whole family at once. Cook the 'grown-up' food without seasoning, put a little to one side for your baby and purée it. Then season your own food the way you like it.

Don't use baby talk. It doesn't help children to pick up anything useful. Use simple, short sentences and look at children when you speak to them.

Turn learning new words into a game. Point at things and get the child to repeat them.

Use body language to reinforce what you are saying: for example, waving goodbye to people.

Expand on what your child says. Always try to add new words for your child to learn. If they point out a fire engine in the street, you can say 'Yes, it's a *red* fire engine'.

▷▷ Toddlers

To cure an early riser, try setting an alarm clock! It may sound mad, but children love gimmicks and your toddler will start to wait for the bell to go off, often falling asleep again before that time comes. Eventually, their body clock will change, teaching them to sleep until your chosen time of waking.

Keep the route from nursery to your room clear of obstacles. If your child comes looking for you at night, you don't want them tripping over things in the dark. Put up a safety gate at the top of the stairs.

If your child is suffering from nightmares, make a point of turning their pillow over to 'turn the bad dreams away'. Leave a night-light or soft light on in the room.

Encourage toddlers to dress themselves by laying out their clothes so they can see the whole outfit. Then make the task a game by setting a clock and challenging them to a race against time.

To get your toddler to wear his coat, put the garment inside out on the floor. Teach him to push his arms in and pull the coat over his head; the coat will then be the correct way round.

Teach little ones their left and right by putting stickers on their wellies.

To teach tying shoelaces, get some liquorice laces and practise making edible butterflies.

When children want to start feeding themselves, dress them in a painting bib rather than a normal feeding bib – it will cover much more of their clothing and is waterproof so can be wiped off.

Faddy eaters may be encouraged to eat if you make mealtimes fun. Arrange food to create patterns or to spell out their name.

Involve toddlers in buying food and cooking – they'll feel much more inclined to taste something they've helped to prepare.

Arrange finger foods in the different compartments of an ice tray – children love 'little things'.

Tantrums and the 'terrible twos' needn't be the end of your sanity. They are just a cry for attention. If you ignore them, the toddler will realise they don't work. If your child is really stubborn, try leaving the room yourself and say 'I don't want to be with you while you do that' – young children hate to be ignored and will soon come and say sorry!

It's never too early … to start learning good manners. Make sure you say 'please' and 'thank you' as well. You want to set a good example!

Dressing up can be great therapy for shyness and can be used to overcome fears. Superman wouldn't be scared of the dentist and Cinderella would always have clean teeth and hair!

When children are cleaning their teeth, use an egg timer in the bathroom so they know how long they should clean their teeth for.

To wean a toddler off a dummy, have a special box which is home for the offending soother. At night, after the child falls asleep, put the dummy in the box – letting the child know it is there if it is needed. At some stage, send the box off to Father Christmas or the fairies, then return it to the child with a small toy in it instead of the dummy.

Make modelling dough out of flour, water and some food colouring. Children enjoy the process of making it as much as the modelling that follows and it's much cheaper than buying it ready-made. If your child makes something really good, this home-made recipe can be baked hard and kept afterwards.

Start potty training when your child can stay dry for a few hours at a time and can understand some simple instructions. Let your child see other children or parents using the loo. Make a star chart – one star for every time they successfully use the potty. And be prepared for it to take time!

Children love magic and surprises. Make special paper by writing messages or the children's names in white crayon on white paper. When they colour the paper in, they'll reveal your message.

Be creative. Use old offcuts of wallpaper and get your child to lie down on the plain side. Draw around them to make a silhouette and then pin it up and get them to colour it in with whatever they fancy.

To make a fun placemat for your child, take one of their paintings and stick it on to a cork table mat. Then cover the mat with some clear sticky-back plastic.

Use sponges and vegetables as stamps. Cut out a simple design for them and then leave them to make patterns on paper by dipping the stamp in paint.

If your children have made thickly daubed finger paintings, a quick blast of hair-spray will stop the bits of paint falling off once it's dried.

Keep a box of odds and ends which you can use for drawing, sticking things together or modelling. Old toothbrushes, old office stationery, large buttons, yoghurt pots, cereal packets and that old stand-by, the washing-up bottle! Keep everything in shoeboxes for a rainy day.

Children's parties needn't be a nightmare for parents. Don't do too much food: children are often too excited to eat a lot. Make sure you've moved all your precious objects out of harm's way. If all the children are under four, they'll need one-to-one supervision. If children are four or five years old, it's best to have one adult for every five children.

If you are going out somewhere busy, like a crowded park or fun fair, tie a brightly coloured balloon to the pushchair. If your toddler runs off and gets lost, he'll be able to find you again more easily.

Encourage your children to tidy their rooms with an egg timer or clock. Make it a race with prizes for the tidiest competitor.

Teach young children to count by marking the back of a jigsaw in numerical order. The little ones can enjoy piecing the jigsaw together using the numbers as a guide and then turn it over to see the finished picture. The numbers will also help you to quickly check if you have all the pieces.

It's important to calm children down at the end of the day. Read them stories and let them know that the quieter they are, the longer you'll read. If they start being noisy, it's end of story.

A fun way to encourage children to eat their dinner is to give them chopsticks instead of knives and forks (not for the faint-hearted or anyone with a new carpet).

To get the kids cooking, but without giving them sharp kitchen implements, get them to use plastic knives and forks.

To make cooking fun for kids let them press all the buttons (on the blender, oven, etc.) while you do the boring stuff of removing all the hot food.

For a healthy and tasty pizza with a difference spread some Marmite on to a pizza base before adding favourite toppings.

To create fun-shaped sandwiches for children use metal pastry cutters.

Children thrive on routine in their daily activities. Try to serve meals at the same time each day.

Eating is a new experience for small children. Don't be surprised if at first a child is cautious and curious, plays with food, is reluctant to try new foods and rebels when forced to eat. Try to be patient, relaxed and maintain a sense of humour – even if they appear to be eating nothing, you'll be surprised how much actually goes in during a day.

Snacks are not always bad for children. Nutritious snack foods can help children obtain required nutrients. Since children have smaller stomachs than adults, they are natural grazers – so serving three small meals with a nourishing snack in between each meal may be more appropriate than serving three large meals.

But frequent snacking may contribute to tooth decay. Clean children's teeth each day and check with a dentist about the need for fluoride.

Children often want to eat one particular food at every opportunity. This is called a 'food jag' and typically occurs among toddlers. As long as the preferred food is nutritious and the jag does not last long, there is nothing to worry about. If you go along with it, the child will probably get bored of the food soon enough.

Children's appetites may suddenly decrease around the age of two due to a decrease in their growth rate. As growth slows, energy requirements are also reduced. So don't worry if a previously hungry hippo turns into a nibbling mouse.

Don't present children with huge helpings – they'll eat much better if confronted with an obviously manageable portion and, if they then manage a second helping, they'll feel a real sense of achievement.

Slice frankfurters into four strips lengthwise and then cut into small pieces which can't block the windpipe and cause the child to choke.

Cook meat at a low temperature (300°–325° F) to keep it tender and juicy. We all remember chewing on a mouthful of meat which just won't go away.

When children are first learning to feed themselves, cut meat into small julienne strips which can be picked up and eaten by hand. Older children who are using tableware still need to have their meat cut into bite-size pieces with the fat and gristle trimmed to prevent choking.

Children usually enjoy brightly coloured fruits and vegetables.

Children like their vegetables crunchy, not soft. Vegetables steamed in a small amount of water, microwaved or stir-fried are not only crisp, but retain most of their colour, flavour and nutrients far better than boiled ones.

Many strongly flavoured vegetables such as cabbage, turnip, cauliflower, spinach, broccoli and asparagus are very acceptable to children when served with grated cheese or a cheese sauce.

Avoid giving raw carrots and whole peas, corn and grapes to children under four years old to prevent choking. Cook and mash carrots, corn and peas, and cut grapes into quarters.

Many older children enjoy raw vegetables served with their own individual bowl of dip.

When shopping with children, encourage them to help select fruits and vegetables, especially ones they have never tried before.

Taste food before adding butter, margarine, dressing, jellies and jams. Since children follow the example of adults, limit your own use of fats and sugars, and use only moderate amounts of these foods in meal preparation.

Seat children at a table for meals and snacks, and discourage them from eating while walking or standing.

Cover the floor directly beneath a child's seat with paper, vinyl or plastic.

Purchase a spoon or fork with a short, straight, broad, solid handle. The spoon should have a wide mouth and the fork should have blunt prongs. Children will begin to feed themselves with a spoon and will learn to use a fork later.

Place food at the level of a child's stomach, where it is less tiring for a child to reach.

Children playing with food should be allowed to leave the table rather than disturb others. This usually indicates that a child has had enough to eat. Don't encourage children to clean their plates when they're no longer hungry. This may lead to overeating or the development of an aversion to food.

Sometimes children behave better and enjoy mealtimes more when they sit down to a meal with the family at a nicely set table. Allowing older children to have candles makes a meal into a special occasion, and little ones can help to blow them out when everyone's eaten well.

Encourage children to try at least one bite of a new food. If, after one bite, children reject it, reintroduce the food later.

Allow children to eat at their friends' homes. These visits offer an excellent opportunity for them to try new foods. Try incorporating these new foods in meals you prepare.

Start nutrition education early by explaining the function of nutrients found in common foods (e.g. milk makes bones and teeth strong).

Meal preparation should not be a burden. Salads, raw vegetables, fruits and ready-to-serve meats, fish and cheese are nutritious and easy to prepare.

Breakfasts don't have to be traditional. Any nutritious combination of foods from all food groups is recommended. Incorporate left-overs when preparing breakfast.

Encourage children to participate in quiet activities before mealtimes. It's difficult to get an excited child to settle down to eat.

Feed children before guests arrive. Children require a lot of attention at mealtimes and it may be impossible to give it to them while entertaining guests.

Children's blood sugar levels often run low quite quickly. If your toddler suddenly seems irritable for no apparent reason, try giving him a little bit of fruit or cheese.

Boring bites can be transformed into magical meals with a few drops of food colouring and a little imagination. Mashed potato can become green grass or blue sea, pasta can be colourful snakes, and rice can be any colour of the rainbow. Even the humble egg boiled in its shell can become jewel red or sunshine yellow. Choose your child's favourite colour and they'll soon start eating up.

Whenever they eat, children should be sitting upright, not lying down or running around. Always supervise at snack and mealtimes, because a child who is choking cannot make a noise to attract your attention. Coughing, on the other hand, is a sign that the child is removing the obstacle naturally. Before intervening, give the child the chance to cough out the food.

The grinding action of a child's teeth is not very effective until at least four years of age. Because of this, foods which are hard or tough to chew, small and round or sticky are most often choked on. These include: frankfurters, raw apples, crunchy or hard-boiled sweets, raw carrots, nuts, corn, grapes, peas, popcorn, chunks of meat, raisins, and peanut butter spread too thickly.

When travelling by car, bus or train with young children, consider their special needs. Pack snacks when taking a trip which will last longer than one hour.

Be sure to keep hot foods hot and cold foods cold. A cooler, which can be stored in a car or below the seat of a bus or train, will allow you to pack a variety of foods which must remain cold.

Raw vegetables, fruits, cheese, crackers and tubs of yoghurt are easily eaten in a car and store well. Pack cheese, cold cuts, peanut butter, jelly and a loaf of bread to make sandwiches on an extra long trip.

Pack tableware, napkins, moist towelettes or a washcloth that has been moistened and stored in a plastic bag.

When travelling by plane, don't expect the airlines to cater to the needs of children, although sometimes they do. Today many airlines are limiting their meal service in order to reduce air fares. It's usually a good idea to bring along sandwiches, fruits, cheese, crackers and raw vegetables, which can be kept for a short period of time without refrigeration. Even though airlines usually provide beverages during a flight, you may want to bring a thermos of milk or cans of juice to prevent children from getting fussy. There will be so much new going on around them, at least the food and drink can be familiar.

Pay attention to the special needs of children when dining with them at restaurants. If you must wait before being seated, take children for a walk outside the restaurant to prevent them from becoming impatient.

Some children expect to eat as soon as they sit at a dinner table and will fill up on appetisers and bread, leaving no room for their main meal. Try to prevent this by asking the restaurant not to put out the bread in advance of the meal and, when you order, inquire about children's portions.

Young children will feel more at home in a restaurant if you bring along their cups and tableware.

Children involved in meal preparation develop a more active interest in food. They can accomplish many different tasks when working one-on-one with an adult in the kitchen. A number of activities children can do successfully at various ages are listed below. Having patience and time to spend with children when involving them in meal preparation is the key to success.

Two- and three-year-olds need to learn about personal hygiene – encourage them to wash their hands before handling any food or eating.

But they love having 'jobs' to do. Try asking them to wash vegetables, wipe the table, tear lettuce, help to shape burgers and meatballs, peel bananas (if the top is started) and clear their own place setting.

Three- and four-year-olds like to feel challenged. Let them break eggs into bowl, measure and mix ingredients, knead and shape dough, pour their own cereal out, and toss salads.

Five-year-olds can make cakes and cookies using baking mixes, help make pancakes, French toast, scrambled eggs, hot cereal and rice (with close supervision), set and clear the table and load the dishwasher.

Encourage teenagers to help out in the kitchen. Put up a notice each day saying what's for dinner. If they get home before you they will know which vegetables to start chopping or to preheat the oven. You may even find dinner waiting for you. (But don't bank on it … !)

For healthy ice-lollies that will still please little ones top and tail a pineapple and cut downwards into 6-8 chunky wedges, then freeze.

Give the kids a treat with home-made creamy banana ice-lollies. Blend a banana with some milk, then pour into moulds, add a stick and freeze.

When making your own ice-lollies, put any piece of real fruit in to pep up the taste and make them healthy.

To remove home-made ice-lollies from their mould place the mould under running warm water.

Keep insects out of the children's drinks when having a picnic. Cover the tops of beakers with clingfilm and push a straw through.

Children will love bananas if you coat them in melted chocolate and roll in coconut.

Dilute pure fruit juice with sparkling mineral water when serving to children.

Do your kids' hands get messy when eating ice-lollies? Just take a disc of card, put the stick of the lolly through the card and, as the lolly melts, the juices will just drip on to the card and not on to the children's hands.

Give kids small cups to drink from – they're easier to carry and so less likely to be dropped. If they do get dropped, there's less to clean up.

For fun cup cakes top them with a marshmallow a couple of minutes before removing from the oven.

Children don't usually like ice-cold milk – try pouring it a short time before serving to take off the chill.

Serve milk in plastic cups with covers that fit or unbreakable cups with weighted bottoms. Fill cups halfway to make milk more difficult to spill; this will also make the task of drinking milk seem less awesome.

Only offer flavoured milk on special occasions. Children should develop a taste for plain milk, which has fewer calories than flavoured.

If children refuse to drink milk, try to include milk-based soups, cottage cheese, yoghurt, cheese, custard or cereal with milk in their diets.

If a child is over the age of two, serve low-fat milk rather than whole milk.

Young children often prefer the taste of bland, sweet fruits over tart fruits. Serve tart fruits from time to time to develop a child's taste for all fruits.

Peel, core and seed fruits for very young children. Fresh, dried, canned and frozen fruits and juices make nutritious snacks and desserts.

To reduce the chance of cavities clean children's teeth with a moistened washcloth or gauze, especially after they have eaten dried fruits.

Do not offer sweets as a bribe or withhold them as punishment.

Since children know that sweets exist, serving sweets on special occasions may be a more sensible approach than excluding them completely. By sometimes including them in your child's diet, you avoid making them into a big deal.

While you should avoid feeding gumdrops, jelly beans, hard-boiled sweets, nuts and popcorn to very young children, many other childhood favourites can still be enjoyed.

Milk and fruit juices are more nutritious than soft drinks and can be stored in a cooler or thermos. Juice will remain cold if you slightly freeze individual cans before packing.

Children love sweets but to keep things under control put the sweets in the freezer for a couple of hours. The paper should peel off easily and the sweets won't be too sticky for little fingers.

Children's tattoos don't always come off easily – use a tiny drop of nail-polish remover on a cotton bud.

If the kids are left with orange moustaches after drinking cordial, rub on some toothpaste and rinse. Lovely clean smiles!

Finally, enjoy your children. The early years will go far too quickly.

►►► Painters & Decorators

Colin Philips; Cyril Cohen; Ray Mansell, Cain Decorators; Mark Vince, Cain Decorators; Paul Pavlo; Robert Smith; Dave Jenkins; Keith Myles; Scott Warroll

Before you start decorating, rub your hands in petroleum jelly. You'll save time at the end of the day when the paint washes out easily.

Always clear and prepare the area you are going to decorate – remove as much as you can from the room and cover the furniture and floor with old sheets.

Don't get paint in your hair – wear a shower cap.

Cover your spectacles with clingfilm so that if you get paint on them, you can just peel the clingfilm away.

If you are removing wall fittings and want to remember where they were, push a matchstick into the hole. Even if you are wallpapering, you can ease the matchstick through the paper.

An old fish slice makes a good paint scraper and because it doesn't have such sharp edges, you can let the kids help scrape the paint off.

You don't need a roller or expensive brush to paint a wall. A sponge works just as well.

If your paintbrushes have hardened, soften them by dipping them in a pan of boiling vinegar for a few minutes.

When stripping wallpaper, thoroughly soak all the paper at once with a 7-in/18-cm brush to make the paper easier to remove. Or use a paint roller dipped in hot water and washing-up liquid to wet the paper.

Always buy paint and wallpaper with the same batch number – there can be a slight variation in colour from one batch to the next.

If you have to buy a tin of paint or roll of paper with a different batch number, use it in places that won't show as much (behind furniture, for example).

Avoid paint drips all over your hand, wind a rubber band round the thick end of the brush to catch any drips.

When painting ceilings, put the handle of the paintbrush through an old sponge to catch any drips.

Don't wear slippy shoes up a ladder – an obvious tip but a sensible one.

When painting from a ladder, always paint from the outside in so you don't stretch away from yourself which can make you overbalance.

It's difficult to work up a ladder while carrying a pot of paint and a brush. Make life easier by placing a small tin of paint inside a larger empty tin. Tuck the brush in the gap between the two and you can carry everything you need and still have one hand free.

Don't spoil your newly painted wall with ugly ladder marks. Pop a pair of clean socks over the ends of the ladder.

The smell of new paint can linger for ages. Stir in a couple of drops of vanilla essence to disguise nasty fumes.

To get rid of the smell of new paint, leave a cut onion in a recently painted room.

Paint perfect straight lines by putting a rubber band round the bristles of your brush. This keeps them together in a stiff shape making it much easier to control where you paint.

Protect your walls when painting close-resting pipes by sliding a sheet of cardboard down behind the pipes as you work.

Painting railings can take hours. You can finish really quickly if you dip a flannel mitt in the paint and then run your hand up and down the railing a few times to coat it.

Don't waste turps by throwing it out each time. Pour any unused liquid into a screw-top bottle. After a few days the sediment will settle leaving you with lots of clean turps at the top.

Intricate mouldings are fiddly to rub down with sandpaper – use a small pumice stone instead to get into all the corners.

When rubbing down window-frames, try using wire wool instead of sandpaper; it won't scratch the glass.

Keep paint off window glass – put masking tape around the edge of the glass. Be sure to leave a tiny gap between the tape and the frame; this will allow the paint to seal the join between the glass and the putty. Remove the tape as the paint starts to dry; if you leave it too long the adhesive will stick to the window.

Keep paint off odd shapes such as taps, hooks or doorknobs by covering with kitchen foil to protect them.

Never paint from a large tin of paint, pour a small amount into a paint kettle. This keeps the majority of the paint free from dust.

If you find your paint has got grit in it, stretch the leg of an old pair of tights across a clean paint kettle and pour the paint through it.

If you are switching paint colours regularly, and you don't want to keep washing out your paint kettle, just line it with kitchen foil. When you've finished with one colour, just throw the used foil away and replace with a clean sheet.

If a window sticks after painting, run a thin knife around the window and frame to release it.

To prevent your windows sticking, start painting early in the morning and leave the windows open all day until evening.

Keep a pair of shoes or slippers outside the room you are decorating, so you have something to change into and you won't walk paint all over the rest of the house.

Wrap your paintbrush in clingfilm or kitchen foil when you take a break. This will help to keep out the air so the brush remains ready for use.

Never stand brushes in water when you take a break – it can swell the wooden handle and rust the metal ferrule.

To soak a brush without leaving it in the bottom of a jar, drill a hole halfway down the handle and push a pencil through it, then balance the brush across the opening of a jar.

To clean brushes put the paint cleaner in a plastic bag along with the paintbrush. You can then rub the bristles with your fingers to get all the paint out.

Support your pasting brush by tying a piece of string across the rim of the bucket. You can rest your brush on the string when not using it and it's useful for wiping off excess paste too.

Even the pros get small blisters under wallpaper. They get rid of them by making a tiny clean cut with a sharp knife and then pressing down with a little extra paste.

Don't spend hours washing out rollers each night, just rinse out and place in a plastic bag and they will be ready to go in the morning.

When you have finished with your pasting brush, rinse it in salted water before washing. This gets rid of the paste and leaves the brush nice and soft.

Keep any left-over paint or wallpaper in case you need to do the odd bit of repair work later on.

If you've only got a small amount of paint left don't leave it in a large tin. Put it into a screw-top jar, label it, and it will keep for years.

Store paint tins upside down to prevent a skin from forming.

To stick down a corner of wallpaper, damp the back with egg white. Let it go a bit sticky and then press down.

If you have to repair a bit of damaged wallpaper, tear a piece of matching wallpaper into an irregular shape (don't cut it because the regular straight lines will show up). Paste the patch and stick over the damaged area, making sure the pattern matches.

Sometimes, when a house gets really grubby, for instance if it has been empty for some time, it can be cheaper and more effective to simply redecorate.

Always keep white spirit in a jam jar with a lid to stop any evaporation.

Wear surgeons' gloves to keep your hands clean when painting.

To clean your palette use a mixture of white spirit and soap.

▶▶▶ Pest Controllers

Pauline Pears, Ryton Organic Gardens, Warwick; Peter Bateman, East Grinsted;
David Jones, London; Paul Hoyes, Foreward Environmental, Bristol; Clive Evers,
Southend on Sea; Tony Stephens, Lingfield, Surrey

▷▷ Small Pests

The most effective weapon against unwelcome creepy crawlies is
the vacuum cleaner. Use it regularly and make sure you always
clean under the furniture.

Woodlice like the damp. Sprinkle talcum powder around the
kitchen and bathroom floors to create dry surfaces. The woodlice
will soon look for alternative accommodation.

Woodlice are fond of house plants so don't put plants on window-
sills and ledges; it will only encourage the woodlice to come into
the house.

Get rid of booklice – give them a good blast with a hair-dryer on its
hottest setting.

Human hair deters the most determined rabbit from nibbling
garden plants. If you're a bit thin on top due to the stress of your
unwelcome visitors, ask a barber or hairdresser for cuttings to
sprinkle around the base of the plants.

Bedbugs love a cosy bed so contrary to everything your mother told you, don't make the bed! Simply leave the bedclothes folded back and the bugs will leave in search of a warmer home.

Sleep with your window open at night – this will keep the temperature too low for the bedbugs.

If you suffer from asthma, pop your pillow in the tumble dryer for 20 minutes on a hot setting to kill off any bedbugs that might be lurking there.

Beetles and small flies often lay their eggs in flour and sugar. Defy them by removing food substances from their paper packets and sealing them in airtight containers.

Moth eggs won't survive intense heat. If your clothes can stand it, give them a quick tumble dry on a high setting.

Little spiders grow up ... into much bigger spiders. Plug up any holes in outside walls, however tiny, to stop the little ones crawling in.

Ants avoid any surface that has been treated, so keep them out by drawing a chalk line around the area you want protected.

Ants hate salt and pepper, so sprinkle a liberal dose wherever you need it to get rid of them.

To get rid of ants, sprinkle curry powder.

Aphids can wreck plants in hanging baskets. Spray the baskets with soapy water to kill off the aphids.

Worms on a golf putting green needn't be a handicap – try spraying soapy water on to the turf. All the worms will come to the surface and you can simply remove them to a more convenient place.

Entice slugs from your drain – pour turpentine down the drain. The slugs will come out and you can get rid of them permanently.

Or try putting a piece of board or hardboard down on the ground. The slugs will hide underneath it to get out of the sun. When you've got a fair crop, lift the board up and wreak vengeance!

To make a slug trap, bury a tuna can up to its neck in the garden. Put some beer in the bottom and leave it for the slugs to drop into.

Stop slugs coming into the house – lay a line of salt across the doorway. The slugs won't cross the line.

Keep flies away – hang up bunches of elderflower.

If bees have taken up residence in your chimney, light the fire. They'll soon leave and won't risk coming back – well, would you?

Never swat a wasp. Many species give off a distress signal when swiped and, before you know it, you could be surrounded by its family and friends!

When a wasp lands on you, he's looking for something to eat. Keep very still and he'll soon realise that there is no lunch laid on, and he'll fly off.

Attract wasps with a jar filled with jam. Add a splash of detergent and they'll drown more easily.

Mosquitoes hate vitamin B, so you could try eating copious amounts of vegetable extract (like Marmite) to stop them nibbling you.

For a useful mosquito deterrent set out a pint of stout – it's a pleasant way to keep them at bay.

Drive annoying insects away from you on a summer's day by drinking some tonic with a slice of lemon. The combination of quinine and citrus will put off most pests.

Catch lots of fleas in one go – fill a hot-water bottle with hot water, cover with double-sided sticky tape and then drag the bottle round the infected area. The fleas will jump on to the warm bottle and get stuck on the sticky tape.

Moles hate any foul-smelling liquid – try pouring cleaning fluid or old flower water around the entrance to mole hills.

Alarm moles into leaving. Set an alarm clock and push it down the mole hole. Once it goes off, the moles should leave home.

Keep foxes out of the garden by spreading lion dung around the edges. You don't have to gather it yourself: just ask at the local zoo.

▷▷ Mice

You think you've got mice but you're not sure? Sprinkle flour where you believe them to be and next morning check it for footprints. If you're lucky, you can then track them to their hole.

Block up small holes to keep mice out. Mice can squeeze through the tiniest hole. If you can fit a pen through a space then it's big enough for a mouse.

Deter mice from entering your home by attaching a bristle strip to doorways.

Attract mice with their favourite titbits. Mice prefer fruit-and-nut chocolate to cheese … unless they live in Birmingham where the local rodent population have a yen for tuna (we kid you not; an earnest postgraduate student spent two years studying the phenomenon).

A humane way to catch a mouse is to use a wide-necked jar. Fill the bottom with broken chocolate biscuits (unless you're in Birmingham) and lean a ramp against the jar. The mouse will climb in but won't be able to get out. You can then release him outside.

A refreshing way to evict a mouse is to squirt minty toothpaste around the edges of its hole. Mice don't like the smell.

Double your chances of catching a mouse by placing the trap at right angles to the wall. Mice feel insecure in the middle of a room and are more likely to skirt the edges.

▷▷ Squirrels

Keep squirrels and birds out of roof eaves and rafters by screwing chicken wire into tight balls and pushing it into any awkward holes or crannies.

Squirrels hate loud noise so try playing heavy-metal music at full volume. The neighbours will hate it but, more importantly, so will the squirrels.

▶▶▶ Photographers

Maddie Attenborough, The Portrait Studio; Justin Quinnell; Nick Mather; Ray Lowe;
Duncan Elson

When you're travelling, don't attract thieves by carrying your
camera in its expensive carrying case. Put it in a normal canvas bag.

Make your camera batteries last longer – warm them underneath
your armpit before use.

Learn from your mistakes and from your successes. Make notes on
photos you've taken.

If you do drop your camera in the water, keep it submerged in a
plastic bag full of water to stop the film from drying out and getting
stains on the negatives. Take it to a developer as soon as possible.

Protect equipment from sand and water on holiday, take a large
piece of bubble wrap, fold one-third back on itself and staple the
two sides together to create an envelope for cameras and lenses.

When going through X-ray machines at the airport, make sure
your films are wrapped in cooking foil to stop them getting foggy
when they are being passed through the machine.

Don't 'snatch' at a picture – when you're squeezing the shutter button, press it gently. If you do it too quickly, you can end up shaking the camera and getting a blurry picture.

A lens hood stops stray light coming into your lens so stick black tape around the edge of a lens on a compact camera to stop some of that reflective light.

You can make a lens hood from a washing-up liquid bottle, painted black and cut out to fit around the lens.

A margarine tub lid is good for DIY vignettes. Cut a hole in the middle of the lid, hold it over the lens, and your pictures will have hazy edges.

To create a soft edge to your shots, put sticky tape around the edge of your lens.

Add a new look to photos – stand on a wall. Getting up high changes the perspective and the nature of the shot completely – a trick that works wonders.

If you are taking photos with a timer, don't place the camera precariously on a wall. Half-fill a plastic bag with pasta, shells, sand, scrunched-up newspaper or beans and put the camera on that. It makes a soft and manoeuvrable base for the camera to rest on.

▷▷ Portraits & People

Shoot from the hip – literally – to capture spontaneous shots. People quickly become self-conscious if they see you holding up a camera.

To get the best portrait shots focus on the eyes.

Ask people to take off their sunglasses so you don't get any reflections and you can see their eyes.

At weddings, don't tell everyone to smile because the end result is bound to look forced. Instead, ask everyone to blow a raspberry. They'll feel so silly they'll end up laughing and you can then take a lovely natural shot.

Once you've tried the raspberry technique, try pulling out a pair of frilly knickers to make everyone laugh for a second fun shot.

If you have an important set of photos that you are afraid might get lost during the developing process, take a photo of your name and address on the first frame so that there is a record of who the photos belong to. Also, stick a label with your name and address on the film canister.

Get your subject to close their eyes and blow a raspberry before you take a shot of them. This helps to relax their jaw and mouth where tension and nervousness can show most.

To get a good portrait shot use the automatic wind-on. Take two portraits in quick succession (keep your finger on the shutter button); the second shot is usually the more relaxed ... and therefore a better picture.

When taking a picture of a large group, it's a good idea to get yourself into an elevated position so that you can include the people hiding in the back.

To soften the image, put a cigarette paper, clingfilm or stockings over the lens. Or just breathe on the lens.

'Red eye' can spoil a shot. Avoid the problem by putting tracing paper over the flash. Or you could increase the light in the room.

If your subject is wearing glasses, check for any reflections in the viewfinder.

When taking a photograph of someone with a receding hair line, shoot from lower than eye-level.

If your subject is an older woman, don't use a flash because this shows up the wrinkles ... and she won't thank you for that!

Try shooting towards the sun but use a flash to fill in the face so you can see the features. Shooting at this angle means that your subject is nicely backlit.

If there's not enough light, ask someone wearing a white or pale shirt to stand close by so that you can bounce some light off them. Or you could ask someone to hold up a white handkerchief.

To take a shot of people on a sofa, put a telephone directory on the sofa for the person in the middle to sit on. Sofas tend to dip in the middle, leaving one person looking a lot shorter than everybody else.

When taking pictures of children, get down on their level so that they fill the frame.

To keep a small child happy while you take a photo, give them a piece of sticky tape to play with. They'll be amused for ages while you concentrate on getting great shots.

To take a picture of a group of children, you want all of them looking at the camera at the same time ... which can be difficult. Blow a whistle to get their attention and quickly take the picture.

When in a photo booth, put an A4 sheet of white paper on your lap to reflect light under your chin, thus avoiding double chins. This is also flattering for people with fuller faces.

To show off your cheekbones in a photo booth, place black paper or card on either side of your face (out of shot) for the Dietrich look.

▷▷ Landscapes & Still Life

When in the great outdoors, take only photographs and leave only footprints.

To keep a camera still, get a piece of string and attach one end to your camera. Make a loop at the other end and hook it under your foot. This creates tension which will help to steady the camera.

For a muted effect shoot through a magnifying glass.

Place Polaroid sunglasses over the lens to give landscape pictures a dramatic effect.

Early morning or late afternoon light creates a wonderful mood. The long shadows can make startling effects.

Taking a picture at an awkward or low angle can be made easier by resting the camera on a small bean bag. You can make your own bean bag by sewing 2 oz/50 g of dried beans into a cotton bag.

Don't be put off by shooting in the rain – you can get some wonderful results. Just pop your camera inside a clear plastic bag and when you're ready to take your shots, tear a hole in the bag for the lens to poke through.

Alternatively, snip the corners off a freezer bag and thread the camera straps through so you can cover the camera in the rain. Just raise the bag when you need to take a photo.

If you're going to be in really damp conditions, wrap your camera in clingfilm until you're ready to shoot.

If you are in a foreign country and you want to take a photo of one of the locals without being too intrusive or rude, take a Polaroid of them first and give it to them as a memento. It's a good way to get the ball rolling.

If you want to get Biro marks off a photograph, rub the mark with some silver polish wadding. Then rub the same spot with some cotton wool ... and the mark vanishes!

▶▶▶ Picture Framers

Kitty Anderson

If you tear the paper when framing a picture, stick the torn edges together with some flour and water for an invisible join.

To mend a hole in paper, mash some of the same paper type with a little flour and water and fill in the hole. Allow the repair to dry.

Never use transparent masking tape to hold a picture in place because, in time, the tape will exude a damaging rubber solution.

To mount delicate items use stamp hinges.

To draw the eye towards a picture use a dark mount.

A grey mount is best for bright pictures because it doesn't distort the colours.

The correct size for a mount should be, on average, one-fifth of the picture size.

To cut an oval or round mount, draw around a bowl or dish.

You can pull a group of different pictures together by using the same colour mount for all of them.

When hanging two pictures next to each other, the gap between the two should be the same width as the mounts.

When framing pastels, always use a mount to separate the glass from the picture. Otherwise, your beautiful picture will smudge.

Wet backing paper before sticking it down; this way it will firm up as it dries and remain taut.

To give paper an authentic distressed look, gently wipe over with a used tea-bag.

For an attractive effect on plain frames, apply one colour and allow to dry. Then add a contrasting colour and gently rub the frame with wire wool so that a little of the first coat shows through.

To add lustre to old master reproductions, use a suede or leather mount.

Clean gilt picture frames with a mixture made from one egg and a teaspoon of bicarbonate of soda.

To stop a picture slipping sideways, wrap sticky tape around the centre of the wire.

To hang a very heavy mirror or picture, brass chain is stronger than picture wire.

If you're hanging a picture above a seat, make sure there's enough space for someone to lean back without knocking the picture.

Don't hang a lone picture against a bold wallpaper pattern because it tends to disappear into the pattern. Group it with other pictures if possible.

Nails will take more weight from a hanging picture if driven pointing down into the wall.

Don't damage your pictures. They should never be hung in direct sunlight or above radiators or heaters.

Hold panel pins in place using an old comb.

To remove a dent from a canvas, gently dab the back with some damp cotton wool. As the canvas dries, it will contract and flatten out the dent.

To judge whether insect holes in a wooden frame are fresh, check for fine dust on the floor and surfaces below the picture.

►►► Pigeon Fanciers

Mr Francis

To help make your pigeons go faster, put them on the train when transporting them. They prefer it to modern-day transporters.

For faster flight, try something called 'widowhood'. Separate the hen from the cock, then put them back together for a short time during the night. Then separate them again and the cock should fly home faster to be reunited with his mate!

To help get a ring on a pigeon, smear it – the ring, not the pigeon – with petroleum jelly.

To buy food at the best price, get it directly from the farmer at harvest time.

To stop your bird's food getting wet, place an old jam jar at an angle in a ball of cement and leave it to set. This makes a good, sturdy feeder and the food will stay dry.

To help the birds when they are moulting, feed them linseed as well as regular corn.

Look out for your hen bird – watch the cock bird and ensure he doesn't punish the hen too much.

To keep the peace over the winter, separate the sexes.

To cut down on fighting, make sure that the number of nesting boxes corresponds to the number of pairs. If there are too many boxes, some pairs will use more than one and this can start fights.

▶▶▶ Plumbers

George Wingfield; Andy Greenfield; Simon Mitchell; The Institute of Plumbing; National Association of Plumbing

Always know where the main stopcock is. If you have an emergency, like a burst pipe, you will need to get to the stopcock quickly. If you don't know where it is, put this book down and go and find your stopcock – try looking under the kitchen sink.

Make sure your stopcock is in good working order. When you have found it, make sure you can turn it on and off. To turn it off, go clockwise; you will have done it properly if no water comes out of the kitchen tap when it's turned on. If you can get water from the tap, the washer probably needs replacing.

Ensure that your stopcock doesn't jam. Open and close it several times a year. When you have opened it, give it a quarter turn clockwise. This should stop it jamming without interrupting the flow of water.

To make sure your main stop valve opens and closes freely, avoid painting it as this can make it inoperable.

When changing the washer on a tap, start the job in the morning. That way, if you have the wrong size or you need some other equipment, the shops will still be open.

Always put the plug in the sink when you are taking a tap to pieces just in case you drop anything – you don't want it disappearing down the plug-hole.

To prevent scarring on chrome and gold tap fittings, use a thick cloth between the jaws of a wrench whilst carrying out any maintenance.

To prevent limescale build-up, clean your shower heads at least every three months.

To lubricate new O-ring seals, use petroleum jelly, not oil.

To open up a drain-cock, you don't need a special key – you can use a pair of pliers. The drain-cock is at the lowest part of the system for when you need to drain the parts that cannot be drained from the kitchen or bath taps.

Drain-cocks sometimes become clogged with debris. You can clean them out using a straightened paper clip but be prepared for some flooding!

To clean out a blocked loo pan, use an old string mop. A couple of plunges should do the trick.

To stop an overflow from your cistern, place a wooden spoon across the cistern and tie the lever arm, attached to the ball float, to the spoon. If you need to flush the loo, you will have to release the arm to fill the cistern. Tie it up again when you have finished.

If the ball float in your loo has a leaky valve and the cistern is about to overflow, you can make a temporary repair. Unscrew the float and empty it (you may have to make a hole to get the water out). Screw the float back on and wrap it in a plastic bag to keep water out. You can then replace the float with a new one later.

To clear blockages in sinks or basins, cover overflow holes with a damp cloth to build up pressure while you use a plunger.

If your pipes have frozen, you can melt the ice by putting hot-water bottles over the pipes. Or you can use a hair-dryer to blow warm air onto the pipe. Don't use a blow torch or anything similar … you may end up setting the house on fire.

If a pipe has split, wrap torn strips of fabric tightly around the break, put a bucket underneath to catch any drips and call a qualified plumber.

▶▶▶ Public Speakers

Miranda Powell

Practise speaking in public by going to a local lecture or public meeting where you can ask a question out loud.

Get used to the sound of your own voice. Keep practising your speech out loud.

Ask someone to video you while you practise so that you can see where you are getting things right or wrong.

Try your speech out on a friend. Ask them to eliminate any irritating habits, such as 'I mean' and 'you know'.

Try to appear confident – even if you're not! Don't cross your arms or legs. Stand tall.

Avoid confusion. Find out how long you are required to speak for; there's nothing worse than talking for too short (or too long) a time.

Keep perfecting phrases – use a thesaurus.

When you rehearse your speech, always do it standing up so that it will feel like second nature on the day.

Don't try to learn your speech off by heart – it's hard enough to give a good speech without putting this sort of extra burden on yourself. Nobody minds if you put your speech on paper and refer to it from time to time.

Put your speech on to small cards – a phrase or point per card – so that you can speak clearly and succinctly.

Make sure your cards are stiff. You don't want your notes to wobble as your hands hold them; people might think you are trembling with nerves!

Don't be afraid to use a microphone. It's much easier once you get used to it and it's better than having people in the back rows straining to hear what you are saying.

It helps to feel that you have something in front of you. Ask for a lectern or a table.

Keep your audience interested. Try to involve them as much as possible.

Encourage a few laughs. It actually helps the audience to stay alert because people take in lots of oxygen when they chuckle!

If you get lost or forget what you should be saying, try a big smile for a moment. It will disguise any nerves and give you a moment to get back *en route*.

▶▶▶ Publicans

Anton Paul

Save money when throwing a party by buying beer in small barrels or firkins. Your local landlord will advise you on what to buy and where to get it. It tastes much better, too.

If you haven't got time to chill beer for your guests, just chill the glasses instead.

People often say they like dry white wine best but in blind tastings medium comes out on top. Choose medium for the safest bet at a dinner party.

All wines benefit from being decanted – even if you only use a simple jug.

Don't risk your own glasses. All drinks retailers now provide free glass hire when you buy your booze from them.

If champagne starts to fizz over while you pour it, discreetly dip one of your fingers into the glass!

Keep the bubbles popping. Champagne bubbles go instantly flat if they come into contact with detergent so make sure your glasses are squeaky clean. Fill the glasses to the top so the bubbles last longer.

Store wine horizontally to keep the corks soft.

Get your wine ready before your guests arrive – white wine needs to be chilled for about an hour and red wine should be opened at least an hour before you intend to drink it.

Tie your tools down! When you throw a party, tie the bottle opener and cork screw on to a length of string attached to something immovable. They have a habit of disappearing just when you need them.

Remember the 'designated drivers' and non–drinkers. Always have enough soft drinks. Try mixing fruit juice with mineral water rather than just having lots of fizzy drinks.

Make drinks fun by adding food colouring.

It's difficult to judge how much people will drink so for a big event buy your drink on a use-or-return basis. Be on the safe side and order more than you think you'll need.

To avoid wax on your tablecloths, put a beer mat under the candles.

▶▶▶ Removers

Dennis Auld; Matthew Mackay

Avoid being charged overtime. Don't move on a Friday, over the weekend or over a Bank Holiday.

Shop around for the right price – removal firms usually give quotations free of charge. Get quotes from two or three firms before you make your final choice.

You can cut the cost – some removal firms charge less if you do part of the packing or unpacking yourself. Discuss this beforehand with your removal firm.

Give your removers a clear idea of how much they're going to have to move – don't forget to show them the contents of your shed, garage, loft and cellar.

When moving a piano, call your nearest concert hall or theatre and ask if they can recommend a specialist remover.

Don't be tempted to move yourself long distance. It is often cheaper to hire professional removers rather than make a large number of long journeys in a hired van.

When moving large objects yourself (such as a freezer or cooker), check the size of van doors and try to hire one with a ramp or a hydraulic lift.

To move a freezer with food still inside ensure that it is no more than a quarter full, that it is on maximum freeze for at least 24 hours before disconnection and that you don't open the door while it is switched off.

To transport a fridge always carry it upright.

When moving your washing machine, make sure you immobilise the revolving drum first.

To make unpacking easier, put your carpets in the van last so that they can go down first before any furniture.

To protect furniture during the move use rugs to cover anything that could be scratched or damaged.

Protect your hands while packing and unpacking – wear gloves.

If you have to provide your own boxes, make friends with the local supermarket. Banana boxes are ideal for moving house.

Start collecting old newspapers well before you move. You will need a lot for packing.

Ask your local electrical retailer if they have any spare boxes with polystyrene shavings that you can use for your TV, video, computer and hi-fi system.

Use a coding system to label boxes. This makes it easier to identify which room a box should go into for unpacking; for example, you could use a colour-coding system: red for the kitchen, blue for the dining room and so on. Label the side of the box, not just the top.

Don't pack boxes full of books because you won't be able to lift them (or you'll do your back in) – only fill them half full.

Prevent creased carpets – don't fold them, just roll them.

To help the new occupiers of your home, collect all the relevant keys of the house together and clearly label them.

Keep children amused and as unsettled as possible – make sure that you keep their favourite toys handy and that they aren't packed away at the back of the van!

If you're not sure how to move your pets safely, call an animal welfare organisation in advance for advice.

Before you move, make sure you've told the electricity, gas, water and telephone suppliers, organised the disconnection of the cooker/washing machine, cancelled the milk and papers, sent out your change of address cards and got a bottle of champagne ready to put in the fridge of your new home.

Pack a box of essential items for the actual day of the move – kettle, tea, coffee, mugs, pens and notepaper, light bulbs, torch, string, hammer, pliers, nails, adaptors, loo paper and aspirin. You will also need cleaning equipment and lots of bin bags.

Don't run out of money on the day – you may want to buy a take-away meal, make an emergency dash to the shops for supplies, buy a bottle of wine or even tip your removal men!

When you arrive at your new home, make sure the entrance hall is protected from dirty footmarks as people tramp to and fro with furniture and boxes.

►►► Restaurateurs

Patricia Sedgwick, Crosby Lodge Country Hotel, Carlisle; Judy and David Green, Teviotdale Lodge Country Hotel, Hawick; Giles Hine, Corse Lawn Hotel; Nick Jefford, Lygon Arms Hotel, Broadway; Steven Morris, Grafton Manor Hotel; Richard Niazi, Sarastros, Drury Lane, London; Mini Chutrakal, Busabong Tree, London

Always set your dining room table with candles. Apart from looking pretty, they disperse strong smells.

To make candles burn brightly, soak the wicks in vinegar.

If you get candle wax on your tablecloth, heat a spoon over the candle. Then place a piece of wet newspaper over the wax and rub the hot spoon over the newspaper to melt the wax which will then come off the tablecloth and stick to the paper.

When serving soup to children, stir an ice cube into their portions to cool it down quickly.

A few grains of rice in the salt cellar will ensure it stays dry and fresh.

To keep brown sugar really fresh, put a small piece of brown bread in with the sugar.

Keep flowers fresh for longer – add a splash of lemonade to their water.

To transform instant coffee into a more sophisticated offering, add a few cardamom seeds. Serve the coffee black … and remember to remove the seeds before serving!

To bring out the taste of fresh coffee, put a pinch of dried mustard powder into the percolator.

Dirty ashtrays look so ugly. Keep them clean with an old shaving brush.

Don't panic if you've forgotten to heat the plates. Just splash with hot water and pop them in the microwave for a few seconds (check that your china is microwave proof first).

To make your plates gleam like new, rinse in a weak solution of water and vinegar.

To serve up pasta on heated plates, drain the pasta over the plates to warm them.

Good–quality china will really sparkle if soaked in denture-cleaning tablets.

It really is simple to impress your guests with hot cleansing towels after a dinner party. Just wet some clean flannels with water and a splash of eau de Cologne, loosely wrap in clingfilm and heat in the microwave for about a minute.

Inexpensive firelighters can be created from the stubs of burnt-down candles, orange peel or matchboxes filled with old matches and a bit of candle wax. Waxed milk cartons are excellent for bigger blazes.

Once your fire is going, a few digestive biscuits thrown in make it burn like fury.

For a pretty Christmas napkin ring, dry a slice of orange with the middle cut out.

Rejuvenate fizzy drinks that have gone flat – add a dash of bicarbonate of soda.

Keep your mineral water fizzy – give the plastic bottle a good squeeze before screwing the top back on.

If you suspect a champagne bottle has been shaken up but you need to open it, hold it absolutely horizontal before easing the cork out.

To keep champagne really fizzy, dangle a teaspoon in the top of the bottle neck.

When you're pouring champagne, put a little in the bottom of each glass before topping them up. This stops them from overflowing and wasting all the bubbly!

It's messy when fizzy drinks overflow. To avoid this, pour fizzy drinks into warmed glasses and then put in lots of ice to chill the drink.

Wine will chill much quicker with the cork out – ideal if you're in a hurry for a cool glass of wine.

For a really fast chill, put wine in an ice-bucket and sprinkle salt onto the ice.

Don't worry if you have to decant a bottle of wine or port at very short notice. Just pour it out very quickly to get lots of air into it.

If you don't have a cocktail shaker, use a smaller glass inverted inside a pint glass.

If your decanter looks stained or dull, fill with vinegar and crushed eggshells. Replace the stopper and give it a good hard swill around. Once rinsed with warm water, it will look as good as new.

To clean your decanter, half-fill it with warm soapy water and 2 tablespoons of rice. Swish the mixture around and pour out after half an hour. Rinse the decanter and stand upside down to dry.

If the stopper gets stuck in a decanter, put a few drops of cooking oil around the neck and leave in a warm place for a while before loosening the stopper.

To separate glasses that are stuck together, put cold water inside the inner one and place the outer one in warm water. Gently increase the temperature of the warm water until the outer glass expands and the inner glass can be lifted off. Easy!

Twist the wine bottle when you pour to avoid messy drips, for the true professional touch.

Keep cartons of double cream fresher for longer by turning the carton upside down in the fridge.

To make really light whipped cream, add a dash of icy cold water just before you do the final whip.

For an instant and healthy milkshake, whisk half yoghurt with half milk.

Make a truly de luxe creamy porridge by stirring in a scoop of quality vanilla ice-cream during cooking.

If honey is too runny give it a 10-second blast in the microwave on the high setting. This will thicken it up slightly.

Stop the sides of cheddar cheese going hard and waxy – spread a thin layer of butter over it before you wrap it up and put it away for the night.

Always store cooked foods above uncooked food in a fridge. This avoids raw juices dripping on to cooked food, which is the quickest way to food contamination.

Eggs will stay fresher for longer if stored pointed end down.

There's nothing worse than a stale-smelling fridge. Put a few charcoal bricks at the back to keep it smelling fresh and clean.

If you've got ants in your kitchen, direct them towards something sweet in one corner and annihilate them there.

Kill off germs in kitchen cloths – heat damp cloths for several minutes in a microwave.

Soap lasts longer if stored in the airing cupboard for a few months.

When freezing big bags of ice, sprinkle the cubes with some soda water to stop them all sticking together in lumps.

Don't despair if you burn a pan – boil up some sliced onions and water in the pan, and leave for several hours.

To treat a burnt pan, boil up some water and vinegar in it and leave overnight. It will be easier to clean in the morning.

If you have a discoloured aluminium pan, boil up a weak solution of rhubarb or tomatoes in it. The food acids lift the stain.

To clean baked-on food from a cooking pan, put a sheet of fabric conditioner in the pan and fill with water. Leave overnight and then next day the food will just lift off with a sponge.

Polish up cutlery using a cork, soaked in water and scouring powder. Rinse and buff with a soft cloth.

Clean a grotty roasting tin (not aluminium or non-stick) with a solution of washing soda and water boiled up in the tin. Rinse and then dry in a cool oven.

To remove barbecue fat stains from your patio, cover with cat litter, grind with your heel, leave for half a day, then sweep up.

Pep up your potted plants – put some old tea-bags in to their soil.

Make a quick chilli sauce using left-over vegetables. Pop them in a pan with some chillies and stew them gently.

To clean perspex and get rid of scratches, rub with toothpaste, then buff up with a cloth.

If sliced ham or tongue has dried out, soak it in a little milk for 5 minutes; this will restore its flavour and texture.

Does the meat seem a bit tough? Squirt a little lemon juice on to it before carving.

Your bacon will be really crisp if you trim the rind with pinking shears before cooking it.

If you need to reduce fat, but love the taste of bacon, try using turkey rashers as a substitute – they're virtually fat free.

For a low-fat gravy try separating the meat juices and fat by pouring them into a jug and adding ice cubes. The ice will cool down the gravy quickly, allowing you to spoon off the fat straight away.

Make your own marinade for pork: use a tablespoon of honey mixed with grated ginger – sweet and spicy.

For a more subtle flavour in chilli con carne use lemon or lime rind grated into the mix.

Try placing a layer of cream crackers or Pringles on top of the sauce in a shepherd's pie or cottage pie – they'll absorb the juices from the sauce and keep the mashed potato fluffy.

To tenderise meat cover it with slices of kiwi fruit for about 15 minutes.

At Christmas baste your turkey with fruit juice for that extra bit of taste.

To roast a turkey evenly begin roasting it upside down and only turn it right side up after about 45 minutes.

To add a bit more flavour to the turkey, before cooking the bird, lift up the skin and rub olive oil and herbs on to the meat.

To stop a turkey sticking to tin foil during cooking place a piece of celery along the breast bone.

To skim the grease off stock during cooking drop in a cold piece of lettuce for 10 seconds. The grease in the hot stock will stick to the lettuce leaf.

If you have left-over turkey, take the stuffing out before putting the bird in the fridge and refrigerate in a separate bowl. You risk bacteria growing if you leave the stuffing inside.

To tenderise the meat in stews add three or four wine corks to the pot. The corks release chemicals which both tenderise the meat and reduce cooking time. Just remember to remove them before serving!

To make top-quality meat gravy wait until the fat has solidified and then remove it from the liquid.

To get the skin off chicken more easily dip your hands in flour before trying to remove the skin. This will make the whole process much less slippery.

To make sure the centre of burgers get properly cooked poke holes in the centre before putting on the grill.

Keep poultry moist while roasting by placing a bowl of water in the bottom of the oven. Make sure you use a heat proof bowl or roasting tin.

Before opening a packet of bacon, roll it up. It will make it easier to separate the slices.

To tenderise tough cuts of meat rub both sides with a mix of vinegar, olive oil and perhaps a little salt. Then put it in the fridge for two or three hours before cooking.

Freeze meat in the coldest part of the freezer.

Save time struggling to get corned beef out of the can – pour hot water over the unopened can for a few minutes and the meat will slide out easily.

A turkey is only as good as the food it eats, so try to find free-range birds which have been fed on a variety of grains.

Roasting a chicken? Put some vegetables in a Pyrex bowl and cook in the oven at the same time to save an additional ring on the cooker.

Mince or finely chop left-over meat from your Sunday roast to make cottage pie on Monday.

To peel an orange easily drop into hot water for about 5 minutes. Dry and peel as usual.

To get more juice out of a citrus fruit warm it in the oven for a few minutes before squeezing it.

To get the juice out of a citrus fruit more easily when squeezing it roll the fruit back and forth over a hard surface before cutting it in half.

Liquidise watermelon for a refreshing drink. You don't even need to pick out the seeds because they'll sink to the bottom.

To bring out the flavour of strawberries when cooking them in desserts, add a touch of balsamic vinegar to the recipe.

To pep up pineapple chunks sprinkle with black pepper.

Pineapple juice helps ease a sore throat.

When you buy or pick a quantity of berries, there are often small twigs or leaves mixed in with the berries. The quickest way to get rid of the twigs and leaves without harming the fruit is to pour them from one container to another across the path of a fan.

To keep strawberries fresh in the fridge for as long as a week, wash them (but don't remove the green stalks) and put in a sealed glass jar.

If your roast potatoes take an age to brown, sprinkle a little flour over them as they cook.

For perfect mash drop a teaspoon of sugar in with your boiling potatoes – it will make them more floury and they'll fluff up better.

Carrots will keep fresh in the fridge for weeks if you trim the tops and bottoms and put them in a plastic container.

To turn oven chips into a crispy and tasty treat sprinkle with sea salt during cooking.

For a delicious alternative topping for shepherd's pie add cream cheese to the mashed potato.

Stinging nettles make a tasty supper dish. Boil new shoots for 2–3 minutes, drain and serve with butter.

A good way to use left-over mashed potato is to make savoury croquettes. Try adding finely chopped onion, tomato, parsley, even tuna and grated cheese. Mix well, form croquettes, roll in flour and fry.

Try putting salad dressing into a spray bottle so that you can control the amount you use – there's nothing worse than soggy drowned lettuce.

A cheap and easy alternative to using haricot beans is to drain a tin of economy baked beans and rinse off the tomato sauce. Remember they're pre-cooked, so just adjust any recipe accordingly.

Use a balloon whisk to stir your rice – you'll find it keeps the grains separated and fluffy.

If you can't get the last drops of salad cream out of the bottle, add some mustard powder and a little vinegar – it makes a great salad dressing.

Peanut butter will spread easily if you add half a teaspoon of sunflower oil to it and stir in well.

Like capers? Take a bottle, drain the vinegar and replace with olive oil. After a couple of weeks, the oil sweetens the taste.

Spice up your sex life with a carrot! Carrots are full of beta carotene, which produces sex hormones.

Don't throw away left-over lentils – fry them in a big pan with a splash of oil until dry. It makes a great topping for toast.

When cooking asparagus, wedge the bundles upright in the pan using potatoes.

Don't throw away elderly garlic bulbs. Plant in a sunny spot and water. The resulting garlic shoots are excellent in salad.

Keep a nettle patch. Don't allow it to flower, but pick the nettle tops to use in cooking. The cooking gets rid of the sting and the taste is like spinach.

For an exciting spread for sandwiches freeze some really good quality virgin olive oil in a plastic container and, when the olive oil is cold and thick, spread it on.

Never store apples and carrots together because the apples give off a gas which makes the carrots go bitter.

And never store potatoes and onions together either. The potatoes will spoil faster.

To stop potatoes falling apart while you boil them, turn the heat right down and boil them for longer, rather than cooking them too fast.

To make celery that bit crisper put it in a bowl of iced water and leave it in the fridge for a few hours.

The brighter the colour of a dried bean, the fresher the bean.

For a subtle garlic flavour spear a clove with a toothpick and dip it into the pan for 30 seconds every 3 minutes.

To preserve garlic after peeling place it in a jar and cover with olive oil. If you store it in the fridge, it will keep for up to 4 months.

The stronger broccoli smells the less fresh it is.

For crisp baked potato skins brush the potato with a little oil before cooking.

A good artichoke will make a slight squeaking noise when handled.

Wrinkled green or yellow peppers aren't bad – they just have a mellower flavour.

Buy cooking potatoes of similar size to avoid different cooking times.

For quick-cooking roast potatoes remove the centre lengthwise with an apple corer. For a sumptuous flavour, place rolled bacon strips in the hollow.

Singe the root end of your onions – then they'll store for much longer.

Left-over Brussels sprouts and potatoes from your Sunday roast make lovely bubble-and-squeak. Just fry all the left-overs together.

Leave your bubble-and-squeak in the pan to go nice and crispy before serving. The crispy bits have more taste.

Boil cabbage with salt, pepper and butter – the strained juice makes a great drink to aid digestion.

Keep boiled potatoes firm by adding a little vinegar to the boiling water.

Keep cauliflower white by adding 2 tablespoons of lemon juice or white wine vinegar to the cooking water.

Try cooking corn-on-the-cob in equal parts of milk and water to tenderise the kernels.

Alternatively, top with a couple of knobs of butter, a generous amount of pepper and wrap in tin foil. Roast in the oven for 20–30 minutes for a really intense flavour.

Freshly grated horse radish will pep up tired mashed potato.

If you find canned vegetables taste tinny, drain then blanch in boiling water for 1 minute and rinse in cool water.

Keep fresh herbs longer – grind in a food processor, add 4 tablespoons of vegetable oil and refrigerate.

When a recipe calls for the leaf of a fresh herb to be added during cooking, add the stem of the herb instead. The stem has a stronger taste and, because it has less chlorophyll than the leaf, it won't add a green tint to the dish.

Or just mix dried herbs with fresh parsley and no one will notice.

Save empty spice jars – the plastic bag refill packs are cheaper than buying replacement jars.

Always bruise a bouquet garni slightly with a mallet or rolling pin to release the aromatic oils before placing in your pot.

For a home-made bouquet garni place bay leaves, thyme, parsley, cloves, allspice and black peppercorns on to a foil square. Fold and seal, then pierce with a pin to release flavours.

Alternatively, if you have a tea ball, just pop the ingredients in and hang over the rim of your pan.

Chop mint the easy way – sprinkle some sugar on it first.

Freeze chopped chives in ice cubes for convenience – it saves fiddling about when you're in a hurry.

Make consommé look more appetising – drop a lump of sugar into the soup before serving.

For a quick party dip beat milk and onion powder into Philadelphia cheese until you have the desired consistency.

To make a tasty dip for guests mix half a packet of mushroom or onion soup with a small carton of cream and chill for a few hours.

Scoop out green or red peppers to make containers for mayonnaise, salad dressings, sauces and dips when entertaining.

For a special custard for adults pour in a small glassful of apricot or cherry brandy just before serving.

Add a touch of luxury to coffee with one teaspoon of vanilla ice-cream instead of milk.

Surprise guests? No desserts? Take two ginger biscuits and sandwich them with some gently whipped cream. Serve with coffee.

To chill beer, wine or champagne quickly add 4-6 tablespoons of salt to the ice and water in the ice-bucket. The bottles should chill in about 20 minutes.

Stop last-minute panics at dinner parties. Boil your vegetables in advance, then run them under the cold water tap. Just before serving, boil the kettle and pour the boiling water over the vegetables. Leave for 30 seconds and serve.

Before serving cheese at a dinner party, warm the cheese knife in the oven. This makes it easier to cut through the cheese and spares your guests embarrassment.

Keep picnic food cool on a hot day. Put the food in a bowl. Take a larger bowl and put ice in the bottom. Then put the smaller bowl inside the larger one – a portable refrigerator.

Add a measure of Bailey's Irish Cream to custard for a really special flavour.

Experimenting with new ingredients? To test ingredients before adding them to the mix, take a spoonful of the dish and add a drop of the ingredient to be added for tasting, rather than risk spoiling the whole.

To keep bread rolls served in a bread basket warm line the basket with foil and then cover with a napkin.

You'll find party sandwiches stay fresh if you place paper napkins over them and sprinkle with cold water regularly.

You can't beat iced tea or coffee when it's hot. Why not freeze any left-overs from your usual brew in ice-cube trays. You'll have plenty of ice to chill your drinks without diluting them.

When serving something cold such as paté, ice-cream or a cold soup, always add lots of flavourings because the cold will numb the palette.

To slice kiwis easily just use an egg-slicer. Remove the skin of the kiwi by edging a teaspoon around the slice, between the flesh and the skin.

Never store vinegar in a metal container – the acidity will affect the metal.

Never cover an entire oven rack in foil – it stops the air circulating so your food will take longer to cook.

Different types of baking dish produce different results. Dark, dull pans produce crispy crusts (so suitable for pies); shinier ones give more delicate results (so good for cakes).

To make cutting raisins and other sticky things easier coat the blade of your knife with vegetable oil.

To keep fruit and veg in your fridge nice and fresh place a dry sponge at the bottom of the salad drawer – it will absorb excess moisture and stop food going rotten.

Store kitchen bits and bobs such as piping bag ends in empty film canisters to save losing them.

Reuse good quality storage bags – just wash thoroughly and dry.

Plastic containers from your supermarket are great for storing herbs, leftovers or for freezing stock.

A simple way to remove a frozen dessert or jelly from a mould is to loosen the edges with the point of a knife and give the mould a blast with a hair-dryer for a few seconds.

Dental floss pulled tightly will cut through cheesecake and other similar puddings with ease.

If you keep salt for seasoning in a small bowl instead of a shaker or grinder, you'll be less likely to oversalt a dish because you'll have total control of the amount you use.

Filter coffee left–overs are excellent for removing grease from stainless steel.

If you want beautiful, smooth icing on a cake, try using an artist's palette knife.

For uniform hamburgers, meatballs, etc. use an ice-cream scoop.

As a rule sharp knives are safer than blunt ones.

If you want perfect cheese curls, try using a potato peeler.

To make neat butter curls freeze the butter for a few minutes first.

There is no actual evidence to suggest that combining 'grape and grain' makes for worse hangovers – except that those who mix their drinks are probably drinking more.

Hold a bottle of chilled white wine by the neck rather than the body of the bottle so that your hands do not warm the wine inside.

If you're tasting wine, always make sure your glass is tulip shaped, curving inwards towards the rim, then, when you swill the wine around, it doesn't splash out all over you.

When tasting wine remember to swill it all around the mouth as different parts of the tongue pick up different flavours.

It is more polite to half-fill your guests' glasses with wine rather than fill them right up to the top – they'll also get the full effect of the aroma.

Plain glasses are better for wine because you can't see colour and clarity through cut or patterned glass.

Impress your guests with expensive wine first – then bring out the cheaper stuff when everyone's slightly merry and they'll hardly notice the difference.

Feeling hungover? Vitamin C is the most important ingredient in any hangover cure – the soluble, flavoured vitamin tablets on the market now are virtually designed for hangovers.

If you're tasting lots of wine, here's an easy way to clean your glass. After each wine pour a thimbleful of the next wine into your glass, swill it around and pour out – so you're effectively cleaning the glass with the new wine, leaving no trace of the old.

Choosing between two wines? Taste the first, then the second, then back to the first – wines have lots of complex flavours and you'll notice subtle differences if you do this a few times. Keep going until you're sure.

Magnums of wine will always be of superior quality to the same wine in a regular sized bottle as the ratio of wine to air is greater, so, if you can afford it or if you're entertaining, go for a larger bottle.

If you find a wine you like, look for the name of the producer rather than the name of the wine. Wines of the same name will often be made by many producers with varying degrees of quality. Better to stick to a producer you trust and try out their range of wines.

Used too much chilli or curry powder? Rescue the day by adding 2 tablespoons of milk.

Egg sandwiches always whiff, so try chopping the cooked egg and then storing it in the fridge in a covered container overnight. This should reduce the smell when you come to make up your sandwiches.

Don't get in a muddle at the supermarket check out – put loose items that need weighing, like fruit and veg, on last to allow you time to pack your bags.

To stop pasta sticking together while boiling add a little olive oil to the water.

If you turn up at a restaurant having booked a table to be told they haven't actually got one for you, the restaurant is in breach of contract and you're entitled to compensation.

And there is such a thing as a free lunch – a restaurant is actually obliged to ask you if you enjoyed your meal. If they fail to do this and you didn't really enjoy the food, you are not liable to pay the bill.

▶▶▶ Sculptors

Paul Astbury; John Mills, Chairman of the Royal Society of Sculptors; Hilary Brock

To make interesting hair for figures, squeeze clay through a fine sieve.

If you're making an ambitious piece of sculpture, make sure you can get it out through the door when you've finished!

To keep clean when you are working, wear an old dustbin liner. It's much easier to throw away each day; you don't want to have to wash out aprons covered in clay all the time.

You don't need expensive tools. Try experimenting with hair rollers, straws or tea strainers for interesting effects.

To prevent your tools sticking to the clay, keep a jar of cool water handy and dip the tools into it regularly.

To seal up a clay model that has cracked, wait for it to dry totally, then use a very sharp knife to cut away the clay from inside the crack. Mix that clay with some vinegar, then replace it in the gap. It will seal perfectly.

If you are in a hurry, you can speed up the clay drying process with a heat gun ... but be careful!

Create an interesting and lighter effect with your clay. Before you fire it up, mix the liquid clay with some polystyrene balls. When it comes out of the kiln, it will be a totally different texture.

Experiment by brushing some oil paint on to your clay before you fire it. You can get some amazing effects. Red oil paint leaves an iron residue and blue leaves traces of cobalt.

▶▶▶ Second-Hand Car Salesmen

Gary Redman; J. M. Littleton

▷▷ Inside the Car

To judge whether a car might have done more miles than the clock claims, look at the gear stick and the steering wheel. If either is very well worn, it indicates that lots of miles have been clocked up.

To check a car's true mileage, look at the driver's seat and foot pedals. Wear and tear on these can signal heavy use.

It's a good move to buy a car that has genuinely been on the road in recent months. Take a look at the tax disc; one that was bought two or three months ago is ideal. But, be suspicious of brand new ones. It might be a clue that this is a trade car which has been recently 'tarted' up.

'Buy dirty, sell clean'. Never buy an immaculate car at an auction. It is a sure sign that someone from the trade has got hold of it and is now trying to get rid of it.

Look under the carpet in the boot. If the floor has ridges in it, the car has been shunted from behind at some point and should be avoided.

▷▷ Outside the Car

Never buy a car in the dark – you are bound to miss something.

Try to judge what sort of owner a car has had by its stickers. AA or RAC stickers show a caring previous owner. Greenpeace or charity stickers show that the owner has cared as well. However, avoid any boy-racer stickers, which might mean that the car has been put through its paces!

If you're choosing a metallic car, give it a good rub to check that no one has smeared oil on to it to disguise faded paintwork.

Be cautious of cars with black shiny tyres. Why have they been tarted up? All revamps should alert you to possible cover-ups and possible problems.

Are the number plates the original ones with the supplier's name on them? If not, they may have been replaced after a crash.

Tap along the bodywork. If filler has been used at some point, you will hear a duller sound than everywhere else.

To see if the car has had an easy life, crouch down a few feet in front of the bonnet and look down the sides of the vehicle. Any little bumps or ripples will show up a treat and, a bit like human wrinkles, you can decide what kind of life the car has led so far!

Another mileage tip. Look for little stone chips on the bonnet. They indicate that the car's likely to have done plenty of motorway driving, which clocks up lots of miles but causes less wear and tear than hundreds of short journeys.

If you can only afford a high-mileage car, go for the newest car that has done all the miles in a short time.

▷▷ Under the Bonnet

When buying at an auction, always check the oil and water levels. Occasionally, dealers put a car that has a smoky engine into an auction. They will have drained all the oil out first so that the car will appear to run perfectly at the sale … but it will quickly get into trouble when you drive it away.

When you open the bonnet, check to see whether the wings have been beaten out. This indicates a previous crash of some sort and the car is best avoided.

Check all the gaps on a car, such as spaces around the tops of the doors. If any are wider than another, there's a good chance that the car has been rolled at some point. So don't touch it with a barge pole!

▷▷ Test–Driving a Car

Does the needle on the speedometer go round smoothly? It's a delicate instrument and one of the first things to react to a bad knock or two.

Take the car for a really good spin. Just around the block a couple of times is no good. Many faults won't show up until the car is truly warmed up.

Don't test–drive with the radio on or the windows open. You must eliminate as much noise as possible so that you can hear any unusual sounds.

Beware of the loud-mouthed salesman who talks non-stop while you're driving. He's probably trying to distract you.

▷▷ Looking After Your Car

When washing your car, don't use washing-up liquid because it contains salt which can cause rust to form.

Remove rust spots from chrome bumpers. Dip kitchen foil in Coca-Cola and rub off the rust spots.

Always keep a supply of hand wipes from fast-food outlets and plastic gloves from petrol stations to keep your hands clean when you have to do any minor repairs.

When you've got your new car, put the registration number on a post-it sticker on the dashboard until you remember it.

►►► Secretaries

Leigh Thomson, BT; Sue Blake; Sharon Hinds, Birmingham TEC

Every good secretary has an emergency survival kit with spare birthday cards, a blank card or two, some peppermints (in case your boss had a heavy lunch), some aspirin, a pair of tights and a sewing kit.

If you can't get the plastic hub out of the centre of the sticky tape, push two or three £1 coins through the middle to shift it.

For meetings, always order one or two extra teas and coffees in case someone changes their mind or an extra person turns up late.

When setting the table for a meeting, turn the cups upside down so that afterwards you'll know which ones have been used and which are still clean.

If the photocopier is broken, send the document through the fax machine on 'copy'.

If you are photocopying a long document, jot the page numbers in pencil on the back. At least if there's a jam you will be able to sort the sheets out afterwards.

Leave jobs like photocopying until a lunch hour so that the phone won't go unanswered.

Photocopy the boss's diary schedule for the day for easy reference and to make notes on.

Write down the ten most used numbers and sticky-tape them to the phone. Many secretaries speed-dial them into their phone and are then lost when someone asks for the number.

Every time you answer the phone, jot the person's name and company down. Once they've rambled on and asked to be put through to the boss, it's easy to have forgotten their personal details.

Always let the phone ring twice before you answer it so that people think the office is busy.

If you know you have something vitally important to remember for the next day, ring your own answering machine at home and leave a message to remind yourself.

If you want to sound confident and authoritative on the phone – stand up. It really does work!

To make a good impression, learn the names of your boss's kids. Even if your boss is in a foul mood, you can ask how little Tom or Jane is.

When someone calls to complain, don't pass them around the phone system to different people. Tell them your name and then say you will make sure someone gets back to them immediately.

Tie a pen around your neck so you'll have one handy at all times.

Clean an eraser by rubbing it on blotting paper.

If you need to take a long lunch, leave early rather than return late. It's much less noticeable.

Wear blue and earn everyone's trust.

▶▶▶ Security Guards

Ben Thompson

Stop a thief from sneaking up in the night by putting gravel down on your pathway or drive. The thief will go for a house with a quieter approach.

A dog is the best deterrent of all.

If you haven't got a dog, borrow a friend's and make a tape of occasional barks to play when you're away from home.

Trick thieves into thinking you have a dog by leaving a dog bowl outside, hanging a lead near a window or leaving the odd dog toy or chew around.

To stop thieves walking off with your planters and tubs, put several stones in the bottom of each tub before filling and planting. They will then be too heavy to lift.

Prickly plants and cactus make a great deterrent. Line your window ledges with them.

Use a baby alarm for extra security. Plug one half into your home and give a neighbour the other half so they can listen out for intruders while you're away.

Burglar alarms cost a lot of money but a dummy box stuck on the outside wall will put off most intruders.

Make sure you can find your keys in the dark – stick fluorescent tape on them.

If you've lost your own keys but have managed to break into your own home then it simply isn't secure enough.

▶▶▶ Small Animal Breeders

Pamela Milward; Belinda Francis

During the summer months, drinking bottles for small animals often get covered in green algae. To get rid of it, fill the bottle with sand and water, shake it vigorously and rinse it out thoroughly. The sand scours the algae off the glass.

To clean a small-necked water bottle, fill the bottle with a little water and a chain from a plug. Rattle it round for a bit to remove the stains.

Stop water bottles from freezing by adding a few drops of glycerine to the water.

To get into awkward nooks and crannies when cleaning a cage, use an old toothbrush. It's a great tool.

Keep flies out of cages – hang old net curtains over the cage.

▷▷ Hamsters

Hamsters are very active at night. If you want a good night's sleep, don't keep their cage in your bedroom.

When waking your hamster, make soft noises, talk to him gently, and move the cage to and fro so that he's not rudely awakened and frightened.

To clean a hamster's cage fill a jam jar with sawdust, put it on its side and encourage the hamster to explore it while you do housework on the cage. This also works if you want to create a hamster loo in one corner of the cage.

If your hamster escapes, put some of his food in the bottom of a bucket and lean a small, hamster-sized ramp up the side. The hamster will smell the food, go and investigate and drop to the bottom of the bucket with no means of getting out again.

Hamsters are great swingers. Hang a cardboard tube from the top of their cage to make a fun swing for them.

Baby hamsters love porridge and similar cereals.

Teach your baby hamster to enjoy being handled by always feeding him straight after playtime.

To prevent your hamster from going into a state of hibernation, warm him up gently in your hands – not by the fire.

If your hamster bites, use a small fishing net to catch him and save your fingers from nips.

To stop hamsters biting scoop them up from below when you want to pick them up. If you pick them up from above, they think they're being attacked and become aggressive.

To groom your long–haired hamster, use an old comb or toothbrush.

Give a hamster something to play with – cotton reels, jars … anything as long as it hasn't got sharp edges and isn't toxic.

Give your hamster something to chew on – attach some white wood to the side of the cage. Alternatively, use a clothes peg.

To help hamsters get over a cold, feed them a mixture of lukewarm milk, water and a drop of honey.

When buying a hamster, try to do so in the evening because they will be more active.

A healthy hamster should have a smooth, well-rounded body, with no bald patches on the coat. The eyes should be bright and clear. The ears should be clean and, if you're buying a young hamster, should have hair on the outside.

Male and female hamsters are equally good tempered.

You can keep two hamsters in one cage depending on what kind you want to get. Short dwarf hamsters and Russian hamsters are sociable souls and will go together. But it's best if they've been together since birth and are of the same sex. All other hamsters should be kept separately because they are territorial.

Feed your hamster once a day in the late afternoon or evening.

An adult hamster eats only a tablespoon of food or less a day.

Avoid iceberg lettuce and citrus fruits. Give small amounts of juicy fruits, such as tomatoes, strawberries or pears.

Hamsters are rather partial to yoghurt, but don't give them a rich variety like chocolate or caramel. No more than a teaspoon two or three times a week as a treat.

If your hamster does bite you, put him back in the cage and leave him for a couple of hours so he can calm down.

Don't use cottonwool or anything similar as bedding because it can be dangerous if eaten.

If your hamster escapes, try leaving some sunflower seeds in each room of the house. Shut all the doors and go to bed. The next morning, you'll be able to tell which room he's ended up in by the absence of seeds. Once you know which rooms he's in, get his cage and leave it with the door open and food inside.

Alternatively, put a pile of food in the centre of the floor and surround it with a ring of flour. Then just follow the footprints till you find the escapee.

▷▷ Guinea Pigs

Guinea pigs are partial to left-over cooked peas.

Treat your guinea pig – give it some toast.

Recycle your guinea pig's droppings and left-over food. Sprinkle them on the garden to grow sprouted oats which, when peeled, can be fed back to him.

Don't leave uneaten food in the cage because it will quickly go off.

Stop males from fighting. Put a few drops of lavender oil on their bottoms. It confuses their sense of smell.

Get your guinea pig used to being handled – support the whole body when you lift him up and hold onto him with the other hand so he doesn't make a dash for freedom and end up injuring himself.

You can keep a guinea pig in with a rabbit – they seem to get on rather well.

Give your guinea pigs hay all year round. The floor of the cage should be covered in it.

Guinea pigs' mouths are right underneath their heads, which means they have to feed from the floor so don't leave their food where they can't reach it.

Guinea pigs can't 'make' Vitamin C, so you must ensure that their diet includes Vitamin C-rich food (broccoli, carrots, swede or any dark green leafy vegetable).

Spinach leaves drive guinea pigs wild.

Avoid rhubarb and beetroot leaves because these are poisonous.

Lettuce leaves have a high water content, so aren't very nutritious.

Guinea pigs love melon, tomato and weeds.

If you like the grunts and squeals that guinea pigs make, start to make a regular noise just before you feed your pets. Like Pavlov's dog, they'll start squeaking themselves into a frenzy.

If your guinea pig starts to rumble, it means that it's not happy.

A happy guinea pig is a leaping guinea pig.

You can keep male (buck) guinea pigs together as long as they are introduced to the cage at the same time.

Guinea pig females are pregnant for around sixty-three days. Avoid handling a pregnant female because you could damage her unborn babies.

When guinea pigs are born, they are the spitting image of their parents – a full coat and eyes open.

When trimming a guinea pig's toenails, put him on a tennis racket. His toenails will poke down through the gaps of the strings, making them easier to clip. Avoid cutting into the quick.

One way to avoid clipping toenails is to give your guinea pigs a hard, abrasive surface to walk on so that their nails wear down naturally. Bricks (without holes in them) are the cheapest and easiest alternative.

Guinea pigs can be very chatty and have a full range of sounds. Try not to alarm them (such as picking them up unexpectedly) because they tend to shriek at full volume.

It's not a good idea to give your guinea pig the run of the house because it's all too easy to lose him behind the furniture. If you really want to have him indoors, build him an indoor run.

If you've just laid a new lawn, give it a chance to settle before introducing your pets on to it. New grass is often treated with weedkiller, which can harm animals.

Guinea pigs have been farmed for fur and food for over 2,500 years in South America.

Another name for a guinea pig is a cavie.

Not too hot, not too cold. Guinea pigs can cope with cold more than heat, so don't put their cages too near radiators or pipes.

Make sure the cage is sheltered from the sun.

While guinea pigs aren't rocket scientists, they're not stupid either. They can be trained to use a litter tray when out of the cage and will come when called. Training takes time, but the potential is there.

▷▷ Rabbits

Cool your rabbit down in summer. Chill a ceramic tile in the fridge and then place it in his hutch.

Use sawdust on the floor of the cage rather than wood shavings or straw. Sawdust is softer and more comfortable.

Hang a carrot on the cage using a metal skewer. It will stay fresh longer and remain free from sawdust so your rabbit will enjoy it more.

Amuse a house rabbit – tell it some jokes … no, seriously, put his food in a washing ball from a washing machine. This will keep him happy for hours.

Prepare a crunchy snack by baking left-over bits of bread.

Rabbits need bulk so make sure they get hay as well as root vegetables, green food and mixed cereals.

Don't let rabbits graze where dogs have been. They could pick up tapeworm.

Make nail clipping easy. Rabbits are pushovers when it comes to putting them in a trance. Simply lie your rabbit on its back and gently stroke its tummy until it drifts off. You can then clip the nails without fuss before snapping your fingers and bringing it back to the real world!

Handle your rabbit frequently so that it gets used to it. Always be gentle. Pick the rabbit up with both hands, placed just behind the front legs. Don't pick a rabbit up by the ears or the scruff of its neck.

If a rabbit panics while you are holding it, put it down on the floor. Rabbits have powerful hind legs and you could get badly scratched trying to restrain it.

Rabbits like to climb. Put shelves in their hutch.

If the hutch is to be kept outside make sure it's in a sheltered, draught-free area.

The bigger the cage the better – it should be at least four times the size of the rabbit and a lot more if he's going to be confined for most of the day.

Rabbits come in different sizes – for example, Netherland Dwarf rabbits are tiny (weighing in at 2 1/4lb/1kg), while the Belgian Hare (which isn't a hare, but a rabbit just to be confusing!) can weigh up to 9lb/4kg.

Paper bags and cardboard boxes make great places to hide in. Rabbits also have fun playing with cardboard loo rolls, bits of paper to shred, small towels, things to jump on and hide under.

Keep an eye on a rabbit when it's loose in the house. Rabbits are great chewers and think nothing of sinking their teeth into electric cables, rugs, plants and so on.

You can train a house rabbit to walk on a harness and lead – but don't take them for long walks in unfamiliar territory. Stick to the familiar.

Always make sure your pet has enough water. If you keep the hutch outside, remember that the water in its bottle can freeze in the winter, so don't fill it right to the top because the water will expand as it turns to ice and crack the glass.

Hay is an essential part of a rabbit's diet because it provides roughage. Apple tree twigs are also a good source of roughage.

Don't suddenly change your rabbit's diet – the bacteria in its stomach which breaks down its food needs time to adapt to any changes.

Rabbits produce two kinds of droppings – the good and the bad. The first sort is made up of partially digested food and is usually passed at night. These droppings are full of nutrients which the rabbit eats so that they are absorbed into its small intestine. The other kind are large, round and stay on the ground.

If your rabbit develops diarrhoea, give it a weed called shepherd's purse, which should help its condition.

Rabbits are able to suck in their cheeks when they eat, which stops sharp, tough things like twigs from getting into their mouths.

Placing your hand round its ears will help calm a struggling rabbit. But never pick up a rabbit by its ears because this will cause it a lot of pain and distress.

Don't pick up a rabbit with your bare arms because you could get badly scratched.

If your rabbit starts circling your feet and biting your ankles, it could be sexually frustrated. Neutering can reduce aggressive behaviour.

Rabbits are territorial. When you open the cage, let them come out on their own; don't reach in and drag them out, because they could bite you.

If your rabbit gives you a nip, let out a sudden high-pitched, loud screech to let him know he hurt you. Keep on squealing every time you are nipped; soon your rabbit will get the message and be more gentle.

Put ice on the spot where your rabbit has nipped you to ease the pain.

You can put your rabbit's hutch on an overgrown patch of vegetable garden. They'll help to keep the weeds down and their droppings will fertilise the earth.

Netherland Dwarf rabbits can be martyrs to their teeth because sometimes their teeth don't fit together properly, which makes eating difficult.

Give your rabbit something to gnaw on like a log or piece of hard-baked bread. It's better they chew away on something like this than on their cage.

Lop rabbits have extremely long ears, which can grow over 24 in long. The Dwarf Lop makes a good pet because it doesn't need any special care and has a nice, friendly nature.

Angora rabbits are one of the oldest breeds and can look spectacular, but they do need a lot of grooming and special housing.

Don't keep buck rabbits together in a cage because they will probably fight each other all the time.

If you keep doe rabbits together, they will often experience false pregnancies.

A pregnant rabbit pulls at its fur to make a soft nest for its young.

If you want to breed from your rabbits, put a doe and buck together. Obvious really, isn't it? The female rabbit will immediately start to produce eggs once she is placed with a male. Rabbits are pregnant for around thirty-one days.

Rabbits can be house-trained – you can teach them to use a litter tray. Unlike cats, they don't damage the furniture, but can scratch the carpet.

Clean litterboxes often to encourage a rabbit to use them. Rabbit wee is really smelly so you won't want to leave used litter hanging around.

If your rabbit has an accident on the carpet, clean the stain with white vinegar or soda water.

If you let your rabbit in your house, don't encourage it to climb the stairs. If it falls, it could damage its back badly.

▷▷ Gerbils

When buying a gerbil, look for an animal that is bright-eyed, alert and inquisitive. If it's dozy and disinterested, it could be ill.

If you want to restrain a gerbil – hold it firmly by the base of the tail. Try to avoid grabbing the tail any further along because you could damage it.

Wooden cages are hard to keep clean. Gerbils also tend to chew large bits off, so stick to a metal cage.

A gerbil's idea of a des res is an old coconut shell. It may not be much to you or me but it's a palace to him. Place it in his cage.

Stop sawdust from getting everywhere. Stand the cage in a cardboard box with the sides cut down. The sawdust collects in the bottom of the box and can be shaken out every few days.

Gerbils are very gregarious and hate to be kept on their own. Two same sex pairs will bond as closely as a mated pair and be happy as Larry.

Gerbils make ideal pets because they are desert animals. This means that they make very efficient use of food and water and hardly wee at all. That means you don't have to clean their cages as much as other rodent pets.

Give a gerbil a bit of wood to gnaw and it will also serve as a look-out point for inquisitive pets and help the cage look attractive.

As desert creatures, gerbils are used to dry conditions and like to dig. Give them plenty of wood shavings (about 2 in deep) to burrow in.

Put a dish full of sand in your gerbil's cage – they love to have sandbaths. It helps to keep their fur in good condition. Change the sand every few days.

Hay is much appreciated as a nest-building material.

Don't get your gerbils a hamster wheel to play with – it might catch its tail in the open spaces.

Unlike many animals, gerbils practise a form of birth control. If you have a breeding pair which produces a litter or two then they won't have any more. If, however, you remove the litter, the parents become fertile again.

Gerbils are sexually mature at 60-80 days.

Gerbils are unusual in that they generally mate for life in pairs (or sometimes as a threesome, the kinky devils).

▷▷ Rats & Mice

To lure a rat out from under the furniture, entice him (or her) by holding a rat of the opposite sex a short distance away.

Rats like sleeping in old shoeboxes, or 3-litre wine boxes – with the wine bag removed, of course!

A cheap alternative to rat food is out-of-date baby food.

Rat delicacies also include titbits like biscuits (both human and dog varieties), apples and tomatoes. But remember to keep them on a balanced diet.

Pick up rats by their shoulders with your thumb held under their chin to stop them from biting. Don't pick a rat up by the scruff of its neck – it'll take a lump out of your finger.

Rats don't fight as much as mice so you can keep them together more easily. Adult male mice tend to be argumentative with each other so are best kept apart.

Mice can be picked up by the scruff of their neck.

Keep mice and rats amused – fill their cages with cardboard tubes, climbing frames, ladders and exercise wheels.

Rats, mice, hamsters and gerbils are ideal for the novice 'keeper'.

You should allow at least half an hour each day for your pet, even more if you only have one animal.

When choosing a pet, look for a healthy animal. There shouldn't be any bald patches on their fur and they should be alert and agile. Small scars on ears and tails are not necessarily signs of illness but are probably from old fights.

Always try to choose a young rodent as a pet because these animals tend to have quite a short life span. A young mouse or rat can be taken from its mother when it's four weeks of age.

Place the cage in a slightly raised position. Mice and rats react strongly to danger from above, even if it's only you coming to feed them. Eye-level is about right.

Try to put the cage in a busy area. Rats and mice love to see, smell and hear what's going on.

When picking up a rodent, try not to swoop down from above in case you frighten your pet. Allow them to sniff your hand before you pick them up.

If your mouse or rat gets out, put a cardboard tube on the floor with some food inside it. Once it runs inside, close both ends with your hands and return the escapee to its cage.

Rats can be kept in guinea-pig cages because they can't slip through the bars.

If you're worried about your pet mice escaping from a wire cage, see whether you can get your finger through the wire. If you can, a young mouse can get out.

The advantage of wire cages is that mice love to climb and the wire gives them ample opportunity to do this.

Don't keep rats and mice together.

Wood shavings are ideal as litter. They are very absorbent and cheap to buy. Spread them around the cage, about 1 1/2 inches thick. Don't use cedar or pine, though, because they contain toxins.

Rats and mice tend to use the corners of the cage as their toilet. You could try adding a layer of cat litter in their favourite spots. It will help keep the smell down too.

Female mice don't have the same musky odour as male mice.

Mice like their cages to smell familiar. Try changing only half the litter at a time so that a familiar smell remains.

Equally, put back a little bit of old bedding each time you clean the cage, so that there is a familiar smell where the mice sleep too.

Try to avoid too many berries because this can cause rodents to wee more often and make their litter really damp.

Avoid windy pets – don't give them cabbage and onions.

You can keep mice and rats on their own as individuals, but you will have to give them a lot of love and attention to make up for lack of rodent companions.

Rats can be taught to come when you call their names.

Mice are sexually mature at 30–49 days old, while rats can wait a little longer – 30–79 days.

To pick up a mouse grasp the base of its tail firmly and lift its hindquarters. Slide your other hand under its bottom and then lift your hand with the mouse sitting on it.

Give them a challenge – don't make life too easy for them. If you're about to feed them, put the food on a different level so the mice have to climb up to it. Make ladders steeper or give them ropes as bridges.

Mice love empty egg boxes – they're great to chew to pieces.

Rats love to gnaw on things. Try rawhide chew sticks or dog biscuits.

Alternatively, cooked soup bones are a particular ratty favourite.

Avocado goes down a treat with a rat.

Mice adore sunflower seeds, but don't give a fat mouse this kind of treat.

To help a mouse lose weight cut out oily seeds (like sunflower seeds or peanuts) and fatty treats. Give it soaked stale bread or plain boiled wholegrain rice with fruit and vegetables.

Cheese is not an ideal treat for a mouse because mice don't feed on dairy products in the wild. Cheese is, however, a convenient way to bait mousetraps.

Rats and mice can be fed a few treats now and again. Dry, healthy, low-sugar cereals, plain popcorn, dry oatmeal, spaghetti or wild bird seed all add variety to their diet.

A rat will require a wheel that is at least 12–14 ins in diameter.

A cheap but effective toy for mice is a section of branch with holes bored into it. Your mice can use it as a climbing frame and ladder.

Alternatively, an upside-down terracotta flowerpot with holes in the edge makes an ideal hidey hole.

Add a few small branches from a birch, beech tree or hazel bush – it will give your rat or mouse something to clamber up and down and explore from.

▷▷ Reptiles

If you're going to buy a snake, take a pillow case with you to the shop or breeder. You can then wrap the snake in it so that he won't become too stressed while you take it home with you.

If your reptile gets a cold, put a jar of vapour rub in his cage and turn up the heating in the cage.

To handle a lizard properly, pick him up by holding him firmly around his body and forelegs – never by the tail.

To help a lizard adapt to its surroundings, cover the floor with enough sand and gravel for him to bury himself.

To create a perfect basking area, place a rock inside the vivarium.

Margarine pots are excellent wet boxes for geckos.

When feeding a snake defrosted mice, put the food under the hair-dryer for a while. This will make it look and smell more like the real thing.

Never put frozen rats or mice in the microwave because this will build up the bacteria. Always allow them to defrost naturally.

If your snake is having problems eating, feed him at night or when all the lights are turned off. This will make him feel more secure and he should go back to his normal routine. If the problem persists, take him to the vet.

When feeding a snake, ensure that you wrap rubber bands around the end of your tweezers so you don't damage his teeth or mouth.

If your snake has difficulty shedding his skin, get a good dollop of vegetable oil on your hands and stroke the snake from head to tail. You should find that the skin will come off more easily then.

If there's a problem shedding skin from around the eye area, wrap a bit of masking tape around your finger and gently remove the skin with this.

If your snake is laying eggs, she'll appreciate a good hide. Drape a towel over two pieces of wood and she'll curl up underneath. Spray the towel regularly to maintain humidity.

Use old egg boxes for your snake's favourite dish – crickets – to jump around in.

To house an aquatic amphibian, you need the water to be at least 6 in/15 cm deep for the animal to swim in. So make sure you've got a good water-filtration system.

To distinguish toads from frogs, check their skin. A toad has a dry, warty skin, shorter hind legs and a flatter appearance.

To keep your frogs happy, collect moss from trees, wash it and put in with the frogs. Then spray it regularly to keep it damp.

To give your newts a nutritious diet, give them earthworms, tadpoles and insect larvae ... don't give them anything that moves too quickly.

Snakes don't require a lot of space. A cage one half to two-thirds of its body length is sufficient for most adult snakes.

Snakes are shy creatures, so give them somewhere to hide: a cardboard box turned upside down with a hole cut in the side is perfectly adequate.

Don't feed your new snake when you get it home. Give it a few days to settle down and get used to its surroundings.

Temperature is extremely important – the cage should be kept at a temperature of between 80°F and 86°F with an incandescent red light (red bulbs cause less stress to snakes). Don't guess at the temperature – use a thermometer.

Proper lighting is important for reptiles because it aids in calcium metabolism. You need the full source of spectrum lighting that provides UVA and UVB rays.

Most reptiles and amphibians become less active when they are cold. This makes them easier to handle. Put them in the fridge for a short while (in a container, of course). On no account try to speed up the process by using the freezer. Don't leave them in the fridge for longer than a few minutes. If ice crystals form on their bodies, it can cause a lot of pain and distress.

To create a perfect basking area place a rock inside the vivarium.

Snakes eat other animals – when thinking about buying a snake as a pet, it's worth investigating whether you will have a ready supply of rats and mice.

Young snakes will need to eat about once a week. Adult snakes can be fed twice a month. For really large snakes, such as boas and pythons, you need only feed them once a month.

Don't leave live food animals in with your snake – mice and rats can give a nasty bite that can seriously injure a reptile.

Don't handle a snake immediately after feeding. It will be sick. Leave it for a day or two.

Bearded dragons make good pets – they can be extremely tame, but have high energy levels and big appetites with personalities to match.

The more you handle a bearded dragon the tamer it will become. Soon you will have it eating out of your hand (literally) and perching on your shoulder quite happily.

Bearded dragons need a light source for basking and the daily heating of their bodies. You will also need to provide places to hide, so that they can regulate their body temperature.

If you don't want a large lizard, don't get a green iguana. Properly cared for, they can reach 5–6 ft within four to five years.

Green iguanas can live for up to twenty years in captivity and weigh up to 18lbs.

In the wild iguanas feel more comfortable in trees. Make sure you have enough height in their tank to allow them to climb.

Iguanas love to climb, so provide them with branches, ropes or towels to climb up and bask on. Make sure they are securely placed to prevent your pet from falling.

Choosing a suitable flooring or (or substrate) for your iguana's cage is important. Artificial grass, carpet or paper towels are ideal. Always have a few pieces in reserve so that, while a soiled piece is being washed and disinfected, you can put the spare piece in the tank. The clean piece must be completely dry before you replace it.

Newspaper does not make suitable flooring for iguanas because the ink can get into their skin.

Iguanas don't need to eat meat – they can be raised on a strictly

plant-based diet where they can get their protein from plant
materials. Alfalfa is an excellent source of plant protein.

Chop your iguana's food carefully. Although they have a sharp set
of teeth, iguanas don't chew their food – they gulp it down, so
don't give them big pieces.

You can make up a week's worth of basic salad for your lizard
and keep it in an airtight container in the fridge. Just spoon in the
required amount when you need to. A good mix would consist of
green beans, alfalfa, parsnip and fruit.

Add a little extra to your iguana's salad with some left-overs. A
bit of rice or bread will add extra calcium to their diet.

Frogs eat slugs and snails – they make up about 25% of their diet.

You can't get warts from a frog – that's just an old wives' tale.

A group of frogs is called an 'army' of frogs. And a group of toads
is called a 'knot' of toads.

**When a frog swallows, his eyeballs close and go down into his
head**. This is because the eyeballs apply pressure and help push the
food down the frog's throat.

Toads are partial to ants, beetles and woodlice. Earthworms
always go down well.

If you have to handle an amphibian (such a frog, toad, newt or
salamander), make sure your hands are slightly damp. They have
very sensitive skin.

Never mix different species together – many amphibians secrete
toxins which can be deadly to other species.

Always wash your hands after handling your pet.

Grass snakes are harmless to humans – it's only form of defence is to play dead.

Slow worms are not snakes – they are lizards, so don't handle them by the tail. They are usually extremely friendly and happy to be handled.

A slow worm will eat in the late afternoon and early evening. Give it snails, slugs, worms and insects.

▷▷ Pot-Bellied Pigs

Pot-bellied pigs can be kept indoors or out. Give them some shelter if they are kept outside.

In hot spells they will need a pool of water to keep cool.

Even domesticated pigs need to root around, so make sure they have an area of soft dirt or soil to stick their snouts in.

Puberty occurs at around six to seven months of age. If you don't plan to breed from your pigs, you can have them spayed or neutered at around three to four months old.

If your pig does have a litter, the piglets' needle teeth should be trimmed, so that the sow and other piglets don't get nipped by the sharp teeth.

Pot-bellied pigs aren't aggressive, but they can give a nasty nip if their canine teeth aren't removed. You can have them removed when the pig is around four months old.

These pigs don't raise a stink. In fact, they hardly pong at all.

Grooming is important. Brush them down with a soft bristle brush each day. Hooves and tusks will need trimming regularly.

Why get a dog? Pot-bellied pigs are intelligent and can be trained as you would a dog. They respond to litter training, can do simple tricks and walk on a lead.

►►► Soft Furnishers

Ben Butterworth, Cheshire; Courtney Spence, Jamieson Furnishings, London; Juliette Bardon, London; Val Adams, Totnes; David Pugh, Birmingham; Ruth Hyde, London

Change the look of your room – simply throw a white sheet over a piece of furniture. It works rather like correcting fluid, blanking an object out so you can start all over again.

Transparent thread on a sewing machine can be extremely static – to prevent static from building up, place a piece of sponge on the last hook so it cleans the thread as it is pulled through.

The secret of great looking throws is to measure generously.

Keep a throw on the sofa by sewing Velcro on the back of it.

Make soft furnishings last longer – simply spray them with Scotchguard or any waterproofing spray of the kind that you would use on suede shoes.

Wash your feather pillows while imagining you're in the vineyards of France. Dissolve a handful of soap flakes in a bath of warm water. Place pillows in and tread with bare feet to remove the dirt. Repeat and rinse, spin in the washing machine and hang up to dry.

Tired looking pillows can be brought back to life by making an opening in the seam and pumping air in with a bicycle pump. Remember to stitch the seam back up.

Stick curtain hooks into a bar of soap and you'll be able to attach them to your fabric with a lot less hassle.

For an instant spot–remover use shaving cream. Apply, blot into stain, wash up with water and blot dry.

Delicate tapestries or needlepoint coverings can be safely cleaned with a baby's soft hairbrush.

Once dirty, it's impossible to get curtain nets really clean, so wash them regularly.

Make invisible repairs in your net curtains – dab colourless nail-varnish on the torn edge and hold them together until the varnish is dry.

Blast the dust off a pleated lampshade with a hair-dryer.

Or use an old toothbrush.

Wash fabric lampshades in warm water, then dry them with a hair-dryer on cool. This tightens up the material so the shade looks like new.

Leather sofas should be buffed up with a mixture of linseed oil and vinegar. Simply heat equal amounts of each, then allow to cool to room temperature and apply with a clean duster. Your sofa will gleam.

Don't ruin beautiful chintz – always iron the wrong side out to protect the special glaze.

Clean velour upholstery with a solution of warm water and washing-up liquid. Dip some muslin into the mixture and wipe over the fabric.

Vacuum your curtains every few weeks and you won't need to have them dry-cleaned so often.

To avoid taking down curtains when washing windows, drape them through a hanger and hang them from the curtain rod.

▷▷ Curtains

Emphasise natural daylight in a room by using curtain fabrics with a dark background.

To dress a window for decorative reasons only (when you'll never need to draw the curtains) use half as much fabric. No one will know the difference and it will save you a lot of money.

For really cheap curtains, muslin is ideal. Create dramatic effects by swagging and draping metres of the stuff. You can leave it as a plain white fabric or dye it to match your colour scheme.

For a toddler's room, try shower curtains instead of fabric ones. However grubby the little fingers that tug at them, the curtains will always wipe clean and they come in lots of fun designs.

To hang curtains effectively, use the wall space, not the window space. Measure 8 in/20 cm above and 12 in/30 cm either side of the window and hang your curtains in this space.

If you are drilling a hole for a curtain pole, vacuum up the dust at the same time to prevent it from getting everywhere.

Make cheap curtain poles from wooden broom handles. Stain them to suit your decor.

Instead of an expensive metal rod in the bottom of your blind, simply sew in a bamboo stick.

To calculate the length of a pelmet, divide the drop of the curtain by five or six.

Experiment with pelmet shapes – cut out trial shapes in newspaper and Blu tack to the wall. Adjust accordingly until you're satisfied.

To make your window look taller, position the bottom of the pelmet at the top of the window.

Make cheap curtain liners from sheets or old blankets.

Place curtain hooks no closer than 5 in/13 cm apart as it improves pleating and draping characteristics.

When taking curtains down to wash, mark where the curtain hooks go with nail varnish so you know where to replace the hooks for the correct spacing.

To keep curtains hanging straight, put old or foreign coins inside the hems.

If a blind curls up at the bottom, put matched magnets on either side to weight it down.

▷▷ Floors

See if that small-patterned carpet is really going to work. Place a mirror on the carpet so that it stretches out in front of you and gives you a better idea of how it would look on your floor.

Make an inexpensive floor covering by painting a piece of canvas with dyes and acrylics. When dry, coat with tough floor varnish.

▷▷ Cushions

Make stuffing from old pairs of tights. Place a bit of dried lavender inside for a lovely smell.

▷▷ Fabrics

Felt is a cheap alternative to velvet – it's very effective and is half the price.

The armrests of a chair quickly get mucky so clean them up by rubbing with a loaf of bread.

Create your own designer fabrics – tie-dye gingham or muslin.

A simple way to create a circular tablecloth is to fold the material in half. Take a piece of string and attach a pencil to one end and a drawing pin to the other. Stick the drawing pin on the edge of the fold, draw a semi-circle over the fabric, and cut out.

If your old sheets have worn away, don't throw them out. Cut around the edges and sew them up into pillow cases.

▷▷ Lighting Up

Don't throw old lampshades away – give them a quick wash and create a new effect with a different-coloured light bulb.

▷▷ Tools of the Trade

Make a 'third hand' – cover bricks with material and use them to hold down fabric while you work on it.

Clean scissors and needles with surgical spirit. It's a great way to remove fabric glue.

►►► Special Needs Carers

Judith Eaton; Pauline Haller, Guide Dogs for the Blind; Denise Smith; Ray Hill, RNID; Disabled Living Foundation; Elaine White; Martin Hughes

When you are doing sign language, try not to wear multi-coloured clothing because it's very difficult to follow what you are saying against such a busy background.

If someone is trying to lip-read you, don't stand with your back to the light.

For the whole family to enjoy watching a video, get one with subtitles that go along the bottom of the screen. The RNID (19–23 Featherstone Street, London, EC1Y 8SL. Telephone 0171 296 8000) have a list of companies that do this.

If you are inside a house where a blind person lives, remember to put everything back in the same place.

To thread a needle if you are partially sighted, stick a bit of sponge on to a block of wood. Place the needle in the sponge and then use the needle threader. This method allows you to use both hands.

Store all your buttons, needles or whatever, in a screw and nail box with transparent drawers. Everything can be found much more easily.

Fastening a shirt can be made easier if you substitute press studs for buttons.

To identify appliances easily if you're partially sighted, buy different-coloured plugs or mark each one with a large initial of the relevant appliance – a large K for kettle, for example.

To help your guide dog settle in and get to know its new owner, keep the family away to start with so that the owner is the only person to deal with the dog for the first couple of months.

To help people with learning difficulties, make sure the tasks that they do can be broken down into component stages.

Having a shower needn't be difficult – fix a grab rail to the side of the wall, but make sure that the wall is sturdy enough to take the weight.

Turning over in bed needn't be a struggle – treat yourself and buy satin pyjamas … or go the whole hog and get satin sheets as well!

▶▶▶ Surveyors

James Burne; Graham Dickenson

Don't just book your surveyor over the phone. You are entitled to meet your surveyor without cost or obligation to make sure he is the right one for you.

Help your surveyor. Write out a specific list of things that worry you before he does his survey.

A survey should be done in the morning to make the most of natural light.

Good surveyors always take a double look at new extensions and alterations. They are often signs of a past problem or a cover up.

Check out general problems such as flooding in the vicinity with a building inspector at the local council offices. They are generally very helpful.

Encourage natural ventilation and avoid condensation in the loft – don't seal the eaves with insulation.

Cure condensation by cleaning the affected area with bleach, then drying out with lots of warmth and ventilation.

To check whether the roof has had slipping tiles, look for pieces of foam placed underneath the roof slates.

Take a pair of binoculars with you – you want to get a really good look at gutters and roofs.

Be wary of a house that has very large trees close by. The roots can cause havoc with foundations. A good general rule is that no tree should be closer than one and a half times its own height to any building.

If you are checking a property yourself, have a probe around with a screwdriver. If the walls feel a bit soggy, then the house probably has rot.

To find rising damp, tap the wall with the handle of a screwdriver. If it produces a dull sound, there could be a problem. Compare the sound by tapping the wall at a higher level where damp is unlikely to be.

Test out how good the upstairs floorboards are by bouncing on your heels in different parts of the rooms. The boards may give a little in the corners but should be solid and silent in the middle of each room.

Test to see how good the open fire is. Burn a piece of paper in the hearth and ask a friend to see how quickly smoke appears from the chimney. If it's drawing well, it should almost be immediate. If not, call a chimney sweep in.

▶▶▶ Swimming Teachers

Louisa Laughlan

▷▷ Very Small Children

When introducing a child to a swimming pool for the first time, let them sit on the side of the pool for the first few visits and watch the other children. They'll soon be dying to have a go themselves.

When a small child first goes swimming, let them take a favourite bath toy into the water with them.

To boost your child's confidence gradually reduce the amount of air in their water wings as they get better.

To help a child under six months become comfortable in the water, encourage them to play in the bath.

When your child has had her bath, let most of the water out and let her lie on her tummy and kick her legs. Tell your child that she's swimming so that she gets used to the idea.

Teach a child of over six months to breathe correctly in the water by getting him to put his mouth slightly underwater and blow bubbles.

Encourage children's arm movements when in the water. Hold them under the armpits and put a ball just out of their reach; then let them try and grab it.

Get your children used to going underwater by playing 'Ring a ring o' roses' in the shallow end of the pool. On 'we all fall down', everyone has to bob under the water.

Children quickly get cold once they've come out of the water so take a towelling bath robe to the pool edge to pop on as soon as they leave the pool.

To stop little ones catching cold, dry their hair under the hand-dryers in the changing rooms.

▷▷ Older Children and Advanced Swimmers

To put goggles on correctly and stop water seeping in, put the eye pieces on first and then adjust the strap at the back of your head.

To increase the power in your leg movements, wear flippers – but always check at the swimming pool that you are allowed to wear them.

Put your flippers on before getting in the water but stay in the water to take them off.

Stop your swimming cap from sticking together by sprinkling it with talcum powder after use.

Prevent your swimsuit from becoming see-through – stick to dark colours.

An easy way to practise a particular leg movement is to hold on to a float so you can concentrate on what your legs are doing.

To hold your head correctly during backstroke, don't look up at the ceiling – look at a point on the wall you are swimming away from.

Check you are moving as quickly as possible during backstroke – try to do six to eight kicks for every arm stroke.

During front crawl you can get the most movement from your arms by trying to touch your bottom or thigh before bringing it out of the water.

Teach yourself front crawl turns by practising somersaults underwater.

To give yourself confidence when you start to dive, imagine a hole in the water and aim for that.

Avoid slipping when taking a dive by curling your toes over the edge of the pool or board.

Keep your legs together during a dive – place a coin between your feet ... and keep it there!

To judge whether a pool is suitable for synchronised swimming, check that the depth is 10 ft/3 m and the width and length are both at least 40 ft/12 m.

In order for synchronised swimmers to hear the music at all times make sure you have a good quality, battery-controlled cassette player and underwater speakers.

Appropriate music can make a big difference in synchronised swimming – select something with a dramatic beginning and end to grab the audience's attention.

To increase the overall style of a synchronised swimming
performance, all swimmers should act with confidence and poise
even before they get into the water.

Keep you hair in place during synchronised swimming – apply
gelatine at least one hour before the performance. This will wash
out later in a warm shower.

Wetsuits can smell if not looked after – keep yours in top condition
by always rinsing inside and out with fresh water after use.

Get rid of wetsuit smells by rinsing the suit with disinfectant
solution on a regular basis.

Dry your lifejacket quickly – inflate it first.

▶▶▶ Teachers

Susan Cawthorne, Heaton Nursery; Broad Oak Nursery School; Leap Frogs Nursery
School; Rocking Horse Nursery; Acorn Kindergarten; Susan Woodroff; Mary Lapworth

▷▷ Nursery School

To get a child to sleep, stroke its forehead between the eyes.

You can make dinner more interesting by putting food colouring in
milk or mashed potato.

To lure a child into eating boring (familiar) food, put it in a
different container to disguise it.

To make children eat more, give them lots of tiny portions: six peas
rather than none at all which makes them feel as if they have eaten
lots of food.

To keep children entertained during a meal, don't use a tablecloth. Put a sheet of wallpaper face down on the table and leave some pens or crayons lying around. Then they feel as though they are scribbling on the table … very naughty!

Make a pretend cooking hob – take a square, silver cake board and draw four rings on it.

To teach left and right, put little Ls and Rs on cutlery and door frames. Paint L and R on the inside or bottom of shoes with some nail-varnish.

Make a game out of everyday things to help educate your child. For example, they can learn the difference between heavier and lighter by helping you to unpack the shopping.

If you want to encourage children to put things away in the right place, put different-coloured stickers on toys which correspond to stickers on or in different cupboards, shelves, boxes or other items of furniture.

Make your own curtains. Find some plain white fabric and get children to walk all over it with paint on their feet, or cover it with hand prints.

To show children which tap is the cold one, cut a soft, foam tennis ball in half and place it over the cold tap. They will know which one is safe to use, and it's easier for them to grip.

Make your life easier – put some washing-up liquid in the children's paint because it helps it to come out of their clothes when they are being washed.

To make non–dribbly paint, mix it with wallpaper paste (but not one that has an anti-fungus agent in it). It shouldn't end up all over the place.

For easy hand painting, fill a bathroom spray with paint and use it as a spray over hands.

For a novel paint effect, trail some bits of string through a paint pot and then pull across a piece of paper.

Dip marbles in different coloured paints. Put some paper in the bottom of a washing-up bowl and roll the marbles around for wonderful 'snail tracks'.

To blow your own paint bubbles make up a solution of paint, water and washing-up liquid in a large margarine tub. Take a straw and blow into the mixture, creating a froth of bubbles. When you've got a nice pile, you can place a piece of paper on top for a bubbly, coloured print.

An alternative paintbrush can be made by filling a used, roll-on deodorant bottle with paint.

To make textured paint, add sand, tea, rice … pretty much anything really.

Do your own rubbings. Stick cereal, lentils, rice and/or spaghetti on to some paper. Put a clean sheet on top and rub over with a crayon.

Rub a wax candle over some paper. Paint over the top and then lay a clean piece of paper over the picture to blot the extra wetness. Remove and leave to dry.

Make your own balls of gunk – extremely popular with small children! Mix cornflour with water in a tray and leave your children to do what they will with it!

More gungy gunk! Mix soap flakes with white paint – great for playing with. As it gets dirty, you can start to add colour to it. Begin with light colours and get darker as it gets dirtier. You can make it bright red or green and call it blood or snot – children love it!

Create a grass ball. Get an old plastic washing powder ball and poke some holes in it. Fill it with earth and grass seed. Water it regularly.

To make some funky fabric, take two layers of bubble wrap and sandwich confetti, glitter, dried leaves, old sweet papers (whatever you like) between them. Then, place the bubble wrap between two sheets of greaseproof paper and fuse them together with an iron. Use your new 'fabric' to create bags, ties, tabards …

Fill balloons with coloured water and then freeze them. You can then burst the balloon to create an enormous round ice ball!

To make your own DIY musical instruments, use an empty Pringles box and fill it with rice or pasta shells.

Make your own mobiles from coat-hangers. Hang or stick pictures, old cards, bits of ribbon and so on on the hanger.

To make a skittle alley, take old washing-up liquid bottles, juice bottles and even cans, and line then up as your skittles.

To make puppets, use old socks with buttons sewn on for the features.

A good game for children is to cut up a picture and hide the pieces around the house. The children have to find all the bits and, in a set time limit, complete the jigsaw picture.

On rainy days, cut up old birthday and Christmas cards that have photos on the front. These can be used to make cards to play with.

▷▷ **Primary School**

To find the end of the sticky tape quickly, put a button on the end.

Stop powder paints from cracking when drying – put a drop of washing-up liquid in with the water when you mix the paint up.

Hair-spray makes a good fixative for models and collages (but don't let the children spray it on themselves).

When teaching children left and right make sure you stand with your back to the class; otherwise they'll be seeing a mirror image and this will only muddle them up.

Children often get confused by the difference between 'b' and 'd'. The word 'bed' is a brilliant way to show them the difference between the two.

Teach young children to listen to you. Keep your voice quiet. Don't raise it or the sound level of the class will just go up and up.

Keep control of a lively class – use a few simple, key words sparingly. Something like 'Stop' so that all the children know they must respond immediately.

When you begin to teach children to write, let them make letters in sand.

When children move on to writing with pencils, give them the chunky, triangular-shaped type because they are easier for little fingers to grasp.

If you are using water to measure different amounts, colour it first with a little food dye so that it shows up clearly.

When teaching the alphabet, create a physical action to go with each of the letters so that they become easier to remember.

In winter, ask the children to put their gloves and woolly hats back inside the sleeves of their coats when they come back inside. Everything will be easier to find at home-time.

▷▷ Secondary Education

Take time to talk to your children when they come home. You'd hate it if no one asked you about your day at the office.

If your son or daughter isn't concentrating in class, make sure they don't need glasses. Short-sighted children often get frustrated because they simply can't see the blackboard.

If you think your child has more of a problem, make an immediate appointment to see a teacher. There's nothing worse than waiting until parent's evening and *then* saying 'I've been worried all term'. It's frustrating for the teacher and it won't have helped your child.

Don't be intimidated by bullies. Just think of them naked or suffering a severe attack of the squits. Suddenly you'll find they don't look so terrible!

▷▷ **Exams & Revision**

Never revise on an empty stomach. You simply won't be able to concentrate.

Be quiet! Wherever you choose to revise, make sure it's not noisy.

Be comfortable. You need to be comfortable when you revise. Lie on the floor, on the bed, sit in a chair with your feet up … if you fall asleep, that's fine. You obviously needed to.

Surround yourself with cups and trophies while you revise to remind yourself that you can succeed.

Good tip for parents: it's a good idea to forget the state of the bedroom when children are revising!

Allow twice as much time to revise as you think you'll need. There are always distractions.

Be selfish. Ignore that phone call from your panicky friend. They'll be OK – they're usually the ones who end up getting the best grades!

Stick key phrases, dates or words round the house. Put them in prominent positions where you know you'll see them … the back of the loo door, the lid of the biscuit tin, the fridge door.

Don't drink coffee every time you take a break. It will make you jittery. Instead, sip long, cool drinks.

If you're getting really angry with a text, take a photocopy of the author's picture, stick it to a football and kick the ball around for half an hour!

It's really important to keep up your physical exercise whilst you revise. Give yourself an hour's break a day to do your favourite activity. It helps you to process what you've learnt and reduces stress levels.

To relieve stress, try alternate nostril breathing. Cover your left nostril with your finger, breathe in your right nostril, then breath out of your left nostril with the right one covered, and so on. Carry on doing this for 5 minutes and it will help you to relax. Best done in the privacy of your own room!

It helps to feel business–like when revising. Don't dress in sloppy leggings or track suits. You are working after all.

Read your revision notes into a tape recorder so that you can utilise wasted time. You can play the tapes while you're travelling, cooking or just lying in the bath, soaking up the information.

Play your recorded revision notes while you're asleep. It is still one of the best ways to really digest facts and figures.

Prevent eye strain while you're revising. Sit at a desk or table that has a view out of the window. Each time you look up, you will automatically focus on the distant images. In this way, you'll relax and rest the muscles you've been using for close-up revision work.

Help your concentration. Stare at an orange spot on the wall.

If you are finding it hard to concentrate, stand on your head for a few seconds. The rush of blood allows you to think more clearly.

Make up rhymes to help you remember key facts – 'In fourteen hundred and ninety two, Columbus sailed the ocean blue!'

Practise writing in two- or three-hour bursts to prevent an aching hand on the big day. Many points can be lost because of an illegible scrawl.

When you're feeling completely overloaded or think you might explode if you revise one more fact, try focusing on something really simple – an orange dot on a piece of paper – and think positive thoughts.

If you need music on while you revise, make it classical music (or easy listening) so you don't get distracted by the lyrics and end up singing along.

Burn essential oil while you're revising. Put some on a tissue before you go into an exam and hopefully the smell will help you to remember.

Take time out – there's nothing more relaxing than stroking a dog or a cat for a few minutes.

Don't be too ambitious. It's better to revise several subjects thoroughly than cover everything superficially. On the day, you will only get to show a fraction of your knowledge anyway.

Organise your research into sections. Keep scaling them down until you end up with some block headlines and a few key facts.

Double-check the time and place of the exam. Then double-check the number of questions you're meant to answer.

On the morning of the exam, even if you wake up at the crack of dawn, don't keep revising. Just glance through at the headlines and key facts.

Get to the exam in time and check that you will be comfortable. Is the desk wobbly? Is there direct sunlight in your eyes? Can you see the clock? And so on . . .

But don't arrive too early. You'll only get more and more nervous.

Take a lucky mascot with you. If nothing else, a little bit of home is reassuring!

Just before you go into an exam, clench and unclench your hands. It helps to get you psyched up and gets rid of any excess adrenalin.

If it's a long exam, it's good to take a few nibbles along with you but avoid anything noisy or distracting. Break up a chocolate bar into little pieces or take some glucose tablets in with you.

Try to quote from texts that aren't on the obligatory reading list. It makes you look passionate and well-read.

If you feel tired in the exam, rub your hands together, then place them over your forehead and eyes for a minute or two. You will quickly feel revitalised.

▷▷ Inspections

Prepare to let inspectors see your pupils learning and doing . . . not just you teaching. Provide lesson notes with follow-on activities.

Teaching should not just consist of chalk and talk but should involve worksheets, film and video.

Pupils' attention spans are short – so divide the lesson up. The aim is to show that you are pursuing a variety of activities.

Show awareness of differing abilities by setting tasks to suit varying levels. You should have clear aims and expectations.

Keep records of finished work and know about assessment recording and reporting. Your pupils should progress in knowledge, understanding and skills.

Make sure you can show off your classroom control – have a question and answer session, activities in groups or individual work. Are you giving your pupils a chance to hypothesise? Are there links being made with other subjects?

Be organised – store your resources and equipment neatly and make sure it's all labelled so that pupils can select things, use them and then tidy them away.

'Work' noise can be productive so don't be afraid of making it!

How does your classroom look? It should be a stimulating and colourful place with children's work mounted on the walls as well as themed displays.

And remember . . . the inspectors will always miss your best lesson!

▶▶▶ Tennis Players

Charles Applewaite, Tennis Wales; Jonathan Markson Centre; Steve Daly

Get your timing and coordination right – throw one ball up with your left hand and then, rather than hit it with your racket, throw another ball at it with your right hand. The aim is to get the second ball to hit the first.

Also, try saying '1, 2, 3' out loud as you serve to get the timing right. 1 – throw, 2 – racket back, 3 – hit ball.

Make sure you are throwing the ball up to the correct height for serving by standing next to a fence and raising your racket up to your 'serving height'. Tie some string to the fence at the correct height. Practise throwing the ball up to that mark.

Placing the ball for a serve is like placing a plate on a top shelf. Don't throw the ball from waist height.

To help improve your serve, pretend you are throwing your racket over the net. Even better, practise throwing a stick for the dog – it's exactly the same action.

Throwing the ball overarm without using a racket will also improve your serve – it's very much the same action as the one above.

To practise your serve indoors, throw crumpled newspaper at the wall.

To encourage players to serve up over the net, get them to serve kneeling down.

To make sure you are standing in the right position every time you serve, chalk around your feet and hold that position.

Stand with one foot on the other to get your balance right when you are serving.

To help children serve, get them to serve from the service line rather than back on the base line. When they get three out of four serves in, they move back 3 ft/1 m and start serving again from there. This stops them from becoming disillusioned if the serves don't go in at first.

Improve your dexterity – practise with your racket in your other hand.

Practise with two balls going at the same time.

To keep your hands in the right position, line your hand up correctly with the handle of the racquet and then mark that position on your hand with a ballpoint pen.

Bending your knees is important in tennis so pretend that you are playing in a room with a low ceiling and that you aren't able to stand upright.

Improve your reaction time and learn to bend your knees – get someone to roll the ball along the ground to you so that you have to move all over the court, and bend down to return the ball.

Best volleys come from a flat, punching movement so stand with your back to a wall to volley shots back. This will prevent you bringing your racket back behind you.

Hold a ball in your armpit to keep your arm close to your body for forehand volleys.

For a more defensive shot, rather than a harder, more aggressive shot, put your left hand (or right hand for left-handers) in your pocket.

The basic stance for a smash is to have your left hand (or right) up towards the ball as it drops with the racket behind your head. To practise this, try catching the ball rather than hitting it. After a while, you can substitute the action with hitting the ball.

The double-handed backhand is principally done with the left (or right) hand. To practise the shot, stand in the backhand position with both hands on the racket and them remove your right (left) hand and practise the shot with just your left (right) hand placed halfway up the handle.

The forehand ground stroke action is just like throwing a bucket of water.

After hitting a shot, get used to taking one step forward.

To practise your top spin, colour one half of the ball so you can see it spin. Practise adding spin by hitting the ball against a wall and not over the net; it becomes psychologically frustrating if you do a great spin shot which ends up in the net.

To put spin on a ball, imagine a clock face – you are hitting from 6 o'clock to 12 o'clock. Or imagine the ball is a face – you want to hit him on the chin.

Sharpen your reactions by getting someone to throw the ball from between your legs behind you. You'll have to run forward and play the shot.

Don't think about your next move too much – if you do, you could mess it up. Shout 'bounce' and 'hit' as the ball bounces and you hit it; this stops your mind from wandering.

If you are playing on concrete, put two pairs of socks on your feet for support.

If your tennis balls are wet, dry them in the tumble dryer.

To make tennis a bit more fun, get four players to play with two rackets or, like a three-legged race, tie their legs together.

Improve young player's hand-and-eye coordination – get them to keep a balloon up in the air with their hands.

To cheat at tennis, when you are running after the ball, get in a position that prevents your opponent from seeing it when it hits the court and you can call it out.

▶▶▶ Travellers

Alison Keeling, Cox and Kings Travel; Jane Breeden, Virgin Atlantic Airways; Charlie Hopkinson; Fiona Seton, Imaginative Travel

Before going off on holiday, leave half a lemon in each of your rooms at home to keep them smelling sweet.

Put suitcases in bin liners before strapping them to the roof rack of the car. It will protect them from the rain and anything else that's flying around as you travel.

Credit cards get a better rate of exchange than cash or cheques.

Pack an empty pillow case to pop all your dirty clothes in whilst you're away – it saves time sorting the clean from the dirty once you unpack at home again.

Seal all bottles and jars with clear nail-varnish to avoid messy spillages whilst travelling.

Get a neighbour to keep an eye on your house while you are away. They can push post through the door, mow the lawn, take the rubbish out and so on. It will give you peace of mind and help you to enjoy your holiday more.

If you're travelling abroad, check with your doctor about any inoculations that you might need.

Never put your home address on luggage labels. When you arrive at the airport, it only advertises the fact that you are away on holiday for a while and that your house is unoccupied. Put your address inside your suitcase.

Mark your luggage with a ribbon or cord (or funny sticker if you have children) so that you can spot it easily as it comes around on the carousel.

A snappy idea to save space when packing for short trips is to fill empty film canisters with shampoos and conditioners rather than taking a huge bottle.

If space is tight, pack a sarong. It can be a skirt, towel, throw, shawl or useful shield for changing on beaches.

Use two cases when packing, one smaller than the other. Put your clothes and belongings in the smaller case and then pack this in the larger one. You then have another case which you can fill with all your mementos and souvenirs from your holiday.

Make space in your luggage – take the cardboard tube out of your loo roll and flatten the paper. If you can't get the tube out, stuff it with your smalls so that you use all available space.

If you are taking a torch in your luggage, make sure you have put some sticky tape over the switch so that it doesn't get turned on by accident.

Minimise laundry on holiday – stick to dark colours.

Lost passports and documents? Avoid the stress by photocopying the relevant pages and keeping them in your luggage. At least you'll have something to show the authorities if things do go missing.

No insect repellent? Eat plenty of garlic to keep the bugs away – we can't promise a successful holiday romance though!

If you get bitten by mosquitoes, lemon juice is a natural astringent and acts as an antiseptic.

Get really comfy on the beach. Half-fill a carrier bag with some sand and lay it under the end of your towel as a pillow.

Firmly sew some fabric pockets to the inside of your windbreaker
so you can safely store keys, sunglasses, cans of drink and so on
while you're on the beach.

When buying bottled water, turn the bottle upside down. If it
drips, don't buy it, it may be filled with untreated water.

Don't ask for ice in drinks when travelling in Third World
countries – it's usually made with untreated water.

Avoid salad and fruit in Third World countries because they are
often washed in untreated water.

Beware of watermelons! They may look wonderful but the really
plump, juicy ones have usually been left in local rivers to soak up
more water. Avoid them if you don't want an upset tummy.

▷▷ Flying

Combat jet lag on long plane journeys with a ballpoint pen. Take
the blunt end of the pen and press it into the ball of your big toe
several times; this massages a pressure point and relieves tiredness
and nausea.

Prevent swollen feet on long flights by rolling a golf ball under
your feet while you watch the movie. It feels great and stops the
swelling.

To stop your feet swelling, follow a Chinese remedy: put your feet
in brown paper bags and then put your flight socks over the top.

If you feel tired during the flight, a quick blast of cologne is a
great pick-me-up.

Avoid dehydration by drinking lots of fizzy drinks and keeping
your salt levels high with some salted nuts or crisps.

To stop babies' ears from popping when flying, give them a dummy or bottle to suck when landing.

You can carry disposable nappies as hand luggage – although most countries do sell them they are often more expensive than at home.

Spread your children's possessions around the family's luggage – just in case one case goes missing, you should have some of the things that they need.

If you're flying with children, you can always ask if they can visit the flight deck. Not everyone says 'yes' but it's worth asking.

Reduce jet lag – don't wear sunglasses. Try not to put on your shades as soon as you reach your destination. Instead, give your eyes a couple of days to adjust to the new brightness.

If you're worried about your children getting jet lag, make sure they drink fruit juice or water, and try to book a flight that arrives at your destination in the early evening. Then they can start adjusting to 'sleep' time immediately.

Keep luggage more secure – thread a key-ring through all the zip pulls.

If you have to pack glass bottles (such as medicine), wrap them in towels or pack them in old margarine tubs.

Avoid puffy eyes when flying. Place a couple of slices of cucumber over your closed eyes.

If your clothes are creased on arrival, hang them in the bathroom while you take a shower and by the time you're dry the creases will have dropped out.

Take a clothes-hanger with you because in many hotels you can't take the hangers out of the wardrobes. You'll find it useful to be able to hang clothes in the bathroom.

If you get sunburnt and you've run out of cream, dab on some neat vinegar to ease the pain.

▷▷ Caravanners

Prevent your caravan screen from being splattered by flies – just cover the screen with clingfilm when travelling and peel it away when you stop. All the flies will come away with the clingfilm.

If travelling during the winter, always wash your caravan down to avoid salt from the road corroding the surface.

To get your loading right, carry heavy items over the axle, followed by the medium weights, and ending with the light weights at the edge.

To check that everything is OK, stop the car after about 20 minutes of journey time and have a good look around your caravan to check that everything is intact.

To avoid any problems with the refrigeration unit attached to the LPG (liquefied petroleum gas), turn it off before you stop at a garage.

Protect yourself from greasy stains off tow hitches – place a tennis ball over the towball.Or just pop a sock over the top of the hitch when you've parked.

Check if your caravan is level. Put a packet of digestive biscuits on the floor; when they no longer roll, you'll know the caravan is level and then you can treat yourself to a cup of tea and a biscuit.

To keep your caravan level, take large blocks of wood with you. It's a lot cheaper than buying a leveller from the shops.

If you want to keep your table level while you're having a picnic outside, use a couple of rubber door stops. They're waterproof and long-lasting – and come in very handy!

To stop your tablecloth from flying away, use some office bulldog clips.

If you take a large umbrella with you to keep the sun off you while you eat, make sure you don't damage it when trying to push it into hard ground. Take a steel rod, about 6–9 in/15–23 cm long and you can bash that into the ground first.

If you're a light sleeper, don't park the front of your caravan so that it is facing east or you'll be woken by the rising sun.

To avoid getting stuck in the ground during a wet weekend, park opposite a gate or exit downhill from the site.

Take a jack with you just in case – they don't come as part of the equipment in a caravan.

Always remember to take a spare tyre with you. If you have a flat and need to call someone out to help you replace it, they will charge you.

To check your tyres, look between the treads and on the inner side walls.

To make your own water-waste container for half the price, get an old 5-gal/23-l drum, fit it with a sink outlet and away you go!

For easy cooking in a caravan, always take your wok.

To liven up your peas and potatoes, keep some fresh mint in a brown paper bag in the fridge. It should last for about a week and you can add it to the vegetables when you cook them.

To cook delicious potatoes on the barbecue, slice them, add seasoning, then wrap in foil and place on the barbecue for about half an hour.

To save money on gas, buy the large canisters of 29–31 lb/13–14 kg because you generally have to pay to have the bottle cleaned. Go for one big one and you'll only have to pay for one to be cleaned. Or, alternatively, you could put your coffee percolator or kettle straight on to the barbecue after you've cooked the meat.

To cook food in tins without using any gas, open them up and place on the barbecue … saves on washing-up, too.

To keep batteries charged up, take a lead with you. If your caravan battery fails, you can run the electrics off the car battery.

To make more space in your cupboards, see if you can divide them into shelves.

To avoid any breakages, go for plastic crockery and not china.

To stop the contents of your shelves from falling off, place two hooks on either side of each shelf and attach a stretchy net curtain rod across the front of the shelf.

Save money – don't buy a caravan toilet brush – just get a washing-up brush and place it in a plastic beaker.

To ensure that your caravanning is trouble-free, try to have the caravan serviced every year.

To get a good idea of what you want from a caravan, try hiring one first for a couple of days before making a decision and buying one.

When not in use, store your caravan cushions in a dry attic.

▶▶▶ Undertakers

Natural Death Centre; Martha's Funerals; Barbara Butler; British Humanist Association

You don't have to relinquish the body of someone you love. It is perfectly legal to ask to keep the body at home until the funeral.

Remember to register the death within five days. You have to be a relative of the deceased, someone who lived in the same house or have been present at the death.

You may need several copies of the death certificate so make sure you ask the registrar if you can have some. You will have to pay a small sum of money.

Make sure your funeral is just as you want it to be. You can leave clear instructions in your will. It saves family and friends a lot of worry if they know what you wanted.

If cremation is your choice, avoid complications. Remember to state if you have any medical implants. Pacemakers have a tendency to explode in extreme heat.

The most eco-friendly way to bury someone is in a cotton body bag or cardboard box, not a coffin.

Lessen the amount of pollution in the atmosphere – opt for burial rather than cremation.

You can be buried on your own land but you have to get permission from the local planning department and you must inform the environmental health officer.

If you are planning a traditional service with family members carrying the coffin a fair way, it is worth ordering the box to be made from lightweight wood, such as willow. People struggling to carry a heavy coffin robs a service of any dignity.

Customising coffins is increasingly popular. Try jazzing it up with some paint or use découpage to stick on lots of pictures and articles about things the deceased liked.

Decorating the coffin is a wonderful way to get the family involved. Doing this can be a great catharsis.

For an alternative non-religious funeral, call the British Humanist Association (47 Theobalds Road, London, WC1X 8SP. Telephone 0171 430 0908) or the Natural Death Centre (20 Herber Road, London, NW2 6AA. Telephone 0181 208 2853) for information and advice.

To help you record details of loved ones forever … put them on the Internet. Contact Meadow Rest Ltd & Information Net UK (Telephone 01275 341111)

►►► Wildlife Enthusiasts

In the spring you may come across a baby animal. Don't assume it's been abandoned – just leave it alone. Unless it's obviously hurt or in danger, retreat to a discreet distance and keep an eye on it if you're not sure whether the parents are around.

▷▷ Squirrels

Unlike many wild animals, a squirrel does not like being enclosed in a box. So, if you have caught an injured one and intend to take it to a vet, use a cage instead. Make sure it's made from metal – squirrels have sharp teeth.

If you are tending to an injured red squirrel, you will have to contact your local Nature Conservancy Council. They are a protected species and you will need a licence to care for one.

▷▷ Foxes

Keep foxes out of the garden by spreading lion dung around the edges. You don't have to gather your own lion poo, just ask at the local zoo for a batch.

If you are looking after an injured fox, give some thought to its water container. Foxes love peeing in them so you will have to come up with a more suitable solution.

To feed a fox cub don't use cow's milk. Feed them goat's milk every three or four hours. You'll need to use a bottle if the cubs are less than four weeks old. They can go on to solids when they are about a month old.

▷▷ Hedgehogs

If you have to catch a hedgehog, but don't want to handle it, wait until it's rolled into a ball and then gently roll it on to a handkerchief or piece of newspaper which you can use to transport it.

If you want a hedgehog to unroll so you can examine it, hold it in the palm of your hand and gently rock it backwards and forwards. The theory is that the animal will get a bit giddy and unroll to see what on earth's going on.

Alternatively, try and work out where the head is and hold it pointing downwards over a table. The hedgehog should start to unroll and try to reach the surface below. You can then hold it gently by its hind legs.

Hedgehogs are nocturnal animals so, if you find one during the day, there must be something wrong with it.

Hedgehogs drink a lot of water – they need up to a 1/5 of a pint at a time.

Don't feed milk to hedgehogs – water is best.

Hedgehogs are the gardener's friend. They will quite happily keep down the slug and beetle populations for you.

If you're keen to leave food out for a hedgehog, try pet foods and baby foods, not milk and water.

If you need to force feed a sick hedgehog, dribble a solution of warm water and glucose into its mouth with a syringe.

Baby hedgehogs with their eyes closed need to be fed every two to three hours – they will need about 3 ml milk and water with a dash of glucose.

If you don't have a pipette for feeding, you could try a paintbrush or small spoon.

After each feed a baby hedgehog must be cleaned and gently massaged with baby oil or kitchen wipes. You have to imitate the licking action of the mother which stimulates circulation.

Equally, you need to encourage a baby to empty its bowels. Dip a cotton bud in warm water and gently tickle the baby's bottom. Do this before and after each feed.

You must keep baby or injured hedgehogs warm. Wrap a hot-water bottle in an old jumper and put in the bottom of a cardboard box.

Don't release a hedgehog into the wild until it weighs 1 lb 6 ozs (623g). Wait until warm weather (around April time) because there will be plenty of insects around for him to eat.

Try to release a hedgehog where there are other hedgehogs. This means that there is enough food and shelter for them to survive.

Hedgehogs love garden bonfire heaps – they make ideal places to hibernate. Always turn your bonfire over to check for guests before setting it alight.

Secure a piece of chicken wire so that it dangles into your garden pond or swimming pool. Hedgehogs can swim, but might need some help getting out again.

Always check grass and weeds before using a strimmer because these are ideal places to nest if you're a hedgehog.

The gap underneath a raised shed provides excellent shelter for hedgehogs and keeps them out of the clutches of any cats.

▷▷ Deer

If you accidentally corner a female deer, watch out for its front feet. They are great boxers when they need to be, and often use their feet first rather than their horns.

Avoid deer during the rutting season, especially male deer. A fully antlered red stag in rut is quite capable of disembowelling a person.

When caring for an injured deer which doesn't want to eat, it's worth persevering with force feeding. Make up some baby cereal so that it's very thick and squeeze or dribble it into its mouth. A pint, two or three times a day, for a large deer will do the trick.

When feeding a fawn, give it goat's milk in a baby's feeding bottle. You could mix in some cod liver oil or egg as well.

▷▷ Bats

If you have to handle a bat, be careful not to hold its wings because they are extremely fragile. Support its body. Better still, offer it a vertical surface and it will instinctively turn itself upside down and hang downwards, gripping with its hind feet.

During the day, bats become torpid, so won't react if you go near them. After resting, they have to raise their body temperature, which they do by shivering for around half an hour before they can fly.

If you find a bat crawling around the house or garden in the summer, it's likely to be a baby. Pop it in a ventilated box until dusk and then hang the box outside near the roost, where its mother can get at it.

An injured bat will need water as soon as possible – use an eyedropper or syringe.

If you are looking after a baby bat, feed it some skimmed milk through a pipette.

▷▷ Ferrets

Ferrets have a nasty bite. If you're unfortunate enough to be on the receiving end of its teeth, try to let the animal's feet rest on the ground (even though your instinct will be to pull away from the source of pain). Once it feels its feet on solid ground, it will probably be so pleased that it will let you go.

If the ferret still hangs on grimly, try pinching its forehead or a foot to distract it.

Most ferrets are easy to handle, however. Just support its body with your hand. Putting your thumb under its chin means it won't be tempted to bite you.

If you want to catch a ferret, try using a tube. They are incredibly curious and love exploring dark holes. A piece of drainpipe with the cage at the other end is one way to catch them.

▷▷ Wild Birds

To make your own instant bird feeder take the cardboard tube from a loo roll or kitchen paper roll and cover it in honey. Then roll it over some bird seed until it's completely covered. You can then hang it outside and enjoy watching the birds as they eat.

To transport a bird such as a swan or goose chop the corner off an old sack and pop it over the bird. They can put their head through the hole, but their wings and body are kept secure.

When handling birds such as ravens or herons, keep an eye on their beaks which are formidable weapons. If you have to examine them, slip a rubber band over the end of the beak for your safety. Don't leave it there for very long.

When handling birds of prey, wear heavy-duty gloves. Their beaks and claws are designed for ripping and tearing. They should be handled by experts but if you're in a position where you have to catch one, don't handle it more than necessary. Put it in a warm, dark, ventilated box (not a cage) until you can hand it over to an expert.

With birds of prey a hooded bird is a quiet bird. An old sock with a hole for the beak will be an effective hood. Don't try hooding an owl, however – it won't work.

Don't bind the beak of a bird while transporting it because it may want to throw up with the stress of capture.

When feeding birds of prey which might not be used to dead food, try cutting up a day-old chick so that its innards are exposed.

▷▷ First Aid

When out camping or walking, use an inverted frisbee as a water or food dish for your pet.

If an animal has suffered a burn, you must try to take the heat out of the affected area. Plunge the area into cold water for 10–15 minutes. Once the area is cool, you can cover it with a clean, dry bandage or cloth. Don't use oil or lotion.

Alternatively, soak the cloth in very strong tea. The tannin encourages the wound to coagulate quickly and protect the sensitive spot.

If an animal has suffered burns caused by acid or alkaline, remember that an acid substance will neutralise an alkaline one and vice versa. Milk or bicarbonate of soda (2 parts bicarbonate to 98 of water) to neutralise acids; weak vinegar (5 parts to 95 of water) will neutralise alkalis such as caustic soda and ammonia.

When an animal has swallowed something acidic, neutralise the acid with alkaline substances such as bicarbonate of soda or chalk (mixed in barleywater or milk). If you don't have anything alkaline to hand, dilute the acid as much as possible with water.

If you suspect an animal has eaten barbiturates, give it an emetic and keep it warm. Even strong coffee will help.

Lead can be extremely dangerous to animals – two pieces of lead shot can kill a pigeon. The best immediate treatment for mammals is a large dose of Epsom salts, milk, egg whites or strong tea. Send for the vet immediately and keep the animal warm and quiet.

Heatstroke is a killer, so you must do everything to cool down the animal as quickly as possible. Reduce body heat rapidly by showering with cold water, applying wet sheets and towels, putting paws in cold water and trying to get cold air into the lungs. Get the animal to a vet as soon as possible.

If an animal has eaten poison, you need to give it an emetic to cause vomiting or a purgative to empty the bowels. Useful emetics are: salt with water (around 2 tablespoons to a cup), washing soda (about the size of a hazelnut for a dog or cat), Epsom salts or mustard in water (1 dessert spoon in a cupful of water for a pig).

Animals can suffer from bee and wasp stings as well as humans. If you can, remove the sting carefully. Apply a paste of bicarbonate of soda to the afflicted area.

Alternatively, rub half a freshly cut onion over the sting spot.

Tar can be difficult to get off fur (or skin, for that matter). Use margarine, melted butter or eucalyptus oil to get it off.

If creosote is the problem, wash it off as soon as possible using warm soapy water or warm castor oil. Make sure you clean the skin as well as the fur.

If you are involved in a road traffic accident with horses, dogs or cattle, you have a legal obligation to report it to the police.

▶▶▶ Index